THE COMPLETE IDIOT'S GUIDE® TO

Organizing Your Life

Third Edition

by Georgene Lockwood

ALPHA

A Pearson Education Company

International Standard Book Number: 0-02-864318-6
Library of Congress Catalog Card Number: 2002108496

05   04   03   8   7   6   5   4   3   2

Interpretation of the printing code: The rightmost number of the first series of numbers is the year of the book's printing; the rightmost number of the second series of numbers is the number of the book's printing. For example, a printing code of 03-1 shows that the first printing occurred in 2003.

Printed in the United States of America

Note: This publication contains the opinions and ideas of its author. It is intended to provide helpful and informative material on the subject matter covered. It is sold with the understanding that the author and publisher are not engaged in rendering professional services in the book. If the reader requires personal assistance or advice, a competent professional should be consulted.

The author and publisher specifically disclaim any responsibility for any liability, loss, or risk, personal or otherwise, which is incurred as a consequence, directly or indirectly, of the use and application of any of the contents of this book.

For marketing and publicity, please call: 317-581-3722

The publisher offers discounts on this book when ordered in quantity for bulk purchases and special sales.

For sales within the United States, please contact: Corporate and Government Sales, 1-800-382-3419 or corpsales@pearsontechgroup.com

Outside the United States, please contact: International Sales, 317-581-3793 or international@pearsontechgroup.com

Publisher: *Marie Butler-Knight*
Product Manager: *Phil Kitchel*
Managing Editor: *Jennifer Chisholm*
Acquisitions Editor: *Randy Ladenheim-Gil*
Development Editor: *Michael Thomas*
Production Editor: *Billy Fields*
Illustrator: *Chris Eliopoulos*
Cover/Book Designer: *Trina Wurst*
Indexer: *Angie Bess*
Layout/Proofreading: *Vicki Keller, Kimberly Tucker*

Contents at a Glance

Contents

Foreword

We live in a world in which technology has given us the ability to share information faster than ever before. It has expanded our choices and increased our ability to access anything, anytime, anywhere. This means we have much more to organize, in every aspect of our lives, than ever before. At times, it can make life seem overwhelming and out of control.

Do not despair! You have in your hands a book that can change all that, and help you gain control in your life. It captures the essence of organization. Organization is not about neatness or making things tidy. It is not about being perfect or being rigid. Organization is about being able to find what you need, when you need it.

My personal and professional philosophy is that for organization to work, it must be simple, and it has to be fun. By following the clear, step-by-step advice Georgene Lockwood presents in this book, you will be able to create systems that are tailor-made to your specific needs. Systems that are flexible, that grow and expand as your needs grow and expand. Systems that address the ever-changing needs of this fast-paced world we live in. You will learn how to set realistic goals at work, at home, and at play. But most importantly, you will learn how to keep your systems simple and have fun organizing.

Keep in mind that the adage "knowledge is power" is only half-true. The real power of knowledge comes from understanding how to best use that knowledge. In order to do that, it must be organized. Information and organization in and of themselves have no intrinsic value. Their values are essential life tools. Having both information and organization tools in one place makes this book a truly extraordinary value.

Organization is no longer a luxury; it is a basic necessity in every work and home environment. This is demonstrated in the United States alone, by the growth in membership of the National Association of Professional Organizers (NAPO). Founded in 1985 by five Professional Organizers, NAPO now has over 1,100 members (700 of them having joined in the last four years). Around the world, professional organizing associations have been formed to help address this global need.

"The most important step on any journey is the first one." You have taken that first step by selecting this book. I assure you, it will dispense wonderful information and be a loyal and trusted friend on your journey to organization. You, too, will thank Georgene Lockwood for sharing her wisdom with us.

—Gloria Ritter, founder and president of PaperMatters and more inc.

GLORIA RITTER, founder and president of PaperMatters and more inc., has more than 10 years of experience consulting and training companies and individuals in many aspects of organization. She is committed to helping companies and individuals work in an efficient manner in order to be more productive and therefore minimize stress. Ms. Ritter serves on the Board of Directors of the National Association of Professional Organizers. She is also president of the National Association of Professional Organizers–Greater Washington/Baltimore Chapter.

Introduction

Recent events have made it all too clear to us that life is uncertain, and making the most of every day is paramount. To have a vision for one's life and to take steps every day toward that vision is where true happiness lies. Ordering our lives to support us in our vision is one of the most profound steps we can take.

To paraphrase George Bernard Shaw, "Hell is to drift. Heaven is to steer." Taking responsibility for where we're going, setting a course, regularly checking our progress, and staying at the helm are the simple secrets of a happy, rewarding life. But why do we so often feel out of control? Perhaps it's because we know what we need to do, but we don't know how. Consider this book Organization 101, a basic course in how to steer your own ship on the day-to-day seas of life.

This is not a dictatorial, "do-it-my-way" kind of book. It's more like a Chinese food menu. You know, "Choose one from Column A, one from Column B." I've taken good ideas from wherever I could find them—self-improvement technologies, meditation, visualization, psychology, behavioral studies—whatever I've found that works, either for me personally or for people I know. You pick and choose what makes the most sense for you.

Getting organized isn't something to do "someday"—it's essential to getting ahead and leading a joyful, productive life. The degree to which you need to be organized to enhance your day-to-day existence and realize your dreams is something you'll have to find out for yourself. Let this book be your guide. I've structured it so you can first set your goals, tackle any immediate roadblocks, decide which areas are really urgent, and then turn to the section that most applies. It's not all work and no play, either. There's lots of fun stuff throughout and chapters at the end are devoted specifically to life's pleasures.

How the Book Is Organized

To make it easy for you to design your own organization plan, there are seven major divisions to help you:

Part 1, "What Do You Mean 'Organized'?" looks at some past experiences or unrealistic ideals that might be getting in your way, and shows you how to figure out what's really important to make an immediate improvement and feel more in control. You'll also explore some ways to get motivated, to stick to your commitment to organize your life, and avoid some of the "booby traps" we all have a tendency to set for ourselves. You'll learn the "Basic Laws of Stuff" and the "Basic Laws of Time," and how stuff and time work together to make your life either smooth or chaotic.

Part 2, "Stuff Simplified," explores some simple ways you can immediately get rid of things you don't really need and get at the things you do, plus some quick-start steps for handling all the paper that comes through the door.

Part 3, "Systems for Getting Stuff Done," moves into the action areas of your life, and concentrates on the tasks that will speed you toward accomplishing the goals you set for yourself. You'll learn how to set up a central area for managing yourself and your family, and you'll get some step-by-step advice for devising personal systems for your major areas of activity.

Part 4, "Money and All That Stuff," guides you through some simple strategies for budgeting and managing your money, examines systems for handling bills and taxes, and asks some basic questions about planning for the future. You'll find concrete ideas for keeping your finances from becoming a tangled mess, causing you aggravation and costing you money.

Part 5, "Getting People Involved," tackles the ways you may let other people sabotage your organization efforts and helps you get people on your side by encouraging understanding, exploring ways to communicate, and discussing when and how to hire other people to do the work for you.

Part 6, "Now That You're Organized, Let's Keep It That Way!" will help you stay on track with a minimum of effort once you have your plan in place. You'll see how to adapt what you've learned to your particular lifestyle.

Part 7, "Now for the Fun Stuff!" focuses on getting the most out of your leisure time. I've covered everything from trouble-free travel to having a happy holiday to enjoying the family pet, so if anybody asks, "Are we having fun yet?" your answer will always be a resounding "Yes!"

Included at the end of this book are some special resources to take you still further in refining your organization skills.

Extras

To give you additional food for thought—some shortcuts, tips, or resources to expand your knowledge of certain areas—you'll find boxes scattered throughout the chapters that are indicated by their own special icons:

Orderly Pursuits _____

This symbol points you to books, audio- and videotapes, online resources, organizations, things to send away for—anything I've found to help make you a more powerful organizer.

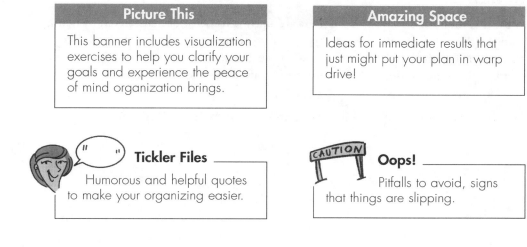

Picture This
This banner includes visualization exercises to help you clarify your goals and experience the peace of mind organization brings.

Amazing Space
Ideas for immediate results that just might put your plan in warp drive!

Tickler Files _____

Humorous and helpful quotes to make your organizing easier.

Oops! _____

Pitfalls to avoid, signs that things are slipping.

Acknowledgments

I have a lot of people to be grateful for in my life. Each time I do a book, I'm simply and subtly reminded. Thanks to my agent, Carole Abel, for creating opportunities for me. Kudos to Randy Ladenheim-Gil, Michael Thomas, and Billy Fields for their intelligence and insight in making a good book better. And, as always, endless gratitude to my family for their love and support. They're the ones who make it all worthwhile, every day, in every way.

Special Thanks to the Technical Reviewer

The Complete Idiot's Guide to Organizing Your Life was reviewed by an expert who not only checked the accuracy of what you'll learn in this book, but also provided invaluable insight and suggestions to ensure that you learn everything you need to know to organize yourself for a better life. Our special thanks are extended to Karen Ussery.

A member of the National Association of Professional Organizers and president of the Arizona Professional Organizers Association, Karen is the owner of Organized for

Success. Her background is in psychology, personal development, and management. She has written over 50 columns on organizing the office for the *Arizona Business Gazette* and currently writes for the *Business Journal*. A native of Phoenix, Arizona, Karen is married and enjoys travel, hiking, yoga, and time with her husband, family, and friends.

Trademarks

All terms mentioned in this book that are known to be or are suspected of being trademarks or service marks have been appropriately capitalized. Alpha Books and Pearson Education, Inc., cannot attest to the accuracy of this information. Use of a term in this book should not be regarded as affecting the validity of any trademark or service mark.

"Bridal Countdown" reprinted with permission from Hazel Bowman.

Part 1

What Do You Mean "Organized"?

Organized people are made, not born. As with other important areas in life, many of us never had anyone to teach us the skills needed to be organized; but with understanding and practice, these skills can be learned.

In these early chapters, you'll learn about beliefs you might have that are undermining your efforts to take control of your time, your relationships, your career—all the things that make living worthwhile. You'll find out how to avoid the biggest trap that seeks to ensnare us all, and the basic rules governing the material things we have and the things we want to do. You'll also learn how to make your organization efforts compatible with what's really important to you.

Chapter 1

The Big Picture: Setting Goals

In This Chapter

- Where you got your ideas about being organized
- How disorganized are you, really?
- The benefits of "getting it all together"
- Setting meaningful personal goals
- Effective resolutions, New Year's and otherwise

Before you dive in and start writing lists, tearing closets apart, and designing new storage, let's begin at the beginning, which is figuring out how you got into this mess in the first place. Did it just "happen," or are there real reasons your life is so chaotic? Rearranging things on the surface isn't going to mean the kind of deeper life changes I suspect you're striving for. You want this to be a permanent step in the right direction, don't you?

Your Mother's Cupboard Isn't Yours

Imagine a child who was never allowed to make a mess. Let's say that child's name is Tony. Tony's parents won't allow him to play with paint because they worry it will stain his clothes or spill. Tony can't play in the dirt because he'll get grimy and disturb the garden. Tony's room is "neat as a pin." There are no stray papers anywhere, no fragments of tape on the walls, and no clothes or toys out of place. To the average outsider, Tony seems like a "model child."

When Tony grows up and leaves home, he figures he's in charge. He can decide to rebel against the way it was at home and say to himself, "Now that I'm a grownup, I can make a mess whenever I want to!" In fact, being a slob may give him a distinct pleasure. It may feel like delicious freedom. But he also may be unable to find the door through all the debris. Or maybe Tony will continue being extra-neat and careful, and rob himself of many of life's pleasures, simply because he can't allow himself to loosen up. Either reaction is just that—a reaction to the way it used to be and not necessarily in Tony's best interest in the present.

How you lived as a child may well help govern how you live now. If someone was always yelling at you to clean up your room, you may still be acting out your old need to be free from such constraints. You may now be "a messy." Or perhaps you're obsessively neat. (Notice I said "neat," not "organized." We'll talk about that in more detail later.) Either reaction can get in the way of real freedom.

Picture This

Close your eyes and imagine yourself as a child in your room. What did your room look like? What do you remember your parents saying about it? Did you share a room? How much privacy did you have? Add lots of details here. Take your time.

Pay attention to any fatalistic words you hear popping up in your mind like *always* and *never*. These are powerful words and can set the stage for some of your adult attitudes. Also, be aware of both verbal criticisms and supportive language. When you set your organization goals, refer back to these memories and see if some of your goals stem from reactions to past events rather than present needs and desires. You may want to revise them accordingly.

There's also the reverse scenario. Maybe you grew up in a terribly cluttered household and vowed that when you were in control, things would be different. But now you may be going overboard. You may spend time compulsively washing, folding, and tidying all your stuff, rather than enjoying the sunshine or smelling the roses. Your desire to maintain absolute control over your environment can prevent you from having fun, and even keep you from reaching your most important objectives.

Throughout this book, I'll be giving you a series of visualizations in the "Picture This" boxes. When you visualize, pretend you're directing a movie. Add as much detail as you can. Notice any emotions that surface as your "movie" plays on the screen. Write down anything that comes to mind during your screening or dictate your thoughts into a tape recorder. Write an essay or story or draw what you see—whatever most helps you get in touch with your visualization experience. What you see and believe in your mind, you create in the material world. If you want to change what you're creating, one of the first steps is to "see" differently.

You Can't Have Everything

Even though we're adults, we may still be trying to gain our parents' approval. This can be especially difficult for women, since housekeeping and making sure the family is well fed, clothed, and successful has traditionally been the woman's job. It's easy to get caught up in trying to be "as good as Mother" (or even better than Mom!), even though Mother might never have worked outside the home or had as many responsibilities or interests.

Recent studies show that although more women are in the workforce, and some even make more money than their male partners, most working women still do the lion's share of the housework and child care. Beware of the Superwoman syndrome. It can kill you!

Again, the important thing is simply to notice your feelings and experiences. Ask yourself the following questions:

1. Of the chores that need to be done every day, every week, or every month (don't forget to include tasks such as bill-paying, driving kids, making appointments, washing the car, and doing household repairs), how is the work distributed? You may want to make a list on one side of a piece of paper, divide the rest of the paper into two columns, and check off which tasks you do and which ones your partner does. Be honest and fair.

2. How many hours does each adult spend working outside the home? Inside the home?

3. Do you feel that the work is evenly distributed? Are those feelings based on the facts? If you asked the other adults in the household how much of the workload they share, what would they say? How does that fit with your picture of how the work is distributed?

4. If you have children, how much do they contribute?

Note your answers and the emotions they bring up. Acknowledge them, learn from them, and move on. You'll have an opportunity to deal with this more in Chapters 8 and 17, when you do some work surrounding the people in your life.

How Come Martha Stewart Doesn't Sweat?

Not only does your upbringing affect your attitudes about being organized; so do the media and the entertainment industry. Personalities like home maven Martha Stewart, and the pages of many home and lifestyles magazines, present as "normal" certain things that are for most of us impossible ways of living. Don't get me wrong. I subscribe to a few of the magazines. I even watch the TV shows on occasion. But do I really believe this lady edits her own magazine, does a weekly TV show, keeps several houses, irons her antique linens, shovels manure in her perfectly manicured garden, and single-handedly cooks up impromptu dinners for 50 from scratch? Naaah.

I enjoy reading home magazines, with all those lovely antiques, exquisite china, and collectibles on every available surface. I even wrote a book about Victorian weddings and the grace, romance, and elegance of those bygone days. When reporters would come to my home to interview me, they expected a vintage home overflowing with bric-a-brac. Instead, they found a contemporary place in the woods constructed with modern materials, an open floor plan, and an easy-to-keep-clean design. Sure, I have a few choice antiques that I treasure, but I work full time, I have a family and a large circle of friends, and I enjoy several time-consuming hobbies. I decided long ago that these things were more important to me than having a showcase home. I never want to be a slave to a house, and I doubt very much that anyone will ever pay me to show mine on TV.

Superwoman and Superman Are Myths

Then there are those guys on the Public Broadcasting Station or The Learning Channel. They know how to fix *everything*. Their Craftsman tools are all in place, and their workshops look like no one ever works there. Of course, that's because after the show is over, someone else comes in, puts everything away, and cleans up for them! And what about those magazines that suggest being a real man means you have to work out, always look great and wear the right jeans, rebuild motors on the weekend, play touch football with the guys, and to top it all off, cook gourmet meals? No sweat, right?

Beware of the images created by movies, TV shows, and advertising. Remember, these people are paid actors. A hairdresser follows them around, their hands never touch a dish or change motor oil, and their homes only exist as movie sets or showrooms.

Advertising especially is about illusions, with sales the ultimate goal. In Advertising 101 students learn how to "create a need" for a new product. If you're "creating" one, that means there isn't one to start with, right? The advertising industry shows you squeaky-clean homes that you feel you must have to be good parents, model homemakers, and acceptable people. Besides living in a perfect home or apartment, you should have white teeth, perfectly clean hair, sparkling clothes, and dry underarms. Don't let yourself get caught in these marketing traps. See them for what they are: fantasies.

Tickler Files

"We are what we think. All that we are arises with our thoughts. With our thoughts, we make our world."
—Buddha

What you're aiming for is a comfortable, orderly, clean, aesthetically pleasing place to live that works well to support your life goals and helps you get the important things, the ones you really care about, done.

How Organized Are You? A Self-Test

Before we continue, let's find out how organized or unorganized you really are. Answer the following questions and you'll have a handle on where you stand:

Yes	No	
❏	❏	Do you find yourself feeling frustrated that you have too little time to do the things you enjoy?
❏	❏	Do you often feel hurried, hassled, or not in control?
❏	❏	When you need to find something, does it often take minutes (or even hours) of frantic searching to finally lay your hands on it?
❏	❏	Do you ever miss appointments or forget deadlines?
❏	❏	Do you have trouble remembering birthdays, anniversaries, important events, and holidays?
❏	❏	Are you usually shopping for special occasions at the last minute (like Christmas shopping on December 23)?

continues

continued

Yes	No	
❏	❏	Do you spend your "time off" running errands, playing catch-up, just trying to keep things from getting out of control?
❏	❏	Are there important things that need to be done to maintain the house or the car that you never seem to get to?
❏	❏	Are repairs made only when something breaks or if it's an absolute emergency?
❏	❏	Do you often pay bills late, not because you don't have the money in your account, but because you just didn't get around to them?
❏	❏	Have you avoided setting up or updating a budget? A will? Insurance? A home inventory? A retirement plan?
❏	❏	Are there piles of newspapers, unread magazines, junk mail, and various other papers scattered around your house or apartment?
❏	❏	Are you embarrassed to have people see your home or office?
❏	❏	Are mornings hectic, spent rummaging around for clean clothes to wear, gulping down breakfast, and running out the door late?

CAUTION

Oops!

If you have big piles of paper that are dangerously close to causing an avalanche, you definitely have some organization work to do. Good thing you bought this book!

If you answered "yes" to two or more of these questions, you can definitely benefit from committing to an "organization overhaul." With this book and a few hours each week, you'll be surprised how quickly you can make a difference.

You know by your answers to these questions whether or not you're on top of it all or under the gun. I suspect there's a heap of work to be done and you may be looking for some help. Well, you've certainly come to the right place!

How Would You Change Your Life?

You picked up this book for a reason. You were looking for answers. You were looking for simple, common sense ways to have your life run more smoothly. Or maybe your existence is out of control completely and you're desperate for a way out of the chaos. Only you can know where you are in the organization continuum. Getting organized, if it is to be more than a temporary cosmetic solution, is really a change in lifestyle.

You're working to change old, deeply ingrained behaviors and adopt new, more productive habits.

Picture This

Take a minute to visualize what your ideal environment would be like. Walk through your house one room at a time in your mind and imagine each space clean and orderly. Imagine yourself getting ready for work in the morning with all your clothes ready to wear. See yourself eating a relaxed, nutritious breakfast. Next, visualize yourself commuting to work and see your office a pleasure to work in. Daydream about what you would like to do with your leisure time. Experience the pride, confidence, serenity, enjoyment, and overall sense of well-being that living in this fantasy place gives you.

So what do you really want to change? Actually, the better question to ask is, "What do you *want?*" I'm not talking about what your parents wanted for you, or what you think you should want, or what the media tells you to want. But what do *you* really want?

As you begin your plan for getting organized, you will keep in mind what's truly important to you and make sure the systems you set up support your goals.

Setting Your Organization Goals

Okay, you've been honest with yourself about what your life is like. You've thought about how you'd like things to be different. Now let's decide on some concrete areas to work on—your own personal plan, broken down and in the order of importance that most makes sense to you. Once you know what matters most in your life, then you can use this book to help you accomplish your goals. You don't need to read it from cover to cover at first. But even if you do, be sure to come back to this first chapter and narrow down those areas you know you need to get a grip on. Concentrating on these right away will have a significant impact on your life.

Doing the exercises I've given you will make the information presented here more effective for you. Write down your thoughts and make a plan. Consider drafting a written contract. Share your plan or contract with a buddy. Having a "partner in crime" can drive your likelihood of success up another big notch. Make sure you pick someone who'll be "in your face" about what you say you want. Do the same for your partner. Put due dates on your contract or plan and tell your buddy to get on your case when the date is drawing near. Meet in person or by phone with your buddy every week or month to review your progress, and celebrate when you meet a deadline. Have the same commitment to the other person's goals that you have for your own.

Be fair to yourself. You need to look at any special considerations you may have. My husband and I, for example, both work at home in separate businesses. We have a much larger volume of paperwork, supplies, and equipment than the average household does. Managing these areas takes more of our energy than is required by most people.

Friends of ours own and operate an animal-training business from their home. They need to concentrate on daily cleaning of certain parts of their home and deal with lots of strangers coming in and out. If you have a large family with children of varying ages, your considerations are different than a couple's whose children are all grown and gone. Different still is a household consisting of one individual. While you do your self-assessment, be aware of the realities of your circumstances and know that your plan needs to take these into account. You'll probably need to tackle the special challenges your particular lifestyle presents first.

> **Oops!**
>
> Using your spouse or your significant other as your "buddy" in setting your goals could have some pitfalls. Your partner may be one of the challenges you'll be dealing with later (see Part 5). But if he or she is the supportive, nurturing, team-player type, by all means, enlist your partner's help!

As you get serious about setting your goals, think about the rewards. Visualize the final result you're aiming for. Draw a mental picture of how being organized would look in your life.

Wishcraft

Now, get out that pad and pencil. We're going to do some broad-based goal-setting. Make a separate sheet for these eight major areas of your life:

- ◆ People (you'll get help with this in Chapter 8)
- ◆ Work (Chapter 9)
- ◆ Food (Chapter 11)
- ◆ Clothing (Chapter 12)
- ◆ Shelter (Chapter 13)
- ◆ Money (Chapters 14 and 15)

- ◆ Health (Chapter 16)
- ◆ Fun (Chapters 21 to 26)

On each sheet, make a random list under the main topic of how you'd like that area to be. Don't hold yourself back or censor yourself. No matter how irrelevant or unachievable your wishes and desires may seem, write them down. Include your "if onlys"—the things you'd like to have or do if you had more time, money, or skill. By including everything, you'll get clearer about what you really want.

For example, under "Food," your goals might be to eat more healthful foods and perhaps lose some weight. How can being organized help you meet these goals? By having the proper foods on hand, by actually planning your meals to stay within certain nutritional guidelines, and by having the right equipment for preparing those foods handy, your chances soar. If, however, your goal is to become a gourmet cook and start your own catering business, then your kitchen and your meal-planning would look completely different.

On the sheet for "Money," your goals might be to get out of debt or secure a better-paying job. Your goals would reflect your desire to change your current situation. Developing a plan and organizing your life around that plan can certainly help you get out of debt or find that new position. If you're debt-free and make enough money in your current job, the way you organize the financial areas of your life might be directed instead toward putting money away for retirement or financing a future project that's important to you.

The point is, if organizing your life is going to be lasting and meaningful, you don't just "get organized"—you *organize with purpose*. It's up to you to discover what that purpose is.

Orderly Pursuits

Some recommended books to help you further with goal-setting and planning are: *The Magic Lamp: Goal Setting for People Who Hate Setting Goals*, by Keith Ellis; *The 7 Habits of Highly Effective People: Powerful Lessons in Personal Change*, by Stephen Covey; and *Wishcraft*, by Barbara Sher.

Narrowing Your List

Continue writing your "wish list" for each category until you've done all eight. Now, on each sheet, circle the one wish that, if it was fulfilled, would have the most significant impact on your life right now. To add a little perspective, think about what would make the most difference in your life if you only had a year to live. I'm not getting morbid here, I'm just trying to inject a little urgency into this exercise. Funny how such a thought cuts through the chaff and gets to the kernel of wheat in a hurry!

As you read this book, use these sheets as a reminder when you begin to list specific tasks taken from each chapter that will help you achieve your goals. You can save the back of each sheet for that, if you like. These are the actions you can take to help you reach the goals you just decided are most important to you. In this way, wishes are transformed into goals, and goals into tasks; ultimately, all is magically turned into results.

Going back to one of our earlier examples, let's say under "Food," you listed as your primary goal "to lose 20 pounds and eat more healthful foods." When you turn to Chapter 10, you're going to be looking for the tips and projects that will help you organize your kitchen, and adapt them to cooking healthier meals that will work with your new eating plan. In Chapter 15, you'll learn more about adding a regular fitness plan to your schedule and planning for a healthier lifestyle.

If you put on the "Work" sheet "perform better in my job and set up my office so I can find things," you'll want to pay special attention to Chapter 6, on handling paper, and Chapter 9, on "Work Systems." I know you'll find at least three simple things you can do immediately to get headed in the right direction.

Setting Priorities

Now, take your sheets and number them in order of priority, with number one being the most significant for you right now. If you feel the most important immediate area to work on is your relationships, then the "People" sheet will have a number one on it. If your doctor told you to lose 50 pounds or you're likely to have a heart attack, then "Food" and "Health" might share the number-one spot. You get the idea.

How and what you organize first will depend largely on your priorities. If you decide that weight loss is a top-of-the-list priority, then your kitchen and food systems will need special attention, as will your activity level. If your career is in high gear and you want to focus on furthering your education and getting ahead, but you've got the health thing pretty much in hand, other areas jump to the top of the list.

Next, on each sheet choose two more wishes (goals) with a very high priority, and circle them. That should give you three circled wishes on each sheet. Decide, in order of importance, which should be number two and which takes the number-three spot. If you're having problems with goal-setting and decide to do some extra work and read one of the books I've recommended, you'll have an even more finely honed set of goals and priorities to work with. *The Magic Lamp* covers all aspects of goal-setting, including the things that get in the way, *The 7 Habits of Highly Effective People* focuses heavily on developing a mission statement, and *Wishcraft* will give you additional exercises to help you pinpoint your goals.

Finally, place the individual lists of three goals for each category on one sheet that you can put in your daily calendar book or on the wall near the desk or table you use to manage your daily affairs.

CAUTION

Oops!

If you don't have a calendar/planner or a central planning place, you'll make the task of organizing much more difficult than it has to be. We'll deal with this in more detail in Chapter 7. For now, get an organizer and put it someplace where you'll be able to refer to it often.

Commit or Fail

Let's examine your motivations for a minute. Are you doing this because someone close to you is on your case? Has something happened (like you blew an important appointment because you forgot or couldn't find the materials you were supposed to bring)? Or did you just spend two hours looking for a wrench you know you have, and finally ended up driving to the hardware store so you could buy a duplicate to complete the job?

Those kinds of aggravating events can sure be the beginnings of getting motivated. But what if you take this trigger incident and broaden it? What if you made a decision to overhaul the larger areas that are out of control, where lack of organization seems to be holding you back and affecting your enjoyment of life? If you look at these incidents in their broader context, the motivation can be even greater and longer-lasting.

This is going to take some work on your part, but it need not be overwhelming. You know the old saying: "How do you eat an elephant? One bite at a time." Well, that's what you're going to do—eat an elephant! I'm going to help you, but you're going to have to dig in with both knife and fork. Sure, you can just slap on some quick fixes and they'll probably make a difference, at least for a while. But think of what a difference it'll make if you work on the big picture and set up organization systems that will put your life in high gear. You can have it all if you're willing to make the effort and see it through.

The Master Plan: Keep It Flexible

This is not going to be like the diet fads many of us have experienced—something you go on for a week until you get tired of counting calories or denying yourself what you enjoy. Gradually it goes by the wayside. Why don't these diets work? They're too rigid. Expectations are too high. They make you feel deprived and stifled. They focus on the symptoms, not on making deeper lifestyle changes.

Experts agree that the best way to lose weight is to change your lifestyle to support healthful eating and regular exercise. You need information to make that change. Which foods? How to cook? Which exercise? How to stay motivated? That know-how—some of it general, some of it specific to you (what foods you like and which exercise you most enjoy, for example)—will let you create a plan that will help you achieve a more healthful lifestyle.

It's no different with getting organized. You need to do the following:

◆ Gather general information.

◆ Collect information about your specific likes, dislikes, strengths, and weaknesses.

◆ Identify goals.

◆ Set up a plan.

◆ Break up the plan into simple tasks.

◆ Schedule tasks, and work toward your goals a little each day.

◆ Develop ways to check progress and reward yourself for achievements.

It's important to do this brain work up front, before you start tearing apart your closets or canceling all your magazine subscriptions. You've already made a good start in the goal-setting area. And there's an added bonus: The techniques you learn here to get your life in order can be transferred to any other area of your life you'd like to change. Figure out what you really want, make a commitment to get it, get the information you need to achieve your goal, and work at it a little each and every day.

Orderly Pursuits

Software programs can help you define your goals. I've heard good things about GoalPro 5.0 (Pentium® 1 - 200mhz or better, Windows® 95/98/ME/2000/XP).

Be willing to adapt your plan as you begin to implement it. Think of your life as continually "under construction," and be open to changing things as you go along. It's been said before in many ways that life is the greatest do-it-yourself project you'll ever undertake. Acquiring the tools and skills you need will make you a better craftsman.

You Deserve a Break Today

Another fundamental concept for changing behavior is providing rewards when you do what you set out to do. Probably the greatest reward of getting your life organized is having more time to spend doing the things you most enjoy. Why not make a list of these things, and when you achieve one of your goals, reward yourself with some time spent doing one of them? I enjoy certain crafts and playing several instruments. When I've done something that was especially difficult or took special discipline, I reward myself with some time in front of the piano or a couple of hours of crafting.

Be good to yourself. Changing your old ways will not be easy. We all resist change. It makes us uncomfortable. It can even be scary. Reward yourself as often as possible, even if it's just to look yourself in the mirror and say, "Well done!" Create small rewards for small things, bigger rewards for bigger things, and don't forget to include some rewards just because you love yourself.

Rewards for getting organized will be inherent. There's the good feeling you get when you can finally walk into your walk-in closet again. The feeling of a burden being lifted when you're out from under all those books and magazines and you can finally face the daily junk mail undaunted. There's the simple pleasure of spending an afternoon lazing in a hammock with a glass of lemonade in your hand, knowing that the house isn't going to fall down around your ears. You're prepared and up-to-date at work, so when you choose to do something fun, you feel completely guiltless, and everything you need for your downtime will be right there where you put it.

Some rewards are even greater than you may realize. When you're in control of your belongings and your time, it's easier to create a bigger vision and work toward it. You have the luxury of contemplating the grander, more philosophical—even spiritual— things in life. So, now is probably a good time to ask yourself, "What's my vision of the future?"

You remember the age-old interview questions: "Where do you want to be tomorrow? Next year? In five years?" Well, ask yourself now. Give serious thought to these familiar questions. Then move on to two even heavier questions: "What do I want on my gravestone? What do I want said in my eulogy?" Whoa! Cosmic, you say? Well, maybe. But answering these questions thoughtfully and honestly should set the stage for you to get the most out of this book and to start thinking with the bigger picture in mind—what getting organized can actually mean for your future.

Putting the Resolve in This Year's Resolutions

Each time we replace last year's calendar with a new one, we hear all about resolutions to be made (and probably broken) for the coming year. Usually these involve something we need to give up or deny ourselves, or they highlight bad habits we need to break. More often than not, these are the same resolutions we made the year before.

Amazing Space
I want you to have a life you love. I'd like to see you take your dreams seriously and be able to achieve them. You deserve to wake up every morning excited about the day and what it will bring, knowing that you are prepared and clear about the prize you're going after. You deserve to be a *winner*.

But from now on, you can look the new year square in the eye filled with excitement and expectancy. You'll view it as a time for congratulating yourself on your achievements and for setting new goals that are meaningful, realistic, and fueled by your innermost desires. You'll expect that the coming year will mean you'll have more of the things you wish for in your life and you'll be doing more of the things you love to do. Now that's a Happy New Year!

The Least You Need to Know

- Your upbringing has shaped your organization skills and habits.
- Setting standards too high actually interferes with lasting change.
- To ensure true success, set goals that are based on what you really want, not what others want for you.
- Being fair to yourself and rewarding yourself often will keep you motivated.

Chapter

2

It's All About "Stuff" and "Time"

In This Chapter

- ◆ Taking inventory of what you have and where it came from
- ◆ Examining your buying habits
- ◆ Making better decisions about the stuff that gets into your life
- ◆ Learning about the dynamics of time

There are two essential elements you need to consider in devising your plan to get organized: *Stuff* and *Time*. It's simple, right? Well, yes and no. The two concepts may seem simple, but being honest about how they really operate in your own life can be a challenge. If you're willing to take a little time up front to examine your personal habits and beliefs, however, you can make some powerful discoveries that can lead to far-reaching changes.

Stuff includes all the physical things you own, things you spend time accumulating, maintaining, and disposing of; things you think about, worry about, and protect. Stuff also includes what you want or need to accomplish each day. There's always lots of "stuff to do."

Time is how you measure your life—the minutes, hours, days, weeks, and years. Everyone has the same amount of time in each day—no more, no less. The difference between people is how they choose to use their time. One of the most compelling reasons to get organized is to have more time to do the things you want to do. No more lost time spent looking for things, fixing or replacing things that broke because they were stored poorly, or going out and buying duplicates because you can't find the originals. By learning the dynamics of time and how to manage it, you can get the "must-do" things out of the way quickly so you can do the fun things. And you can learn to arrange your life so the must-dos really are *musts*.

How Did You Get All This Stuff?

Before we get into the nitty-gritty of organizing your life, we need to start at the beginning—the sources of all the stuff in your life.

Stuff comes into your life in four ways:

1. **You take it.** When you first leave your parents' house to go out on your own, you take some stuff with you. Maybe a small box of books, a few pieces of furniture, stuffed toys, your old test papers and book reports, a scrapbook, and a handful of extra kitchen utensils your mom doesn't need anymore. You know— a little stuff to get you started.

   As you go through your daily life, you bring home more stuff. All those free items (note the magic word—*free*) that agencies, companies, and organizations offer you just for being such a nice person—and a potential customer. Sometimes you pick up stuff in the supermarket from a smiling lady at the door, from a prominently placed brochure rack, or from a shelf, or maybe you send for it in the mail. Still, this is stuff you decide to bring into your life in one way or another. And, hey, it's *free!*

2. **It's given to you.** As time goes by, people give you stuff. There's a chair from Aunt Margaret, Grandma's framed pictures of the Statue of Liberty, Cousin Charlie's used golf clubs. It's hard to say no, and besides, this stuff, too, is *free!*

   Then there are those gifts you receive for all occasions. It starts with gifts for graduation, then your first apartment. Loving relatives and friends send you housewarming gifts. Next, there are birthday presents, perhaps wedding gifts, gifts for anniversaries, and, of course, we must not forget Christmas. Maybe the gift is really not your taste, or you have absolutely no use for it, but gee, it's a gift! It's the thought that counts. And, by gosh, it was *free!* So it ends up in the attic, a storage closet, the basement, the breezeway, or any other place you tuck away things you never use.

3. **You inherit it.** Relatives and family friends die. Somehow their stuff finds its way into your stuff. You can't throw away Grandpa's pipe collection, even though you don't smoke. You can't pitch Mother's hand-crocheted doilies, even though you wouldn't be caught dead using doilies. By golly, they're *free!* So you integrate these possessions into your own or store them, keeping them safe to pass on to the next willing (or perhaps unwilling) party.

4. **You buy it.** Ah, now here's where it gets serious. When you're given things or inherit them, when someone offers you something for nothing, your desire to please, or at least not hurt another's feelings, and your love for the giver or the departed are strong motivators to keep stuff. But that doesn't explain why you buy so much useless stuff for yourself!

> **Tickler Files**
>
> "Actually, this is just a place for my stuff. That's all I want, that's all you need in life, is a little place for your stuff. You know? I can see it on your table. Everybody's got a little place for their stuff. This is my stuff, that's your stuff. That'll be his stuff over there. That's all you need in life is a little place for your stuff."
> —George Carlin

Why We Buy

How conscious were you when you made your last purchase? How did you decide to buy that item? Had you seen it on TV or in a magazine? Did you notice your neighbor with it and decide you just *had* to have it? Let's look at some of the influences on our buying habits.

According to *American Demographics* magazine, in the early 1990s there were 1,220 TV stations in the United States. Radio stations numbered 9,871. There were 1,763 daily newspapers and 11,328 magazines. All these are avenues that advertisers use to reach potential buyers. Private and public agencies spend approximately $400 billion a year to get you to buy their products or services, change your attitudes, or influence your decisions. That's $1,600 a year just for one person: you.

The average American watches between 30 and 40 hours of television a week. If you fall within this average, in a typical day you watch well over 100 TV commercials.

Besides what you get over the tube, you're exposed to various forms of print media and radio. And let's not forget all those billboards, posters, bumper stickers, bus and cab displays, direct-mail packages, and telemarketing calls, not to mention the names of companies plastered on mugs, hats, and memo pads. It's estimated that every day another 100 to 300 sales messages of one kind or another pass by you, either visually or through audio media. The Internet is fast becoming another major marketing tool. Even though Americans represent only 6 percent of the world's population, we consume more than 50 percent of the world's advertising.

Is it any surprise that you wonder how that thing got in your shopping cart in the first place? Why your cabinets and closets are crammed with stuff you never use? "Where did that come from?" you ask. "What was I *thinking?*" But instead of admitting you made a shopping mistake, you keep all that stuff, convincing yourself you can't possibly get rid of it, since it's still "perfectly good." Sound familiar?

> **CAUTION**
>
> **Oops!**
>
> Don't let today's images of "the good life" in ads, TV programs, and movies pass you by without examining them. Are the images skewed toward a luxurious, materialistic lifestyle? Just notice what's being presented, and compare it with your own values and beliefs about what "living the good life" really is.

How to Control the Habit

The first step to controlling the stuff you accumulate is to be aware of how, when, and why you decided to get it in the first place. Take your notebook and keep a running list of the number of times you go shopping next week. Include on it the amount of time spent, what you bought (you can use general categories, but be fairly detailed), and what time of day you went. Notice whether you went alone or with your spouse or a friend, how you felt when you were shopping, whether you went because you had something specific to buy, and whether you stuck to your original purpose or came out with additional items or something else entirely.

Next, take a leisurely walk through your house, look at all your stuff, and ask yourself where it came from. If you bought it, try to remember how you came to the decision to buy it. How often do you use it? What purpose does it really serve in your life? What impact would there be if it was lost or stolen?

Notice that I'm not saying you should cover your ears every time you hear a commercial, nor am I asking you to unplug your TV and put it in the attic. I'm not even suggesting that you skip reading your morning paper or tune out your favorite talk radio host. All I want you to do is to become more conscious of the hidden persuaders around you, and take more conscious control of your buying decisions and your own mind. This is the first important step in organizing your life.

Be more critical of the *way* you view or listen to the mass media, too. The next time you see an advertisement, here are some important questions to ask to help you become a "consumer critic":

♦ What claims does the ad make, both obvious and subtle?

♦ Are the claims substantiated?

♦ What methods are being used to influence your thinking? Pricing gimmicks? Sex appeal? Vivid images? Demonstration? Staged testimonials? Peer pressure? Supposedly scientific studies? Guilt? Fear?

♦ What is the ad's key point? Is it directly related to the product?

♦ How much do you really know about the product from the ad?

♦ Is there some item you already own that performs the same function as well or better?

♦ If this stuff is so great, how come you got along without it until now?

Make it a game when you go shopping with your spouse or kids to keep these questions in mind. This way, you'll help to teach others critical thinking while you hone your own skills.

> **Tickler Files**
> "Society drives people crazy with lust and calls it advertising."
> —John Lahr

Buy! Buy! Buy!

The irrational accumulation of things we don't use, don't need, and eventually don't want is what I call the Acquisition Trap, and we all fall victim to it now and again. The Acquisition Trap is a system of assumptions, beliefs, and ideas about the nature of material things and what they can do for us. This system, which often works on us unconsciously, influences many aspects of our lives: where we live, how we work, and who or what we associate with our purchases. The Acquisition Trap seduces us into believing that owning something will make us sexy, or successful, or smart, and that a particular object or possession represents love, happiness, self-esteem, joy, or knowledge.

> **Orderly Pursuits**
> If you'd like to learn more about living with less and staying out of the Acquisition Trap, check out *Voluntary Simplicity: Toward a Way of Life That is Outwardly Simple, Inwardly Rich*, by Duane Elgin. In addition, the Simple Living Network website, www.slnet.com, offers a free e-mail newsletter and lots of resources for a less acquisitive lifestyle.

Owning a library of beautifully bound books won't make you an educated person. Reading them will. Wearing a certain scent won't make you irresistible to the opposite sex. Your overall appearance and personality is what attracts others. Toting a $500 briefcase won't make you successful in business. Experience, determination, and creativity will.

Be aware of the Acquisition Trap and decide whether you yourself might be caught in it. This isn't about beating yourself up, or feeling guilty—it's just about paying attention to your habits, which can ultimately lead you to living a freer, more organized life.

Less Stuff, More Time

As you begin to apply the ideas in this book, you'll make new decisions about what stuff you have and what stuff you want to devote your time to acquire and maintain. You'll be paring down, examining your work habits, gaining control of your finances, and arranging your life so you can have more fun and spend more time with the people you love. You'll begin to free yourself up to focus on the people and activities that actually give meaning to your life. You'll voluntarily eliminate the excess and concentrate on the good stuff. You'll purge what doesn't work for you and organize the rest. To help you stay on track, I've devised the following "Ten Basic Laws of Stuff." Refer to them every time you get the urge to collect more stuff. I hope they'll remind you why you really don't want to!

The Ten Basic Laws of Stuff

Law number one: Stuff breeds. The more you have, the more you need. Well, okay, if you leave two objects in a dark corner, they don't actually reproduce, but sometimes it sure seems that way. Let's say you buy a computer system. This basic system consists of a keyboard, the computer itself, and a monitor. Oh, and of course there are all those manuals. After you get the computer out of the box and set it up, the first thing you probably decide you need is a printer. Next you need a printer stand and some paper. Oh, and an extra printer cartridge. Then you need an antiglare screen for your monitor and some stuff to clean it with. But the stuff to clean the antiglare screen is different from the stuff you need to clean the monitor screen itself, so you need to get that other stuff, too. If you have a mouse, you'll probably need a mouse pad and a cleaning kit to keep it working properly. Next, you'll start buying software, extra disks, and a CD-ROM drive and burner. And so on, and so on.

Lots of things operate like this. Consider the food processor and all the special attachments, racks, and caddies that go with it, not to mention cookbooks and whatever else you need to get the most out of your appliance. Maybe you're thinking about starting a collection of some kind? All those collector plates need hangers, or holders, or shelves. Those baseball cards need albums or boxes to keep them in. The cute little porcelain figurines need a display case or even a piece of furniture. Even the stuff used to store other stuff, like Tupperware, just begs for something to hold all those lids when you're not using them!

Law number two: The useless stuff crowds out the good stuff. The more you have that's useless, obsolete, broken, or just plain junk, the harder it is to find (and find places for) the stuff you really value and use often. Finding the good stuff takes twice as much time and doubles your blood pressure in the process. The more you have in your life that's extraneous and without purpose, the less time and energy you have for the good stuff.

Law number three: Dust loves stuff. Bugs love stuff. Rodents love stuff. Moisture loves stuff. When you store something unused for long periods of time, odds are that when you finally need it (if you ever do), it'll be useless anyway.

Law number four: Stuff loves to stay where it lands. It takes time and energy to put things away. That's why the coat or sweater that's flung over the chair tends to stay there forever.

Law number five: Stuff expands to fill the space available. The bigger the house and the more storage space it has, the more stuff tends to accumulate.

Law number six: Over time, stuff becomes invisible. Ever notice how once you put something on your bulletin board, in a few days you can no longer see it? Things fade into the background through familiarity. I call this the "Disappearing Stuff Phenomenon." After that scrap of paper hangs on the bulletin board for a while, it can be plainly visible, but you still won't see it.

Law number seven: Stuff costs you money more than once. Don't fool yourself that the only cost of an object is its purchase price. First you pay to buy the item. Now you have to get it home. This may involve driving your car, taking public transportation, or incurring shipping charges. Next you have to store it, which may mean buying a container or a shelf to put it in. If it's valuable, you may need a security system,

> **Amazing Space**
>
> You can make the corollary to Law number four work for you. The easier you make it to put stuff away, the more likely it will be. Refer to later chapters for tips on how to coordinate storage space with your daily habits.

not to mention paying additional insurance premiums. If you move to another house (which will probably be bigger, because you need more storage), you need to pay to move it.

And if all this isn't enough, finally, your stuff continues to "cost" even beyond the grave, when you saddle your family with the unpleasant task of getting rid of it after you die. Think about the real cost of stuff next time you rush out to grab that "bargain."

Law number eight: Stuff has a powerful effect on your state of mind. Clutter can be oppressive and depressing. If our possessions are in need of repair, that can add to our feelings of depression and failure. Stuff can weigh us down, and we feel burdened by it and what we have to do to get and keep it.

Law number nine: Stuff takes on value only when it is used. Unused stuff is just junk or clutter. How often you use it gives it increased value. Less use, less value. Stuff that may seem not to have any utilitarian value can add beauty to your life and therefore is being "used" by your senses and your soul. These aesthetic additions to your environment should be chosen with great care, to give you enjoyment every time you look at them. If you don't love it, lose it!

Law number ten: Stuff doesn't make you happy; you do. I think this law speaks for itself. You know the drill: Money can't buy happiness. Well, it's the same with stuff. Both are just tools to help you achieve your own happiness.

Try spending an entire week without bringing any more stuff into your life. Call a moratorium on shopping, use what you already have as much as possible. During this time review the "Ten Basic Laws of Stuff" and see if you don't become more aware of how stuff gets into your life.

Picture This

The following visualization will help you understand how strongly stuff affects your mental state. Picture yourself in a room—for example, your office or garage—where everything is uncluttered, well positioned, and clearly labeled. Take a moment to notice the positive associations evoked by this smoothly functioning and spacious setting. Now imagine the stuff in the room beginning to expand, as paper spills out of the drawers and files onto the floor, labels get switched, and boxes begin to crowd out the elbow room. What are your emotions now?

The Ten Basic Laws of Time

The other half of the equation to be covered in this chapter is *Time*. In a way, I discussed time indirectly when I talked about how having less stuff can give you more time to do the things you love most.

But time has its own properties and dynamics. And stuff struggles with time in our lives, requiring us to make constant day-to-day choices that affect how the former affects the latter. Experts tell us how to "manage" our time, but it helps to know a little bit more about its very nature. We couldn't very well have the "Ten Basic Laws of Stuff" without giving equal time to the "Ten Basic Laws of Time," now could we?

Law number one: Time can be neither created nor destroyed. Phrases like "making time," "buying time," or "saving time" actually reflect the misconception that time is a *thing*. Time is a concept humankind has created to measure and give proportion to the cycle of birth and death. Of course, we need this concept to make sense of our existence, but every now and then, it's worthwhile to remind yourself that your ideas about time are just that: *ideas*. It's up to you to make use of the time you have in a way that's meaningful and leaves you feeling satisfied and rewarded. You are in complete control of your time, even if you think you're not.

Law number two: Nobody gets more time in a day than you do. Ever notice how some people seem to get so much done in a day or week? You'd swear they had 36-hour days instead of the meager 24 the rest of us get. But remember, we all have the same period between sunrises. It's just that some people know the secrets for using time to the fullest. Soon you'll know them, too.

Law number three: Time isn't money, it's your life. It's fashionable these days to talk about time as it relates to "the bottom line." I prefer to think of time as a collection of moments, filled with possibilities and beyond price. Certainly, we need to know if our efforts to earn a living are producing an adequate wage for time spent, but along with a growing bank account should be deposits of love and joy in the "bank book" of life.

Law number four: The value of time is created by opportunity and choice. What makes one moment more fulfilling than the next? I'd like to suggest that the opportunities we find or create and the choices we make are what give our time value and pleasure. Even missed opportunities and bad choices can be valuable if we allow ourselves to learn the lessons they can teach us.

Law number five: Once time is lost, it can never be reclaimed. When you find yourself "wasting" time watching TV or engaging in idle gossip, remind yourself that these moments are gone forever and can never be retrieved. Imagine how you might want them back if you suddenly found out you had a short time left on the planet. Don't squander your most precious asset.

Law number six: Time invested in planning, preparing, and organizing is vital to making the most of your time. You may rebel at the idea of regularly scheduled planning sessions and careful preparation for both mundane and important events. In the beginning, it may seem that getting organized would take up too much of your time. But by the time you finish this book, you'll understand why time spent planning, preparing, and organizing will more than repay itself in the long run.

Law number seven: You can always begin where you are. The first step to managing your time and moving toward your goals is to start. You know, "just do it!" Take stock of what tools and skills you have, make a plan, and take action. Once you begin the process, you'll figure out what else you need along the way.

Law number eight: Identifying your personal time-wasters leads to mastery. Who knows where the time goes? You do! If you can't seem to remember, keep an activity log for a week and you'll see clearly where the black holes are that suck up your valuable time. Write down all the things you do and for how long, even the mundane things, then total the categories up for each day. Once you've identified the nonproductive uses of your time, write them up as a list and post it where you can see it each day. Be honest. How much time do you spend watching TV? On the phone? Chatting with your neighbor? Reading through junk mail? Knowing your time weaknesses will help you avoid them.

 **Tickler Files**

"Planning is bringing the future into the present so you can do something about it now."
—Alan Lakein

Law number nine: Time seems to expand when you set limits. The more you make conscious decisions about where, how, and with whom you want to spend your time and energy, the more of these commodities you'll seem to have. Setting limits means saying no to some things and yes to others. Bowing out of activities that don't support your goals and dreams frees up time for what really counts. Taking people up on offers of help or paying someone else to do certain tasks are ways of saying "yes" to more time for yourself.

Law number ten: The secret is to enjoy the passage of time. If you're doing more now and enjoying it less, something's definitely wrong. Just being busy doesn't mean you're productive or happy. Do the work to identify your goals, create systems to achieve them, and allow yourself the time to enjoy the rewards. Time will be your friend, not a high-pressure enemy.

Organization is not an end in itself. You can't do it once and for all. It's an ongoing process, especially if you're an active person with lots of interests, goals, and people in your life. Sure, if all you do is get up in the morning, eat, read the paper, eat, watch TV, eat, stare into space, and go to bed, it's probably pretty easy to be organized.

But if you're running a business, managing a household, pursuing hobbies, doing things with friends, serving in community organizations, taking classes, or whatever else you do, there's a lot more to being organized than throwing out the newspaper each day, washing the dishes, and turning off the tube. In fact, you picked up this book in the first place because you have a busy life. You want to get more out of life and be in control of your time and space. With your willingness, some soul-searching, and the information contained in this book, you can transform your life from merely okay to *awesome!*

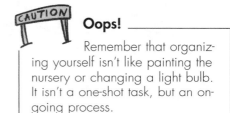

Oops!

Remember that organizing yourself isn't like painting the nursery or changing a light bulb. It isn't a one-shot task, but an ongoing process.

The Least You Need to Know

- Unstuffing begins with understanding how things get into your life in the first place.

- The media and advertising have a powerful influence on your buying decisions.

- There are basic principles of stuff and time that operate in everybody's life.

- Getting control of your stuff and your time is the beginning of gaining control of your life.

Chapter 3

Excuses! Excuses!

In This Chapter

- ◆ How to break old habits and form new ones
- ◆ Common excuses and how to stop making them
- ◆ Breaking the grip of procrastination
- ◆ Finding the time to get organized
- ◆ The cost of organization

If getting organized is so great, why doesn't everybody do it? Well, nobody said it was going to be a snap. There's effort involved, and sometimes the greatest effort goes into overcoming the obstacles we put in our own way. There are four main reasons people fail to get organized:

1. They have limiting ideas and beliefs about what they can and cannot do.

2. They procrastinate.

3. They believe they don't have the time to get organized.

4. They think the tools for getting organized will cost too much.

Recognize yourself in any of these? Well, in this chapter, we'll take a closer look at each reason and show that beginning to get organized this very minute is not only possible, but essential to achieving your goals. We'll also analyze the many reasons we give for why we don't or can't get organized, and expose them for what they are—excuses preventing us from getting what we really want in life.

How Habits Help or Hinder

A habit is what develops when you repeat something often enough that it becomes the customary way you do something. It's "business as usual" in the behavior department. If a habit doesn't seem to benefit us, we talk about "breaking it," much as we talk about taming a wild horse. Habits are hard to break, and the longer you've had them (the more times you've repeated and reinforced them), the more difficult they can be to change. The good news, though, is that you already know how to break an old habit. Really, you do! Since you got these habits through repetition, the way to change them is through the same process—repetition. And if we can break habits, we can also make them. Pick a new behavior, repeat it every day for three to four weeks, and it's yours.

Oops!

Ideas, assumptions, and habits of thinking that served you in an earlier life situation may no longer be in your best interest now. Holding on to old patterns can block our efforts to make important changes. Be aware and let go!

Bet you never before thought of a habit as something you did "on purpose"! Habits can be things that just happen or things we create consciously. We can create the habits we want to have.

When you're trying to make a major change in the way you do things, another area to look at is your beliefs. We all have automatic reactions to things, and many times we've acquired these reactions, these ways of thinking, *without* thinking. So they may not be suitable for our present lives and goals. It's time to examine some of those beliefs and see whether they might be getting in the way of getting your act together.

Excuses for Stuff

If you're wondering how you ended up with all this useless stuff in your life, read on. These could be some of the things you tell yourself and other people that give you permission to live in a junkyard.

I Might Need It Someday

Maybe yes, maybe no. There are several things to consider here. If you don't throw the item away, will you even be able to find it when you need it, and will it be in any useable condition by then? Chances are, if you haven't used it in the past two years, you won't need it in the next two. On the off chance you do, you can probably get it somewhere else. Besides, you're getting organized for the life you live today. If tomorrow brings different challenges, you can always revise your plan and arrange to have on hand the tools you need.

I'm Just Sentimental

Okay, be sentimental. I consider myself a sucker for things that remind me of the people I love or experiences I treasure. But how about being selective? And how about taking those mementos and turning them into something you'll enjoy every day, like a collage or an album? When it comes to memories, not all experiences and people are created equal. Pick the ones that are truly special and memorialize them. Ask yourself, "Is this really important to me, or am I just keeping it out of habit?"

One way I satisfy my sweet tooth for the past without taking up a lot of space is by keeping a journal. Through my written descriptions of people and things, I can relive my experiences again and again. The composition books I use to record my memoirs take up far less space than boxes of out-of-focus photographs or shelves full of knick-knacks. Some people more artistic than I am add sketches to their journals, and even poems or songs. An occasional photo to accompany the text might be an added way to enhance your personal chronicle. You can reread your journals as part of your annual New Year's ritual. You've created something that has meaning, not just accumulated more stuff.

More Is Better

The habit of stocking up can come from a variety of sources. It can be a way of feeling more secure—prepared for hard times. People who survive a major economic crisis, whether personal or on a larger scale like the depression or a war, can overdo it in times of plenty to make up for what they lacked in times past. And

Orderly Pursuits

When you are considering buying in bulk, keep in mind the difference between irrational hoarding and wise preparation. (Refer to Chapter 13 for a fuller discussion.) Keep on hand whatever you'll really need in case of natural disaster or other emergencies, but don't turn your home into a warehouse.

wholesale clubs and discount stores make it easier and cheaper to add to the stockpile. We need to apply a little good sense here. How many people are in your family, and how fast will they consume the goods you're amassing? Will you be able to store them in the meantime, and will they still be fresh when you get around to using them? Do you have room to store them so you can easily see what you have, so that you won't end up buying duplicates?

So be realistic. It's not a bad idea to store some essentials in case of a natural disaster, or to avoid having to run out to the market constantly. But make sure you rotate them with fresh items, and give some serious thought to what you really need.

I'm Saving It for My Kids

This one is closely related to the "sentimental" excuse. If you believe you're filling your attic and basement with things to pass on to your progeny, ask yourself, "Is this something they'd really want?" If you already have adult children or grandchildren, you can ask this question with specific personalities in mind. If you're saving things for children who are yet to be, you might want to honestly ask how likely you are to become a parent or grandparent, and whether the average child of the new millennium will care about this stuff. Remember, tastes change.

> **Amazing Space**
>
> Try to limit your collections to things you can display or store easily; "trade up," getting rid of the lesser examples you have and acquiring better ones as you go along. That's a good rule for decluttering on many fronts. If a new one comes in, an old one goes out!

If you're pretty sure it's something any generation would love, why not pass it on now? Your children or grandchildren might enjoy using these family heirlooms, and you can experience the sense of connection and history that seeing them cared for in the here and now can bring.

One caution. If it's something you're truly ready to give away, do just that: Give it away. No strings, no conditions. If the recipients hate it, they should be free to refuse it or pass it on. And promise them you won't be heartbroken if they break it.

It's Really Old

Ah, we've finally hit upon my own personal clutter trap. I love history, and I'm especially attracted to things from the nineteenth century. Victorian antiques could easily be my nemesis. But just because it's 150 years old doesn't mean it's worth having. (I have to keep telling myself this.)

Unless you're actually in the business of buying and selling antiques, even valuable old junk is still junk if all it does is clutter up your house.

It's Still Perfectly Good

It's only perfectly good if it's good to you now. Even if something's in tip-top shape, if you never use it, it's just a perfectly operating piece of junk. Pass it on to someone who really needs it, or sell it at a garage sale, and make room for the things that are truly "perfectly good" because they have usefulness and meaning for *your* life now or just enjoy the "breathing room."

It Was a Bargain

Need we go back and review the basic principles of advertising we discussed in Chapter 2? Remember, sales are gimmicks to get people into the store. Many times stores run a sale to get rid of something that's going to be discontinued soon, or that a manufacturer has too many of (could it be it's not selling well for a reason?).

Unless the item is something you use regularly, or you made a careful decision to acquire something, researched the make and model you wanted, and it happened to be offered at a special price, a sale really isn't a bargain. Consider that when you're clipping all those coupons, too. Same principle. What should get you into a store is the fact that you need something specific and are prepared to buy it. Just think of all the time you'll save when you give up reading and shopping those circulars!

They Call It a Timesaver

Even if this isn't one of your bugaboos, I'll bet you know someone who can't resist the latest newfangled thingamajig. Some people are just gadget freaks. They love all sorts of whose its and whats its, and can always think of an excuse to get them. Usually it's in the interest of making some task easier, saving money or saving time. Well, always build into the true cost of that gadget the time it takes to earn the money to buy it and to maintain the space you store it in. Add in the time it takes to find it, get it out, and use it, *plus* the time it takes to clean it after the task is done.

The Big Put-Off

Putting off 'til tomorrow what we need to do today is known as procrastination. We all do it now and then, but for some it can become a chronic condition. Sometimes knowing why we do something that has a negative effect on our goals and desires can be the beginning of changing how we behave. Now that we've looked at some of your excuses for keeping or acquiring more stuff, let's dive into the reasons you have for just not "getting around to getting organized."

Some underlying causes of procrastination are …

- You're not really committed.

- There's something you don't want to face.

- You don't know how.

- You have some belief that's getting in your way.

- You're setting too high a standard.

- You're afraid you'll fail.

- You're trying to do too much at once.

- You haven't clearly defined your goals.

- Your energy level is low.

- You aren't convinced of the benefits.

The fact that you're reading this book and have gotten this far says to me you're at least somewhat committed to unstuffing your life and getting things on an even keel. If you didn't do the exercises in Chapter 1, go back and do them now, especially if you skipped the goal-setting section. When you have a mission and you know why you're doing something and what the benefits will be when you accomplish it, your excitement will be uncontainable.

If you're still dragging your heels, ask yourself what you're afraid of. Is it a possible conflict with your spouse? Are you afraid you might fail? Is it resistance to change? Let me ask you to put these concerns aside for now. We're going to deal with them in various ways throughout this book, and you'll have lots of small, specific steps you can take to help you confront your fears and accomplish your goals.

Examine your beliefs, as well. Look for things you hear yourself saying often like "I can't," or "I always,"

Oops!

Keep a vigilant eye on the hidden time demands of so-called time-savers. For example, a food processor does a lot of things more quickly than preparing food by hand. But unless you're cooking in quantity, the time it takes to chop onions by hand will be a lot less than the time it takes to take out the processor, use it, clean it, and store it again.

or "If only," or "Once I have … then I can." Replace this language with "I am," "I want," or "I can and I will." Concentrate on what you have control over, and the skills and resources you already possess. Focus on acting upon, rather than being acted upon and reacting to. Be proactive.

Picture This

When we don't have the benefits of a course of action clearly in mind, we will it put off. Visualization helps here. Picture yourself at work where you can find everything in your files and never forget an appointment. See yourself dressing in the morning with a wardrobe that's well planned, easy to choose from, and always clean, pressed, and mended. See yourself preparing a meal in a sparkling, efficient kitchen where everything's within easy reach.

If your energy level is low, everything becomes a chore. Are you in poor health, not getting enough sleep, partying too much, or experiencing temporary depression? If you answer yes to any of these, give yourself the physical and emotional attention you need first, and then get to work.

Pulverizing Procrastination

Now that you've had a conversation with yourself about some of the underlying causes of your procrastination, here are some tips for breaking through the bottleneck:

- Tackle it head on. Ask yourself, "What's the real reason I keep putting this off?"

- Take one step. Do *something* right away to get you started. Action produces momentum. Get started.

- Do the hardest thing first. Do the easiest thing first. (See which approach works better for you.)

- Clear the decks. Set aside time, clear a work area, and assemble the tools you'll need to get started. Make an appointment with yourself and write it in your calendar.

- Break down your plan into small tasks. Write down the larger tasks and divide each into its smaller parts or "bites" (remember the joke about how to eat an elephant?). See if the task can be broken down in terms of time or physical space. Do five files, clean one cabinet, set the kitchen timer and spend 10 minutes on the task.

- Do something toward your goal every day, even if it's a very small thing.

- Set deadlines for yourself.

- Set a fixed time to take on a task every day or week, and stick to it. This will help form a habit and it'll take less energy over time to get it done.

- If one way isn't working, try another. Adopt a "whatever it takes" attitude.

- Don't let too much attention to detail or perfectionism get in the way. Visualize the end result and be realistic about it.

- Enlist some help. Finding someone to share a task with can get you started and keep you going. Enlist your kids, your spouse, or a buddy. Set specific goals, check in with your buddy regularly, and enjoy a reward together when you follow through.

- Do it now! Get in the habit of doing things right away. If you have something to put away, do it. Don't put it on the counter on the way to the garage, or on the stairs to be put away later. Finish it. The sense of completing tasks on a regular basis will reinforce itself.

- Increase your rate of motion. Set a timer, challenge yourself, make the time go faster. Create momentum using whatever tricks work for you. Get wise to yourself.

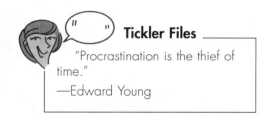

Tickler Files

"Procrastination is the thief of time."

—Edward Young

If you keep putting things off in spite of all these efforts, maybe you *really* don't want to get organized. Either shelve the idea until you're ready to commit some significant thought and energy to it or, if you're not ready to give up just yet, hire someone else to do it. Perhaps hiring a professional organizer will be the jump start you need, and you'll be able to finish the job yourself.

Making Time

Do you think you can't afford the time to get organized? Actually, you can't afford the time *not* to get organized. Just consider all the extra steps, the time wasted, the duplicated efforts, the frustration, the feelings of losing your grip, the missed appointments and important events, and the lost moments. Getting organized will fill your pockets with time to spare.

But I Don't Have the Money to Get Organized!

Organization is a state of mind, not a thing. It doesn't have to cost a lot of money to get organized. In fact, you can't afford not to. There are lots of low-cost or even re-cycled solutions to storage and organization tools, and I'll point them out to you throughout this book. Wherever possible, I've given you several alternatives, including budget-conscious ones, for the materials suggested.

Spending money on the right tools will save you gobs of dough in the long run. Quality storage containers and tools will quickly pay for themselves. Weigh the cost of something that will help you get and stay organized against the cost of chaos. I think you'll find it's worth it in the long run to spend money on quality items that will do the job well and last a long time.

So, Stop Making Excuses and Go!

Let's face it. People who are always making excuses are a drag. Just think about the people in your life who do it and how you feel about them. Not high on your list of folks to while away the hours with, right?

Don't be one of those people. Start today. Take your first step toward achieving what you truly desire. If you keep making excuses and procrastinating, you give up control. Why drift through life when you could be at the helm, steering? Concentrate on what you can change, and begin.

Orderly Pursuits

Be sure to consult some good books on managing your time, an inextricable part of getting organized. Two good books on time management are *Time Management from the Inside Out: The Foolproof System for Taking Control of Your Schedule and Your Life* by Julie Morgenstern, and *First Things First: To Live, To Love, To Learn, To Leave a Legacy* by Stephen Covey.

The Least You Need to Know

◆ Habits are made through repetition and can be changed the same way.

◆ By looking at your beliefs in light of your goals, you can spot obstacles to your progress.

◆ Procrastination has a variety of causes, and there are simple steps you can take immediately to combat it.

◆ You can't afford the time or the money it costs to stay disorganized.

Chapter 4

When Stuff Rules Your Life

In This Chapter

- ◆ Defining clutter disorder, hoarder's disorder, and compulsive spending disorder
- ◆ Understanding the relationship between chronic disorganization and Attention Deficit Disorder (ADD)
- ◆ Determining if your relationship with stuff is seriously out of control
- ◆ Getting help and support for recovery and growth

Most of us recognize ourselves in the first three chapters of this book. If you weren't struggling with clutter and disorganization, chances are you wouldn't have picked up this book in this first place. Even the most organized people have to do periodic tweaking, can find themselves getting behind, and may sometimes be prone to procrastination. But there's a line beyond which disorganization becomes a personality disorder.

In this chapter, we're going to discuss some serious personal issues. It's beyond the scope of this book to fully cover their complexities, so I've given you some basic information along with resources to lead you to the real experts—books, support groups, and mental health professionals.

If you're dealing with some of these issues, I do hope you'll reach out and get the help you need.

Hoarder's Disorder and a Case of the Messies

There are folks for whom the terms *messy* or *disorganized* just don't quite express it. The chaos in their lives is extreme and chronic. The debris and mess seriously hampers their ability to function day to day, and may even have a negative impact on their ability to have a happy marriage, parent their children effectively, hold a job, and maintain healthy, satisfying friendships.

Tickler Files

"Anything that can get you evicted, get your children taken away from you, keep you from inviting people into your home, or get you charged more by retailers and the tax authorities because you can't find the paperwork needed to pay them on time, is a real problem."

—alt.recovery.clutter FAQ

CAUTION **Oops!**

Ignoring the signs that there's a deeper problem operating in your life can mean serious repercussions later on down the road. People who recognize their needs and seek help are smart and courageous!

This extreme behavior can come under a variety of names and categories. It's not always easy to diagnose exactly what it is or where it comes from. Sometimes labeled "clutter disorder" or "hoarder's disorder," this is a new area being explored in psychology, and few therapists are trained or experienced in treating it. Extreme cluttering and disorganization may also be manifestations of other psychological problems or even neurological disorders. But, as with many other debilitating behavioral problems, professionals can be located to provide treatment, and self-help groups—both local and online—have been formed to offer the support and information needed to make great strides in conquering the problem.

According to Sandra Felton, founder of Messies Anonymous and a self-professed "messie," approximately 15 percent of the population is in this category. She describes her life, before she got help, as a real struggle:

> I had big houses, little houses, no children, children, maids, no maids. But under all circumstances I was a Messie. This was not only frustrating, but surprising, since I was quite capable in other areas of my life.

Are You a Compulsive Clutterer?

But how do you know if you're in the "extreme" category? There are warning signs. Ask yourself the following questions, and if you answer yes to several of them, this may be the time to come to grips with what's happening and seek professional help.

Yes	No	
❏	❏	Have you read all the books, hired a professional organizer, and repeatedly tried to get started decluttering your life, yet you seem never to be able to do it?
❏	❏	Is the accumulation in your house a severe health or safety hazard?
❏	❏	Do you have a deep fear of people coming to the house and seeing the clutter and dirt? Do you pretend not to be home, so you don't have to open the door?
❏	❏	Do you lose sleep over lost papers, money, or other valuable items?
❏	❏	Do you chronically miss appointments and important occasions, even though you have the best intentions of making them?
❏	❏	Are you often referred to as unreliable or disorganized by others?
❏	❏	Has the safety of your children ever been compromised because of clutter or disrepair in your home?
❏	❏	Do you regularly pay late payment fees or penalties not because you don't have money to pay the bills, but because you can't find them, can't remember to deposit checks, or are unable to keep track of your checkbook balance?
❏	❏	Do you avoid leaving the house or cancel appointments for lack of clean or mended clothes?
❏	❏	Do you drive a vehicle with expired insurance or registration, even though you have the money to pay these fees?

These could be indicators that your disorganized habits go deeper than normal. If you're not sure, seek the help of a professional, and be open about your behaviors and concerns. There's a lot we don't understand about disorganization and related disorders. Only recently, for example, have they been linked to Attention Deficit Disorder, obsessive-compulsive disorders, and certain speech pathologies, such as stuttering. In the most extreme cases, there may be stacks of newspapers from floor to ceiling, clothes covering all the floors, broken furniture and appliances left blocking doors and windows, and boxes of saved paper, plastic bags, jars, and cans filling basements and porches. Sufferers may be unable to leave their homes, handle their finances, or have meaningful relationships.

Picture This

Close your eyes and visualize being enveloped by a huge pink bubble. With this bubble around you, you can be, have, or do anything you want to—you are confident and nothing can harm you. Inside the bubble you feel bliss and happiness. Imagine that you are unconditionally cared for by others, enjoying their respect and esteem. As you bask in the warmth of your own worth and worthiness, say to yourself "I am never alone. I have a wise and loving friend within me. If I need help, I can ask for it anytime."

Attention Deficit Disorder and ADHD

A condition related to clutter disorders is Attention Deficit Disorder (ADD) or ADD with hyperactivity, ADHD. Persons with ADD often have trouble setting priorities or planning in what order to do a series of tasks or activities. They may start something, but be unable to finish. People suffering from ADD find their mind is so cluttered with competing thoughts and messages, it is hard to function. It's no wonder that mental clutter manifests itself in physical clutter and disorganization.

If you're not sure whether or not you or someone close to you might have ADD or ADHD, there's a quiz available online to give you some clues. You can find it at Mental Help Net at mentalhelp.net/. Just type "ADD Questionnaire" into the Search box.

Education professionals are becoming more informed and better able to identify ADD in children. This disorder can severely inhibit a child's ability to learn in a conventional educational setting, and can lead to behavioral problems if not treated. If caught early, however, many positive steps can be taken to circumvent the negative patterns that can develop in ADD children as they grow into adulthood.

Shopping When You Don't Need More Stuff

Compulsive shopping/buying disorder can be another culprit in the fight against clutter and disorganization in a person's life. In this instance, the accumulation of stuff is an offshoot of the problem. The main cause, however, is a compulsive need to buy things, even when they are not needed and they are not serving any purpose in a person's life. Compulsive shopping disorder can cause financial ruin and destroy relationships.

If you're not sure whether you might have a compulsive spending problem, ask yourself these questions:

◆ Do you continue spending on credit, even though you're unable to pay off your current credit card debt?

◆ Are you facing bankruptcy or at least serious financial problems, yet are unable to curb your spending?

◆ Do you often have arguments with your partner, family members, or friends about your spending?

◆ Do you have a closet stuffed full of clothes you never wear, some with the price tags still on, yet find yourself shopping for more?

◆ When you're in a store, do you find you cannot leave without buying something?

◆ Do you spend inordinate amounts of time shopping or thinking about shopping?

◆ Do you shop to avoid pressure, to escape or fantasize, to increase your self-esteem, or to feel more secure?

◆ Do others regularly make comments about your excessive spending?

◆ Do you often spend money you don't have on things you don't need, or perhaps already have several of at home?

If you answered yes to any of these questions, you may be suffering from compulsive shopping disorder. If you're not sure, ask a professional to help with a diagnosis.

Compulsive spending is only one type of obsessive-compulsive disorder (OCD). Other OCDs manifest themselves in the reverse behavior of disorganization or out-of-control spending, such as compulsive neatness. Both extremes can mean that stuff somehow rules your life and interferes with your enjoyment of

Orderly Pursuits _____

Here are two books to help with understanding and overcoming compulsive spending: *Born to Spend: How to Overcome Compulsive Spending* by Gloria Arenson; and *Can't Buy Me Love: Freedom from Compulsive Spending and Money Obsession* by Sally Coleman and Nancy Hull-Mast.

Tickler Files _____

"Clutter is anything we don't need, want, or use that takes our time, energy, or space, and destroys our serenity. It can be outgrown clothes or obsolete paper. We may be selective in some areas, but not in others. Objects may be strewn about or wedged into drawers; neatly stacked or stowed in storage."

—The Twelve Steps of Clutterers Anonymous

regular activities and other people. If you can't stand to see something out of place, if you have to constantly straighten and clean, if it's difficult for you to relax without thinking about tidying up or cleaning, then you may have OCD. Again, if you're uncertain, seek the help of a professional to get a more accurate diagnosis and devise a treatment strategy.

Other Disorders and Conditions

There are other mental health issues and possibly infectious diseases that may influence an individual's ability to manage his or her life and stay organized. Some of these are depression, bipolar disorder, chronic fatigue syndrome, and fibromyalgia. If you're not sure what may be exerting its influence in your situation, a healthcare professional, a professional therapist, counselor, psychologist, or psychiatrist can help you sort it out. If you suspect a particular culprit, by all means share your suspicions with your mental health professional.

It's important that you identify the source of your problem and get help. You don't have to live with anxiety and chaos! You deserve better. If you or someone you love needs help, lead the way.

Never Fear—Help Is on the Way!

All the disorders and conditions I've mentioned can be treated. There's excellent help out there, and the resources in this chapter should help you at least get started on the road to recovery. There are varying degrees of distress, of course. But for some people the situation is grave, and drastic measures need to be taken.

Don't wait to seek professional help if you feel this is the case. If, however, you feel the situation is less severe, you can still take steps to help yourself, armed with good information and the support of other people who suffer from the same problems. In fact, for some, the ongoing support of people like themselves, in addition to working with a mental health professional, is the best route to real recovery.

Hoarder's Disorder

One option for recovery is to find a 12-step group that is designed to work on your specific problem. Similar to alcohol and drug recovery groups and based on the principles of Alcoholics Anonymous, these groups follow a defined structure and set of principles, and have produced some dramatic life-changing results. They're free, and if there isn't one in your area, it's easy to start one on your own. Some 12-step groups for clutter disorders are:

Clutterers Anonymous
P.O. Box 91413
Los Angeles, CA 90009-1413
admin@clutterersanonymous.net
www.clutterersanonymous.net

For info send a long first-class SASE with twice the minimum first-class postage to:

Messies Anonymous
5025 SW 114th Avenue
Miami, FL 33165
(800) MESS-AWAY (637-7292)
www.messies.com

> **Amazing Space**
>
> If you join a group, you'll probably find lots of resources available there that you can borrow or share, rather than purchase on your own. This can be the first step toward eliminating clutter in your life. You'll have partners that can catch you when you begin to repeat old, destructive patterns, and cheer you on when you make new, more constructive decisions. You're not alone anymore!

Founded in 1981 by confessed "messie" Sandra Felton in Miami, these groups use her books to guide in the recovery process. Her latest is *The New Messies Manual: The Procrastinator's Guide to Good Housekeeping*. Felton also gives seminars nationally.

Other Disorders

Some organizations for other disorders and conditions that offer information, referrals, and support are:

Obsessive-Compulsive Disorder

Obsessive-Compulsive Foundation
337 Notch Hill Road
Branford, CT 06471
(203) 315-2190
info@ocfoundation.org
www.ocfoundation.org

Obsessive-Compulsive Anonymous
P.O. Box 215
New Hyde Park, NY 11040
(516) 739-0662
hometown.aol.com/west24th/index.html

Orderly Pursuits

Bipolar disorder and depression touch people in all walks of life. One of the more well-known personalities who has gone public with her bouts of this mental illness is actress Patty Duke. Her book (with writer Gloria Hochman) is called *A Brilliant Madness: Living with Manic-Depressive Illness*. A second recommended book on the subject is Kay Redfield Jameson's *An Unquiet Mind*.

Compulsive Spending/Shopping Disorder

Debtor's Anonymous
General Service Office
P.O. Box 920888
Needham, MA 02492-0009
(781) 453-2743
www.debtorsanonymous.org

General Emotional Disorders

Emotions Anonymous International
P.O. Box 4245
St. Paul, MN 55104-0245
(651) 647-9712
info@EmotionsAnonymous.org
www.emotionsanonymous.org

Attention Deficit Disorder

National ADD Association
1788 Second Street, Suite 200
Highland Park, IL 60035
(847) 432-ADDA
mail@add.orgwww.add.org

This organization will help you find ADD professionals and support groups in your area, whether you're an adult with ADD or the parent of an ADD child.

Bipolar Disorder and Depression

National Depressive and Manic-Depressive Association
730 N. Franklin Street, Suite 501
Chicago, IL 60610-7204
(800) 826-3632
www.ndmda.org

Chronic Fatigue Syndrome

The American Association for Chronic Fatigue Syndrome
515 Minor Avenue, Suite 18
Seattle, WA 98104
(206) 781-3544
info@aacfs.orgwww.AACFS.org

Finding a Local Group

When attempting to locate any self-help group in your area, first check with the headquarters of the proper organization, and ask for a local contact person. If you're close enough, you may be able to join their group. Otherwise, call the contact person and pick her brains. She'll probably have lots of ideas to share about how she got started, and what to avoid in starting your own group. If you decide you want to do that, put up a notice on bulletin boards at local churches, the library, the post office, Laundromats, health-food stores, and any other public place where you think you might find people who'd like to work with you on starting a group. Leave your name with local mental health professionals, as well. If you have a community self-help clearinghouse or hot line, let them know of your desire to form a group and ask them to refer people to you.

Next, put a notice in the public service announcement section of your local newspaper. Consider any newsletters of organizations that might reach people for your group. Contact professional organizers in your area and let them know what you're trying to do. A professional organizer often knows people who might benefit from such a group. To find one, contact the National Association of Professional Organizers, P.O. Box 140647, Austin, TX 78714; (512) 206-0151; www.napo.net; e-mail napo@assnmgmt.com.

Going Online

Even if you decide not to join a group, you may want to subscribe to an organization newsletter for support, subscribe to an online mailing list, or check in with an online newsgroup. For online resources, try some of the following:

Mailing Lists

Decluttr mailing list

Decluttr@MAELSTROM.STJOHNS.EDU

To subscribe, send this message to listserv@MAELSTROM.STJOHNS.EDU: Subscribe Decluttr (Your) FirstName LastName.

This list and its monthly archives are public. You can subscribe to the list in an index (table of contents) format or a digest (one mailing with all messages for the day) format.

The Flylady mailing list and website

I discovered the Flylady a couple of years ago and I can't help but sing her praises. Basing her system on the "Slob Sisters" system outlined in the *Sidetracked Home Executives* book series, Marla Cilley has improved on their ideas and created a support system ideal for those who need daily help getting their housework done and clearing their lives of clutter.

To subscribe, go to the Flylady website at www.flylady.net. While you're there, check out the archives and get started on your routines and periodic "27 Fling Boogies." All can benefit from the Flylady's wisdom, but her principles are especially helpful for those suffering from depression, ADD, or ADHD.

Compulsive Spenders mailing lists

There are several mailing lists for people with compulsive spending disorder. To sign up, register at group.yahoo.com and type in "compulsive spending" to get a list.

Bipolar Disorders Information Center

Their main website is www.mhsource.com/bipolar/index.html.

Subscribe to the bipolar mailing list at www.mhsource.com/bipolar/mailinglist.html.

Roses and Thorns

A mail list for diagnosed mood disorders, such as depression, bipolar disorder, and seasonal affective disorder (SAD). To subscribe, point your browser to www.esosoft.com/hauser/.

Newsgroups

alt.recovery.clutter

This is a place where people who have cluttering as a problem can discuss methods of dealing with it, share experiences and tips, support each other, recommend books and find contact information for organizations. It doesn't speak for any particular organization. They have created a FAQ (list of frequently asked questions) available at www.faqs.org/faqs/alt-recovery/clutter/.

alt.support.depression.manic
soc.support.depression.manic
soc.support.depression.misc
soc.support.depression.treatment

These four newsgroups are for those suffering from bipolar disorder (also known as manic-depression).

Other Online Resources

www.pendulum.org

Bipolar Disorders Portal at Pendulum Resources.

www.cdc.gov/ncidod/diseases/cfs/index.htm

Chronic Fatigue Syndrome Home Page from the Centers for Disease Control and Prevention.

If you don't see what you're looking for here, click on your favorite search engine and put in any of the terms I've mentioned. You'll find tons of information for each, including help understanding what these disorders are, clues to help you decide what might actually be going on in your own particular case, and resources for finding professional help and support groups in your hometown. If you don't have access to the Internet, check the Yellow Pages of your local phone book, or call the nearest mental health facility.

Don't underestimate your own ability to do this. Once you've identified a problem, you can begin to solve it. Many of these disorders can be overcome or minimized with hard work and persistence. However, if you really try to do it on your own and you're just overwhelmed or can't seem to get out of your own way, reach out and join with others who can help show you the way and support you in your efforts. A support group can give you a sense that you're not in this alone, plus provide some solid ideas and approaches you can try in your own life.

I have nothing but admiration for people who face their illnesses and work on their own recovery. I hope in some small way I've helped you or someone you love find a way. May you gather the courage, energy, and self-love to triumph and be well!

Tickler Files

"It is hard to fight an enemy who has outposts in your own head."
—Sally Kempton

The Least You Need to Know

◆ If disorganization and clutter interfere with a person's ability to function, there is likely a more serious disorder that needs to be addressed.

◆ While each disorder has its own particular symptoms, conditions such as Attention Deficit Disorder (ADD), hoarder's disorder, and bipolar disorder all can lead a person to live a highly disorganized life.

◆ Seeking professional help and joining a support group are effective ways to overcome or at least live with emotional disorders and diseases that affect the ability to organize and manage one's life.

◆ There are many resources online for information on clutter-related disorders and diseases. Using a search engine will probably provide you with much of what you need, if it's not listed in this chapter or in your local phone book.

Part 2

Stuff Simplified

These next chapters will get you into the unstuffing mode. By reducing the amount of clutter that comes into your space, as well as getting rid of what's already there and in your way, all the rest of your efforts at organizing your life will go more smoothly. First we'll tackle the paper monster, or should we say monsters? (The ones that live and breed in your home, your office, your car, and your mailbox.) By the time you're through with this part, you'll be ready to tackle anything!

Chapter 5

Utterly Uncluttered Space

In This Chapter

- Simple principles you can adopt right away for immediate results
- Questions to ask yourself when organizing your stuff
- A 10-step program for clearing out the clutter
- The real costs of having too much stuff in your life

You're impatient, I know. I am, too. So why not get started right this minute? Get out of that chair! Don't even think about going for that remote!

So, you haven't quite got your goals set and your plans made like I told you to do in Part 1. Well, I'm going to give you 10 quick and easy steps to get you started on the right track. They're basic principles you can begin using immediately to make the rest of your organization efforts fall right into place.

Getting Started

Pick one room or area to begin. It can be as big or as small as the time you have available. If you can, pick an area that supports your highest priorities. Key areas would be your bedroom (to ensure a peaceful night's sleep) or the kitchen (the hub of the house), but you choose. Decide not to get distracted. As you note larger projects like building storage or buying storage solutions, put them down on a single list. Don't worry about any order or deadlines for now. This list will become your Master List, but for now you don't need to think about what it's called. Just keep a running list of anything that needs to be done or that you'd like to do someday. Record any ideas that pop into your head while you're plowing through your stuff.

Next, set up five boxes. Label them *Trash*, *Put Away*, *Mystery*, *Pass On*, and *Fix It*, or use your own labels if you like. If you have a recycling program in your area, you may want to set up another box labeled *Recycle*, or just bring the plastic recycling bin with you.

The purpose of the *Trash* and *Recycle* bins or boxes is obvious. The *Put Away* bin is for stuff that doesn't belong where you found it. It may be other people's junk (or treasures) or simply items you know belong somewhere else.

The *Pass On* box is for stuff to hand down, give to charity, or sell at a garage sale—anything you're not keeping that is too good to throw away.

The *Mystery* bin is for things you just can't figure out what to do with. Maybe you don't have a place for it (you'll need to find one if you decide to keep it around). Even worse, you may not know what it is (true mystery stuff)! If at all possible, ask the questions in step one (discussed later) and make a decision now to trash/recycle it, pass it on, or put it away. But if you're just not sure where it goes right now and it takes a lot of time to decide, you'll at least have a temporary place for it.

> **Amazing Space**
>
> Set a time when you'll return to the *Mystery* box. Be ruthless as you go through it and decide which of the remaining four bins the stuff belongs in. Most of it can go out the door through the *Trash*, *Recycle*, or *Pass On* bins. The more you use this system, the fewer "mystery" items you'll have as time goes on.

The *Fix It* bin should only be used for items you really believe are worth fixing. If it's been broken for five years and you've lived without it this long, don't bother. More about this bin later.

Now, armed with your pad of paper and your bins, you're ready to begin working through the 10 steps.

Step One: Use It or Lose It

One of the greatest favors you can do for yourself, starting today, is to get into the stuff-cycling habit. Don't let it land—keep it moving. If it's in use, it's moving. It can move on to someone else who has a use for it, to a local charity, to the recycling center, or to the trash. The key word here is *use*. For starters you can vow today not to let anything come through the door unless you're sure you're really going to *use* it.

Take your chosen area and go through it, item by item. Ask the following questions and follow through with the action discussed after the question:

- **When was the last time I *used* this?** If it's been more than a year, give serious thought to putting it in the *Trash* or *Pass On* bin. If you're sure you need to hang on to it, go on to the next question.

- **How often do I use it?** If you don't use it very often and it's in a location where regular daily activities occur, put it in the *Put Away* bin. You need to find a place other than that reserved for more useful items. But, before you do that, ask yourself the next question.

- **If I don't use it very often, could I borrow, rent, or improvise the few times I might need it?** If the answer is yes, put it in the *Trash* or *Pass On* bin.

- **Is it a duplicate?** If it is, you probably bought another one because you were unhappy with the old one or you couldn't find it. Keep the best one and toss or pass on the extra one. Put the item where you use it most.

- **Is it out of date?** Food that's past the expiration date or clothing that'll never be back in style? Throw old food away or add it to the garden compost, and pass on clothes. Expired medicines should be flushed down the toilet for safety's sake.

Oops!

Don't throw out, give away, or sell anyone else's stuff without asking. How would you like it if someone did that to you?

- **If I didn't have this anymore, what impact would it have on my life?** This is a deeper question, but ultimately one you need to ask. Imagine that the dog chewed it up or a flood carried it away or a burglar took it. Is this item something you'd have to run right out and replace? This exercise will probably direct still more things into the *Trash*, *Recycle*, or *Pass On* bins.

- **Do I value this item?** If the answer is yes, put it where you'll use it, display it, or put it in your treasure chest.

- **Am I keeping this because I'd feel guilty if I tossed it?** Consider that people give you gifts because they want to please you. If you don't use it or like it, pass it on to someone who will—a family member or charity. It will make you feel good, which is the whole point of gift-giving! Let go of that guilt!

◆ **How easily could I get another one if I needed it?** If it's a hard-to-find item and likely to be used even once in a while, then it may be worth keeping. Store it in a way that'll make it easier to find later.

One idea for the *Pass On* box. How about sharing? Is there someone you know who would use an item more than you do? Give it to them so they can store it, with the condition that you can borrow it back when you need it. Consider this solution for stuff like camping gear, bicycles, tools, and sports equipment.

Step Two: Put It Away

When you can't find things that are useful or even valuable, it's like not having them at all.

In this step, you'll work with your *Put Away* box. Remember that putting stuff away is a habit that can be formed. Start today. When you take something out, put it back where you found it. It's worth the extra steps. When you see something lying around, ask, "Where does this belong?" and put it there *now*. If it doesn't have a place, put it in your *Mystery* box. Applying other principles in this chapter, you'll find a place for it shortly.

As you're putting things away, think about the principle of prime real estate. The storage closest to where you spend the most time and engage in most of your activities is *prime real estate*, and it has the most value. Put the things you use most often there. By moving something to where the task is done, you activate it. *Secondary storage* is for stuff you use, but not every day. The *deep freeze* is for rarely used items such as seasonal stuff or tax records. Be careful of this one, though. It can become a clutter trap all too easily. Remember, the key word to keep uppermost in your mind is *use*. If you only think you *might* use it, don't store it at all. Put it in the *Mystery* box or part with it altogether.

Oops!

Beware of saving things for garage sales. They either end up accumulating in the garage or find their way back into the house again! If you really have enough for a garage sale, put the ad in the newspaper right away!

"But where do I put it when I put it away?" you ask. We'll look at storage solutions more closely in later chapters, but for now we're looking at general principles, and storage has its own set of simple rules. When looking for places for things, here are some important principles to remember:

◆ Get stuff in the general area where it will be most useful. If you found golf balls in the kitchen junk drawer, put them with the golf clubs. If the hair dryer somehow ended up in the living room, make sure it finds its way back to the bathroom.

◆ Choose containers that are uniform and covered. Units with drawers are generally better than those that stack, because stacked boxes have to be moved if you're to get to the ones on the bottom. Make sure labels will stick to them.

◆ Make sure the location and containers will keep your valuable stuff safe from the Destroyers. Who or what are the Destroyers? If you're a clutterer, you know them intimately, I'm sure. They're dust and dirt, moisture, sunlight, and pests. Pests include insects and vermin, and even domestic animals can do damage. Something valuable stored poorly can become junk overnight.

◆ When creating space for the things you're keeping, see if you can add:

> Shelves
>
> Inserts (step shelves, drawer inserts)
>
> Racks
>
> Poles
>
> Hooks
>
> Pegboards
>
> Containers
>
> Carts on wheels

Amazing Space
When you've got stuff in your hands, recite, "Don't put it down. Put it away!" Make it your mantra. *Away* means in its place or in one of the five boxes.

◆ Add getting these items or doing these projects to your master list and move on.

◆ When considering storage, also consider how easy the container or storage unit itself will be to keep clean.

Step Three: Give It Away (Now)

Put the stuff you're saving for posterity in the *Pass On* box. We talked about this already in Chapter 3. Well, now's the time to start giving your loved ones those things you've been saving for them. Pack up Grandma's china and give it to your daughter-in-law, *now*. Pack it up and ship it, haul it there yourself, or ask your kids and grandkids to come and get it. The important thing is to pass on all this wonderful stuff now so it gets to where it's supposed to end up, before you're six feet under. Make sure you let everybody know this stuff is on its way, and reassure them you're not planning on kicking the bucket for a long time. You just want to live to see them enjoy it!

Step Four: Take Just 15 Minutes

Give yourself 15 minutes in the morning to pick up one room. Take that 15-minute coffee break and start revamping your files or working on your goals from Chapter 1. Instead of watching TV, take 15 minutes to apply the "Don't use it? Lose it!" principle to a section of your living room. Take 15 minutes and sort stuff in your boxes or bins from one small drawer. Before you hit the sack, give yourself 15 minutes and put the day's clutter away. You'll wake up a lot more refreshed, and your life will be that much more orderly the next day.

Use a kitchen timer. Somehow that ticking away in the background helps you move a little faster. The timer can become your best friend!

It's amazing how seemingly trivial 15-minute intervals can produce noticeable results, and joined together, they can help you make powerful progress toward achieving your goals.

Picture This
Take a moment to visualize the power of 15 short minutes. Mentally walk through your day, picturing all the times when you could easily set aside 15 minutes for your organizing tasks. Fifteen minutes first thing in the morning; before you fly out the door; the length of a coffee break; a fraction of your lunch hour; half a TV show; the last thing you do before you go to bed. Make a list of the times that are well suited to your schedule.

Step Five: Group Like Things Together

Keep office supplies in one cabinet or drawer. Having them scattered all over means you have to look several places every time you're looking for a paper clip. Do the same thing with cleaning supplies, canned or packaged goods in the kitchen, tools, or whatever. Grouping makes things easier to find, and you'll know what you have so you don't end up buying more than you need.

Other ways of grouping might be to gather all the things for one task together in one container or location. You also might group clothes by color, size, category, or season.

Step Six: Consolidate and Compress

Consolidating is a natural outgrowth of step five. When you start grouping like things together, space seems to appear from nowhere. Putting things that were once scattered in several places into one compact container means they take up less space.

There's a cost associated with being spread out all over the place. Remember our earlier discussion about the cost of space? One way to reclaim it is by consolidating what you have. You might find out you have unnecessary duplicates, including broken items that you've replaced. If you've replaced the broken item already, put it in the *Pass On* box and give it to Goodwill Industries or a similar charity. Your broken item will give work to someone who needs it and money to a worthwhile organization. If you haven't gotten a new one, chances are that since it's been broken all this time, you don't really need it anyway. If you need the item and it's broken, put it in the *Fix It* box and either fix it or send it out to be repaired this week.

> **Amazing Space**
>
> Open your eyes to clutter. Really *see*. Look at your stuff with a critical eye. Put distance between it and you. Become unattached.

If you find lots of duplicates as you consolidate, keep the best one and pass the others along. If it's something you keep in quantity, like paper clips or rubber bands, be honest about how many you'll use in six months or a year and share the rest. Unless you're planning on opening an office supply outlet, stocking up beyond a reasonable point is probably a poor use of your space. Here are some other areas where you can consolidate and compress:

- Consolidate clothes by getting rid of duplicate, outdated, ill-fitting, and unused items. If it needs mending, put it in the *Fix It* bin and do it this week.

- Use existing containers that are just taking up space, such as jars, drawer units, bins, boxes, sectional boxes and chests, dividers, baskets, caddies, racks, and shelves. Use them or lose them!

- Apply the consolidation principle to tasks as well. Find a downtown shopping area or mall where you can get a lot done without driving all over creation. I shop downtown, leave my car, and walk to the post office, bookstore, food specialty shops, and the bank. Not only do I get a lot done in a short period of time, I also get some needed exercise.

- Look for other areas where you can "fold" time. Cook double batches at one time and freeze one. You only have to clean the kitchen once, but have prepared two meals. We'll "up the ante" on bulk cooking even more in Chapter 11.

Step Seven: Alphabetize

I never realized the power of this simple idea but, believe me, it will help you sail through your day in ways you didn't know were possible. As you work through whatever spaces you've decided to apply the 10 steps to, and after you group things together and consolidate them in containers or on shelves, consider whether putting items in alphabetical order would be an appropriate next step. It's not worthwhile for everything, and I'm not encouraging obsessive-compulsive behavior, but you might be surprised how much easier it is to find things and put them back where they belong when they're in alphabetical order.

Alphabetizing saves me time every single day. I can quickly find a spice when it's on the rack in alphabetical order. My files are much easier to use when they're in alphabetical order. Books, videos, you name it—you'll save oodles of time, all the time, if you just use the old A-to-Z method.

> **Amazing Space**
>
> You might consider getting a labeling machine. I'm not a great advocate of gadgets, but this is one that can save a lot of time. Look for one that allows you flexibility in label size, and make sure the type styles are readable from a distance.

Step Eight: Label It

This is another powerful tool that produces many of the same results alphabetical organization does. I label everything I can get my hands on. I don't look through the wrong drawer, because it's labeled. I don't wonder what's in that box, because the contents are on the label outside.

Step Nine: Go for Quality, Not Quantity

Another way to pare down is to buy the best. This may not seem like a way to reduce the junk in your life, but it very well can be. If you have a tool that works well every time, chances are you won't need another for a long time. You may not think you can afford it, but if you examine the true cost of buying inferior merchandise, you may find it's actually cheaper in the long run to buy the very best.

Let's take the vacuum cleaner, for example. If you buy an inexpensive one or one that's poorly designed and can't handle many jobs, you'll need several other devices to do the work you need to do. One appliance, carefully chosen for its power, utility, and features, should cover almost any job you might encounter. Where do you think all those half-working appliances in your basement or garage came from, anyway? They probably ended up in these way stations because you bought something else that did the job better. Why not do it right the first time?

While you're sorting, if you come across something you just know doesn't work right or you avoid using because it's of inferior quality, toss it get something that works.

Step Ten: Think Multipurpose

Why have six tools when one can do the job? Marketing experts work long and hard to create new products, but there's a good chance you already have something in the house that'll do the job just as well. Look for appliances and tools that can handle many jobs, not just one. They'll take up less space, cost less in the long run (although they might be expensive to buy initially), and cut your maintenance time down as well.

Your *Pass On* box should be full of items that do a single task that can be done just as well by something else you have on hand for another job.

And Now What?

This is not a once-and-for-all thing. You'll probably find yourself unstuffing several times a year using the 10 steps, but it gets easier as they become habit and as you learn to keep stuff from accumulating. Don't let more clutter in the door. Shopping is not a hobby. With each purchase you think of making, ask yourself first, "Do I have a *use* for it?" Then ask, "Do I have a *place* for it?" Put it back on the store shelf unless and until you do.

Picture This

Close your eyes for a few minutes and imagine the area you've just subjected to the 10 steps. See yourself and your family using that area. What activities are conducted nearby? Who uses it most? What things would be most handy in that space? Now, open your eyes and look at it anew. Quickly run down the list of 10 steps and see if you can go still further with your unstuffing program. I'll bet you can!

Remember, junk costs you other things besides money. It can even get in the way of job advancement and good relationships. It robs you of time, energy, peace of mind, and perhaps, ultimately, happiness. If it doesn't add to your life and help you accomplish the things you believe to be most important, *lose it!*

Now that you've applied the 10 steps to at least one area of your life, review your progress. Pat yourself on the back for what you've accomplished. Reward yourself. Now, plan the next area to give the 10-step treatment. Pick a time and write it down on your calendar. You're off and running, so don't stop now!

The Least You Need to Know

- ◆ There are basic principles you can learn that can be applied to all areas of organization.

- ◆ By applying the 10 steps to any room, you can get a head start on putting it in order.

- ◆ Part of successful unstuffing is identifying the items you simply don't use.

- ◆ Smart storage habits, consolidation, and grouping like things together can help you streamline your space.

Chapter 6

Mastering the Paper Monster

In This Chapter

◆ The myth of the "paperless society"

◆ How to control paper—immediately

◆ Keeping paper findable

◆ Cutting down on junk mail

◆ Using computers to reduce the paper in your life

Way back when, we were told that the computer age would bring about the beginning of a paperless society. With the advent of word processing, databases, electronic spreadsheets, and e-mail, we wouldn't need to put things down on paper anymore. Everyone would have a screen on her desk and one in her pocket, and the written or printed word would become quaint and outdated. Reading bound books in conventional print, the pundits assured us, would be a thing of the past.

But take a look around you! The "paperless society" is actually suffering from a paper glut. Some 68 million trees and 28 billion gallons of water are used each year just to produce catalogs and direct-mail sales pitches. Junk mail fills 3 percent of American landfills and its disposal costs $320 million in American tax dollars. Forty-four percent of all junk mail is thrown in the trash, without ever being opened. Add to that all the office paper, personal correspondence, newspapers, magazines, and books and, well, you get the picture.

In this chapter, you're going to take another giant leap toward unstuffing your life and getting a grip on all the paper you get, handle (sometimes again and again), and save (usually for far too long). I'm going to give you 10 simple ideas, plus some ways to implement them, that will keep those piles of paper from piling up in the first place.

Paper—We've All Got It!

No one's immune to the paper glut. Even if you personally refrained from generating a single piece of paper this week, chances are you'd still have a substantial pile all your own before the week was through.

We all have bills, correspondence, receipts, bank statements and canceled checks, insurance and tax papers, legal papers, reading material, instructions and warranties, addresses, reminders and invitations, keepsakes and photos, recipes—the list goes on and on. It's whether or not we confront the paper in our lives, deal with it, systematize it, and dispose of it that makes the difference between being on top of the paper pileup and being buried by it.

Here are 10 simple ideas you can use right away to get paper under control forever.

Idea One: Stop It!

One way to spend less time and energy handling paper is by reducing the amount that comes into your household in the first place. You can lower the amount of junk mail, for example, by stopping it at the source.

One of the fastest and easiest ways to remove your name and address from the many mailing lists that are bought and sold between direct marketing companies (who generate the junk mail in the first place) is to send your name and address on a postcard to the Direct Marketing Association (DMA):

> Mail Preference Service
> Direct Marketing Association
> P.O. Box 9008
> Farmingdale, NY 11735-9008

Make sure you give them all the different incarnations of your personal mailing information. If your name appears sometimes as John Doe and others as J. P. Doe and yet again as John Doe Sr., you need to let them know. Your name and address in various forms will be added to the Direct Marketing Association's delete file, and its 3,600 members will be notified. It may take several months for you to see results, so be patient. You'll need to repeat this procedure every five years, because that's how long your information will remain in the delete file.

If you notice a reduction in some mail, but continue to receive other unrequested mailings, that may mean a particular company doesn't participate in DMA's program. In this case, you'll have to contact the company directly. You might make up a form letter and simply make copies.

Orderly Pursuits

Consider joining the Stop Junk Mail Association. For $20, they will delete your name from a variety of sources and lobby to protect your postal privacy. Call or write to Stop Junk Mail Association, c/o 3020 Bridgeway, Suite 150, Sausalito, CA 94965; (800) 827-5549.

Dealing with credit card companies requires a slightly different approach. The law requires these companies to refrain from disclosing customer's personal information for marketing purposes if the customer requests. Call your credit card company's 1-800 number for customer service or write to them directly and ask about this.

You may also be able to attack the problem from another angle, by contacting credit bureaus. Depending on which state you live in, these bureaus may be required by law to delete your name from their marketing mailing lists if you request it. There are three major credit bureaus you should contact—Equifax, Experian, and Trans-Union—and all three can be reached with the same toll-free number: (888) 567-8688. You'll be calling the "Opt Out Request Line," and by giving them your information when asked, you'll kill three birds with one stone.

Another place you might want to contact to have your name deleted is National Demographics and Lifestyles. This company collects buyer profiles and sells the information. Write to:

National Demographics and Lifestyles
List Order Department
1621 18th Street, Suite 300
Denver, CO 80202

Staying away from buyer's clubs or special buying programs is another way to reduce the number of promotions and coupons sent to your home. Another source

Oops!

If you order or request a catalog from a mail-order company, ask that the company not pass your information on to anyone else. Otherwise, your mailbox will begin to fill up with unwanted junk mail all over again.

companies use for mailings is the telephone book. Having an unlisted number, or having only your name and number (no address) in the book, is another way to cut down on the number of solicitations you receive.

Whenever you get the chance, make a formal request that your name be kept private and that no mailings other than those you specifically request be sent. Here are some other big list-sellers that you might want to write or call:

ADVO, Inc., Delivery Services
6955 Mowry Avenue
Newark, CA 94560

Donnelley Marketing
Database OperationsMarketing Database Operations
416 South Bell
Ames, IA 50010

Metromail/Experian Maintenance
List Maintenance
901 West Bond
Lincoln, NE 68521
(800) 407-1088

Even the post office sells your name and address! Didn't know that, did you? When you move and fill out those little change of address cards, they sell the information to bulk mailers. Better to skip those cards entirely and contact your correspondents individually.

This may all seem like a lot of effort, but it really doesn't take more than writing a letter, addressing a few envelopes, and sticking them in the mail. The reduction in unsolicited mail can be dramatic. Remember to keep a list of the companies I've given you (or refer back to this book), since you may need to repeat the process in five years or so.

Another important paper reduction technique is to cancel subscriptions to publications you don't really read. Consider combining subscriptions with someone else who shares your interests, or using the library. Bet if you had to make a trip to the library to read publications, you'd see in a hurry which ones really mattered to you!

Idea Two: Decide Now

When paper in its many forms first comes in the door, make a decision about it right away. Don't allow it to pile up. Set up a system to keep it moving, and decide immediately where in the system it goes.

Sorting Into Three Categories

Paper falls into three basic categories: *Action, Throw Away*, and *Pass On*.

An action might be to read it, do something with it (like pay a bill), or write to be taken off a list. It might go in your tickler file, you might need to transfer the date to your calendar and then throw the piece of paper out, or it may need to be filed for reference. Maybe you need to write a letter in response. Whatever the action is, those papers are the ones you keep. The rest gets trashed or given to someone else. When the piece of paper first enters your life, ask yourself:

♦ Would I miss this? What would I do if it was gone?

♦ Can I get this somewhere else?

♦ Does having this piece of paper support the goals I've set for myself?

♦ Can I reduce or consolidate this?

♦ If I decide to keep this, how long will I need it?

♦ Where can I keep it so I can find it when I need it? (This last question leads into how you sort and file paper, which I'll discuss shortly.)

> **Amazing Space**
>
> Because warranty or product registration cards might generate more junk mail for you, consider not sending the card next time you buy something new. You're covered by the manufacturer's warranty whether or not you send it in. If you feel you must send in the card, fill in the bare minimum and indicate you do not want your information passed on. Keep your receipt along with the product model and serial numbers for warranty and recall purposes.

A word of advice: Keep up with reading material daily. If you can't, you have too much. You'll never get to it anyway, and when it's in huge piles, you won't want to. So get rid of it and start being more selective right now!

I make a habit of reading through the day's material every evening after work while I listen to the TV news. Those are two activities I can easily do at one time. If certain reading material requires more serious concentration, I might put it on my bedside table and read it before I go to bed or over my morning cup of coffee the next day.

Dealing with What Remains

Once you make the first set of decisions about what to act on, what to trash, and what to pass on, you then need to decide what to do with what you have left.

I open my mail at the kitchen counter where I have a trash can. The recycling bin is right outside the door, and on a nearby shelf is a horizontal organizer with slots for various things. Stuff for my husband goes in the "Jim to Read" slot. I have my own "To Read" slot as well, which I empty each night, as I mentioned.

Bills and receipts go to my office, where I have another organizer at my desk. My husband's mail-order business involves catalog requests; there's a slot for them in the kitchen organizer because he usually fulfills them in the evening so they go out in the mail the next day. There's also a "To Mail" slot. That's for items that already have postage and are ready to go into the mailbox. There's another slot for the post office, which is for items that need special postage or handling. That way, whoever is headed out to the mailbox or post office can check the slot (even from as far away as the front door) to see if anyone else has mail to go. This system works for us. You might find another one that works better for you. Whatever system you choose, make sure it makes it easier to handle the mail right now!

Personal Action Items

The next decision level concerns your own personal action items. Decide now how you're going to sort all your own personal paper—past, present, and future. The usual categories most people use are *To Do, To Pay, To Read,* and *To File.* Some people add a *Pending* category, as well. That can become a catchall and a "black hole" for paper, however, so be careful.

Since I work at home, my "paper action system" is on one end of my desk in my office. That's divided into "To Do," "To File," and "To Pay"; I also have a separate "Correspondence" slot. I reserve Fridays for bill-paying, filing, and correspondence, so I appreciate having these all mapped out for me when Friday rolls around.

Oops!

Be careful about bulletin boards: They can become catch-alls instead of organization tools. If you must, use one only to post material you refer to regularly and make a vow not to clutter it with anything else.

You'll deal with filing in even more detail when you get to the chapters on work and finances. What you're working on here are some general systems to get you started. As you're sorting your action items, ask these questions to help you get rid of still more paper, *before* it finds its way into your action system:

- Is there enough time to do this, or is it already too late?

- Do I really want to do this and does it support the goals I've set for myself?

- Will doing this really make a difference for others or myself?

- What would happen if I never did this? What would happen if I never read this? What would happen if I never filed or replied to this?

If you have paid bills in the pile, file them. If you don't have a filing system for paid bills, put aside some time to set one up. It took me all of one afternoon to set up my own files. I included both household and business, and organized them according to the categories I use in my Quicken personal finance software. These are set up for tax purposes, so they make what used to be an end-of-the-year scramble, a breeze.

You may want to look at how your taxes were prepared for some of the categories, and then include anything else you'd like to track or need to be able to put your hands on quickly (more about taxes will be discussed in Chapter 15). Adapt and adjust your system to your own personal needs, and always remember you can change and improve it at any time.

Remember, too, that paper is the same as other stuff as far as storage is concerned. What you need at your fingertips should occupy *prime real estate*. Other paper that needs to be accessible, but isn't used as often falls in the category of active files and occupies *secondary storage*. And, last, you have paper that belongs in the *deep freeze*, of which there should be *very, very little*. All I keep in the *deep freeze* is support material for books I've already completed and previous years' tax information. The rest is either *active* or *essential*, and those are in systems that are easy to access and regularly purged.

That's how I do it, and it works for me. Some variation on this system is likely to work for you. The important thing is to set up a process that helps you make immediate decisions regarding the paper in your life. Get your system up and running right away, and reevaluate it in a couple of weeks. I say "right away" because paper is the single greatest contributor to clutter and disorganization. If you find you still have piles of paper around, critically examine what the paper is and where the system has broken down. Then fix it!

Amazing Space

Consider adding a section in your filing cabinet called "Pass Ons," with separate folders for out-of-town family and friends. You can save articles and the like that you think they'll enjoy or that relate specifically to their jobs or hobbies, and send with your weekly correspondence.

Idea Three: Handle It Less

You've heard people say to handle paper only once. This is a guideline, not a rule. It's often impossible to handle a piece of paper only once, but you want to make a decision as quickly as possible about where it goes. Don't allow it to pile up, handling it many times, moving it from here to there, from pile to pile.

If you make the effort and implement idea two, you'll find you're physically dealing with paper far less. If you constantly police yourself, reduce the amount of mail you get by following the suggestions in idea one, and apply the principles in this chapter daily, you'll spend less time shuffling paper and more time doing the things you want to do.

Idea Four: Move It Along

If paper belongs with someone else, get it going! Have envelopes and postage handy (plus a chart of rates for various sizes and weights, and a postage scale) so you can hand off things as quickly as possible. As I mentioned before, I keep folders in my filing system for just this purpose if the people to hand things off to aren't close by. When I see an article, get a flyer, or print out a useful message from the Internet, I immediately put it in their folder, and once a week or so I send off the items to them. It's an important way to let them know I'm thinking of them, but I don't want it to turn into a "paper problem" for me, so I empty the folders on a regular basis.

Orderly Pursuits

Sharing is a great way to get paper out of your life and even save money. I share my copies of *Publisher's Weekly* with writer friends in my area, and they save various publications for me. Consult professional associates or people with the same interests who might be willing to swap with you.

Another way to "pass it on" is to recycle. That may mean actually sending your useless paper to a recycling center or simply giving it to someone else who might have use for it. Give old magazines to doctor's offices or nursing homes. Our local library accepts donations of some magazines and books and sells them to raise money.

You may want to pre-address some envelopes (you can use computer-generated labels) for the people you regularly send items to. You're more likely to keep up with it if you've got everything prepared in advance.

Idea Five: Don't Open It!

If you know it's something you don't intend to do anything with, don't open it—put it directly into the trash. The time it takes to open and read it isn't worth the effort.

This is especially effective with expiration notices for magazines you've decided not to renew, contests, catalogs, and offers. Rip up or shred credit card offers without opening them and throw them away.

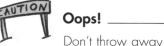

Oops! _____

Don't throw away unopened mail unless you're *absolutely sure* it's not something important. You may be throwing away a check or a bill!

Idea Six: Distinguish Between Short and Long Term

We all have paper we need to save for various reasons, but most of us end up hanging onto it much longer than we have to.

Find out from your tax preparer, financial advisor, and lawyer what documents you need to keep and for how long. We'll discuss this at length in Chapter 15, but you might want to start asking some of these questions now, since this is the "Quick Start" part of your organization plan. Weigh the cost in storage space and time required to hold onto these documents against the costs involved in recreating them in the event you might need them in the future. What is the likelihood? How difficult would it be to obtain them again?

Make sure to purge your files regularly (every three to six months), using the guidelines your professional advisers give you. Mark the date on your calendar as an appointment with yourself. It's easy to forget and just allow these mounds of paper to accumulate. If you keep going through them regularly, replacing the oldest year's with the newest, you'll still only need the same amount of storage. That means that once you set up storage systems for these long-term records, you'll probably never have to add to them to any appreciable extent.

Some people use an accordion file with monthly tabs (or make 12 hanging files) to file all bills paid and receipts collected by the month in which they occurred. If they ever need to return something or a bank statement seems off, they can find the info you need with a minimum of digging. The same accordion file is reused year after year. As you move into a new month, you can take the stuff from that month's slot that's now one year old and shred it, burn it, or toss it. You'll need to separate out tax related stuff and put it in separate files. Find a system that works for you and maintain it.

Idea Seven: File So You Can Find It

There are many filing systems—some so complicated only the person who set them up can use them. So let's spend some time discussing how to set up a household filing system that works.

My basic advice is to keep your system as simple as possible, make it alphabetical wherever possible, label everything clearly and boldly, and be sure it is easy for other people to use. It should be self-explanatory, whenever possible. Even home filing systems need to be clear and understandable, in case you're not there and somebody else needs to retrieve something. What if you're stranded in Bora-Bora and need to tell someone how to get a copy of your birth certificate to you? It should be simple for anyone (even the house-sitter) to do if your files are set up right.

A Three-Category System

A basic filing system falls into three categories: *working*, *reference*, and the *deep freeze* (archival).

Working files get *prime real estate*, the space that's closest to you. Depending on whether you have a home office or not, these might be in your office or at your central planning station, wherever that may be. We'll talk a little more about the "central planning station" later, but you need a central place to store the supplies and information you rely on to keep everything moving. This can be in a closet or cabinet, wherever it's easy to get at and closest to the activities of planning, paying bills, handling correspondence, and keeping regular reference materials. These files include current projects and current financial information.

Next are your *reference* files. These are things you need to refer to fairly often, but they're not part of your daily life. These files might include information on hobbies, career, housekeeping, your family history—whatever is currently in your life, but not essential to the daily workings of your household. If you have room to keep both the working files and the reference files in the same place, that's great. If not, reference files should still be accessible.

The final part of your filing system is the *deep freeze*, and there should be practically nothing there. In our household, because I'm a writer, we probably have more in this category than most people. I need to keep support files for the books and articles I write. I weed them out, then they go into banker's boxes and get stored in the garage. As I mentioned earlier, the only other *deep freeze* files we have are past year's tax records and support material.

Picture This

Imagine what would happen if everything you own was destroyed in a fire, flood, or other disaster. What would you need to pick up the pieces? How would you identify yourself? If you died, how easily could your survivors handle your estate and other affairs? Actually visualize what would happen. Then take a look at your files and records and come up with a plan that would deal with these two circumstances. Consider off-site backup and who should know where things are (and what they might need).

Now let's talk about categories for your household files. Here's a list of those I think almost every household should have. We'll discuss several of them in more detail when we get into organizing your financial life later on in this book, but for now, consider setting up hanging folders for each of these categories right away. You'll want hanging folders, which you never remove from your file drawer, *and* regular file folders.

◆ Auto (gasoline, loan information, repair records)

◆ Bank statements

◆ Birth and other important records (copies of birth, marriage, divorce, adoption, citizenship, death, and military records would go here; keep originals in a safety deposit box)

◆ Budget

◆ Contributions/charities

◆ Credit cards

◆ Heating (fuel and service)

◆ Home repairs, improvements, and equipment

◆ Income tax (current year and prior year's form as filed)

◆ Insurance (auto, homeowner's or renter's, health, business, life)

◆ Inventory (a copy of this should be kept in a safety deposit box, along with supporting photos and/or video)

◆ Investments (stocks, bonds, pension, mutual funds, savings; you might want to break this out into separate sections if you have a lot of investments)

◆ Medical (divided by person; receipts; might want to include dental or break that out into a separate folder)

◆ Safety deposit box (information on the box itself, as well as copies of important documents kept there and an inventory of everything in the box)

Some other files you might have are:

◆ Legal (case information including expenses)

◆ Pets (this could also be put in Medical)

◆ School (transcripts, registration information)

◆ Social Security

Tickler Files

"Order marches with weighty and measured strides; disorder is always in a hurry."

—Napoleon I

Don't Forget Computer Records and Documents

Even if your computer records and documents aren't in hard copy form, they may still be important pieces of information that need to be organized and probably backed up. Make printouts of documents that really belong in your files and would be hard for a person who's not computer-oriented to find. A man we know died quite suddenly, and all his financial information was on his computer, which no one else in the family knew how to operate. It took months for his widow to learn that she had been well taken care of, so she could stop worrying. If you do keep important records on computer, make sure someone else knows how to access them, or back them up with actual paper printouts that are clearly labeled and filed so anyone can find them.

Idea Eight: Keep It Where You Need It

If you often use certain information that's on paper, put it where you need it. I keep a file for all my instructions for electric tools and appliances right near the kitchen. It's close to most of the appliances we use, which are in the kitchen, the laundry room, and the garage just off the kitchen. I have a separate one in my work area for all the office equipment and computer stuff I use there. It's clearly labeled, so if someone needed to run the equipment when I wasn't around, they could quickly and easily find the information they needed to do it.

Remember, current action files belong in *prime real estate*. All other files should be in *secondary storage* or the *deep freeze*. If it's in the *deep freeze* and your tax consultant or lawyer hasn't told you that you need to hang onto it, maybe you ought to consider getting rid of it.

Keep phone message pads by the phone. Ditto with the family address and phone file and the phone book. Keep the TV, cable, or satellite guide by the TV. If you have places designated for these things, they're less likely to walk away. Just keep in mind the idea of *prime real estate* and the importance of location, and you'll find you can lay your hands on the important papers you need when you need them.

Idea Nine: Tailor Systems to Special Needs

Some activities involving paper require special handling. Perhaps you work at home, or maybe you work outside the home but handle the paperwork for the business at home. Maybe you're a sales representative or an officer for a charitable organization or professional association. Other kinds of paper don't quite fall into the usual categories; these include greeting cards, recipes, photos, or your kids' school projects.

As you examine, purge, and sort the many kinds of paper in your home or workplace, these are the items you might not know what to do with. These types of paper may need special systems to handle them in a way that preserves them and makes them easy to get to.

I'll be specifically tackling home office solutions, recipes, photos, and keepsakes in later chapters. You may want to skip ahead if you're really motivated, or for now you can simply start grouping items together in temporary containers until you reach those sections.

> **Amazing Space**
>
> If you're most likely to read magazine articles while relaxing at night, soaking in the bathtub, or waiting for appointments, tear them out and keep them where you're most likely to read them, then get rid of the rest of the publication. This will keep magazines from piling up.

Idea Ten: Use Computers to Cut Paper, Not Make It

You already know that computers haven't eliminated wasteful paper. Far from it! If you're a computer user, you know from experience how much paper it can generate. Luckily, computers can also reduce paper. For example, just this year I stopped several subscriptions and now use online newspapers and magazines to get most of my news. If there's something I want to save or have someone else read, I print it out and file it or pass it on, but I'm very selective. Sure, I'm generating some paper, but it's still far less than I had with the paper subscription.

Think seriously before printing something out. It can become a bad habit. Before you hit the print button, ask yourself:

- Can I work with it on-screen?

- Do I really need to save it? What are the chances I'll need to refer to it again?

- Can I archive it on a disk rather than work with a hard copy?

> **Picture This**
>
> Put your imagination cap on, pick a room, and scan it for any paper items that fall into the "special" category. Can they be grouped together in categories? Integrated into the filing system you set up earlier? If not, what storage or display format would make them most useful to you? Consider things like file boxes, albums, display cases, frames, and anything else that might be used for that purpose.

Incidentally, things get lost on disks because of poor filing, just as they do in paper files. The same rules apply to both: purge often, label clearly, and only save what you really need.

Use e-mail to reduce the amount of paper going through the postal system. Don't feel compelled to print out and save every message. Of course, one of the advantages of e-mail over, say, a telephone conversation, is that you can make a hard copy of what was communicated for future reference. This is especially handy for job-related information, directions, travel information, and the like. Again, ask yourself the important questions and don't hang on to these printouts longer than you need to.

Get It Online

With so much valuable research information on the Internet and more electronic versions of newspapers and magazines available online all the time, survey these areas and see where you might be able to eliminate paper versions altogether. There are many services available that deliver news and weather to your electronic mailbox daily for free. I no longer own an encyclopedia, but subscribe to *Britannica Online* instead. I also get newspapers and newsletters online. This not only reduces the paper coming into my home and office, but it also makes the material much more useable, since I can now search it, cut and paste it into other files, and print out *only* what I really want.

Put Paper in Its Place

Many of the same principles I gave you in Chapter 5 for dealing with stuff apply just as well to taking care of paper. Consolidate and compress. Put it on one sheet. Reduce it with a copier. This technique is especially effective with keepsakes—keep a part of it, a swatch, or one picture that's representative. Consolidate keepsakes—put them in a scrapbook or album or make a memory wreath or collage.

When you finish with Chapter 7, about setting up your own Central Control or Life Management Center, you'll reduce your paper even further, because you'll have a simple system for keeping important information in one place all the time. You'll stop putting notes on a zillion different snippets of paper, and you'll learn to have a single place to plan and keep track of details.

For now, reward yourself for getting on top of your own personal paper mountain. If paper starts to build up again, stop it in its tracks! Set aside some time every day at home and at work to do your paperwork. Use small bits of time (remember the power of just 15 minutes and your timer?) to handle it throughout the day. The amount of time you gain by getting control of paper is enormous. The joy of being able to put your hands on the information you need, when you need it, is real.

> **Amazing Space**
>
> Be creative when thinking up ways to save space. Take a tip from a clever quilter who reproduced various images of her parents and transferred them to a quilt for their fiftieth wedding anniversary. Included in the quilt's fabric were swatches from old dresses, tablecloths, and baby clothes.

The Least You Need to Know

- Paper can support or hinder your goals.

- You can't get organized until you get control of paper.

- You can reduce the amount of paper you handle every day by stopping it at its source.

- Systems can be set up to sort and file paper, keeping it under control and easy to retrieve when you need it.

- Some kinds of paper need special systems to be handled effectively.

- Applying the 10 ideas regularly will help ensure that you never again end up with a paper pileup.

Part 3

Systems for Getting Stuff Done

In Part 3, you'll develop systems for accomplishing goals in each of the major spheres of your daily life: work, relationships, grooming, food, clothing, and shelter.

First, you'll carve out a place at the helm of your ship, a hub or center from which to manage your life. You'll also create a portable system you can take with you wherever you go and manage just as effectively. Next, you'll zero in on each life sphere, one at a time. When you finish this part, you'll see even more dramatic changes in your day-to-day life. So, roll up your sleeves and let's get to work!

Chapter 7

Creating a Command Center

In This Chapter

◆ Carving out a place to run your life

◆ Schedules, lists, and time management systems

◆ Commanding, delegating, and co-managing

◆ Taking it with you

Many people have likened life to a ship on an ocean. Personally, I prefer to think of life as a starship exploring unknown worlds in space, *Star Trek*—style. And if life is a starship, then you're the captain, and somewhere on board there needs to be a "bridge." The bridge of a ship is where the captain (supported by a highly trained and obedient crew) navigates and handles crises. This is Information Central, where all the various departments of the vessel report in and get their orders.

To manage your life effectively, you need to create your very own bridge. You can call it whatever you like: the hub, the nucleus, the office of the president—you may even want to make a sign so there's no mistaking it. Around our house, we call it the Command Center.

A Room All Your Own

Where you locate your Life Management Center is up to you. Just make sure it's in the center of your life's activity. If you share your space with other people, it needs to be a place that's accessible to everyone. This is where you funnel all the information about everyone's schedules, chores that need to be done, mail that needs to be sent, bills that have to be paid, and everything else that goes on in your household.

Oops!

Don't let yourself get distracted by others who inadvertently take your supplies without returning them. Consider tying the tools down (seriously). Just put a long string around the scissors, stapler, tape dispenser, and so forth, and secure it to your desk. Make it known that anyone caught with the captain's stuff will be lost in space forever!

Your Life Management Center should be near a phone, have a good, uncluttered working surface to write on, and have wall space to hang a calendar and any other information that needs to be posted, such as lists of chores. Ideally, your current files will be located there as well. If that's not possible, consider having a rolling cart that you can store elsewhere and bring to your center when you have filing to do or need to refer to something.

I find it helps if you can locate your center close to the door that is used most often to go in and out of the house. That way, you can easily grab letters to be mailed or immediately handle the incoming mail, and it's convenient to take a quick glance at the calendar or daily list as you start and end your day.

Stocking Up: Basic Life Management Supplies

Certainly an effective manager or captain needs to have the "right stuff" to get the job done. Basic tools and supplies kept all in one place make it more pleasurable to do the job, and more likely you'll want to start it in the first place.

Here's a list of some basic supplies you'll probably want on hand:

Paper/letterhead

Business envelopes

Mailing supplies, including overnight mail forms and supplies if you use those services

Letter opener

Stamps in denominations most often used

Supply of greeting cards, note cards, and postcards

Ruler

Stapler

Glue stick

Tape

Post-it notes

Paper clips

Scissors

Calendar

Bulletin board for posting schedules and other important information (and nothing else!)

If you use a computer for your planning and/or finances, you may want to keep it in your command center. Remember, there's always room to adapt your command center to your particular situation. We have. Our main command center is in my office, since I'm the one who pays the bills and handles our social calendar. My computer is there, and all the supplies I need are in a rolling cart by my desk. Next to the kitchen we have a miniature command center. That's where the shared calendar is, and where we keep duplicate supplies for last-minute mailings or note writing. Make the concept fit your own life.

You've Got Mail (or Other Messages)

If handled poorly, phone messages and written notes from members of the family can be a major source of frustration and even disaster. If members of the household need to communicate and are on different schedules, ensuring these messages are passed on is imperative. One thing you can do is set up a message board in a prominent place, either one that can be written on and erased, or a bulletin board sectioned off with a space for each person. Or

Orderly Pursuits

If you have multiple phones in your house, lost phone messages can become a problem. Consider getting carbon phone message pads. You write down the message, tear it off, and pass it on, but if one gets misplaced, there's always the carbon record to refer to. You can use one for every phone in the house.

you could use the horizontal compartmentalized organizer I mentioned earlier, and assign a slot for each individual. Or you can make a board with clips, putting each person's name above their clip. There they can check for mail, notes, or phone messages whenever they get home. Find the one that works (experiment) and stick to it.

Whatever method you choose to take and receive messages, make sure everyone is aware of the setup, and give it time to become a habit. The more permanent and prominent the message center, the more likely it will be a success. Magnets on the refrigerator may work for some, but a more defined location is usually necessary for a more complicated household.

This Is the Captain Speaking!

One more aspect of setting up a Life Management Center is adapting it to your life situation. One essential question in any enterprise is "Who's in charge?" There can be many answers to that, depending on your living arrangements. But one thing is for sure—when it comes to your own personal responsibilities and interests, the answer is *you.* You are always the one in charge, and the more you accept and believe that, the more empowered you'll be in your life.

But what about the spheres outside of your immediate influence? Let's take where you live, for instance. If you live alone, the answer's pretty obvious. You decide how everything is organized, what you eat, what color the sheets are, when the bills get paid, and what TV shows to watch. But many of us share our space with someone else. It could be a significant other, a roommate, or an entire family. Now the question of who's in charge becomes a little more complicated.

When you set up a Life Management Center, it's important to consider other people and examine the real dynamics in your particular household. In our house, for example, I'm pretty much the home manager. When my husband and I were first married, I tried different approaches, but it became obvious that he preferred letting me handle the organizing, scheduling, bill-paying, and most other activities involving the running of the home. He liked to be consulted, and he was always willing to help, but he preferred to let me handle the details. At first I resisted the responsibility, but then I realized it gave me a lot of freedom to manage things the way I wanted. I also knew I was probably more skilled in these areas.

If you're "in command," so to speak, you'll be doing a lot of delegating as well. You may delegate to your partner and children, and you may also delegate to various outside contractors to handle certain jobs that no one in the household wants or has time to do.

In another living arrangement, two or more adults may be more equally involved in the organization process. It's very important here that you consult the other person when you design these basic systems. First of all, they'll be more likely to use them if they've been part of the planning process. Also, they may have some good suggestions for making the system work better. You may need to divide up areas of responsibility for it to work effectively.

Add children to the household and you have yet another wrinkle (or two or three). Depending on the age of the child, you may do more delegating (and following up) or work more in partnership. You'll need to devise systems they can use as well. It may be as simple as positioning the message board at a lower level, or printing rather than writing in script. A system of incentives and rewards will likely become part of the mix as well. Be sure to include children, even young children, in the organizing process.

Schedules, Lists, and Time Management Systems

As soon as you hear the word *schedule*, does the hair on the back of your neck immediately stand up? Are you unpleasantly reminded of school, or punching a clock, and does every fiber of your being revolt? Try and keep an open mind. I promise we won't divide up every minute of your day. But having schedules and lists, and some kind of a system for keeping them, is essential for getting your life under control.

Think of your planner/organizer system as your Mobile Command Center, an extension of the well-organized hub you've established at home. If you set it up right, it'll give you ultimate control, whether you're at work, traveling, or just pushing a cart at the grocery store.

A planner/organizer eliminates all the little scraps of paper scattered all over your desk, in your pocket, on the kitchen table, and stuck to the visor in your car. You'll save hours of time you would have spent looking for things, or trying to recreate what happened last week. Everything will be at your fingertips in one central place.

There are many prefabricated systems you can buy through the mail or at an office supply store. Or you can set up a notebook of your own if you think that would work better for

Orderly Pursuits

The major personal planner manufacturers are on the World Wide Web, complete with product information and lots of helpful articles and tips. Check out Day-Timer at www.daytimer.com/; DayRunner can be found at www.dayrunner.com/home.htm; and FranklinCovey's URL is www.franklincovey.com/.

you. Just make sure it's a size that's portable and flexible, yet large enough to handle all the aspects of life management we're going to discuss.

I've used several different planners over the years, and for a long time found one of the smaller versions of the Day-Timer to work best for me. It was large enough to give me room to write, yet small enough to fit in a purse or briefcase. Other excellent planning systems include DayRunner and FranklinCovey. I must confess, I've now converted over to a PDA with backup on my laptop computer, but for many years the paper system worked just fine.

Most planners are supported by various computer software programs that not only complement the paper planners, but also print out the forms they use. You'll find addresses and phone numbers of the major companies that offer organizers in Appendix A at the back of this book, so you can send for information or order products through the mail, or look for them at your favorite business products supply store.

The cheapest alternative to buying a premade planning system is to use a small ringed binder with dividers. However, you may still like the convenience of having pre-printed forms that you can use however you wish. Just make them up yourself and photocopy.

Planner/Organizer Essentials

Whichever system you choose to use, make sure it has the following features. Your ideal system:

- Is portable enough to take anywhere
- Is refillable (a spiral notebook won't do)
- Is durable and can be kept secure
- Has a calendar section with options for daily, weekly, monthly, and annual calendars
- Has calendar pages with ample room for appointments, phone calls that need to be made, and a daily To-Do list
- Is organized alphabetically
- Has address/phone pages
- Has a variety of other forms you can use if you need them, such as expenses, mileage, sources, and notes

The two obvious uses for your planner are to keep track of appointments and schedules on your calendar, and to record addresses and phone numbers. But this isn't using your system as a true life management tool. Your planner is a way to constantly remind yourself of your mission, your goals, and your priorities. It's also a convenient way to chart your progress.

The alphabetical address/phone section is a sophisticated database. Say what? That's right. It may not need a computer chip or power supply, but it's your own personal data bank. Think of it as an alphabetical filing cabinet for all the information you want to have at your fingertips, no matter where you are. This A-to-Z filing system can empower you to make decisions on the spot, save you time over and over again, keep you on track, and make managing projects a breeze.

Here's how to make it work for you: Make a list of all the information you might need if you were suddenly stranded in a faraway city and forced to manage your life from a hotel room or simply "on the road" for the day. Your list might include these categories:

◆ Banking (account numbers, phone numbers; don't write your PIN number, though!)

◆ Computer information/settings/support phone numbers

◆ Family (clothing sizes, Social Security numbers, birth dates, blood types)

◆ Food (master shopping list, menus, allergies)

◆ Home repairs (vendors, account numbers, list of what was done and when)

◆ Investments (list of stocks with symbols, phone number of broker, account information, rollover dates, and so on)

◆ Legal (attorney's phone number and address)

◆ Medical (list of doctors and dentists, medical history, health insurance information)

Oops!

Try to avoid all the extra sleeves, pockets, checkbook organizers, and credit card holders that simply add bulk to your planner. They not only can be a nuisance, but also can be costly—if you lose your planner, you'll lose all your important cards and checks, too.

You get the idea. This is just to get you started. Add as much of your own data as you can think of. Once you begin thinking of your planner this way, you'll come up with more and more categories. I keep one for book ideas and others for various writer's organizations I work with. I have another that's my personal wish list for things I'd like to have or accomplish, and I even have a rewards list to remind me of nice things I can do for myself when I've done a job well.

If you're working on a particular project, or serve in a leadership position in an organization, it's helpful to have on one sheet information all the other people involved, plus any other pertinent information you might need. Then, wherever you are, you can turn to your planner and handle whatever comes up. For instance, you can go down the list and call each one to schedule a meeting, or just to keep in touch. Use the blank sheets provided with your planner creatively, or adapt one of the preprinted forms. DayRunner has a form called "Sources" and another called "Project," either of which could be adapted for this purpose. Have important lists, forms, corporate objectives, or records reduced at the copy shop, and file them in your "data bank."

Pretty soon you'll be relying on your planner/organizer as you would a partner. It adds confidence to know that wherever you are, you can quickly put your hands on all the important information you rely on in your everyday life. It helps you handle emergencies, and it enables you to take advantage of waiting time. Just grab your planner/organizer whenever you leave the house, and you're all set.

The power of any planning/organizing system is imparted only when you use it! If you think of it as your partner, you'll want to consult it on a regular basis. Use it for as many aspects of your life as possible. Make it user-friendly by setting it up in a way that works for you and pleases you as well. Use forms and paper fillers that encourage you to use them. A little color may add to your enjoyment.

For starters, you'll probably want to consult your planner/organizer first thing every morning and at the end of the day. As time goes on and you customize it more, making it more and more useful, you'll find yourself turning to it throughout the day.

> **Amazing Space**
>
> Whatever time you choose for updating your planner/organizer, make sure you add it to your routine. Use it to review your goals, track your progress, and reward yourself.

Just as with any filing system, your planner/organizer needs regular maintenance. Go through it periodically (a great use for one of those 15-minute snippets of time) and update or purge information. Put some planning time into your schedule—whatever works best for you. How about Sunday evenings, before the work week begins? Or Friday afternoons, when the week is drawing to a close? Maybe short periods every morning or evening work best for you.

The Master of All Lists

One of the most important lists you'll keep in your planner/organizer is what I call the Master List. You actually started it in Chapter 5. This is kind of like a To-Do list, but it knows no priorities and no boundaries. This is where you dump anything that comes up during the day—tasks you'd either like to do or feel you need to do that suddenly pop into your head in no particular order. Don't worry about when you'll get to it, or whether it's urgent or not—just get it down on paper. You'll consult this list when you're actually doing your planning and scheduling, and then you'll set priorities and decide which activities most support you in getting what you want out of life. This list is simply a repository for all your ideas.

Your Master List will contain everything from making important business calls to cleaning the gutters, from fixing your daughter's bike to making a doctor's appointment. The purpose of the master list is to catch the fleeting thoughts you have that reveal your motivations and desires. Your brain is working on many different levels, even when you're occupied with something else. It's a powerful computer and is often triggered by associations or visual input in an unpredictable way. The beauty of the Master List is that you capture the thought *and* get it off your mind by putting it in writing.

Some things stay on my Master List a long time. Some things never get done because I later decide they're not important. That's the key word—*decide*. The master list lets me decide what to do about each item, and that puts me in control.

Although this isn't a book strictly about time management, many of the tools and concepts are the same. If you feel time management is an area where you need more work, several good books are available to help you, which I've listed in Appendix B. But here I've given you some of the basics, which should get you well underway.

The Calendar

The rest of your planner/organizer should contain a calendar section. I prefer a weekly form that lays out an entire week on two opposite pages. If you have a lot of appointments, you may prefer having one day on a page. Whatever your style, you'll need to have enough room to put down appointments and things to do. I divide each page into three sections: Appointments, To Do, and Phone Calls. Since I make all my phone calls at one particular time of the day, I like having a list of people to call in one place. I recommend you write down all appointments in your book, rather than trying to rely on your memory.

You can add monthly tabs to your calendar as well. I keep my master list at the end of the month's forms, along with my mission statement and project sheets for that month. You may choose to file these things in your alphabetical data bank. Do whatever works best for you and prompts you to refer to them often.

Oops!

Try not to make notes on your calendar pages. For this purpose, use a separate pad (most systems come with a place for that) or notes sheets. This will make your calendar more useful for later reference.

Whichever method you choose, keep your calendar section clean and functional. You never know when you may need it to recreate the past. The one and only time I was audited by the IRS, I brought in my bank records and my planner/organizer. After just a few minutes, the auditor could see I had a record of every trip, every business lunch, and every appointment. He told me to go home, and that I kept very good records. Most of it I could hold in one hand!

Backing Up Is Smart to Do!

Make sure you have a backup for all the essential information you keep in your planner/organizer. Just as you would need to recover from a disaster that destroyed your records at home or at work, you'd likewise need to recreate the important information in your planner/organizer if it was lost or stolen.

One simple way to back up is to keep a file folder with photocopies of the important information in your planner. For me, these include the telephone/address section (updated periodically to include new additions), specialized phone lists, family information, and a few information lists that I could recreate, but only with some serious time and effort.

If you're working from a computer program and printing out your pages from there, you have an automatic backup, which is one of the advantages of this arrangement. My only caution here is that you could end up using two systems, but fail to have all the information on both. If you're not diligent about transferring information back and forth, it could cause confusion and missed appointments. The same is true if you use a desktop program and a handheld computerized personal organizer. You need to be sure information is shared between both devices on a daily basis.

You'll need to decide what system works best for you based on your own traits and personality. Just keep it as simple and streamlined as possible and you can't go wrong.

Personal Management for Road Warriors

If you're one of those people who spends a lot of time on the road, your Life Management Center will most likely need to be a mobile one. There are new and better products available on the market every day for those who make a living out of their car or flying from city to city on a regular basis.

The principles are still the same, however, and you'll simply need to have a scaled-down system for handling the same tasks. If you use a cell phone or receive a lot of phone calls at your hotel room, you'll need a way of taking down messages so you don't lose them. If I'm traveling, I prefer to keep everything in one place, including phone messages, so I keep them in my personal planner. That way, there are no little pieces of paper to lose. Everything's secure in my small, portable PDA. You'll also want to keep a list of phone calls you need to make when you return.

> **Amazing Space**
>
> Consider buying a zippered plastic envelope that's three-hole punched to fit in your planner. Use it to hold business cards you collect on business trips (with careful notations on the back, of course!) for the next day back at the office.

You may need some sort of portable filing system to keep track of important receipts and papers generated during the day. These could include personal and household items, as well as those related to work. Labeled folders in one of those portable plastic file boxes is a workable solution. Instead of having receipts in your pockets or flying all over the car, you'll deposit them in their folders—one for business, one for personal. Of course, you can organize this in whatever way most suits your particular situation, but you get the idea.

If you're a laptop user, much of your information can be kept electronically, including personal files, so you can manage both your work and personal life on the go right from your computer. If you're using personal organizing software, this may be the place to keep it, rather than on your desktop at home. Just make sure that whatever option you choose (laptop, PDA, desktop, or paper), you use it consistently and don't have partial information in a variety of different locations. Instead of making life less complicated, this can really foul you up. If one system doesn't seem to be working, try another. Simpler is usually better.

Make It So!

Now that you've got control of your starship, you can explore any territory with confidence. You know you have one place to handle your finances, plan the week's menus, check on the kid's soccer game, or plot the overthrow of your company's competitors. With your Life Management Center and its satellite, your planner/organizer, you're ready for any mission.

The Least You Need to Know

◆ Setting up a central place for managing your affairs gives you control and saves time.

◆ Having basic supplies on hand helps your Life Management Center operate smoothly.

◆ When setting up Life Management systems, be sure to take into account your personal living situation.

◆ Having a personal planner/organizer will make you more effective at home, at work, and on the road.

People Who Need People: Interpersonal Systems

In This Chapter

- Priority one: taking care of yourself
- Nurturing relationships as part of your organization plan
- Setting people priorities
- Keeping track of important dates and events
- Using organizational tools to have more fun with the people you love

We've spent a lot of time talking about organizing "things." But besides getting control of your possessions, an important aspect of organization that most experts overlook is getting control of your relationships. What do I mean by *control?* I'm talking about establishing successful relationships with the people you value most in your life through planning, scheduling, goal-setting, and plain old-fashioned organizing. You didn't think organizing your life could help you with your relationships? Think again!

Take Good Care of Yourself First

The first person you need to provide for in your overall organizing program is *you*. The very fact that you're reading this book and taking steps to carve some order out of chaos shows you care about yourself and are trying to make your life better. Let's begin, then, with the premise that you're no good to yourself or anyone else—family, friends, co-workers, *anyone*—unless you're "taking care of business" with the most important person in your life—you.

> **Tickler Files**
>
> "Friendship with oneself is all-important, because without it one cannot be friends with anyone else in the world."
>
> —Eleanor Roosevelt

Maybe you have trouble thinking of yourself as #1, but it's true. You are and you have to be. Your goals regarding health, mental attitudes, physical appearance, and spiritual well-being all need to be essential parts of any organization plan.

In Chapter 16, I'll share more information on health and fitness, but in a discussion about planning for the people in your life it is extremely important to start you thinking about yourself and your own well-being as you engage in the organization process.

"Unstuff" Your Relationships

Just as your home or office can be full of stuff that falls into the category of "junk," useless things that only get in your way, so, too, your social life may be filled with "junk relationships." This can be a hard thing to face honestly. None of us like to discard people, and we don't want to be discarded. But if we haven't been steering our own ship well in other areas of life, it's likely that our relationships, too, may be foundering on rough seas.

There's no polite way to say it—you need to get people who don't support your goals and share a positive outlook out of your life. You need to learn how to say "no" to these people and concentrate your time and energy on those who add substance and sustenance to your life.

Relationships, like "stuff," tend to fall into three categories:

1. There are the people who deserve to occupy *prime emotional real estate*. They're the closest to you and often the ones you're most likely to take for granted or ignore. Sometimes they're not as demanding as people who are actually less important to you.

Although we constantly hear that the world is becoming smaller and technology is making it easier to stay "in touch" and "connected," technology also brings with it increasing demands on our time. There are lots of stimuli vying for our attention. We may spend more time with TV people than with the people we say are most important in our lives. You can use your organization program to see that this doesn't happen.

2. Then there are *secondary* people. You like them and care about them, but they're not fundamental to your existence. They're not at the core of your life. This probably includes people you encounter at work, in your community, at your place of worship, or while pursuing your various interests. You enjoy their company, they play an important part in these particular spheres of your life, but if you were to lose contact with them through a move or other change, you might not see them regularly, or might lose track of them altogether.

3. Last are the people who are better put in the *deep freeze*. I know that sounds harsh, but I think you know what I'm talking about. It's essential that you have an honest talk with yourself about the people you devote time and energy to who might fall into this category. Do some people you spend time with add nothing to your life?

Picture This

Close your eyes and clear your mind. Visualize the people you spent time with this past week. If necessary, write down a list before you begin this visualization. Put the face of each person in front of you, one at a time. Note how you feel when you visualize that person. Recall what time spent together is like. Is it rewarding? Do you eagerly await seeing them again? Is this a person you've identified as one of the key people in your life (see "Creating a Quality Circle," further on in this chapter)? How much time did you spend with the ones you love most?

I look at it this way: The people who are most important to me are held in the highest esteem in my life. I give them priority over all others. What's left goes to the next level of relationships, and I simply don't have a place in my life for the third kind.

Take a "People" Inventory

At the beginning of this book, we spent some time talking about your personal challenges and your mission in life. This was a "broad stroke" process to help you identify what's important and what you really want. Now I'm asking you to take a similar inventory of your relationships and implement some incremental changes to make them better and stronger than ever before. The goal of this book is not just to help you be an organized person. There are plenty of sharply dressed people with tidy offices and showplace houses, whose lives are falling apart. I want you to have it *all*, and the only way for you to do that is to include it *all* in your Life Plan.

Take a look back at last week. Who did you spend time with? How much time? Write down the names and, next to them, the approximate times. Use the visualization I've given you earlier to help you accomplish this. Now, look at your schedule for this week. Who are you planning to see? Add them to the list if they're not already there.

> **Amazing Space**
>
> When you "de-junk" your relationships, you have more time to nurture those with potential to be more rewarding. Could you grow closer with certain relatives or friends that have gotten pushed into the background with more frequent visits, phone calls, or letters? You might be surprised what happens when you make the effort!

Next, make a list of the people who are most important to you. Your spouse, partner, or person you're dating? Your children? Your parents? Siblings? Extended family? Friends? Co-workers? List them on a separate sheet in the order of their importance. How does what you're actually doing stack up against what you say is most important to you?

Now that you've taken your "people inventory," the next step is to decide what results you want with the people who mean the most to you. To get you started, try asking these questions about the key people you've identified. Again, I suggest you write them down. For each person ask:

◆ What's the current state of our relationship?

◆ Do we communicate often enough?

◆ What are some of the areas between us that could be improved?

◆ What would I have to do to make those improvements?

◆ How would improving that relationship make me feel?

◆ What are five small things I could do today to contribute to making that happen?

◆ How can I use my current organization plan to include my goals for improving my relationships with this person?

◆ Is there a phone call or visit I need to make? A letter or card I really need to send?

Maybe you need to schedule a night out with your spouse. Maybe you could improve the interaction between you and a partner or your kids by streamlining some of the daily chores and working together on the process. I'll bet if you start today to focus regularly on your "people priorities" and include them in your daily and weekly planning sessions, you'll see immediate results.

Creating a Quality Circle

In the 1970s, an idea was introduced to American management from Japan that many people believe helps improve productivity and quality, especially in manufacturing. The concept was called "Quality Circles," and it has helped build strong project teams and strengthen communications. I'd like to suggest applying a modified version of this principle to your relationships.

Somewhere I read that we can't have quality relationships with more than 10 people at one time. I'm not sure I can even manage 10! That's not to say we can't know and interact with more, but we can only give of ourselves to 10 people or fewer in a deep, intimate way.

Let's look again at your list of the most important people in your life. How many people are on it? Are you certain these are the people who are vital to your happiness, who truly mean the most to you? Are they at the core of your life? Do you hold a similar place in their lives? If not, pare your list down to those relationships that are key to your happiness. I'll bet when you're finished you'll have 10 people or fewer by default.

Think of this as your own personal quality circle and nurture it every day. Hold these people in the highest esteem and give them the best you have to offer. Organize your life around them. They form your support system in difficult times and are the ones you celebrate with in joyful times. Being committed to their happiness and well-being will contribute to yours.

You Remembered!

Just by focusing more on the people you care about and eliminating unrewarding relationships, you'll find it easier to remember and keep track of important events like birthdays, anniversaries, school plays, or whatever. But if you tend to be forgetful or remember too late to make the occasion as special as you'd like, I have a foolproof method for always being on top of it.

What makes it foolproof is that it actually involves several systems, not just one. It's what they call in computer jargon "redundancy." Most of the time, organizing involves eliminating duplication, but in this instance duplication works in your favor.

Here's how I do it. In my personal electronic planner I keep an events calendar. It's really just a list of regular events that occur each year pretty much at the same time. Toward the end of any given year, I use my events calendar to fill in important dates for the coming year on my daily calendar pages. I put the actual date on the calendar *and* an early reminder 10 days before. I *also* put these dates on the communal family wall calendar for the year, so I can help my husband keep track. Any annually recurring events like birthdays and anniversaries need only be entered once. The planner's program will keep them perpetually year after year.

The same program exists on my laptop, so everything in my electronic planner is backed up. You can set it to sound an alarm to remind you as well. This method might not work for everyone, but it works for me because I use my computer pretty much every day. The 10-day lead time allows me enough time to order a gift or send a card, and the second reminder the day of the event nudges me to call and wish them a happy birthday, too.

If you're using a paper system, one way to create "redundancy" is to put all these events on both your family wall calendar and your personal planner. Remember to build in the 10-day cushion, so you have time to get a gift or send a card.

Another good idea is to keep a list in your planner/organizer (under "G" for "Gifts") of outings, books, or gifts you hear people say they'd like—their personal "wish list" kept by you. If you come across something in a magazine or on TV that you think they might like, jot down the information and transfer it to this list. You could also have this in a file folder if that's more convenient for you, but I find that having it with me in my planner/organizer allows me to act on it whenever the opportunity arises. If I'm in a store, for example, and I have some time to browse, I'll refer to my list so I have my giftees in mind. At the beginning of the year I review that list and put out feelers to see if these things are still appealing to my "giftee." If not, I cross it out; if so, I decide whether I need to do some advance planning and build that into my calendar.

Orderly Pursuits

If you use a computer rarely or not at all, you might consider a telephone or mail reminder service. Look in your Yellow Pages under "reminder services" or "personal assistant" or check one from a nearby city if you live in a small town. Some personal assistants will even buy gifts, send cards, and run errands for you. For a fee, of course!

When a new year begins, set aside some time to review special events coming up unique to that year. Note, especially, landmark events, like 25th or 50th wedding anniversaries, decade birthdays, baby's first Christmas, confirmations, bar mitzvahs, and similar once-in-a-lifetime events. This gives you even more time than the usual 10 days to plan something really special. Draw up a plan and schedule various tasks into your calendar.

One year for a special Father's Day, for instance, I decided I wanted to do something really different for my husband. I investigated a Jeep tour I'd read about. He's a Western history buff, and the tour involved traveling over some rough road to an old mining town and following a historic Arizona stagecoach route. I found out I needed to book at least a month in advance and had to have at least four people to go on the tour. I had time to invite one of our favorite couples and make it a total surprise. This took some advance planning and organization, but because of my system, I was able to pull it all off without a hitch and in plenty of time. No telling what might happen next year!

Another thing that will save you time and keep the pressure off is to buy greeting cards in advance. You can keep them in a box with dividers especially for that purpose. Since you have your personal planner with you (see why it's important to have and use one?), you'll know which events are coming up and who you need to have cards for. If you do buy cards in advance, make sure you have a place to keep them where they won't get soiled or wrinkled and where they're easy to find any time. You might organize them by month and put a sticky note on ones you have specifically earmarked with certain individuals in mind. Then when you reach your 10-day reminder, you'll just go into your box and grab the card you planned for in advance. Don't just buy for specific occasions—have a few extra for those unplanned-for times when a get well, birthday, or "thinking of you" card would come in handy.

Letters! We Get Letters!

Do people really write letters anymore? Well, *I* do! When you simplify and organize your life, you have time and energy for some of the social graces that make daily living kinder and gentler. With more reliance on the telephone and e-mail, I certainly send letters through the mail ("snail mail" as it's often referred to in cyberspace) less than I used to, but it's still a part of my daily life.

Sometimes I write because I have to clear up a question on a bill or change an address on an account or for similar reasons. This generally falls into the category of business correspondence, and I'll discuss that later in Chapter 9. But on some occasions a personal note, postcard, or letter is appropriate.

Be creative in thinking of ways to keep up with your correspondence. Sometimes I sit out in the hammock and jot off a short postcard message to a friend with a quote or a thought to let her know I'm thinking of her. You might write letters for an hour or so in bed, just before drifting off to sleep. Or you can bring your basket and write while others might be watching a TV program you're not all that interested in. Remember those small 15-minute gems of time I mentioned earlier in this book? When you have your letter-writing supplies handy, it's easy to make use of those 15 minutes to stay in touch with loved ones.

If you have a lot of correspondence, how do you keep track of it? I find a file folder system works best. In the drawer where you keep your personal files, why not have a correspondence file? You may want to photocopy important letters you've written and put them in the file. You also may want to keep letters sent to you that are especially meaningful and note on them when you answered. I don't advocate keeping routine correspondence and cards, but keeping carefully selected mail has its place. I have separate folders for my children and keep copies of e-mails and letters that I know someday will be part of our memories together. These can become material for memory books or scrapbooks, which we'll discuss shortly.

> **Amazing Space**
>
> One way to encourage personal letter-writing and make it quick and easy is to have all your supplies—stationery, stamps, return address labels or rubber stamp, stickers, and pens—in a box or basket you can take with you anywhere.

There are lots of systems for keeping addresses and phone numbers, from the most old-fashioned (a handwritten address book) to the most newfangled (contact software or a handheld electronic personal organizer). I'm of both the old and the new school here. I keep an address/phone book in my household management notebook, which stays in the kitchen and which everyone has access to. It's actually just a printout from my computer program. By the way, this household management notebook also has my cleaning routines in it, emergency information, the recipes I use on a regular basis, and some other useful information that the family needs access to regularly. Not everyone in our household is a computer buff! I also keep a Christmas card list (redundancy again) in a label program in my computer, which I update every year. This allows me to generate labels anytime for most everyone we stay in contact with.

Some people favor a 3 × 5 card filing system so they can make notations on the cards. Others keep everything in a computer program or personal electronic organizer. You decide what's best for you, but be sure your system is portable and easy to update.

To E-Mail or Not to E-Mail?

With the rapid increase in the number of people who have computers at home and in the office, the use of e-mail has skyrocketed. If you aren't hooked up yet, you might want to look into getting an e-mail account as a tool for uncluttering your life. Depending on how you use and manage it, e-mail can make a big difference in how well you stay in contact with the people in your life that really matter, but who may not be close at hand.

The Benefits of E-Mail

I find e-mail indispensable for both personal and business correspondence. Some of the benefits of e-mail are:

- ◆ It's easy.

- ◆ It's cheap.

- ◆ It's fast. In fact, in most cases it's immediate.

- ◆ E-mail gives your correspondents hard copy at the touch of the button, but generates paper only when they choose.

- ◆ You can send items of interest, photos, and even sound files as attachments to e-mail.

- ◆ You can use e-mail to transmit short messages that would otherwise end up in chatty phone calls taking far more time out of your schedule.

I use e-mail to communicate regularly with my children, who are spread out all over the country. This way, when we speak on the phone or get together, we can cut right to the heart of the matter, since I already know most of the day-to-day gossip and happenings in their lives through our regular e-mail correspondence. By writing several times a week, they know I'm thinking of them, and I can remind them I love them any time of the night or day, whenever the spirit strikes me. This makes our phone conversations even more focused and intimate.

I also use e-mail to send electronic cards for special occasions (they're free!), in addition to sending one via "snail mail." This makes a friend feel doubly special. Electronic greetings often have musical accompaniment and animation, adding another dimension to their card. If I've somehow forgotten an event or just learned of one, an electronic greeting is a last-minute solution.

Orderly Pursuits

For a nifty selection of electronic greeting cards, check out the Blue Mountain Arts site at www. bluemountain.com/. There's something to send for just about any holiday, even those that might be obscure to many of us, and there are some greetings available in French and Spanish.

E-mail is great for firming up visiting arrangements, and transmitting directions and flight information. I would urge caution here, however. Print out the information, and always confirm by telephone closer to the date. That's good e-mail etiquette in any case, and will prevent misunderstandings. E-mail just doesn't have the urgency or impact that phone or face-to-face communication does. In some instances it's a great supplement to voice communication, but not a complete substitute.

Things to Watch Out For: "Netiquette"

Just as there are polite rules of behavior in other areas of social interaction, there are also rules (commonly known as "netiquette") governing communications in cyberspace. Here's a short list of do's and don'ts for e-mail correspondence:

◆ Do read over an e-mail message you've composed before you send it. Remember, there are no emotional clues, no voice inflections, no pauses or facial expressions to tell the reader that something's intended with humor or being said with a smile or a sarcastic grin. Make sure there can be no misunderstanding.

◆ Do learn to use emotion symbols (known as "emoticons") whenever truly useful. Many use <g> to mean "grin" or :) to mean "smile" (look at it sideways and you'll see a smiley face). For a comprehensive list of emoticons and other e-mail shorthand go to www. computer-user.com/resources/dictionary/emoticons. html. You can also use descriptive words in parentheses to make the meaning clear if you're not sure it will be clear to the recipient.

◆ Don't forward long posts or files unless you really think the recipient will benefit from or enjoy them.

◆ Don't send chain letters or information about multilevel marketing schemes. It's rude and, again, takes up a person's time even if it's just to open your message, read part of it, and delete it.

◆ Don't rely solely on e-mail when making important arrangements. Always confirm or reiterate via phone or in person.

◆ Do quote part of someone's previous message when replying to his e-mail; this reminds him of the "thread" of the conversation. Many e-mail programs automatically duplicate the message being replied to in the body of the reply. But don't overdo it. Having to read through the entire message again is a waste of time. Just quote the pertinent parts.

Amazing Space

If you don't want your e-mail stuffed with junk, ask others to take you off their joke-of-the-day, recipe, or other mail list. It's just a waste of your time if you don't enjoy it. Likewise, don't subject other people to your own mail list without their permission.

Oops! _____

Be sure the person you're e-mailing is a regular user of his online connection, especially if you're contacting him with time-sensitive information. Otherwise, your message can sit there forever, and you'll wonder why you haven't gotten a response. The reverse is also true. Don't send an e-mail message or give out your e-mail address and then not log on for two weeks.

◆ Do exercise care with grammar and spelling. Not only do poor communication skills reflect on you, they also indicate how much you value getting a clear message across to the recipient. The less clear the communication, the more room there is for misunderstanding.

◆ Don't use all capital letters. It makes your message LOOK LIKE IT'S BEING SHOUTED! And we all know it's rude to shout.

Putting People in Their Place

What do you do when you really need to tell someone to give you some space or let him know he's intruding on your privacy or time? If you're truly committed to simplifying and organizing your life, this may well be necessary at some point.

Generally I find honesty is the best policy. If it's not a good time for people to call, say so. If they just drop in without asking, tell them you can't see them right now and ask them to call next time. If you need uninterrupted time to get something done, don't answer the phone. Let your voice mail or answering machine take it. You decide who has access to you and when. Use the various means available to you to control your time and your life.

I have caller ID, for example, as well as an unwanted call screen, and I use them to eliminate calls from telemarketers and control calls from people I know who are habitually inconsiderate of my time and my needs. My home is my castle, my quality circle is my first concern, and my time is precious. I use every trick I can find to protect them and me. You can, too.

Scrapbooks and Other Memory Devices

Since we're on the subject of people, let's talk about the things we tend to accumulate as keepsakes to remind us of special people and important moments we spend with them. These can include letters, cards for special occasions, photographs, memorabilia, and just about anything else that reminds us of a special event or person. But these things can accumulate, and unless they're organized in a meaningful way, they just become part of the clutter.

A "new" trend (actually, it's quite old-fashioned) is the making of scrapbooks or "memory books." This is a great way to unstuff your life of sentimental clutter and keep only the best or most memorable things. You discard a lot. What you *do* save goes into an archival quality album with acid-free paper, so you're protecting your precious memories from the ravages of time, adding your own personal comments and artistic sense, and putting them into a form that can be passed on and appreciated by the whole family and future generations.

Keep materials to a minimum, even though that may be hard to do. There are lots of products on the market to enhance your scrapbook—stickers, rubber stamps, special papers, glitter, and much much more. Just keep it simple and basic, buying only what you need. Put your best photos and mementos in your album and get rid of the rest.

Another way to pare down keepsakes is to incorporate them into a collage or other display that, again, only uses the best or most memorable objects. Still another idea for kids and adults alike is to keep a "memory box." Use the size of the box to limit what is retained, and weed it out periodically so it contains only the most special trinkets and photographs. I also find that my personal journal and the descriptions of events I write there often make it less necessary to save these things. An illustrated journal (a few choice photographs can be added to enhance the text) makes an even more personal way to remember the past without cluttering the present and future. Scrapbooks can also be made richer by the addition of journal-like commentary on its pages.

Orderly Pursuits

To learn more about preparing scrapbooks, check out *Making Scrapbooks: Complete Guide to Preserving Your Treasured Memories* by Vanessa-Ann. Or point your web browser to Vickie's Scrapbooking Village, www.playhere.com/scrapbooking/.

Spontaneity Has Its Time and Place

Making an inventory of people in your life and planning time around them may seem too structured, too scheduled, not spontaneous. That doesn't have to be true if you make sure there's unstructured time in your plan. This may seem like a contradiction—organizing yourself to be spontaneous? It isn't. By getting physically organized and mentally focused (they reinforce each other), you get the "must-do's" done more efficiently. You release yourself from the nagging feeling that things are out of control and getting further away from you. You feel confident knowing that you're making time for the people and activities you really care about. This actually allows you to be more spontaneous and provides the emotional freedom to let go.

One quick thought about intimacy and romance. I believe it's essential to have planned times for intimacy, as well as spaces in your life where the unexpected can happen. Think how much more passionate you can be when you can relax and know that your life is humming along on an organized plan. You'll feel strong and energized knowing you're well on your way to achieving the goals you've set for yourself. Bet you didn't know that being organized can be sexy!

My friend Karen and her husband actually schedule at least half an hour every day to snuggle. They usually set time aside around 5:30 P.M., when they're both done working for the day (they both work at home), as a way to connect with each other. It's absolutely precious and jealously guarded time for them. No phone calls, please!

People Time, Quiet Time

There's a time to be with people and a time to be alone. And time alone spent in silence is especially healing and renewing. Remember, included in your quality circle is *you!* Make sure you schedule time each day (yes, I said *day*, not week!) to listen to your own inner voice. That's how you know if you're on the right path and you've got your goals and priorities in the right place. That's how you know if your people time is being spent wisely and if you're happy.

So, tend to the people you care about most, but always leave time for solitude and having important (or even frivolous) conversations with yourself.

Orderly Pursuits

Want some terrific ideas for gifts (many of them "nonstuff" ones) you can give the one you love? Get yourself a copy of Gregory Godek's *1001 Ways to Be Romantic* and his sequel, *1001 More Ways to Be Romantic*.

If You Can't Have Fun, Why Get Organized?

Getting your life in order may seem like hard work. And in fact, it *is* hard to honestly assess what you're doing and change old, deeply ingrained habits. But as I'm sure you're beginning to see, the rewards are enormous. Granted, cleaning out your dead files, throwing out old newspapers, and getting a DayRunner won't automatically make you spouse of the year, superdad, and megafriend. But let me ask you a question: If you have more time to spend with your loved ones, if you're more relaxed when you're with them because your life is under control, and if you're making sure you include them in your overall Life Plan, could this possibly *hurt?* I think you know the answer!

The Least You Need to Know

◆ Your own health and well-being are the hinge upon which your entire organization plan revolves.

◆ There are three types of relationships. The first type is most important and occupies *prime emotional real estate;* the second type is maintained with what remains; and the third type should be eliminated entirely.

- ◆ A redundant reminder system will ensure you never again forget an important recurring event.

- ◆ Correspondence is easily managed by assembling all the supplies in a central place and using small blocks of time.

- ◆ E-mail can be an effective way of keeping in touch if you observe a few basic rules.

- ◆ Spontaneity (and even romance!) is made possible by organization and planning.

Work Systems: Getting Ahead Without Getting a Headache

In This Chapter

- ◆ Applying basic organization principles to your work life and career goals
- ◆ Unstuffing your office
- ◆ Getting control of work-related paper
- ◆ Organizing your home-based business

According to professional organizer Stephanie Winston, a typical manager loses one hour a day to disorder, costing his company as much as $4,000 a year if the manager earns $35,000 annually.

Other experts theorize that 10 percent of a manager's salary is lost to office chaos, and believe disorganized companies are targets for double-billing and other scams, because they don't have a handle on their records and procedures.

But there's an individual, human cost as well. If people are disorganized at work, they live every day feeling overwhelmed, ineffective, and pressured. Not sure whether you're disorganized in your job? Check if any of these have happened to you recently:

❑ You missed an important appointment or meeting because you forgot or lost track of time.

❑ You forgot to return a phone call and the caller had to phone you a second time.

❑ You had to do something over because you couldn't find the original work.

❑ You missed an important deadline.

❑ You spent hours looking for a piece of paper you needed in a hurry, only to find it sometime later in a pile on your desk or stuffed in an obscure file folder.

❑ You passed up a possible job, career advancement, or business opportunity because it was too much trouble to put your resumé in order.

❑ You spent evenings or weekends working at home because you couldn't get the job done during regular business hours.

Oops!

Besides taking a toll on your own mental and physical well-being, both the reality and the perception of you as a disorganized person may be keeping you from a promotion or from moving into the career you want. How likely would *you* be to trust additional responsibility to someone you thought of as "disorganized?"

If you checked one or two of the above, you probably have a less-than-perfect work life. If you checked three or more, it's probably darn near out of control, and you're way more stressed out than you want or need to be.

Never fear. Together, you and I will conquer the work front the same way we began whipping things into shape at home. So stop making excuses, stop procrastinating, roll up your sleeves, and let's get to work on work.

Goal-Setting Fine-Tuned

More goal-setting? Absolutely! Only this time you're moving into advanced goal-setting, fine-tuned specifically for work and career. Let's start with a few questions first (feel free to write your answers down on the lines provided or on a separate piece of paper):

♦ How satisfied are you in your current job? Do you plan to be there a year from now?

_____

_____

◆ If you're dissatisfied with where you are now, what are you specifically dissatisfied with? Could any of these be related to your own performance or lack of organization? How could getting organized improve your present job satisfaction?

_____

_____

◆ If you plan to seek a new job in the next year, how would getting organized right now support both your job-hunting efforts and your goals in your new position?

_____

_____

◆ What are your broader career goals? Where do you want to be five years from now? Ten years? Twenty? What additional skills, education, or experience do you need to realize these goals? How would getting organized support you? Do you have a career strategy or plan for getting where you want to be? What would one look like if you did?

_____

_____

◆ Look at your current working environment. What feelings does it create for you? Which elements do you have the freedom to change? (Look at "Designing Your Work Environment" later in this chapter for some specific areas to consider.)

_____

_____

◆ Can you take the basic principles of organization you learned in Chapter 5, Chapter 6, and Chapter 7 and apply them to work? (Don't worry if the answer is no on this one. You'll be getting some help!)

_____

_____

Picture This

Would thinking of yourself as an entrepreneur, even though you work for someone else, have an effect on your attitude and ultimately your results? Close your eyes and visualize your position as your own company, with you as president and CEO of your job. Imagine you are solely responsible for making the company grow and that all of the people you work with are part of your corporate team. Imagine you are responsible for motivating these people to help you grow your business. How does this feel? How does this shift in viewpoint change the way you see your job? Act on this shift in perception and see if it doesn't improve your attitude and performance.

Unstuffing: Work Version

Before you try to get organized at work, you'll need to pare down. Sound familiar? This unstuffing stuff seems to apply to *everything!* Commit to getting rid of the clutter and junk around you and streamlining your work space, just as you've already begun to do in other areas.

Start by mapping out some time. Come in an hour early. Stay an hour late. Use your lunch hour or a series of breaks to get started. Whenever you choose to make time, focus exclusively on implementing your organization plan and don't allow any interruptions.

Remember your boxes for sorting? We're going to use the same basic system for unstuffing your work space. This time your boxes will be labeled *Trash* (or you can just use a large wastebasket), *Put Away* (most of this will likely be filed), *Pass On* (waiting to be handed to someone else in the company; or it might mean you need to delegate it), *Mystery* (for stuff you just don't know what to do with right now), and *Action* (for stuff you need to do something about).

Keep the stuff you put in the *Mystery* box to a minimum. You either have to find a place for it, identify it (a true mystery), or eventually trash it, so if you can make those decisions now, you might as well. But if you just can't figure out what should be done about a particular item, this is the place for it temporarily.

Do the same thing here that you did earlier with your living space. Tackle one small area at a time (a drawer, cabinet, or shelf). Remember the power of "just 15 minutes."

You can also try taking everything except your computer and phone off the surfaces in your office and putting back only what you absolutely need to get through the day. You may be surprised at how little you actually put back. And you know what that means: "If you don't use it, lose it!" When you make decisions about personal items, be selective ("quality, not quantity"). Give them a special place and keep them to a minimum.

As you do your sorting, ask the same basic questions you asked when you unstuffed your home space:

◆ When was the last time I used this?

◆ How often do I use it?

◆ If I don't use it very often, could I borrow it the few times I might need it?

◆ Is it a duplicate? If so, which one works best?

◆ Is it out-of-date?

◆ If I didn't have this anymore, what impact if any would it have on my work? What's the *worst* thing that could happen if I tossed this and then needed it?

As you answer these questions, more should be finding its way into the *Trash* or *Pass On* bins or boxes. Be ruthless. Remember, just because someone sent it or gave it to you doesn't mean you have to keep it.

Next, follow the "directions" on your *Trash* and *Pass On* bins. That's easy—just do it. Now let's take a look at the *Put Aways*. Chances are you're dealing mostly with paper here, but there may also be supplies and personal items. Are you hoarding things like artwork, knickknacks, photographs, funny calendars, souvenirs, sneakers, umbrellas, food containers, or coffee mugs? For now, just group these personal items together and put them aside.

Take a look at your pile of supplies. You may find you actually have three rulers and two staplers. Look for duplicates, keep the best, and either pass the others on or trash them if they don't work well. Decide on a place to keep supplies. You'll probably end up with two places: one for what you need right at your fingertips, such as tape, a stapler, staple remover, and pens; and one for supplies you don't need very often, like tape refills and extra staples. Keep *prime real estate*—the drawers, shelves, cabinets, and surfaces closest to you—for the most frequently used things.

Even if your company won't supply a rolling cart, you may want to consider buying one for supplies. I use this in my home office and couldn't be without it. It cost about $30, has five drawers, and sits on casters, so I can move it out of the way when I don't need it. Remember to label the drawers so you don't have to rummage through each one looking for a pair of scissors or a letter opener.

Orderly Pursuits

Check the resources list at the back of this book for lots of mail-order supplies— filing supplies, rolling drawer carts, rolling file carts, baskets, racks, office furniture, phone equipment, and just about anything else you can think of to help organize your office space.

If the rolling cart idea doesn't work for you, consider drawer dividers and step shelves for cabinets to maximize your storage space. Again, if your company won't pay for them, it's worth getting them yourself. You can always take them with you, and when others in the company see how well they work, you may even get reimbursed.

Keep personal items to a minimum. Make them simple and meaningful.

The remaining papers need to be either filed or acted upon. First we'll tackle the filing (what's in your *Put Away* bin), and then the To-Dos (what's in your *Action* bin).

Your Files Aren't Another Trash Can!

How much of what's in your files is outdated or no longer useful to you? Probably about 80 percent! As you clean up the stuff strewn around your office, file only what you really need. Then set up a time to go through your existing files and do some serious weeding. When that's done, commit to purging them at least twice a year, and more often if you can. Perhaps you can key those purging sessions to events like the New Year and "spring cleaning." You don't have to do your file purge all at once. Take 15 minutes and do a little every day. Before you know it, you'll have more file drawer space than you ever imagined possible.

Another important issue is whether it's easy to find something once you file it. My advice is to keep your filing system simple. Not only does it save you time, it also makes it easier for someone else to handle things in your absence. In fact, when you get that promotion, it'll make it easier for the next person in your position to take over!

Here are some tips for improving your filing system:

- Alphabetize. Don't separate individual files into various conceptual divisions and then alphabetize within them. If it makes sense, use separate drawers for broad divisions like Projects, Personnel, and so on, and alphabetize the whole drawer. Of course, sometimes you may need to use another type of system, but for most filing, alphabetical is the way to go.

- Label clearly and boldly. Make sure you can read the subject headers quickly and easily, even from a distance. Black and bold is best. There are label programs for your computer that allow you to select an easy-to-read font in any size and print out labels whenever you need them.

◆ For each item you're filing, ask what word comes to your mind first and use that as your category. Use a noun for file categories. For example, "Files, Organizing," not "Organizing Files." Remember that the word you choose to be first will determine where the file goes alphabetically.

◆ Be careful you don't duplicate categories—Records, Medical and Records, Health, for example. Pick one and be consistent. If you use a computer, use the same name for paper and computer files.

◆ At least in the beginning, keep a list of all your file categories. That'll prevent you from creating duplicates and make the system easier to revise.

◆ File the most recent document in the front. When you open the folder, your documents will always be in chronological order.

◆ Use a hanging folder and a regular folder for each subject. This may seem like extra work, but in the long run it isn't. If you never take the hanging folder out of the drawer, you'll file the manila folder in the same place every time. Guaranteed!

◆ Consolidate and compress wherever possible. Can you make a list on one piece of paper and eliminate several others? Can it be reduced or copied double-sided? Can several pieces relating to the same project be clipped together?

> **Amazing Space**
>
> If your secondary storage space is limited, you may want to keep only a bare minimum of extra supplies in your office and go to the supply room when you start to get low.

> **Oops!**
>
> Avoid having files called "Miscellaneous" or "Other." These are traps, and you usually can't find things in them anyway.

Don't forget to unstuff your computer files, too. Many of the same principles apply—file things under names you'll find easily, avoid catchall file names like "miscellaneous" or "stuff," consolidate files, and avoid duplicates. Use the "search" or "find file" function to find files when you can't. Use a compression program to save on disk space. A software program like Norton Utilities can help to regularly "defragment" your hard drive to optimize space as well. Keep your computer desktop clean and uncluttered. Purge computer files when you purge paper ones.

And Speaking of Paper

In Chapter 6, we talked at length about controlling paper at home. Now, how can you apply what you learned to handling paper in the workplace? Let's review.

Stop It!

Get rid of as much junk mail at work as you can, using the technique I've already shown you for the home front. Ask to be taken off mailing lists. Stay away from surveys and questionnaires. And when you subscribe to a publication, send a form letter requesting to be kept off mailing lists and not to sell your information to anyone else.

In addition to junk mail delivered by the post office, you may also need to combat junk e-mail, also known as SPAM. This fast and cheap way to target upscale consumers has lots of e-mail subscribers up in arms. It takes valuable time to download, open, read and then trash those useless messages, and it overloads online resources already pushed to the limit carrying important stuff that we really want!

Here are some steps to stop SPAM:

1. If the sender gives you a way to "opt out" in the message, you can do so. I feel that it should be the other way around—we should decide if we want to receive the stuff in the first place—but at least you may be able to stop more from coming. Some determined spammers only use your reply to confirm your e-mail address and sell your name to still more spammers!

2. Go to the Junkbusters site (www.junkbusters.com) and the Netiquette site (www.netiquette.com) and fill out their opt out forms. Again, this may have little effect, but it's a start in letting online marketers know your preferences.

3. If there's a toll-free number in the SPAM you get, call and complain.

4. Complain to your own Internet service provider (find out who the right person is). Some ISPs have standard addresses for this purpose, such as "postmaster@ yourisp.com" or "abuse@yourisp.com." You can ask that your provider install a junk e-mail filter, which will filter out SPAM from known offenders.

5. You may also be able to install a filter on your own computer or your Internet Service Provider may have one. If you're not sure how to do this on your own, call your ISP or an independent computer consultant.

6. Be aware that most spammers get your name and e-mail address through postings to electronic bulletin boards, mail lists, and newsgroups. You may want to

use a second web-based e-mail address (many of these are free) to participate in these, so at least you'll be able to get your important mail without having to wade through a lot of SPAM.

7. Be careful about registration forms and surveys on the Internet. If you fill one out to access a site, give as little information as possible, and tell them you don't want your information to go anyplace else.

Internet activists are attempting to get Congress to regulate online marketing and the proliferation of SPAM. Until they do, you can at least take some steps to reduce the amount you get clogging your mailbox (snail mailbox, that is).

Review your subscriptions at work and see if you can't cut them in half. Be realistic about the time you actually have for reading. If you've got reading material backed up for more than a week, trash it and start fresh.

Can you use an electronic or paper clipping service or Internet mailing list to stay on top of subjects you need to track? Is there a printed or electronic newsletter that does a good job of summarizing the latest developments in your field? Even though some of these options may seem somewhat expensive initially, in the long run they'll save you precious time and money (add up the cost of all those subscriptions, for instance). In addition, information is often easier to absorb on one particular subject when it's gathered in one place.

If you have a secretary, see if your mail can be opened and sorted before you get it. Deal only with priority mail during the business day, and quickly sort through the rest at the end of the day, during your homebound commute (if you don't drive to work), or during your afternoon break.

> **Amazing Space**
>
> If you're on a publication pass-on list within the company, try requesting to be taken off the list if the information in the publication isn't crucial.

Don't be a paper-generator. Limit memos and letters whenever possible. Try to avoid getting into the "CYA" habit. Most of the time this causes unnecessary accumulation of paper to prove something actually occurred, in case you're asked to defend yourself. If this is really necessary in your present company, you might want to think about changing jobs. Don't print out e-mail messages or online information unless it's absolutely necessary! Whenever possible, file it digitally.

Decide Now

When you sort through mail or other papers, put them into categories as quickly as possible. Be ruthless. The paper in your hand either gets trashed, is passed on, or goes in one of three compartments: *To Do* (or *Action*, if you prefer), *To File*, or *To Read*.

If you decide something needs to be filed, make sure it's something you really need to keep. Keep it only if it meets one or more of these criteria:

- Can't be found elsewhere
- Supports you in the goals you've set for yourself
- Has been reduced or consolidated as much as possible
- Is up-to-date

Make sure you file it where you'll be able to retrieve it when you need it. Have a clear idea of how long you'll really need a particular piece of paper. If you purge your files every six months (or more often, if you can manage it), once a particular item's usefulness has passed, you'll be pitching it in the circular file, and freeing up space on a regular basis.

File So You Can Find It

Treat your files at work the same way you do at home. There are your current Action or Working files, Secondary or Reference files, and Archival files (the Deep Freeze!). Keep your Working files close at hand in your filing *prime real estate*. You may even want to consider one of those rolling files we talked about earlier, or a divided holder next to your desk.

Secondary files that you only refer to periodically can be less accessible. Archival files should be put in storage, preferably out of your office, and should be kept to an absolute minimum.

Whatever you use for current project files, make sure it's not a catchall. Some people like having some sort of rack or holder to keep them in view. Rather than having a holder out on the desk for current files, other people prefer an in-the-drawer system or rolling file. This is an especially good option if you're easily distracted. In the morning, the desk is clear and you can focus on whatever tasks you decide should get your attention first. Then in the evening, everything can be put away off your desk for a fresh start in the morning. I've tried both and both have advantages and disadvantages. You decide.

Everything's filed in alphabetical order—hanging folders first with a matching manila folder within it. If there is more than one subdivision within a hanging folder, then the manila folders are also filed alphabetically. That's the simplest and quickest system I know, and it works best for most people. In some cases, you may need to use a chronological or numerical filing system instead.

I color code my files using just four colors for the four major types of files I have: Working, Reference, Financial, and Personal. Each has a separate file drawer (or two). I do this because I work at home and use my filing system for work, household, and personal information, and this helps me keep things where they belong. Color coding works for some people, but for others it's an unnecessary complication. One drawback is having to store different colored supplies. Again, you decide. Don't be afraid to try one system and scrap it if it doesn't work for you.

Be sure your documents are dated and the source is identified before you file. This is especially important when clipping newspaper or magazine articles. Should you later need to quote the piece or place it in a chronology, you'll be glad you took the time.

Oops!

Before you make any radical changes in the way you handle and store files and records, be sure to review your company's policy, and your department's, to make sure you comply with financial and legal requirements.

Observe good filing practices with your computer, as well. Use color coding only if it really helps. Keep files and folders off your desktop and tucked away under pertinent category folders on your hard drive. Purge often. Put as much in the trash as possible, use portable media (floppy disks, larger disk media, tape cartridges) to "file off" and store a big chunk, then organize the rest on your hard drive. Don't duplicate digital with paper files unless absolutely necessary. Choose the form that makes the most sense.

Back Up or Else!

Another important consideration for electronic files is backing up. We all know we should do it, but most of us back up sporadically at best. I suggest you keep two sets of backup disks for your files. One you leave at work and a second you take home with you and rotate once a week. That way, you're always assured a fairly recent copy of your work, regardless of any disaster that might occur. Since I work at home, I exchange a set of backup disks with another home worker. We meet for breakfast once a week and exchange our latest versions. If you don't have someone to switch with, consider keeping a set in your safety deposit box. Especially if you own your own business, having backup can mean the difference between surviving and going under in the event of a fire or other disaster. You may even want to consider a commercial off-site backup service.

If you tend to forget to make a backup, make it a ritual. How about every Friday afternoon? Or every Monday morning? I generally use Fridays for "housekeeping" in my office—filing, tidying up, nonurgent correspondence. This is my time to do a weekly backup. On important documents, I back them up to a floppy every day. There is also software you can buy that automatically reminds you to back up. Whatever you do and however you do it, back it up!

A final note: Be careful about taking files out of the office without adequate backup. The same is true of computer files on disk. Think of the hardship it would cause if they were lost or damaged. Make sure you have duplicates of absolutely critical files.

Life Management Center: Work Version

In the office you'll have a different version of the Life Management Center you set up at home. This one is specifically geared toward supporting you in your career goals. Depending on what kind of work you do, it may involve a planning board, project calendar on the wall, or other specialized tools.

You'll also need a way to integrate the schedules of other people in your department and overall deadlines. Some companies do this through software on a networked computer system. If yours has one, learn how to use it effectively and train others as well.

> **Amazing Space**
>
> If you use a paper planner/ organizer, use a pencil for writing down appointments and To-Dos that may change. Try a colored pen or highlighter to emphasize important appointments or reminders.

An indispensable tool, however, will still be the planner/organizer that you set up in Chapter 7. This is what integrates all the things that are important to you in your life, and helps you keep a balance between work and home. Enter everything that comes to mind that you need to do on your Master To-Do List as you think of it. You can keep a separate one for work and home if you like, but I prefer to keep everything on one list, so I'm sure to include both when I'm planning either for work or for my personal life.

Your Master List is simply a data bank of things you want or need to do. You're the sorter. Review your Master List whenever you do your planning (I recommend mini-planning sessions first thing in the morning and last thing in the evening, every day) and see what should be transferred to your Daily To-Do List and when. Make sure you include deadlines and phone calls you need to make (or times you've asked others to call you) as well.

Prioritize the tasks on your Daily To-Do List. Some people like the A-B-C method:

Oops!

What seems to be most urgent is not necessarily what's most important. Keep repeating this over and over to yourself. Don't let only the "squeaky wheel" grab your attention. You decide what's important.

"A"—Top priority items;

"B"—These things are important but don't absolutely have to get done today;

"C"—It would be nice if these things got done, but they could probably be put off indefinitely.

Personally, I don't think any C items should be on your list at all. Keep them on your Master To-Do List and only add them to your daily one when you decide they're important enough. So, all that's left are As and Bs. I prefer to number them in order of priority, from number one to whatever. Anything I don't get to at the end of the day gets put on the next day's list and most likely gets a high priority number.

Assigning a task number-one priority doesn't necessarily mean it's the one you do first. It simply means that of all the tasks on your schedule for that day, it's the one that you most want or need to get done. Take advantage of your peak performance times for tasks that require the most concentration or creativity.

Remember, what determines priority is the place a particular activity has in supporting you in your goals, not whatever comes up first or shouts the loudest.

Use the organizing principle "Group Like Things Together" when you plan your time. It's often more efficient to do all the things that require certain tools or skills at one time, like writing letters or making phone calls, than it is to scatter them throughout the day.

Don't forget to write down planning time on your schedule, block out time to be with family and friends, and make appointments with yourself to take care of your needs for relaxation, learning, and spiritual development. Always keep in mind the whole picture of who you are and are aspiring to be, and integrate that into your daily work planning and organizing.

If you're not accomplishing all the tasks you set for yourself in a day on a regular basis, that usually means you're wasting time, asking yourself to do too much, allowing too many interruptions, or suffering from The Big P: Procrastination. If it's the latter, go back to Chapter 3 and review the section on procrastination. You can't afford not to conquer it.

In conjunction with a planner/organizer, some people have a "tickler" file. A tickler file is simply a set of 31 numbered files representing each day of the month and a set of 12 files behind them for each month of the year. As invitations, tickets, conference brochures, or anything with date-specific importance comes through your hands, you can file it in your tickler file. When the event draws near, you'll have all the information you need. Make sure to file the information in the file for the date you need to act on it, *not* when it's due. If, for example, you get a memo about a project that's due two weeks from now and you don't intend to work on it for another week, put it in the numbered file for seven days from now, to remind you to start on it. Keep information for later months in the 12-month folders. Be sure to check your tickler file every day. It's not a bad idea to check ahead for the following week on Monday morning and Friday afternoon, as well.

> ### Amazing Space
>
> A tickler file system should occupy *prime real estate* (as in, under your nose), and checking it must be a habit. The system only works if you use it regularly. If you forget to check it, things can get lost and you can forget to take important actions when needed.

Tickler files don't work for everyone, but if your work is very date-oriented, it might be the right system for you.

Designing Your Work Environment

The environment you have in your work space has a direct effect on how well you work. That applies to offices away from home as well as home offices. Often, if you work for someone else, you simply accept the environment you're given and fail to realize how much you can actually do to adapt it to your own needs and working style.

Look around your office or cubby and ask these questions:

♦ What's the furniture in this room really like? Is it functional? Is it in the best spot? Is it attractive? Is your desk the right height? Your computer keyboard? Do you have space to spread out? Is there ample room for you to stretch out your legs or lean back? How comfortable is your chair? What are your options in this company as far as furniture is concerned? Can you make changes? If not, what can you do to adapt what you already have using add-on drawers, step shelves, desk pads, or other removable accessories?

◆ What are the predominant colors in this room? How do you respond to them? Is there a way to add color through wall decorations, furniture choices, or office accessories?

◆ How does this room filter out sound? Is there a way to improve it? How does sound affect you when you work? If there's music piped in, does it help or hinder you? Can you eliminate it if you want to? When might you need to do that? Is there a quieter place you can retreat to when noise becomes a serious distraction?

◆ Where are your light sources? Is there any natural light? What kind of blinds or curtains do you have to control natural light? What kind of light fixtures do you have? Are they adequate? Are they located in the best places? Are they fluorescent or incandescent (incandescent is easier on your eyes)? If you have a fluorescent fixture, does it buzz? (If so, the ballast may need to be replaced.) What is the strength of the light bulbs in your fixtures? What are your options for changing and improving your office lighting? Are there any ways you could improve the situation by bringing something in yourself?

◆ What's the temperature in your office? Is it too cold? Too warm? Does it fluctuate? Can you control it in any way? Can you control the sunlight into your office, thereby having a certain amount of control over the temperature? Would the addition of a small fan or space heater help? Would wearing layered clothing that you can add or shed make a difference? Do you include getting some fresh air as part of your daily routine? Is there a way to get fresh air into your work space?

◆ How about humidity? Is it too damp or too dry? Would the introduction of a room humidifier or dehumidifier be an option?

◆ What's the location of your phone jack? Is it conducive to where you want your desk, computer, and modem to be? Can you have your phone jack moved or an additional one put in? How about electrical outlets? What are your options here? Can you get extension cords or power strips? (Be careful about overloading electrical circuits, protecting critical equipment, and the safe locating of cords and wires.) Would the addition of a headset, cordless headset, or speaker phone greatly enhance your comfort and efficiency?

◆ Do you store food in your office? How does that affect your working environment, and does that support you in your health and fitness goals? Does having food nearby distract you or encourage you to procrastinate? Do you tend to eat lunch and take breaks in your office, rather than resting your eyes and your wrists or stretching your legs?

◆ What comforts or accessories can you add to make this a better work space? A better chair, a cushion, or backrest? A wrist pad or mouse pad for your computer? An antiglare screen? A mat or footrest? How about a rolling cart for supplies or a rolling file cart?

◆ Do you have your space set up to maximize your movements, and have you allotted *prime real estate* to the tasks you perform most often? Are all the supplies you need to perform a task located in the right place? Can you obtain more or better storage to accommodate your needs?

◆ Have you managed your total work environment to bolster your energy level and help you stick to your health goals? Are you taking regular breaks from your computer screen or other work? Are you getting up from your desk regularly and moving? Have you considered buying equipment like an air filter, ionizer, or aromatherapy diffuser to enhance your work environment?

◆ Have you given consideration to the care and feeding of your mind, heart, and soul when you survey your work environment? What's your overall sense of well-being in your current work space?

◆ Are your goals, dreams, and visions somehow projected and presented for you on a daily basis?

Orderly Pursuits

For suppliers of office phone equipment, check out your local business supply store or chain, such as Staples (www.staples. com/) or Office Max (www. officemax.com/), Radio Shack's Duofone products (www. radioshack.com/) and the Quill business supply catalog (www. quillcorp.com/).

By the time you're done asking yourself these questions, you'll probably have a list of things to do and requests for your purchasing department or office supply center (or you may need to buy things personally). Don't delay, since these "environmental" improvements can have an immediate impact on how well you perform your job and how you feel about it. These things are so easy to take for granted or ignore. Take a few minutes today to focus on them and make the necessary improvements.

People Power

Do you manage people? Work in teams? How's your relationship with your boss? Your secretary? The mailroom personnel? How can you organize yourself to make these relationships better? Being organized reduces stress, not only for you, but also for the people around you. Order increases efficiency and promotes creativity; it has definite effects on your ability to perform and your level of satisfaction. Here are six strategies for increasing your people power:

1. **Delegate.** That doesn't mean sloughing off work on other people. Delegating means giving other people the authority and freedom to do a task that you might otherwise do yourself. Make sure you thoroughly explain the task, communicate what's expected, and empower the person you've asked to do the task to perform it thoroughly and well. It may not be done exactly the way you would have done it, but if the end result is acceptable, then allow the person the freedom to handle it his or her own way. Agree on when and how progress will be reported and reviewed. To make sure you don't lose track of who's doing what, you may want to set up a simple form and record what you delegated, to whom, when, and when it's due. If you learn to delegate effectively, you'll have more time to attend to higher priority tasks, and the person you've delegated to will have a valuable opportunity to learn and grow.

2. **Network.** Use your friends' and colleagues' knowledge and experience. If you're asked to do a project or implement a program that others you know have done, pick their brains. And make yourself available to them for the same purpose. I regularly let writer friends of mine know what projects I'm working on. Since they see a lot of information daily on a variety of topics, just as I do, they often pass on news or magazine clippings or make me aware of experts, books, or online sites I should know about. Sometimes they suggest people to interview or relate personal experiences I can incorporate into my story. I reciprocate in kind. By sharing our resources, we can cover a lot more ground than we ever could alone.

Orderly Pursuits

Use professional organizations as a means of networking. Locate the most prominent in your field and find out what resources they offer. The International Association of Business Communicators (IABC), for example, gives briefs on various types of communications programs and holds regular networking meetings, as well as national conferences.

3. **Collaborate.** A "buddy system" often makes tasks easier or helps you stick to a particular project. Is there a colleague you can get to work with you? How can you make it to his or her advantage to do so? This technique is effective at work, but can also be applied to many other areas of your life.

4. **Prepare.** Organize and plan carefully for meetings ahead of time. They'll be more productive and take half the time. If your department has regularly scheduled meetings, try eliminating one and see whether it really makes a difference. You may just be meeting out of habit, rather than need.

5. **Listen.** Use Stephen Covey's rule in *The 7 Habits of Highly Effective People:* "Seek first to understand, then to be understood." By listening carefully and fully comprehending the problem before you try to give advice or attempt a solution, you'll save time in the long run and be much more effective in your dealings with people in all areas of your life.

6. **Learn to say no.** Just because someone calls, walks in your office, or asks you to do something doesn't mean you have to give him your time right then. Make decisions about how to organize your time, and be firm about not allowing other people to sabotage your efforts. Be polite, but don't be afraid to say, "No, I can't do that," or, "I'll talk to you about it later." If it's something you want or need to do, but you're busy with something else, schedule a time then and there when you'll meet with or call the person to discuss it. Thank them for respecting your time.

   If you already have too many commitments, resign or beg off some. What committees or boards are you on that don't really serve you or make the best use of your time and resources?

Picture This

Saying no is very difficult for some people. Close your eyes and imagine yourself in various situations (be as specific as possible) where you might be asked to do something where saying no would be a good idea. See yourself saying no firmly and politely. Say it out loud when you're by yourself, and hear yourself taking control of your time and what you need to do. Repeat the process over again until you really feel comfortable doing it, then try it out. Notice how powerful the word *no* is.

Shortcuts

What can you streamline? Standardize? Customize? Computerize?

Look for ways to standardize forms, formats, routines, and checklists. Create procedural manuals whenever possible. This saves time with new employees (make sure it's kept up-to-date). Create form letters for regular types of correspondence. You can change them slightly if need be, but you won't have to put in the mental energy creating a new letter each time.

Set up style sheets for regular correspondence or flyers in your desktop publishing or word processing software, so you don't have to reformat each time. Keep a file with directions to your office or meeting place and send with confirmation e-mails, or print out and send with correspondence. This eliminates those "how do I get there again?" phone calls and e-mail messages.

Use checklists. When you travel, use a packing checklist. When you make a sales call, use a check-list or a phone interview sheet to make sure you've covered everything. Make up a fax cover sheet that you store in your computer. Copy enough to have on hand when you need them.

Orderly Pursuits

Write thank-you and follow-up letters while you're on the road (a great way to use flight time); at least do a draft, which you can tweak after the event. You can address envelopes ahead of time, too.

Use binders when they make sense. There are all kinds of inserts and plastic sheets you can use to customize a binder to suit any number of purposes. A binder can be used to organize business cards, slides, computer disks, specific business trips, newsletters, professional organization information, and any sheets of paper you want to last a long time (use plastic sheet protectors). Recycle binders you may have gotten as handouts at conferences or from public relations firms. Think about how binders might be useful at home, as well. I have one for stain-removal information that I keep in the laundry room, one for general household and emergency information that's accessible to everyone, and another for holiday planning.

Learn how to use all your fax machine features, and consider having a fax modem with good fax software installed in your computer, too. You'll save the time printing documents and putting them through the fax machine.

Get a mouse that allows you to customize its functions. You can program it to double-click or print, for example, and save time on repetitive tasks.

Make an effort to really learn your computer's capabilities. Take the time to read software manuals to help you understand program features. You'll be amazed how little of your computer's power you're actually using! If you don't understand, get help with a tutorial, a book, or a class that addresses your particular software. It's not cost effective to spend $500 for a program and only know how to use a fraction of its features. Once you know what it's capable of, you can make an intelligent decision about which features are most useful for you.

Put all important lists on your computer so they're easy to reprint for others or revise and reprint for yourself. Consider keeping shopping lists, phone lists, instructions, directions, personal goals lists, or any others you refer to regularly, on disk or on your hard drive. Most major manufacturers of paper-based organizing systems have software that allows you to print out all their standard forms and any others you might invent.

Ring Around the Workplace: Phone Control

The telephone is a tool. In fact, it is your servant! So how come it feels like it rules your life? Take charge and use these techniques for a happy, productive "phone relationship." Get control of your phone and you get control of one of the greatest sources of interruptions and time wasting:

- Have a specific time for making and returning phone calls and a specific time when you can encourage other people to reach you in your office. If possible, have your answering machine, voice mail, or secretary take messages at other times.

- Change your voice mail message as needed to let people know your schedule and when they should call; then make sure you're available when you say you'll be. Don't answer except at the allotted time. Do the same for returning calls, and keep your word.

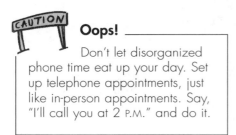

Oops!

Don't let disorganized phone time eat up your day. Set up telephone appointments, just like in-person appointments. Say, "I'll call you at 2 P.M." and do it.

- When recording a phone message on someone's answering machine or voice mail, leave a specific time when she can call you back. Always repeat your phone number, even if you think she's already got it, and give your full name.

- Do phone messages have a way of disappearing? Both my husband and I use a two-part carbonless phone message book, available from business supply stores. This ensures that if one of us somehow misplaces the original message, there's a backup. This method has come to our rescue more than once!

- If you make a lot of telephone calls or make extensive notes from your calls, consider buying a telephone headset. Make sure it's comfortable and has good sound quality. The model I have is also cordless and clips on. Just about anyone could benefit from a headset phone. It frees your hands to do computer file maintenance, open mail, write short letters, or sort papers while you're on hold, and it beats scrunching the phone between your shoulder and ear. Besides, you look mighty funny that way and your neck will thank you!

- Learn to make phone calls quickly and get to the point. Answer phone calls the same way. Decide on the focus of the call, prepare (make a list of points to cover before you dial), and stay on track. If you know you're going to be calling someone who tends to chat a lot, make the call just before lunch or a few minutes before quitting time. Hunger or the desire to go home can be great motivations for keeping it short. This is also a good time to call someone who's difficult to reach.

◆ Treat e-mails and faxes the same way you would other mail or phone calls. Pick specific times to go online and collect your e-mail (twice a day is good). Respond immediately to anything you can, and add to your schedule those that are really a To-Do. If an e-mail message contains information you need to retain, print it out and put it in the *To File* slot. If you need to pass it on to someone else, either forward it electronically or print it out and forward it. The same basically applies to faxes. They either go in the *To-Do* slot, where they are scheduled in your planner/organizer, or they get filed, passed on, or discarded.

Business Correspondence Made Easy

Now let's move on to organizing your business correspondence. We've talked a little bit about e-mails and faxes, which, along with letters and memos, make up the bulk of your correspondence. You can apply your basic sorting system to all of them. Some goes directly in the trash. Some might need a short notation and can then be returned to the sender or passed on to the appropriate person. Some may simply need to be filed. And some requires action, which might include a more extensive reply. Throughout the day, think of these categories—*Trash, Pass On, File, Action*—and continually get things off your desk or desktop and into the appropriate place.

Now for some tips to lighten your load when it comes to business correspondence and to streamline the process:

◆ When only a brief reply is needed and the original doesn't need to be kept on file, return the original letter with your notation at the bottom. That gets it off your desk, saves paper, and reminds the sender what was said originally.

◆ Use e-mail to reply whenever possible, rather than a written letter. It's quicker to write, doesn't generate paper, and is cheaper and instant. Make sure the recipient is someone who checks his e-mail frequently, however, if the message is urgent.

◆ Schedule time to fully learn your e-mail program. Features you may not even know you have allow you to send messages to more than one person, copy to other people, automatically file or delete messages, send attachments, sort, and filter.

◆ When you have a choice between a letter or fax and a phone call, choose the telephone. It usually takes less time and creates less paper. Use the hints for effective phone management presented earlier in this chapter.

◆ Write in clear, concise English using action verbs and nouns. Write short sentences and paragraphs.

Orderly Pursuits

Need some quick help with your writing style? One of the best books I know on effective business writing is Robert Gunning's *How to Take the Fog Out of Business Writing*. You know if your writing can use help. If it can, get it!

◆ Don't create more information in your written communications than anybody needs! Don't write a 10-page proposal when 1 page will do. Aim for tighter writing. It promotes clearer thought (you have to focus and be clear yourself to write concisely) and results in greater understanding.

◆ Don't print e-mail messages unless you really have to. Enter the information in your planner if it's about an appointment or a meeting. File electronically whenever you can. If you must file a hard copy, print it out and put it in the *To File* bin immediately.

Make Your Daily Commute Count

What does your morning commute into work look like? How about the trip home? Not a pretty picture, huh? Isn't it time you revamped how you get from here to there?

Please don't use your morning commute for breakfast. Make a point of getting up early enough and doing whatever it takes to have a quiet, well-balanced breakfast before you make the trip to the office. Eating on the run is bad for your digestion and doesn't set you up for a good day. Besides, you can mess up your clothes or spill coffee all over your car. More stuff to do!

If you drive, you can make the drive time count. Use it for "self-talk" about your goals for the day. Listen to a tape that'll help increase your management skills or teach you something new. Play an audio book. Carry a small tape recorder with you and record thoughts and ideas to follow up on later.

If all your brain cells aren't activated first thing in the morning, at least listen to some music that will set you up for a great day. Make a tape of songs that inspire you or relax you or simply make you feel "up," and play it on those days when you could use an extra lift.

Does your car look like your desk used to? Are there fast-food wrappers, overdue library books, and papers all over the place? That's no way to start out your day.

Schedule part of this weekend to clean it. Vacuum the inside and wipe down the surfaces that collect dust. Wash it or get it washed if it needs it. Make sure the windows are clean and the wipers work properly. Take the ole buggy in for an oil change if you've been putting that off. Surround yourself with order, competence, and things that look and feel good, and you'll start a trend!

Put together a commuter survival kit in a sturdy container with a lid. It could include a box of tissues, a simple tool kit, a first aid kit, a flashlight (keep the batteries in a separate plastic bag; they'll last longer), and some flares. In cold climates, make sure you have all the necessary implements to handle snow and ice removal, plus extra clothing and a folding pair of rubber boots in case you get stranded. Always carry water. These simple emergency preparedness steps will go a long way to promoting peace of mind every day.

How about car pooling? If this can work for you, use the days you don't drive to catch up on your reading or as planning time. This works as long as everyone in the car pool has the same goal; otherwise you may end up losing the time socializing. Don't allow a car pool to make you too tied to a routine, either. It can actually limit your ability to stick to your organization plan. It may be necessary to beg off of the car pool now and then so you can come in early or stay late. You, not the car pool, control your schedule. Use it to help you find more time, but don't let it rule your time.

If you use public transportation to get to work, get in the habit of using your commuting time to support you in your goals. On the morning commute you may want to listen to a motivational or instructional tape or an audio book. Use travel time for daily planning or to catch up on your reading. If that's not enough to keep you busy, there's personal correspondence, catalog shopping, keeping a journal, paying bills, filling out medical insurance claims, or doing a favorite craft if it's portable enough. Make a list of your personal favorites for your planner/organizer. Try varying your routine on different days, so you're not bored and don't get in a rut.

If your place of work is close enough that you can walk or bike there, consider integrating your exercise into your daily commute. Add a portable tape player and you can listen to a book, learn a foreign language, or work on your business skills while you get in shape. Or use this time as "quiet time" for observing what's around you and communing with nature. One consideration, however, is whether you have facilities for showering and dressing once you get to work, if the workout is going to be a vigorous one.

Try not to use your commuting time for work. Use it instead to set up your day, unwind at the end, and make the transition from work to home.

Picture This

Imagine yourself in total control of your work environment. See yourself using your time effectively; meeting your deadlines and handling crises. Make it real. What are you wearing? How do you feel? Visualize yourself walking through the workday with all the right tools at your fingertips. What does this picture do for your self-confidence? Where can you imagine it leading? List all the benefits you'd gain. List all the ways not being organized and confident will cost you, financially and emotionally.

Taking It on the Road

Many of us are going mobile. We're traveling more for both business and pleasure, which creates its own organization challenges. Going on a business trip to a trade show or an industry convention doesn't have to mean coming back with a backlog of paperwork, tons of phone calls and correspondence, and a general feeling of disorganization and inefficiency. Don't put off dealing with the accumulation of business cards, literature, receipts, or papers to be sorted through. When you delay making decisions, clutter builds up.

Use travel time and evenings in your hotel room to keep on top of it all. Have folders that duplicate your office sorting system in your briefcase: *To File, To Do, To Read.* As you sort through paper for filing, especially if you can't do it right away, jot the filing category on top. This speeds up filing when you get back to the office. On your first day back in the office, schedule time to deal with the accumulation of mail and paperwork. Don't put it off or it will soon grow into a mountain instead of a small hill.

Keep an envelope for your receipts, and write notes on them while the purpose or other details are fresh in your mind. Write notes on the back of any business cards you get—anything you've agreed to do, where you met the individual, or any other pertinent information. Then transfer the card information to your computer contact software, or put the card in your office card file, after you've taken any necessary action.

Make sure to add to your planner/organizer any deadlines or promises you made. Any other ideas that come up can be added either to your idea list or your Master List of things to do.

Use e-mail to your advantage while you're traveling. You can stay in touch with the office when it's most convenient for you. These days, most hotels have phone jacks set up for computer data. Write snail mail letters and e-mail them to your secretary to mail out while you're gone. By the time you return, you'll either already have a reply or will have one shortly. Use e-mail to keep in touch with family when schedules conflict. It's not a substitute for a phone call, but can be a great way to help keep the home fires burning when you're far away. E-mail is just one more way of keeping our people priorities straight. It's also a good way to reinforce your commitments to employees when you can't be in the office.

As a final suggestion, carry a small amount of personal stationery and stamps with you, and write any necessary thank-you notes during your trip. You can mail them when you get home or as you go.

> **Amazing Space**
>
> Mail literature you've accumulated from trade shows, don't carry it home. Trade show companies sometimes provide boxes and mailing points specifically for this purpose. If you only need to glance over some of the literature and have room for it, read it over on the flight home and dispose of it at the airport when you arrive.

When Home Is Your Office

The very things that make working at home the envy of many office workers provide the greatest organization and time management challenges for those who do it.

The benefits of a home office are clear. Whether you work as a telecommuter for a distant corporation or manage your own home-based business, you're in control of your work space. Too hot? Open a window or turn on the air conditioner. Need some exercise and a breath of fresh air? Step outside and walk around the block for a half hour. Hungry? The fridge is right over there.

Working at home isn't for everyone, however. Some people find they just have too many distractions to be productive. There's laundry to be done, dishes to wash, and golf clubs that beckon. To succeed as a home-based worker, you first have to decide to succeed and then develop a plan. Yep—commitment, organization, and planning are the keys in this one, too!

Getting Started

If you're new to working at home or just considering it as a possible alternative, you need to realize it takes time to adjust to this new lifestyle. You'll have to set all sorts of limits on other people—like the neighbor who figures that since you don't have a "real" job, you can let in the plumber and walk her dog. This includes your own family as well.

In the beginning, allow yourself room to experiment. If at all possible, plan for becoming a home-based worker in advance, set up your work space, and ease into at least a partial routine before you give up your off-site job.

Get your equipment and supplies, design your office space, write your business plan, and have your stationery printed before you quit your job. Consider using your days off to try things out and get a handle on the challenges you'll face. Take notice of your energy patterns, what distracts you, and where your time goes; you might even keep a log at first.

Go through the questions list in the "Designing Your Work Environment" section earlier in this chapter and broaden it to take advantage of the freedom being a home-based worker affords you. You can repaint, remodel, accessorize, and furnish to your heart's (and budget's) content. It's up to you to make the choices and keep your focus at the same time.

Orderly Pursuits

I highly recommend the book *Working from Home: Everything You Need to Know About Living and Working Under the Same Roof,* by Paul and Sarah Edwards. It's the "bible" of the home-based business movement.

Another advantage of working at home is a greater ability to integrate work and home. It allows you to spend more time with your family, eliminates commuting, and saves on dry cleaning and clothing bills, and it gives you enormous time flexibility. The challenge is to keep the two spheres separate, making sure that family and home concerns don't gobble up work time, and that you're not working day and night and never attending to the rest of your life.

Since the structure isn't defined by someone else, *you* have to define it. Use your Life Management Center and your planner/organizer to give your work life structure. Set regular hours with room for planned deviations. Create routines and rituals that help you stay focused. Some experts even suggest dressing a certain way for work, even if it's just wearing a particular sweater or pair of tennis shoes. If you wore a suit to work before and it puts you in the "work mode," wear a suit at home, at least in the beginning, until you establish some kind of routine. One man even got dressed, walked out the door, got in his car, drove around the block, and then came back to work in his home office to get himself in gear. Hey, whatever works!

Set regular deadlines for yourself. If all you have is the deadline for the completed project, break it down into smaller, manageable chunks and assign deadlines to those. Add them to your planner/organizer.

Define your work area as well. If at all possible, physically separate your office from the rest of the house. You can possibly turn a spare bedroom, a rarely used dining room, a large closet, garage, attic, basement, or finished porch into the perfect office space. It helps if it has a closable door or some other way to mark off a separate space and indicate that you're working and don't want to be disturbed.

Other issues for home-based workers are isolation from co-workers and colleagues, being "out of the loop" when it comes to business access, loss of self-image, and child care. Solutions for all of these can be found in the wealth of books and other publications on the subject, as well as by participating in home-based workers organizations and frequenting online gathering places. Keep priorities in mind by reviewing them daily and periodically reminding yourself of the reasons you wanted to work at home in the first place. Consider the benefits. What would you have to give up if you went back to working outside the home?

Oops!

If you work at home, you don't have to go overboard devoting permanent space to meeting with clients or colleagues. If there isn't adequate space at home, meet at their location, at a rented suite (in some areas, office suites can be rented by the hour or the day), or in a restaurant or club.

Taking Charge

Working at home is about taking full responsibility for your work life, especially if you're self-employed as well. So, take responsibility for …

♦ Preventing interruptions.

♦ Creating a supportive working environment.

♦ Getting the right tools.

♦ Creating the image you want for your business.

♦ Learning about new technology and using it.

♦ Keeping up with your field or industry.

♦ Finding local services and vendors and establishing a good business relationship.

♦ Making a business plan and reviewing it regularly.

♦ Finding a good business lawyer, tax preparer/accountant, and financial planner.

♦ Filing the appropriate papers and obtaining necessary licenses, such as a local business license, resale certificate, seller's permit, employer ID number, business name registration, partnership agreement, or articles of incorporation—find out from your lawyer what you need and then get it!

◆ Investigating and using telephone company services such as call forwarding, call waiting, voice mail, and an accounting feature if these will help you run your business better, stay focused, save time, and help organize you.

◆ Backing up important print and computer files.

◆ Preparing your business for fire, flood, theft, or other disasters.

◆ Giving yourself time to dream, plan, think, and create.

◆ Rewarding yourself and sharing your success with others.

Finally, take responsibility for your own success. You wanted to be in charge. So take charge!

On the Lookout for Your Next Job

How prepared would you be if you got fired or laid off today? If you're currently working at home, what if you decided to get an off-site job? How quickly could you begin to make the transition? What if a head hunter called with the job of your dreams, but you needed to get a resumé in today's express mail? Or what if a job opening was announced today within the company that you really wanted? Would you be able to act on it in a hurry?

An important benefit of being organized is that it allows you to be proactive, rather than reactive. "Proactive" is really just another word for prepared. If an opportunity arises, you don't need to "throw something together," because you've already *got* it together. Have a file both at home and at work that contains your employment records, references, letters of praise, and an up-to-date resumé. If you don't have a resumé, write and design one. Get professional help if you need to.

Review your job readiness every few months. Have enough money in the bank to cover four to six months of unemployment. If you're not in a financial position to do that right now, start working toward it. Even if you switch jobs, you still may need extra money to make the transition between your last paycheck at your old job and the first at your new one.

Keep a diary of your accomplishments with specifics: How much did you actually save the company? How many people did you oversee on that project? What were the results? Who? When? What? Where? How? Why? You'll have everything you need at your fingertips if you need to back up a request for a raise or for your next job interview.

Don't just organize for the job you have. Organize for the job you want. Think of the peace of mind you'd have today just knowing you could handle any change in your job situation and respond to any opportunity.

Your work life is your life. Identify how it fits in to your mission statement. Make it part of your overall organization plan, and you'll not only be more productive, you'll also be a happier person.

Orderly Pursuits

Buy or borrow the book *What Color Is Your Parachute?* by Richard Nelson Bolles. This is *the* classic guide to career planning and job hunting. You'll probably want to reread it periodically, because it's so informative, entertaining, and uplifting. It turns "looking for work" into "discovering your life's work."

The Least You Need to Know

- ◆ The same principles and techniques you used to organize yourself at home can easily be applied to work.

- ◆ Using a planner/organizer effectively helps integrate your work and home lives, and keeps larger goals in front of you.

- ◆ Even if you work for someone else, you can customize your office space to make it more comfortable, efficient, and enjoyable.

- ◆ Working at home offers more freedom and creates unique challenges. Taking responsibility is a key element in being a successful home-based worker.

- ◆ Keeping up with basic organizing tasks on the road will make your first day back in the office a snap.

- ◆ Being prepared for unemployment or new job opportunities alleviates worry and creates possibilities.

Chapter 10

Methods for Your Morning Madness

In This Chapter

- ◆ Starting the day the organized way
- ◆ Saving time on grooming and makeup routines
- ◆ Keeping a lid on clutter
- ◆ Using a modular system to end the "handbag from hell"

What is "beautiful" or "handsome"? You won't catch me opening *that* can of worms! But I think we can agree that "looking good" not only makes us feel good, it can also help create the confidence we need to be more successful.

This chapter will help you make "looking good" easy and fun, by showing you how to pare down and devise simple routines, as well as giving you tips on how to organize the stuff you use to get the look you want.

Unstuff the Bathroom!

First things first. Before we talk about ways to organize what you have, let's get rid of what you don't need. Most bathrooms are booby-trapped, with bottles and tubes of goo tucked everywhere—some of it from another decade. It may be hard to find the sink; you have to duck when you open the medicine chest. The vanity cabinet under the sink is a jungle of pomades and potions.

Out It Goes!

Step one is to go through your cabinets, bathroom drawers, linen closet, medicine chest, dressing table, bureau—wherever you keep various personal care concoctions, bath brews, face paints, nail polishes, hotel samples, and hair tools. Clear them all out (bet they'll fill a clothes basket), clean the drawers and shelves, and start to weed out the pile.

Get rid of old cosmetics and personal products. Here are some guidelines for how long you can keep common items and the best way to store them:

◆ Creams and lotions can be kept up to two years. Pump-type dispensers are best because fingers never touch what's left in the bottle, so you don't add bacteria. Otherwise, dab what you need on a cotton ball.

◆ Sunscreens usually have an expiration date. If there isn't one on the containers, ditch them if they're older than one year. Remember, when you head for the beach, sunscreen should be kept in a cool, dry place—not in a hot glove compartment or basking in the sun.

◆ Toothbrushes should be replaced every three months. Store them so they dry quickly. Dampness breeds bacteria.

◆ Nail polish may thicken or separate with age. Shake it to blend. If that doesn't do it, you'll know it's time to toss it.

◆ Mascara is a real villain for transmitting bacteria that can cause infections. Don't keep it more than three months. Use a permanent marker to note on the tube the date you bought it. You can do the same for toothbrushes. If you're not sure how old it is, toss it out.

◆ Foundation, cover-up, lipstick, eye shadow, blush, and powders are generally safe for one year. Why not make an annual purge on New Year's Day or just before the holiday season?

◆ Hair color has an expiration date on the package. It should be kept out of light and heat.

Three more general points to keep in mind:

- If you can't remember when you bought it, throw it out!

- Get rid of duplicates, items that are broken, and those that just don't do the job.

- While you're tossing outdated, redundant, and useless personal care products, add expired prescription medicines to the pile. Don't play doctor and medicate yourself with old medicines. Get proper medical advice and the right medication. And never, *never* transfer prescription medicines to different containers. The results could be dangerous or even fatal.

> **Oops!**
>
> Don't limit yourself to single-use products. By choosing products with multiple uses, you'll cut down on bathroom clutter. For example, as most outdoor enthusiasts know, Avon's Skin-So-Soft bath oil does double duty as an effective bug repellent. Petroleum jelly has a host of applications. And many moisturizers and makeup bases have sun protection built in.

By following these guidelines and getting rid of old products, you've already done yourself a favor. You can further reduce health risks by becoming a label reader. If a product causes burning, a rash, or breakout, note the main ingredients and move on to something else that doesn't list those ingredients.

An allergic reaction may also be due to preservatives or even an old product whose chemical composition has begun to break down—all the more reason to dump cosmetics and personal care products when it's advised.

Another word about labels: Don't be fooled. The government doesn't regulate use of the term *hypoallergenic*, so don't assume you won't have a reaction when you see this word on the label. "All natural" doesn't necessarily mean allergy-free, either. There are natural substances that are just as irritating as commonly used chemicals, if not more so.

Never share your cosmetics or personal products. This is really asking for trouble. Remember to be conscious of this rule when trying on cosmetics at the store counter. Use personal samples only.

Be careful of professional manicures, too. You may even want to bring your own instruments. There is always the possibility of drawing blood during a manicure and transmitting bacterial infections. Don't be afraid to ask about (and watch) sterilization procedures. Take the same care with your nails at home. Sterilize your nail care instruments periodically in boiling water or alcohol.

Stow It!: Bathroom Storage Solutions

Now that you've unstuffed your beauty and grooming products, you need to find a better way to store them. We all know that bathroom cabinets and drawers were devilishly devised to make it impossible to retrieve what you want, when you want it. Here are some storage suggestions that may work better for you:

◆ Store regularly used products like shampoo, conditioner, and cleanser in the shower. In a smaller shower, consider one of the many over-the-showerhead organizers. In a larger stall, a spring-loaded floor-to-ceiling unit with multitiered shelves works well.

◆ Divider trays in drawers keep smaller items under control. To clean the drawers, you just take the trays out and wash them.

◆ One way to organize drawer contents is by assigning each drawer or drawer section to a particular part of the body. How about one drawer for hair brushes, combs, and accessories, one just for the man of the house's shaving paraphernalia, and another just for special pampering accoutrements—complete with bath oils, scrubs, and moisturizers.

> **Amazing Space**
>
> Can't seem to find any more space in the bathroom? Try hanging a shoe bag on the back of the bathroom door. This is a great caddy for small things you need at your fingertips. Make sure the compartments are clear, so you can see without rummaging around, and group like things together in one compartment.

◆ In some instances, a tackle box, art supply caddy, or box made especially for holding cosmetics or grooming products might make the most sense. This is especially true if you're sharing a bathroom with several other people and need to look for an alternative place to get ready when the bathroom's occupied. You can take your "paint box" anywhere, even when you travel.

◆ Consider a Lazy Susan to move things easily from the back of the cabinet to the front.

◆ Group similar things together in bins or baskets.

◆ Hang hair dryers and curling irons in special caddies or racks specifically made for affixing them to the wall.

◆ An old-fashioned vanity or dressing table gets you out of the bathroom for certain parts of your morning routine. Make sure it's well lit, has a good mirror, and has places for all your makeup, perfume, and hair grooming supplies.

Get a Routine

The time you spend in the morning showering, shaving (for you guys), fixing your hair, dressing, and putting on your makeup can get you ready to meet the world with your best face forward. But if it's hurried and chaotic, you'll start out with a frown. Here are some tips for avoiding "Morning Madness":

♦ The best way to make your morning production smooth is to standardize what you do. By creating a routine, you'll save time, you'll narrow down the products you need, and you won't be faced with making new decisions each morning. Do the same steps each day and your morning ritual will eventually become second nature. Write down the steps to start with, if you need to.

♦ Being well-groomed today means more for men than just having trimmed hair and clean fingernails. Men today have all the gels, mousses, lotions, shampoos, sprays, spritzes, soaps, salves, scrubs, mists, and masks that women do. There are even makeup and hair coloring products especially for men. Decide what your "bottom line" is and build it into your daily routine.

Oops!

Make sure to leave enough time for your makeup routine. Applying mascara while driving is an absolute no-no. At the very least, you could soil your clean clothes. At worst, you could have an accident or blind yourself (no kidding).

♦ Maybe the shampoo bottle says "wash, rinse, and repeat," but unless your hair is especially oily, once is probably enough. It's also a good idea to change hair products periodically. It seems to prevent a buildup. There are special products on the market that eliminate buildup caused by shampoos, conditioners, and styling products. Or try a diluted vinegar rinse.

♦ Use only a small amount of conditioner, and concentrate on hair ends, not on the scalp.

♦ Some men find sporting a beard saves time and is easier on their skin. And they like the look.

♦ Pay attention to the weather and climate conditions. Choose your hairstyle for the day accordingly. Take steps to protect yourself from sun, heat, wind, and cold. Choose skin care products that contain sunscreens and moisturizers.

♦ Switch to a simpler hairstyle. For women, long or short is easiest, but a classic bob is relatively easy to care for as well. Long hair can be swept back, put up in

> **Amazing Space**
>
> One time-saver is to brush your teeth in the shower. It's easy to rinse thoroughly—just put your head in the water! Be careful, though, that your toothbrush doesn't stay damp and become a breeding ground for nasty germs. Let it dry completely between brushings.

a French twist, or made into a braid that's tucked under at the nape of the neck. These sleek hair styles look best on women with high cheekbones and fairly delicate features. Find something that's flattering (get professional help if you need it), and practice fixing it until you have it down to a few simple steps.

Men have similar choices. If you choose to wear your hair long, it can be slicked back and pulled into a pony tail. Shorter hair is probably the easiest of all.

Morning Makeup

In my opinion, less is definitely more when it comes to women and makeup. I'm not a purist, mind you, just a minimalist.

Cosmetics definitely have their place. Makeup can conceal defects like hereditary dark circles under eyes and even birthmarks or disfiguring scars. Makeup can be used to enhance good features and minimize less attractive ones. For some women, wearing makeup makes them feel more confident and prettier. And some products can have health benefits, such as protecting against sun and wind damage. If it has that effect for you, then I'm all for it. To my mind, however, there's no substitute for regular exercise, adequate sleep, and healthy food. Good health is the prettiest makeup of all.

When creating your makeup strategy, find a set of products that work for you, and get rid of those that don't. Practice applying them (there are plenty of books and magazines to show you how) until you have it down to a quick set of steps. You might even consider making an appointment with a cosmetician or color consultant (something to add to your Rewards List?) with the idea of finding a simple routine that makes the most of your makeup time.

What should your routine consist of? One school of thought is to pick neutral colors (your consultant can help you choose which ones are best for you) and use them for everyday. Choose from browns, taupes, grays, champagnes, beiges, gold-tones, coppers, and silvers, all of which go with everything.

Then use color for dress-up, adding reds, plums, berry colors, pinks and oranges, or blues and greens to your special occasion makeup wardrobe.

Ladies, take a tip from the stars. Their makeup artists often pick one strong feature and play it up, then minimize the rest. Do you have especially interesting eyes or pouty lips? Well, make them shine!

You may even want to consider having a color analysis done. Then you can weed out the makeup and the parts of your wardrobe that don't flatter you.

Professional makeup artists and beauty editors also offer these tips:

- Makeup brushes save time and apply makeup most evenly. Professionals recommend natural bristle brushes, like sable, goat's hair, or human hair. The basics in your collection would be a blush brush, powder brush, eye shadow brush, and brow brush. Store upright in a glass, or invest in a brush roll. Wash often (every week to two weeks) with shampoo, use conditioner, and rinse thoroughly. Air dry, then store.

- Makeup sponges work best for applying liquid makeup. Wash and air dry.

- Get yourself a pair of good tweezers and a magnifying mirror. Store tweezers in a handy place like the medicine chest, and always put them back. Some magnifying mirrors attach to the wall and pull out when you need them, saving counter space and time spent searching.

- Use a lip pencil in a nude shade (one that matches your lips) to outline and define lips, then fill in with your favorite shade of lipstick.

- Have two sharpeners, one for lip pencil and one for eye pencils, to minimize the risk of bacterial cross-contamination.

- Cotton (not synthetic) swabs and pads are best for makeup removal. Store them in a pretty jar or clear plastic box with lid.

- Use a metal lash comb (professionals recommend them) to separate eyelashes. Sterilize regularly.

Orderly Pursuits

If you're looking for some extra tips on applying makeup or general grooming tips, here are some books that can help: *The Art of Makeup* by Kevyn Aucoin; *Color Me Beautiful's Looking Your Best: Color, Make-up, and Style* by Mary Spillane and Christine Sherlock; and *Beyond Soap, Water and Comb: A Man's Guide to Good Grooming and Fitness* by Ed Marquand.

Amazing Space

Resist the urge to buy makeup in those large palettes or ensembles. Invariably there are a few colors you like, and the rest just sit there and take up space.

Don't let cosmetics or personal care salespeople load you down with more than you want or need. Find your own routine and stick to it, using the products you've determined work best for you.

If you keep what you use in a box, divider tray, or zippered bag, you won't have to hunt for what you need. Add duplicates of your major makeup products to your handbag, in smaller sizes if they're available.

Daily, Weekly, and Monthly Rituals

Standardize your regular beauty and grooming tasks as much as possible. If your habit is a morning shower and you share the bathroom with several other people, set up regular times for each person and have a caddy or shower shelf (the spring-loaded floor-to-ceiling ones work well for this purpose) for each person's daily care products. I'm more of a bath person, and like to take mine at night before going to bed. This works out well, since my husband takes his shower in the morning. We're not competing for hot water, and all I need to do in the morning is wash up and brush my teeth.

For those longer, more involved beauty rituals, like manicures, hair coloring, hair treatments, masking, bleaching facial hair, and the like, why not make them an opportunity to pamper yourself? Make it a regular Friday night end-of-the-week treat or a midweek pick-me-up, if it's a weekly chore. A little imagination can turn it into a special occasion, when you can indulge yourself at the same time. Start with a good soak in a bubble bath, complete with relaxing music on the portable tape deck and maybe a glass of wine , mug of special tea, or a fruit juice cooler.

Key monthly tasks to a particular time of the month—say, the last day or the first day. Or get creative and schedule your magical beauty rituals for the full or new moon! You might even enjoy experimenting with the natural fragrances and health benefits of aromatherapy. On the market now are some excellent, easy-to-follow books and reasonably priced, high-quality oils, so that anyone can begin to experiment with some simple, mood-enhancing and healing scents. Make sure you know the safety indications for the oils you're using.

CAUTION

Oops!

Don't go hunting around and wasting time looking for your makeup ingredients and tools. Have all the ingredients and tools for specific "rituals" at hand in their own caddy, bag, or basket. One for manicure paraphernalia, another for hair coloring tools, and yet another for shaving and hair removal or bleaching would be handy.

Give Your Handbag a Hand

I always marvel at those women who can carry a tiny purse. You know the kind—they barely hold a lipstick, $20, and a credit card. Heaven forbid you should need a tissue or a nail file!

I'm afraid I just can't pare down quite that much. But I do have a system for keeping my handbag from becoming a catch-all for everything under the sun. I've used it for the last several years and it's served me well.

I've developed what I call a "modular system" for handbag paraphernalia. Which modules I use depends on where I'm going, for how long, and what I'll be doing. I choose the size of the handbag I carry according to what my needs are. The basic modules are:

Module 1: Makeup. This module just includes the basic neutral shades I use for my everyday makeup routine. It duplicates what I have at home on my vanity. In a tinier bag that goes inside this module I keep some bobby and hairpins, plus a couple of barrettes and a hair elastic. There's also a miniature tube of hand lotion; you could add a nail file or clippers, and some clear nail polish for pantyhose emergencies.

Module 2: Emergencies. A few medical supplies (including aspirin, eye drops, a small tube of sunscreen, some lip balm, a small tube of antiseptic ointment, Band-Aids, and a couple of antacid tablets) are in this module, plus a small sewing kit.

Module 3: Mini-office. Here I group a couple of pens, a marker, some Post-It notes, a few 3 × 5 cards, stamps, and a small roll of tape—anything I might need on a business call or if I expect to be waiting and might be catching up on my reading or correspondence. This is basically a companion to any clipped articles I might take with me to read, a book, or something I'm working on. By the way, I always carry some business cards in a holder in the small zippered pocket of my handbag, not in this module. You never know when you might meet a potential customer, client, or interview subject!

Module 4: The Bank. This one has my cash, credit and membership cards, checkbook, and a credit card–size calculator. It's roomy enough to hold bank deposits as well.

> **Amazing Space**
>
> The basic modules are small, zippered cosmetic bags. Make your "module" cases clear or each a different color or pattern, so it will be easy to identify each one and its contents.

By using these modules, I never have loose stuff floating around in my pocketbook. Most of the time I just have the bank in my handbag, since I'm probably running to the grocery store or dropping off a shipment at the post office. If I'm going out for a business meeting, I add the makeup module, the one for emergencies, and the mini-office. An evening out might mean just grabbing Module 1 and stuffing a little cash in it. If I'm going for a day trip in the mountains, I'll definitely take Modules 2 and 4.

Your modules may be made up of different elements, but at least give the modular system a try. Don't forget to periodically go through each module and restock or weed out.

Oh, and what to do with that age-old problem of finding the keys? One solution is to get a clip-on type key chain that hooks to an outer ring on your handbag. Since I don't have any other loose things in my bag, I find just dropping them in one compartment isn't a problem. They're easy to find among the zippered module cases.

Beauty Is Happiness and Good Health

To risk sounding clichéd, beauty really does come from the inside. I find if someone's relaxed, happy, and smiling, he or she is attractive, no matter what his or her actual facial characteristics. There's no remedy for a frowning face, a harried look, tiredness, or bad humor.

With your life organized and your most important goals being achieved on a daily basis, I'll bet by now you're absolutely shining, and people are asking you what's happened! I believe happiness comes from fulfilling your dreams, and there's nothing more beautiful than confidence and success.

Tickler Files

"'Tis not a lip or eye we beauty call,

But the joint force and result of it all."

—Alexander Pope

Another element of beauty that comes from the inside out is health, and there's no substitute for that, either. You know the drill. If you drink plenty of water, eat a balanced diet, and get adequate rest and regular exercise, you're going to look your best. So keep these commitments you've made to yourself, put them on your schedule, and see to it that they become habits. You look better already!

The Least You Need to Know

♦ Weeding out cosmetics and personal care products not only makes them easier to organize, it helps ensure products are fresh and free of bacteria.

♦ You will save time and keep bathroom and handbag clutter to a minimum by establishing a basic routine that you master and follow each morning.

♦ Weekly and monthly rituals can be important times to pamper yourself and slow down.

♦ A modular system using separate resealable bags is one way to keep confusion in your handbag to a minimum. It also makes it easier to switch handbags.

♦ The beauty that's generated from good health and a happy life is dazzling. No makeup can ever match it!

Chapter 11

Food Systems: Getting Your Daily Bread

In This Chapter

- ◆ Setting your food goals
- ◆ Making your kitchen your nutrition partner
- ◆ Designing and equipping a well-organized kitchen
- ◆ How to cut shopping time with lists and menus
- ◆ Cooking made simple
- ◆ Organizing cookbooks and recipes

Whether you're a gourmet cook or you eat "on the fly" most of the time, the kitchen is one of the most time-consuming spaces in your home to keep clean and organized. Having an efficient, well-laid-out kitchen can mean the difference between enjoying meal preparation and dreading it. Before you start moving stuff around or giving away half your appliances, you first need to take an inventory of where you are now with regard to food, and decide what matters to you about the daily rituals that surround putting regular meals on the table.

You Are What You Eat

Take the time to ask yourself some questions before you start your kitchen reorganization. This will give you some insight into the role food plays in your life and help you decide if there are some changes you'd like to make. Your answers will also give you a basis for making decisions about what to keep and what to dispose of as you go. Write them down to help you stay on track.

- What place does food occupy in your life? Do you just "eat to live" or is food a major social event?

- Do you eat out or order in most of the time? Do you cook at home, but use a lot of prepared foods? Or do you cook at home, largely from "scratch" using fresh ingredients? What, exactly, did you do for supper each night last week? If you can't remember, keep track for a week.

- How would you assess the quality of the food you eat? Do you eat a lot of junk or fast food? A lot of prepared or frozen food? Do you consider your diet "healthful"?

- Do you need to lose a few pounds? Are you battling a blood-pressure, blood sugar, or cholesterol problem? Do you have food allergies? What other special dietary or nutritional needs do you have, if any?

- Do you usually eat alone, or with family, friends, or housemates?

- Are you expected to cook for your family or is this a shared activity?

- Do other people share your kitchen? What's their schedule?

- Do you eat on a regular schedule or whenever you can grab a bite?

- What are some things about your cooking and/or eating habits you'd like to change?

How, when, where, and what you eat goes a long way toward setting you up to have a good or bad day. Food can affect your mood, your energy level, your general sense of well-being, and your long-term health. This is a book about organization, not nutrition, but this isn't a bad time to consider the fuel your body depends on to help you accomplish all those things you plan to do.

As you probably know by now, I strongly believe that before beginning a task it's good to see it in a larger context—to know its purpose and ask if it supports you in what you want in your life. Now may be a good time to see a nutritionist or your doctor and take an honest inventory of your health and the role your eating habits have in keeping you healthy or making you sick. If everything's okay, you may only need to look at your kitchen layout, work flow, and convenience. If, however, you want to make some major changes in the way you eat, you'll need to scrutinize these things, as well as which foods you have in your pantry and even the kinds of cooking equipment you use.

Tickler Files

"Tell me what you eat and I will tell you who you are."
—Anthelme Brillat-Savarin

After examining the way you eat now and thinking about changes you'd like to make, write down two or three goals for the way you plan, shop for, prepare, eat, and clean up after your daily meals. Perhaps you'd like to begin eating at home a little more often. Maybe you'd like to get on a more sensible eating program that includes more fruits and vegetables. Are there some diet-related health problems you really need to face and take action to correct? Would you like to entertain more, but find yourself putting it off because cooking for company is such a hassle? Would you like to rein in your budget, and feel you could save money by changing your eating and cooking habits?

Whatever you decide your food goals are, write them down and keep them uppermost in your mind as you revamp your kitchen. Decide on specific actions to help you accomplish those goals and add them to the Master List in your planner/organizer. You can confront the kitchen in an all-day session or work on it piecemeal, one small area at time. Whichever method you choose, you need to understand the design and layout of your kitchen as it is now, watch yourself work, and decide how to minimize your movement and maximize the space available to you.

Unstuff Your Kitchen

After analyzing your space and setting your goals, the next step is to go through your usual unstuffing routine, the one you learned how to do in Chapter 5. Start with any food you have stored in your kitchen cabinets, pantry, refrigerator, freezer, or any other food storage area using the following guidelines. Check them off as you accomplish each one.

♦ Toss out any food that has passed its expiration date. Separate foods that need to be

Amazing Space

Not enough space in kitchen cabinets for food storage? Consider a free-standing cabinet or piece of furniture. If you have wall space, you can install narrow wire racks designed especially for canned goods and other food packages. There are even racks that fit over doors. Look for space in unconventional places!

used up shortly. These will go in the front of the cabinet or pantry shelf when you put them away.

◆ Give or throw away food that doesn't fit your nutrition objectives.

◆ If you have a lot of one item, evaluate whether you can use it up before it becomes dated. If not, pass some on to someone who can.

◆ If you tend to store a lot of canned goods, rotate by putting the oldest in the front, and when you shop again, put the newer cans in the back. Make a written inventory. Plan meals around what you already have.

◆ Clean out your refrigerator and freezer, throw out food that's bad or stale, and put remaining food back, grouping similar things together wherever possible. Freezer items not kept in original packaging should be labeled with name of food and date. Make a written inventory of what foods are in your refrigerator and freezer, so you can plan meals around them.

◆ Group your packaged and canned goods into categories: staples, baking ingredients, vegetables, fruits, meats, sauces, beverages, and so on.

◆ Store food using the same basic principles we've used for everything else: Put most-used items in *prime real estate*, least often used further away; group like things together; consolidate and compress using different containers.

If you anticipate doing a major revamping of your cabinets and drawers, adding shelving or buying inserts and dividers, you may want to put your nonperishable foods into boxes according to category for a short while and put them back when you've got that project completed.

Put the rest of the areas in your kitchen through a similar "unstuffing" process. Use your sorting boxes: *Trash*, *Put Away* (for things that belong elsewhere in the house), *Pass On*, and *Mystery*. Go through cabinets, shelves, and drawers and look at dishes, pots and pans, appliances, and utensils. Ask yourself the following questions:

◆ When was the last time I used this?

◆ Do I have another tool that can do double duty in place of this one?

◆ Are there any duplicates? Which one works best?

◆ Does it need to be fixed?

If you come across kitchen tools that just don't do the job, get rid of them and replace them with ones that work well. Buy quality kitchen equipment and learn how to take care of it. A few excellent knives kept sharp are far more useful than a drawer full of the other kind, and take up less space. Learn how to use a steel and a whetstone properly so you can maintain your cutlery.

Have a few high-quality and easy-to-clean pots and pans in the most common and convenient sizes. When you buy new ones, don't keep the old. Seriously, how many frying pans do you really need if you're not running a restaurant?

The same is true with appliances. Buy quality, not quantity. Also, don't overbuy. If a small chopper is all you ever need, don't buy a professional-size food processor with all the attachments.

Now that you've pared down and have familiarized yourself with what you have to store, let's talk about how your kitchen is laid out and what you can do to make the most of its design.

> **Orderly Pursuits**
>
> There's a place you may be able to locate replacement parts for your small kitchen appliances, other than the manufacturer itself. Check with Culinary Parts Unlimited at (800) 543-7549, or on the web at www.culinaryparts.com, before you toss something out for good.

Make Your Kitchen Do the Work

I'm not a contractor, so I'm not about to guide you through a major remodeling of your kitchen. If you have a chance to do extensive remodeling or build from scratch, and the money to boot, great. There are lots of good books on the market and plenty of experts to help you design your custom kitchen. I'd suggest you consult an organization expert *as well as* a contractor! However, we're going to work with what you already have, which probably has a number of design flaws, and make it the best it can be.

To plan how to use available space to its greatest advantage, a kitchen is best divided into activity areas or centers. There's a preparation center for cutting, chopping, and mixing ingredients, a cooking center that revolves around the stove, a serving center, and a cleanup center that basically involves the sink and dishwasher (if you have one). When you look at some kitchens, you can't help wondering if the designer ever tried boiling water in it, because none of these areas is clearly defined or efficiently located.

The Preparation Center

In the preparation center, lack of counter space is the most common problem. You need adequate space to lay out your ingredients and use a variety of tools and small

Orderly Pursuits

Short on storage for pots and pans? Look up! There are some beautiful racks on the market that hang from the ceiling for suspending cookware. If you have some wall space, you can hang them from a grid system or brackets. Check out the options in mail order catalogs and culinary and decorating stores.

appliances. This area includes the sink, to allow for rinsing foods and washing off utensils. If you feel cramped, get as much off your counters as possible. Keep this area for work, not display. Store appliances that aren't used every day in cabinets or on shelves, or consider the various products available that mount under cabinets and out of the way. If you still don't have enough counter space, see if you can make a fold-down one or add a kitchen island or movable cart with a butcher-block top. You'll want to locate items like knives, bowls, cutting board, and food preparation appliances near this area.

The Cooking Center

From the preparation center, you'll want to be able to move to the cooking area, which includes the stove, and any nearby counter space. A triangular layout between preparation area, stove, and refrigerator works best. If you can rearrange your appliances so they give you that pattern of movement, try to do it. The items you use most should be located in the storage within that triangular area. If you can't arrange things in a triangle, then a rolling work cart may be the only solution. You can assemble items from the refrigerator and roll them to the work area, then take prepared ingredients to the cooking area the same way. This should save you some steps and spills along the way. Pots and pans, hot pads, spices, and other items used regularly during cooking should be located in this area.

The Serving Center

The serving center is best located near where you actually sit down to eat, and your dishes, eating utensils, and serving pieces should be located there if at all possible. I have a counter-divider between my kitchen and dining area, so that's where I set things to be served. The silverware drawer and cabinets that hold the dishes are right next to it, near the preparation center. Just notice how far away your dishes and serving bowls are from where you serve. You may want to consolidate them and locate them closer to where you eat.

The Cleanup Center

When you finish a meal, have a designated place to put dishes. To one side of the sink is a good location. If you're making too many trips from the eating area to the kitchen during the clearing process, that may be an indication that you need to rethink how you're doing things. You may want to have a tray handy, or a rolling cart for stacking dishes and taking them to the kitchen to be washed and put away. It helps if others in the household know where to put dirty dishes as well. There's no sense having them move dishes to one spot, and then you have to move them to another.

Keep one side of a double sink or a dishpan full of hot, soapy water ready to put dirty utensils in as you cook. This avoids clutter and makes them easier to clean later on. If you keep up with dishes, they'll be less of a problem. Unwashed dishes that have been sitting require more elbow grease, more water, and, if you're using a dishwasher, they sometimes won't even come clean without prescrubbing. If you can't get to them immediately, at least rinse them or put them in water to soak.

Orderly Pursuits

Make a list of storage problems you've identified in your kitchen. Then make a series of field trips to organizing, hardware, discount, and decorating stores. Be sure to take measurements of your cabinet spaces with you, and bring a tape measure. Take notes and check what you find against mail-order options.

Advanced Kitchen Storage

Now that you've figured out where to locate the main areas of activity in your kitchen, the next thing to tackle is storage that saves you steps and makes the most of the time you spend there. Some cabinets have adjustable shelves. If yours do, you've got a lot more options. If not, there are all kinds of racks, step shelves, and slide-out drawer units on the market that can make them more efficient and flexible. Check out the resources at the back of this book for products, stores, and mail-order catalogs to help you plan. If your cabinets are very deep and things tend to get lost in the back, a step shelf along the back, a Lazy Susan, or a slide-out unit should help.

Don't overlook the backs of doors, or walls and ceilings as possible storage components. There are grid systems for wall storage (or you might consider pegboard, which can be painted), over- and on-the-door racks, and various fixtures for hanging pots and pans from the ceiling. Just make sure you don't hang anything where you'll bonk your head! Also consider hooks under cabinets for cups or one of those racks that hold stemmed glasses upside down.

Even a small space above a door or between the door jamb and ceiling, might be used for cookbooks or other smaller, uniform items, just by installing a shelf.

When choosing decorating materials, appliances, fixtures, and equipment, think about functionality and ease of cleaning. Keep hardware like faucets, knobs, handles, or pulls simple. The fewer nooks and crannies to get dirty, the better. Keep in mind that paint or wall coverings should stand up to kitchen grease and grime, and avoid fancy curtains or other decorating elements that can give you cleaning headaches. Don't forget to put up back splashes where they're most needed—behind the stove and your work area.

Don't let your plastic food containers sit in a drawer—use them. You only need so many pieces for leftover food storage. If you bought your plastic storage containers at a Tupperware party, you may be able to replace those missing lids. Call your nearest representative (consult the phone book or their website at www.tupperware.com) and find out.

Get rid of containers you never use or have too many of in one particular size. Ditch those without lids, or use them under plants to catch water or to sort similar items in drawers if they're low enough to fit. You can take your containers out of the kitchen if you still have too many. They make great storage for crafts and office supplies, among other things.

If space is at a premium, keep little-used and seasonal items in the high, hard-to-reach cabinets above the stove and refrigerator or out of the kitchen altogether. You may need a step stool to reach them. Cleaning products can be kept under the sink in a portable caddy.

> **CAUTION**
>
> **Oops!**
>
> Be careful what you store in the cabinet under the sink and in all low cabinets, especially if you have small children or entertain folks with little ones. Many cleaning products are highly toxic or, at least, can create a nasty spill.

Speaking of that dreaded under-the-sink area, make sure you do a thorough unstuffing job of that catchall, as well. There are probably cleaning products lurking there you haven't seen in years! Get rid of those you don't use, consolidate wherever possible (can three partly used spray window cleaner bottles be poured into one?), and keep your cleaning products and tools to a minimum. We'll talk about this in more detail in Chapter 13, but you might as well get a head start!

When you're done unstuffing and relocating, make sure anyone else who uses the kitchen knows where stuff is and will be kept from now on. You might even consider making up lists in large type and taping them to the inside of cabinet doors or on drawer faces until everyone gets with the system. At least once a year, do a thorough cleaning of your kitchen storage areas. Make sure you get rid of unused items just as you did in this first session. Reevaluate your work flow from time to time, and move things that don't seem to be in the best place.

Shop but Don't Drop

Now that you've pared down and unstuffed your kitchen, what's the best way to keep the necessary things on hand? Is there a way to make shopping easier?

I believe there is, and the way to do it is to standardize. Don't you find that there are a few basic meals that you and your family enjoy eating on a regular basis? Maybe it's chicken and dumplings or pot roast. Maybe a particular pasta dish, soup, or stew. Or perhaps you grill regularly. I'll bet you could make a list of 15 to 20 meals you prepare over and over again. I call these my rotation meals, and I keep the recipes for them all in my household binder, plus a list of them in my planner/organizer. I know them so well that I can pretty much name the ingredients from memory.

In addition to your personal list of rotation recipes, you'll need an ingredients list. This is a list of all the major ingredients you use in your everyday cooking, a kind of Master Shopping List. That way, if you're out running errands, you can just scan your list and see if you've forgotten anything. Keep a running list for other items that come up in a prominent place where the whole family can add their shopping reminders. A dry-erase board is handy for this.

Another help is to plan your week's menus ahead of time. You may even want to do it for two weeks, to cut down on trips to the grocery store. You may not cook exactly what you'd planned on the day you planned it, but you'll have a pretty good idea of what you'll be doing for the next two weeks.

Buy in bulk when it's practical. If you're only one person, you obviously can't eat a bushel of apples before they go bad, but you could make applesauce for yourself and can or freeze it. Know what you're really capable of using and don't overbuy. Also be sure you have storage space for it. We use industrial shelving in the downstairs storage room for our bulk purchases of paper and canned goods. Buying in bulk cuts down on the time you spend shopping and can save you money, but it's no bargain if you can't find what you bought or it goes bad before you get to use it. In the next section, you'll learn about a cooking method that makes the most of bulk shopping and saves time and work.

Items it truly make sense to buy in bulk are paper goods, cleaning products, nonperishable staples like vinegar and baking soda, personal care products, canned and bottled foods, and some dry foods, like legumes and pastas, that

Amazing Space
I suggest you do your menu planning along with your calendar, so you can figure on easy dishes for busy evenings and skip planning meals for evenings you'll be out.

keep well. You can store up to a six month's supply in a fairly compact area, and you'll save time, effort, and money. Make an inventory and post it near your bulk storage area. Cross off items as you use them up and add them to your shopping list.

Crafty Cooking Strategies

Too busy to create yummy home-cooked meals? Nonsense! I'm going to give you three strategies that'll make it easy to put good, nutritional homemade meals on the table with the least amount of effort. They'll each save you money, too! Pick the one that's best for you.

Cook Once, Eat for a Month

A couple of years ago, I made a fabulous discovery. It wasn't a totally new idea to me, since I had done a scaled-down version when I was a single parent, working full time and going to school, but I had never seen it systematized and explained quite the same way. The method goes by many names—Once-a-Month Cooking, Freezer Cooking, Bulk Cooking, Frozen Assets, Investment Cooking—but they all use the same strategy of bulk buying, bulk cooking, and freezing. If you're serious about using this method, it helps to have a separate chest or upright freezer, but it's possible to do it with just the freezer compartment of an average-size refrigerator.

> **CAUTION**
> **Oops!**
> Why clean your kitchen every day? With bulk cooking, you only make a major kitchen mess once a month. One good scrubbing after your monthly marathon session, and it stays clean until the next time.

The basic idea is that you plan your menus for a month, do all the shopping in one day, then do all the cooking in another day or two, and forget about it for 30 days. I especially find this method helpful when I'm heavily embroiled in a book project and don't want to be burdened with thinking about "What's for supper?" My mental energy can go toward other things, because I took the time to think out our eating plan ahead of time, and all the work is done.

Some of the benefits of bulk cooking are ...

◆ Major shopping is only necessary once a month. You cut down on trips to the supermarket and the extra hidden cost of impulse buys and children asking "Why can't I have this, Mommy?" The fewer number of trips, the less you spend.

◆ You can take advantage of restaurant-size cans and quantity buys on fresh fruits and vegetables from wholesale clubs or food cooperatives. This saves lots of money and often means higher quality.

◆ Bulk cooking is environmentally friendly, since bulk buying usually means less packaging.

◆ Because you're cooking ahead and freezing, you can make the most of seasonal foods and buy ingredients when they're the freshest and least expensive.

◆ Meals are all planned and prepared, so you don't have to think about it. You can concentrate on other things!

◆ Because you're cooking several meals all at once, there's less waste. After cooking whole chickens for several meals, for example, the remaining carcasses and defatted drippings become the base for a soup or sauce. Trimmings from fresh vegetables can be used to make vegetable stock. More dollar savings!

◆ Since the main meal is already prepared, you can concentrate on tasty and nutritious side dishes, like fresh salads or vegetable dishes, if you have the time and energy. You can also whip up a special treat for dessert.

◆ With dinner in the freezer, you're less likely to order pizza or stop for fast food. So, you not only save money when you go to the grocery store, you also save money throughout the month.

◆ You save energy, because you're using appliances for large batches rather than many small batches. In warmer weather, you heat up the house less, especially if you use your slow cooker to thaw and heat up your dish earlier in the day.

◆ You'll actually *use* appliances like food processors, mixers, grinders, slicers, blenders, and slow cookers on a monthly basis, and it will be worth your while to pull them out of cabinets and off shelves, *and* clean them!

◆ You can get the whole family involved in the various tasks associated with bulk cooking, like chopping and slicing.

Orderly Pursuits

In the resources section, I list several good books explaining various versions of the bulk cooking method. One that gives you a total plan you can adapt to your own nutrition goals is *Once-a-Month Cooking* by Mimi Wilson and Mary Beth Lagerborg. Check out the OAMC website, too, at members.aol.com/oamcloop/.

◆ Dinner is always in the freezer when you're caught with unexpected guests or a neighbor is ill and could use a home-cooked meal. In fact, you might actually find yourself asking more often, "Why don't you stay for dinner?"

◆ Having your meals planned and prepared means you're less likely to "throw something together" and eat foods you're trying to avoid.

It might be easiest for you to get a picture of how bulk cooking works if I describe a typical month's cooking. At the beginning of the month, I go through my recipes (we have several favorites I make every month, then others we use less often) and plan the meals for the month. Next, I write up a list of all the ingredients I need to purchase, grouping like things together. So if a recipe calls for two bell peppers, sliced, and another recipe calls for one pepper, chopped, I know I'll need three peppers.

I spend almost an entire day shopping. First I go to the wholesale club, then my regular supermarket, and last I might have certain things to buy at the health food market. That night, before I go to bed, I put two whole chickens in the slow cooker to cook overnight. The meat from these will go into chicken casseroles, chicken soup, and chicken salad. I'll use the bones to make stock the next morning. I also fill a second slow cooker with a double recipe of one of our favorite dishes, or I use it to cook ahead some beans or grains. In the morning, I clean out the cookers and put in each one the ingredients for a double recipe. This creates four meals, and I still have two meals from the night before. That's six total, and I haven't even begun my main cooking day!

For the rest of the day I cook, taking several breaks and making sure to eat lunch. I group processes together (for example, chopping all the onions for all the month's recipes in the food processor). I then package each meal in a freezer container or plastic freezer bag, label it with contents and date, and add it to my meal inventory list, which I post on the refrigerator. I make sure that anything I need to complete the dish, such as a topping, cheese, can of soup, or whatever, is either in a plastic freezer baggie attached to the container when it goes in the freezer, or in the pantry with a big "X" on the can so no one uses it for anything else.

If I need to, I cook another large-batch recipe in the slow cookers overnight and package those meals the next morning. Once I'm done with everything, I wipe down all my appliances, put them away, clean the kitchen thoroughly, and the rest of the month I thaw and reheat, keeping kitchen mess to a minimum. Many times, a month's worth of meals lasts considerably longer. Meals unexpectedly eaten out or quick meals made from fresh ingredients that become available during the month stretch my cooking "investment" still further.

You don't have to cook for an entire month, if that sounds too daunting. Try a week or two to start. Or you can just begin by doubling or tripling every recipe that lends itself to freezing, and start building up your freezer stash on the installment plan, a little at a time.

Quick Cooking, Easy Clean-Up

Another way to get control of meal preparation is to learn quick cooking methods. Quick cooked meals involve a minimum of ingredients that can be easily assembled, are often cooked in one pan or dish, and usually take less than 20 minutes from start to finish. Martha Stewart even has two "quick cook" cookbooks. What more can I say?

Impossible, you say? Not at all! Especially if you have some of the ingredients prepared and waiting on hand in the refrigerator. Here's another use for that slow cooker you've got on a shelf in the garage! Put a batch of a whole grain like brown rice in the pot, add the appropriate amount of water, and let it slow cook while you do other things. Use part of the batch for supper and save the rest for another meal or two during the week. It can be frozen, too. One dish might be a sauté, another a casserole, yet a third a cold vegetable and grain salad.

Put some carrots, onion, summer squash, and zucchini through the food processor using the shredding disk and store in a plastic bag in the fridge. Then when you get home from work, you can toss some of your "vegetable medley" in a wok with a little oil, slice up some chicken breast or throw in a few shrimps or scallops, add some cooked noodles or brown rice, season, and you'll be sitting down to eat in seconds, not minutes. For a meatless meal, leave out the chicken breast or fish or substitute some tofu. If you don't feel like cooking, just toss the ingredients with some salad dressing and eat it cold.

You can probably come up with lots more easy combinations like this on your own. Scan cookbooks and magazines for ideas to add to your collection. You don't even have to follow the exact recipes—just gather combinations of simple ingredients for a quick, healthful meal.

Apply a similar strategy to breakfast and lunch. Use leftover rice, some raisins or other dried fruit, a splash of milk, a little cinnamon, and honey, and you've got a nutritious and *fast* breakfast. Toss leftover noodles with a bit of soy sauce, some toasted sesame seeds, and green onions for a quick, healthy, and inexpensive lunch. Add an orange or apple on the side, or a handful of dried fruits and nuts, and you're all set. Simple food takes less time, costs less, and is almost always better for you.

For this cooking method, you'll want to have in your pantry certain easy-to-add ingredients that require little preparation. Stock up on items like chopped canned tomatoes and cans of mushrooms, soups and broths, corn, bamboo shoots, water chestnuts, beans, and chile peppers. It would be handy to have around items like salsa, corn or flour tortillas, prebaked pizza shells, and quick-cooking frozen vegetables that can be added direct from the freezer, such as peas, chopped broccoli, or spinach.

Slow Cooking: Ready-and-Waiting Meals

Another great way to cut down on cooking time and preparation is to make skillful use of your slow cooker. I own three and I use them all the time. As I already mentioned, a slow cooker can be a very helpful tool if you're following the bulk cooking strategy, but you can use it to simplify meals day-to-day, even if you don't choose this method.

> **Amazing Space**
>
> If refrigerator and freezer space is at a premium, the quick cooking method works especially well. Plan out your week's menus, chop or precook as many components as possible, and shop two or three times a week for fresh ingredients as needed.

> **Orderly Pursuits**
>
> There are lots of Crock-Pot cookery books around. One of the best comes with your appliance, or I recommend the *Fix-It and Forget-It Cookbook: Feasting with Your Slow Cooker* by Dawn Ranck and Phyllis Good. If you don't want to add to your cookbook collection, there are several excellent sites on the Internet for slow-cooker recipes. Try www.cs.cmu.edu/~mjw/recipes/crockpot/crockpot.html and www. justcrockpotrecipes.com/.

Wouldn't it be great if the moment you came home, the splendid smell of a complete, nutritious, home-cooked meal wafted from your kitchen—without your ever having to light the stove? How do sweet-and-sour beef, chicken Polynesian, or three-bean chili sound to you? Again, planning is the key, but in this case you're planning your meals around your kitchen powerhouse, the slow cooker.

Use your Crock-Pot for entertaining, making delicious gifts like chutneys, jams, and jellies, and concocting scrumptious desserts. You can even bake in your Crock-Pot with the right accessories and instructions from the recipe book that probably came with your appliance. Make it your business to learn how to use this marvelously versatile piece of kitchen equipment, and if you don't have one, you might want to whisper in someone's ear!

Constantly be on the lookout for systems, strategies, and methods that save time, use your resources to their best advantage, and support you in your nutrition and health goals. You won't regret it, because mastering this important part of everyday life will reward you in more ways than you might imagine. In later chapters we'll talk about ways to organize and simplify food preparation for entertaining and special events, but take the time now to get the day-to-day preparation of meals organized in a way you can live with. Experiment with the strategies above and perhaps rotate or combine them. Do whatever works for you!

Freezer Science and "Refrigology"

Your refrigerator and freezer are like any other cabinet or closet. Treat the shelves, drawers, and various compartments as ways of grouping like things together. You can add additional storage tools to make finding things even easier. Covered plastic containers, open plastic baskets, and resealable plastic bags all help organize your refrigerator and freezer. Use a Lazy Susan to help reach small bottles and jars like jellies and condiments. If storage items are going in the freezer, make sure they're "freezer-safe" and won't break, crack, or shatter in the extreme cold.

Group like things together on the same fridge shelf. Keep all leftovers in the same place, for example. Use the refrigerator door for storing the things you use most often. That way, you won't be digging in the back all the time, and you'll save time and effort.

Take advantage of individual cooling zones in your refrigerator so that, for instance, meat and vegetables are kept at their ideal temperatures, and butter can be kept soft enough to spread.

Group similar things together in the freezer, as well. Use baskets or boxes, if necessary. Put all frozen vegetables in one box, juices in another, and frozen meals in a third. This is absolutely crucial if your freezer is a chest type, where foods might be layered from the bottom up. Having boxes or bins that can be lifted out with the contents intact makes it much easier to get at the food at the bottom without upsetting everything.

Oops!

A full refrigerator or freezer doesn't work as hard to keep cool, but you don't want to stuff it so much that you can't see what's in there or have to play "catch" every time you open the door.

Food Storage for Emergencies

There's a saying that goes something like this: "There are no emergencies for someone who's prepared." The Boy Scouts teach it, and experience bears it out. Whether it's a natural or man-made disaster or something personal, like a financial setback, illness, or finding yourself unemployed, having a store of food and water, and planning for self-sufficiency in an emergency, gives you peace of mind and can actually save your life!

In Chapter 13, we'll talk more about how you can outfit your house for an emergency, but it's appropriate to talk about emergency food storage while we're on the subject of planning menus, shopping, and cooking.

If you're without power, the Red Cross recommends you first eat up the food in the refrigerator, then the freezer, and finally turn to food in your long-term storage. No long-term food storage? Well, perhaps you should consider building some. Having three to six months of food and water for your family buys an incredible amount of peace of mind and security. It's a lesson our ancestors knew well. They canned and dried food, dug a root cellar to overwinter vegetables, stored grains, and always had a "rain barrel." In our fast-food society, we've all but forgotten what it means to "put food by," but with recent hurricanes, tornadoes, floods, and even terrorist threats, people are rediscovering its wisdom.

You'll want to set up and locate your system based on the particular circumstances that relate to your region. Are you in a tornado region? A flood plain? An earthquake area? Are there alternative sources of water, or is water a problem where you live?

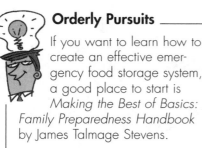

Orderly Pursuits

If you want to learn how to create an effective emergency food storage system, a good place to start is *Making the Best of Basics: Family Preparedness Handbook* by James Talmage Stevens.

You don't need a lot of expensive provisions, but can handle just about any crisis with forethought, planning, skills, and knowledge. Just remember to "store what you eat and eat what you store," rotating your provisions regularly. A fun family project is to throw the breaker for a whole day and night or two and see how well you're able to cope with the lack of electricity. No fair hopping in the car and going to the local fast-food restaurant!

Handy Recipe Rationale

Recipes come from a variety of sources: cookbooks, magazines, newspapers, television shows, friends—maybe even from your computer online service. Of all the recipes that come into your hands, how many do you think you'll ever actually try? This is another time to do some soul searching and examine your true ambitions as a cook. I'll bet right now you could eliminate two thirds of your recipe collection, if not more. And, hey, if you really need another cheesecake recipe in the future, I'm sure you can find one in the library, in a magazine, or on the Internet!

I already mentioned rotation recipes. These are the tried-and-true dishes that everybody in your family loves. If you have recipes you use regularly, and especially if you're trying one of the cooking methods described in this chapter, you'll want easy access to them. There are several ways to store your recipes to make them easy to find and less bulky.

Recipe Binder

One way to keep track of recipes is to use binders with plastic sheet protectors, "magnetic" sheets (used for holding photos), or just paper for pasting onto, as in a scrapbook. You may want to have several smaller binders, with each covering a particular food category, such as one for meats, poultry, and fish, another for desserts, a third for appetizers, and so on. Using sheet protectors or magnetic albums allows you to rearrange or take out recipes, which is an advantage over a more permanent scrapbook. If you're saving tried-and-true recipes in a scrapbook, however, this might be less of a problem.

Recipe Box

This is the old-fashioned method for keeping frequently used recipes, and it works as well as ever. A new twist might be to laminate the recipe cards so they hold up better and can just be wiped clean. If you find the recipe in a magazine, just cut it out, paste it on a card, and laminate it. If it's from a cookbook, photocopy it, cut it down to size, paste, and laminate. Simple and efficient, and it doesn't take a lot of time to keep up.

Recipe File

A filing folder system is another way to keep track. But remember to purge it regularly, as you should any file drawer, and only save those recipes you honestly think you'll use. Depending on how much you cook and like to experiment, you may set aside part of the household filing cabinet for this purpose.

Recipe Database

Proponents of the computer school of recipe-keeping have a point. Why struggle with cumbersome cookbooks, cards that get dirty, binders, or file boxes when you can put everything on the computer? The powerful cookbook software available today comes with several digital cookbooks that even allow you to add your own recipes.

You can create menus and shopping lists and keep track of cholesterol, fat, and calories. Best of all, they're searchable, so you can find that recipe in a flash. If you want a fresh copy, just print it out!

Typing in recipes can be time-consuming, which is a disadvantage. A hand-held scanner and optical character recognition software can help ease the burden, but they're expensive and can't recognize handwritten recipes. However, with so many mail lists and websites on the Internet, where recipes are exchanged in common recipe software formats, there are a great many more options.

The Least You Need to Know

◆ A good time to look at your eating habits and see if you need to make any changes is when you decide to reorganize your kitchen.

◆ The first step toward putting your kitchen on the right track is paring down food, utensils, dishes, appliances, and equipment.

◆ Simplify shopping and meal-planning using a master shopping list and rotation recipes.

◆ Cooking ahead and freezing saves time shopping and cleaning, and is also a boon when entertaining. Other time-saving methods are quick cooking and slow cooking.

◆ Purge your recipe files and cookbook shelf of recipes you will never use. Organize what you have left onto index cards, into binders or file folders, or in your computer.

Chapter 12

Clothing Systems: Easy Ways to Wash and Wear

In This Chapter

- ◆ How to determine your clothing style and design your wardrobe
- ◆ Smart shopping tips
- ◆ Unstuffing your closet and making it work for you
- ◆ Clothing care and laundry tips to keep your clothes looking great

Imagine getting ready for work on a morning where you can walk into your closet and everything in it is ready to wear. Everything fits, it's clean, it's in season, and when you put it on you look and feel your best. Not quite the current picture at your house? There's no reason why it can't be, if you commit now to making some decisions about what kind of clothes really work for you, do some serious weeding of your wardrobe, and possibly invest in some new hardware or storage units for your closet. Add to that an easy plan for doing laundry and keeping up with mending and ironing, and voilà! You're ready for anything.

What's Your Clothing Style?

Think of the people you know who always seem poised and well dressed. They don't necessarily wear a suit and tie or look like they just walked out of the board room or the pages of *Vogue* or *GQ* magazines—maybe their look is quite casual—but their clothes suit their personality and their activities. They're well groomed and their clothes look that way, too. They seem comfortable and natural in what they're wearing.

In addition to understanding your own personal style and how you like to dress, you also need to consider the activities you engage in. If you're a jeans and T-shirt type but your job demands a three-piece suit, you're obviously going to have to make some compromises.

Your off-hours wardrobe might be more of an expression of your real clothing personality, and maybe you can add touches to your otherwise staid work outfits that hint at the other side of your life.

Picture This
If you had unlimited funds and could start from scratch, what would your wardrobe look like? Think about the colors you like. Textures. Cut. Fabrics. If you were to pick one word to label your dressing style, what would it be? Classy? Casual? Sporty? Ethnic? Romantic? Dramatic? Nonconformist? Keep the picture you just made in your mind (or better, describe it on paper) and refer to it as you begin to design a wardrobe and organize your closet. When you see pictures in magazines that fit your style, tear them out and keep them with your wardrobe design ideas.

Take out your organization notebook, planner/organizer, or just a sheet of paper, and make a list of the activities you engage in during a typical week. You'll probably have things on your list like "work," "play tennis," "jog," "garden," "houseclean," "work outdoors," "hike," "date," "go out to dinner"—whatever. Add to this any special occasions or seasonal activities you might expect to come up in a given year. These might include a formal dinner/dance, holiday parties, skiing, or swimming—anything that isn't part of your regular routine.

Now, go into your closet and group your wardrobe into four categories: *Work, Play, Dress Up,* and *Specialty.* The first three categories are self-explanatory. The last category would include seasonal items (the sweater with the big Santa Claus design, for instance), costumes, formal wear, and clothing that's especially for a particular sport or other activity, like a ski jacket or hiking boots.

Unlike some of the other organization projects you've done so far, I don't recommend you break this one up into small sessions. Allow at least two or three hours for your clothing/closet blitz, with a couple of smaller follow-up sessions to accomplish some of the actual redesign projects you choose to implement. Tackling this task all at once will give you a good overall picture of your wardrobe, and investing this time now to get your closet in shape will have a huge impact on your everyday life.

Clothes, Clothes Everywhere and Not a Thing to Wear!

The next process will be repeated for each part of your wardrobe. You're going to "unstuff" your closet and later your dresser drawers or anywhere else you keep your clothes. After this, everything you have in your closet will be clean and ready to wear, and will make you feel good when you put it on.

A Wardrobe Review

Ask these questions as you look at each item:

- Does this fit you *now?* If you plan to lose 30 pounds and are actually on a weight loss program, you may want to put aside one favorite outfit that doesn't fit you now, but will when you're done dieting. However, don't fall into the trap of having different wardrobes for different weights. Keeping "fat" clothes gives you permission to get fat again. Keeping "thin" clothes mocks your efforts and erodes your confidence.

- Does this go with anything else? Is it an odd color or style?

- How long has it been since you wore this? Why?

- Is this too complicated to wear? Too fragile (silk, sequins, fur, and so on)?

- Does this need to be ironed? Mended? Washed? Dry-cleaned?

- Is this in season *now?*

- Does this flatter you? You may want to get a buddy to work with you on this. Sometimes we think certain things look good on us, when they simply don't. Pick a friend who'll tell you the truth, and be open to what your buddy says.

> ### Amazing Space
> Think of ways to express yourself without compromising your career objectives. One woman who likes lacy, old-fashioned clothes, but needs to dress in a more conservative, corporate style at work, wears a variety of antique lace handkerchiefs tucked in her jacket pocket, secured with a vintage pin to express her inner style.

- Is this comfortable? Does it pinch, ride up, or bind?

- Is this a duplicate? How many other items like this do you have? Of the similar items you have, which do you like best or wear most often?

- Does this sock have a mate? Do these hose have a run? Underwear stretched out? Stains? Tears? You know what to do with them!

- Do you have clothes hanging in the closet that still have dry-cleaning plastic over them? If you're protecting them from dust, you're probably not wearing them often enough to keep them!

As you go through your closet, take out the things that don't fit or flatter you and put them in one pile. If you have four black blazers, decide if you really need them all and put the least attractive or lower-quality ones in this pile, as well. This is the *Pass On* pile.

If an item needs to be mended or ironed, put it in a *Fix* pile. Decide first whether it's really worth the effort. One reason you may not have gotten around to it could be you didn't really miss it. If that's the case, put it in the *Pass On* pile.

If you're not sure about a piece of clothing, put that in a *Mystery* pile. This may include items there's nothing wrong with—you like them, they fit you well, are of good quality, and don't need fixing—but for whatever reason you just haven't worn them in a long time. Ask yourself whether the reason you don't wear a particular item is that you don't have anything that goes with it. If that's the case, you may want to set it aside and purchase something that will bring it back into your regular wardrobe. Whatever's left, put it in a bag or box and try living without it for a week or two. If you don't miss it, transfer it to the *Pass On* pile.

Oops!

Be careful of the "If-I-keep-it-long-enough-it'll-come-back-in-style" trap. Even if it does (sort of), the trend won't be quite the same or it won't really fit by then. Get rid of it! Besides, if your wardrobe is full of classic, high-quality pieces, you'll always be "in style."

A good time to seriously reevaluate your wardrobe is any time you experience a change in lifestyle. I went from being a corporate professional, wearing high heels, suits, and pantyhose every day, to a work-at-home entrepreneur. I don't wear high heels anymore, ever! Guess what you won't find in my closet! I also moved from New England to the Southwest, so I don't need a down jacket or heavy snow boots either. Have you experienced a lifestyle change, but your closet hasn't caught up yet? Look at what you've hung onto from old activities, locations, and lifestyles. Think about the way you live now, and get rid of clothes that no longer make sense.

Put off-season clothes in the least-accessible part of your closet or in another closet altogether if possible. Make sure what's up-front in your closet is right for *now*.

Do this for each type of clothing we've identified—Work, Play, Dress-up, and Specialty. Put a limit on clothes you keep as "grubbies" for grungy jobs. One or two sets of clothes for outdoor work or painting should be enough.

Now, all you should have hanging in your closet are items that make you look and feel good and are in good condition and ready to wear. Continue this process with your shoes and accessories and anything else in your wardrobe.

Then, let's see if you can pare down even more! I challenge you to live with only two weeks of outfits or less in your closet. Make them all things you love, that interchange and can be classified as the "cream of the crop." Put the rest away in a safe place, but give yourself some time to try this pared down system. See if it doesn't make your life a lot simpler.

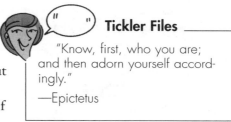

Tickler Files

"Know, first, who you are; and then adorn yourself accordingly."

—Epictetus

Take the *Pass On* pile and give the clothes to charity or whomever you think can use them. Box it up. Do it now! Do the same with the *Fix* pile if you're taking it to the tailor. Put these items directly in your car so you can drop them off the next time you're out and about. If you leave them around the house, they just may creep back into your closet. If you're going to do the mending yourself, schedule time in your planner/organizer this week.

Take a look at what's left in your wardrobe and notice the colors and styles. Does this match the earlier picture you came up with of your dressing style? Make a list of a very few quality purchases that would make better use of what you have and add a little more of your personal style to your wardrobe. Something as simple as a new blouse or shirt or some color-coordinated accessories might pull together several elements and make them more versatile. If you have a lot of neutral colors, you might want to add something with more pizzazz. Or perhaps you need some more basic pieces to enhance the usefulness of what you already have.

Now that you've organized your space, reward yourself with some extra touches. Make the inside of your closet even more pleasant by adding sachets between clothes, lining walls with attractive postcards or art posters, and using scented shelf papers. Colorful hat boxes or baskets work well as organizers. Have an attractive box, basket, or hanging bag in the closet to keep clothes that need to be dry-cleaned, and another for mending.

A-Shopping We Will Go

When you go shopping for new things for your wardrobe, keep these basic points in mind:

◆ Don't buy anything just because it's "on sale." Have a list of things you need to make your wardrobe more complete, and stick to your list.

◆ Fashion = waste. Stay away from clothes that are too trendy. Generally, fads disappear after a short time, and you're left with clothing "junk." The classic styles never change much because they're flattering, easy to wear, and go with everything. If you must keep up with the latest trend, try to limit your purchases to accessories, not major wardrobe items.

◆ Invest in quality. With your wardrobe basics, buy the best you can afford. They'll last and look good for a long time. Plus, you'll get more than your money's worth.

◆ Buy clothes that are easy to wear and easy to care for.

◆ Buy any needed accessories when you buy the outfit. That way, a new item won't sit in the closet waiting for the right pair of shoes, a complementary tie, or the right scarf or pin. You'll have something ready to put on the moment you bring it home.

◆ Keep an inventory of your wardrobe in your planner, and refer to it any time you see something and consider making an "impulse purchase." Ask yourself what it will go with or whether it's a duplication of something you already have.

Oops!

If you buy something that needs to be dry-cleaned after only a few wearings, you'd better love it. It's going to cost you a bundle! Avoid clothes that need ironing or special washing. Read the label!

◆ Wear clothes that are easy to remove when you go shopping and, if possible, have on the same shoes and undergarments you intend to wear with the item you're buying. Don't wear much makeup or jewelry.

◆ If there's enough of a seam allowance, clip a small amount of fabric from the item you're trying to coordinate with, or bring the item with you so you get a perfect match.

◆ Use thrift stores for around-the-house clothes. Who says everything you buy has to be brand new? Secondhand is fine for painting or gardening, and you may even find some items for your other wardrobe needs.

◆ Check over new garments when you get them home. Reaffix buttons that appear loose and reinforce seams in problem areas like the back seam in pants or under-arm seams of blouses or shirts. Make sure hems are secure, and cut off all loose threads. This will save you lots of mending time down the road.

◆ Sew extra buttons on an inside seam allowance and you'll always have an extra if you need it. Lord knows, you'll never find it in the button box!

> **Amazing Space**
>
> Stick with solid colors for basics. That's where your biggest dollars will go, and you'll want them to mix with as many things as possible. Add variety with accessories—think texture, print, color accents, jewelry, scarves, hats, ties, and handkerchiefs for the pocket, belts, and sashes.

The idea is to end up with a wardrobe full of clothes that work well together, flatter your figure, suit your lifestyle, express your personality, and are ready to wear right now. Don't let a wardrobe just happen. Plan it.

When there's a change of seasons, go through what you're about to put away and apply the same process. No sense saving a lot of useless garments until next year. Do any laundering and mending so they're ready for next year with only a little touch-up pressing. Dry-clean woolens before putting them away to avoid moth damage.

When you pull out the current season's wardrobe, decide, sort, toss, and fix again. If you do this every six months, when you make your seasonal wardrobe change, you'll maintain your clothing organization system without really trying.

The Great Hang-Up: Closet Design Basics

Now that you've got your wardrobe pared down and in working order, the next thing on our list is taking a hard look at your closet itself. Follow this checklist and then concentrate on those areas you've checked off as needing attention.

Yes	No	
❏	❏	Does your closet make the best use of space?
❏	❏	Are there areas for hanging long garments, as well as short ones like shirts and jackets?
❏	❏	Can you double up on certain areas with a second rod placed halfway down?

continues

continued

Yes	No	
❏	❏	Is your shoe storage effective? (If there are piles of shoes all over the floor, check "no"!)
❏	❏	Do all special items (such as pocketbooks, ties, jewelry, and hats) already have their own storage solutions?
❏	❏	Are nonclothing items like sports equipment or luggage stored in the garage or attic, if appropriate? If "no," decide where these items are going to go and remove them from the closet. Put them away when you're done organizing.
❏	❏	Are your hangers well used? Good-quality plastic hangers are far better than wire ones. Do you have special pants and skirt hangers? If "no," put these items on the shopping list in your planner.
❏	❏	Can you clearly see what's contained in boxes or other storage containers? If not, consider labeling and/or transferring to clear containers. Add to your To-Do list and shopping list, if necessary.

A number of companies offer custom closet makeovers, and others allow you to design your own closet. If you choose either of these options, you'll want to completely empty your closet and start from scratch.

Closet design systems can double or even triple your closet capacity. If you decide to go this route, be sure to get several estimates. Ask the closet company the following questions to help you evaluate:

◆ Do you remove old rods and repair any wall damage?

◆ Are special hangers needed for your system?

> **Amazing Space**
>
> Put a towel bar or two on the back of your closet door. Hang flat things like scarves on them. Look for places to put up hooks for things like nightclothes, hats, belts, handbags, or a drawstring bag to hold delicate items for hand-washing.

◆ How do hangers fit into the system? Don't opt for a system where each hanger sits in its own groove or grid section and clothes can't be slid along a rod. This is very limiting and very annoying when you're looking for something.

◆ Are the shelves and any slide-out units sturdy? Put some weight in drawers and be sure they still slide out easily when full. You'll want to see an in-store sample.

◆ Will the system you design work with each season's wardrobe? Don't go ahead unless you're sure.

◆ Are there ways to add flexibility to the system with free-standing units that roll out or adjustable shelves? Can it be changed?

If you don't have the money to go the total redesign route, start out by completely measuring your closet and doing a layout on your own before you buy any additional shelving or organization aids. Measure the length of your longest jacket, skirt, shirt, or blouse before you install double rods. That will ensure they're the right distance apart to accommodate all your tops and bottoms. Stores like the Container Store, which sells do-it-yourself storage systems, will do a free consultation. Don't hesitate to ask. Check the resources section in the back of this book for companies that offer closet design products and services.

It All Comes Out in the Wash

What's it like at your house on laundry day? Do you even have a regular system for getting your clothes cleaned, ironed, and mended? If you don't, we can't leave this chapter without getting that part of your life organized, too.

My mother and her mother always did their laundry on Mondays. Monday was Laundry Day. Try as I might to emulate them, it just never worked for me. The system I later devised is a simple one, and the reason it works so well for us is that it's visual—even a child can use it. In fact, I devised it to teach my daughters to do their own laundry.

The first thing we did was get in the habit of sorting as we went along. I bought three kitchen-sized plastic garbage cans. These each hold just about one washing machine load of clothes. One was labeled "Darks," one "Lights," and one "Whites." A separate mesh bag or basket is sufficient for hand-washable items. As the kids undressed at night, we sorted the clothes together. Soon they did it automatically, peeling off their clothes and putting them in the appropriate bin. I taught them to look at labels for dry clean or special care items. Once a bin was full, it was time to do a load. Come

Oops!

If it isn't dirty, don't wash it! Sounds simple, doesn't it? And yet many of us automatically throw whatever we've worn in the hamper at the end of the day. Stop and look first! A simple airing might be enough. Carefully fold or hang and save yourself some work. Train family members to do the same.

washing time, they helped in the laundry room, so they could see how the machine worked and how to measure soap powder and pretreat stains.

As they got older, they had been doing the sorting for so long and had seen the washing procedure enough times they just grew into doing a load when the garbage bin got to the top. The next step was teaching them to sort out their own clean clothes, fold them, and put them away. They were more motivated to do this because they had a limited amount of clothes in the first place and needed what was in the load.

The last step was teaching them how to mend and iron, which took a little more of my attention. Basically, my children were doing their own laundry by age seven or eight. If young children can be taught this system, why not use it yourself? My daughters are now grown and long since out of the house, but my husband and I still use "the garbage can system." It may not be pretty, but it works! I just check when I dress in the morning to see if I need to throw in a load.

Even if you don't adopt my system, come up with your own routine, and make it a habit. If a once-a-week system makes more sense in your life, then do it. Especially if you live in an apartment building and don't have your own washer and dryer, this may be the only logical solution. But presorting like I'm suggesting will still save you time, even at the Laundromat.

Stain-Busters

Even if you never took Chemistry 101, you can still be a stain-removal expert. All it takes is a few basic principles, a "stain-busting kit" containing a few important ingredients, and fast action (stains are harder to remove when they're "set").

Treat stains as soon as you notice them. Learn something about the chemistry of stain removal. It will save you lots of money and time. Have on hand the following products for fighting stains and learn how to use them:

> **Amazing Space**
>
> Too stained to use or even pass on? Cut it up in handy wipe-sized squares and use in place of disposable paper towels. Start a "rag-bag" today!

- **Acetone** (get at your local hardware store; don't use nail polish remover): good for taking out glue or nail polish.

- **Bleach** (both the kind for whites and for colors): removes the stain's color, but not the actual stain.

- **Club soda:** excellent for removing pet stains and odors. Just saturate and blot up.

- **Color remover:** (get at the fabric dye section of your supermarket).

- **Enzyme presoak** (such as Biz): this "digests" the stain with powerful enzymes. Use on protein stains like blood and chocolate.

- **Glycerine** (get at pharmacy): used to soften and dissolve "set" stains, especially on wool and fabrics that don't take kindly to water.

- **Hydrogen peroxide:** another bleaching agent.

- **Lemon juice:** use as a very gentle bleaching agent on delicate fabrics. The effect is intensified by exposing the fabric to sunlight while saturated with lemon juice.

- **Low-alkali soaps** (such as Woolite or Ivory): for delicate fabrics and wool.

- **Oil solvent** (such as Carbona or K2r): use for oil and grease stains.

- **Oxalic acid solution** (such as Zud): used to remove rust stains.

- **Paint remover**: make sure to store this safely.

- **Petroleum jelly:** for softening up hardened grease and oil stains.

- **White vinegar:** for removing hard water stains and any other alkaline deposits.

Orderly Pursuits

Get yourself a copy of Don Aslett's *Stainbuster's Bible: The Complete Guide to Spot Removal.* It tells you how to remove just about any kind of stain from any kind of surface, explains all the household chemistry involved, and even gives advice on how to avoid making stains in the first place.

Ironing, Mending, and Other Unfamiliar Subjects

To have a closet full of useful, ready-to-wear clothes, you have to maintain them. This is one of those tasks that takes only a little effort each week, but can become daunting if left to pile up. Part of the problem can be handled up front during the buying process and immediately after taking your purchase home. Take time to read the labels *before* you buy. Ask yourself if you really want to iron that cotton shirt or hand wash that silk blouse. Consider the dry-cleaning bill if that's what it takes to keep it clean. Look the garment over carefully and reinforce any buttons, seams, or hems *before* they come apart.

You'll still have to do some ironing and mending. Here are some ways to save yourself time and effort, while keeping your wardrobe in tip-top shape:

♦ Learn how to use your washing and drying appliances. Read the manuals and follow directions. Select the right cleaning products for your appliance and water type (you might want to have your water tested and may need to purchase a water softener if it's especially hard).

♦ Dampen a washcloth with liquid fabric softener and toss in the dryer. It's cheaper than disposable fabric-softener sheets and works just as well.

♦ If you go to a Laundromat, set up a caddy with all the products you need, including a stain-treatment kit.

♦ Sort ironing by the temperature required. Dampen as you go.

♦ Have a basic mending kit handy. If you do your laundry at a Laundromat, be sure you bring your kit with you to do small mending jobs while you wait.

♦ Kids mean more repairs and more laundry. Look for shortcuts. Use fusible bonding fabric, iron-on patches, a button puncher, and anything else that'll save time and effort.

♦ If the laundry has really piled up, you can go to the Laundromat and get it all done at once (even if you have laundry facilities at home). If you've got 10 loads to do, you can fill up 10 washers and dryers and do all 10 loads in the time it takes to do one. Go at off-peak hours so you don't have to wait for a free appliance. You'll go home with everything washed and folded and only a few things to iron or mend.

> **Amazing Space**
>
> Take clothes out of the dryer immediately and fold or hang them. You may hardly ever have to iron if you observe this simple rule, and you won't pile up laundry waiting to be ironed. If you forget to take your clothes out of the dryer, throw in a damp towel and redry 5 to 10 minutes to remove wrinkles.

♦ Limit the purchase of items that take special care and make sure you really enjoy the extra work it takes to keep them. I like collecting old linens and handmade items. They take careful washing and ironing. I only use them once in a while and, for me, the extra effort is worth it when I see them out on the table.

Dry Cleaning Made Simple

Did you know a lot of the clothes labeled "Dry Clean Only" don't have to be dry-cleaned? It takes some confidence and maybe a few mistakes before you get the hang of it, but over time you'll find you can really save on the dry-cleaning bill with just a few pointers. Items with linings or inserts of a different fabric aren't good candidates, but simply constructed garments of all the same material can often be hand-washed rather than chemically dry-cleaned.

Here are the basics:

- Before putting your clothes in the closet, air them out—outside or in a covered porch if possible. They may not even need cleaning, just some deodorizing.

- Use a mild liquid, flaked, or powdered soap, not detergent. Dissolve whatever you decide to use completely in a basin or sink before putting in the garment.

- Wash one item at a time, so if colors do run you haven't ruined anything else. Things tend to wash better in plenty of water, anyway.

- Rinse thoroughly—several times if needed.

- Don't wring the garment—gently squeeze. Roll in a towel or several towels until fairly dry, then lay flat or iron to dry. You won't have to dampen a second time when you iron.

If an item does need dry-cleaning, make sure you don't roll it in a ball until you take it to the cleaners. Hang or fold neatly. Tell the dry cleaner any stains you know of and what they're composed of. Check buttons and seams. Repair yourself or ask if the dry cleaner has someone who can do it and what it will cost.

The Least You Need to Know

- You can make dressing, shopping, and clothing care simpler by planning your wardrobe and weeding out what you have to conform to that plan.

- A professional closet job or a do-it-yourself plan that's well thought out can double or triple your clothing storage space.

- Ensure you don't make any more clothing goofs by having a clothing inventory and shopping list, and taking with you samples of what you want to match.

- A carefully planned laundry system will keep your clothes ready to wear and take less time. Even a child can be taught a simple system.

- Regular maintenance as clothes need it saves time in the long run and keeps your wardrobe ready to wear.

Chapter 13

Shelter Systems: Giving Your Nest the Best

In This Chapter

- ◆ Creating a home environment you can live with
- ◆ Organizing to clean like the pros
- ◆ The fine art of preventative maintenance
- ◆ Making your home safe

Your home doesn't have to be just a roof over your head. When it's organized with your goals in mind, it becomes your launching pad for success and your well-deserved retreat from the world. Depending on the attention you pay to your home, it can either be an obstacle course you have to navigate, or serve as a strong "base of operations." It can be your dungeon or your castle.

You've already taken some huge steps to unstuff your life and much of your environment. You've tackled the kitchen, your closets, and your office, and made some important changes in your acquisition habits and your clutter outlook. Now we're going to look at the bigger picture at home. You'll make some decisions about your home's design, how it flows, and its functionality and ease of maintenance. And you'll learn something about cleaning methods as well.

Taking Stock So You Can Streamline

Remember how we weeded out your closet in the last chapter? We're going to use similar criteria of functionality, good design, comfort, and attractiveness to assess the items in your house. Make a list of the contents of each room, one room at a time. This will become the basis of your home inventory. I suggest you start with your living room and your bedroom. List everything—each piece of furniture, pictures on the wall, bookcases, decorative items, electronic equipment, and any other contents.

Picture This

Walk around your house, observing it as if you were a stranger. Better yet, pretend you're a real estate agent helping her client make improvements for a quick sale. Take notes on colors, clutter, and any other characteristics. Try to be objective, not defensive.

Next, imagine your ideal environment. What does it look like? Sound like? Smell like? Imagine yourself on a typical day in your ideal environment. Write down your vision, so you can refer to it throughout this chapter and beyond. As you do your home inventory, keep this picture in mind.

If you also record model and serial numbers while you make your list and photograph ("instant" photos will do) and/or videotape what you have, your home inventory will be just about done. (Remember you're documenting these things, so get close.) If you make a video, have someone read the necessary numbers out loud so they'll be recorded on the tape. Don't forget to include equipment for hobbies, such as sewing machines, shop equipment, and things inside drawers, cabinets, and closets.

Later on, you can do the final steps of your home inventory—writing down estimated costs and attaching receipts for high-ticket items. But while you take stock, you might as well make your time do double duty and create an inventory for insurance purposes as well. If you decide later to get rid of some items, you'll have an idea of their dollar value so you'll know what to ask as a selling price or you can estimate what to take off on your income tax if you give it to charity.

A Streamlining Questionnaire

Once you have your list, evaluate each item, one room at a time, asking the following questions:

◆ How well does this function in my life? In this room? What is it supposed to do and how well does it fulfill its function?

◆ How much space does this object take up? Is there another possibility that would free up space? A dresser, for example, might be unnecessary if closet space were redesigned. A coffee table that included storage space underneath might eliminate the need for a magazine rack or separate video storage.

◆ Are there ways that rearranging things would be more functional? Easier to access? More pleasing?

◆ What does it take to maintain this? Does it require special polishing or cleaning? Does it have special details that make it difficult to clean (like carving or ornate hardware, hard-to-clean fabric, or colors)? If it's not easy to clean, is it truly worth the effort?

Amazing Space
If you have a computer, you may want to record and save your inventory. That way, it will be easy to add and subtract as you unstuff or acquire new, more serviceable items. If you have a laptop, that would be ideal for taking from room to room.

While you're in each room, ask these questions:

◆ Are window treatments and other decorative accessories easy to keep clean? Can they be thrown in the washing machine or do they need to be dry cleaned? Would the room be improved by blinds or shades?

◆ How easy is it to reach surfaces for vacuuming or dusting? Can you easily remove cobwebs from the ceilings? Is there room to get at windows when they need to be washed?

◆ Is there evidence of any household pests like mice, ants, fleas, bees, wasps, bats, or moths? Any indication of water damage from leaks or spills?

◆ Are there pieces of furniture that need to be repainted, reupholstered, glued, cleaned, or otherwise repaired? Are they worth the effort? Would you do this work yourself or pay someone else to do it?

◆ Do furniture, carpets, window treatments, or accessories show signs of wear? Do you notice particular high-traffic areas? How clean are walls, woodwork, ceilings, and floors?

◆ Have you provided adequate light? Heating and cooling? Fire protection (smoke alarms, fire extinguishers)?

◆ Do particular areas seem prone to clutter? What items seem to be creating the problem? Are there any solutions using the furniture or built-ins currently available? If not, what alternatives come to mind?

◆ When you come to the basement, notice whether there are any cracks or areas of dampness. Is there sufficient light? What activities generally take place here? Is there sufficient room for storage and work?

◆ Where are the electrical outlets in the room? Are they conveniently located? Are there enough of them?

If you find areas that need to be unstuffed, schedule time to get rid of the clutter. It will be easier to make rooms work for you and easier to set up cleaning routines without unnecessary clutter sabotaging your efforts. You know the drill. Get out your sorting boxes and get the job done right away.

Spotting Patterns

Now that you've done your evaluation, you'll probably see that items in your notes fall into four basic categories:

◆ Projects to do (including repair and furniture moving)

◆ Things to discard or pass on

◆ Work to hire out

◆ Things to buy

Add the projects to your Master To-Do List and work on scheduling them as soon as possible. Incorporate into your budget the work you need to have done and the things you need to purchase (Chapter 14 will help you with that), and get rid of the stuff you decide doesn't do the job now.

Your budget and schedule may not allow you to do the whole house at once. Tackle the areas that are most urgent in terms of safety or impact, then work on one room at a time until the whole house is in pretty good shape.

Instant Unstuff: Have a Yard Sale!

Want to get your house uncluttered in a hurry? Pick a date for a yard sale and then put into the garage everything you haven't used in a year, furniture that doesn't work for you, stuff your kids have outgrown, and stuff you're just tired of. Put prices on it (low, so it'll *go!*), place an ad in the classified section of your local newspaper, put up some easy-to-read signs in strategic locations (be sure to give your street address), and watch the money come in while the stuff goes out.

Tell your friends, too, and ask them to bring their friends. Word-of-mouth is often the best advertising. Add balloons to your signs and make them colorful to get extra attention.

Go to the bank to get some change—maybe $5 in coins, 20 singles, 4 fives, and 4 tens—and designate a box for cash. Display things on tables, if at all possible, and use a sheet or blanket underneath to set them off. Group like things together (such as kitchen gadgets, tools, clothes, craft items, art work, and books) to make it easier for people to find what they may be looking for.

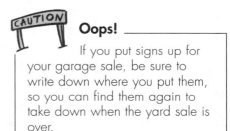

Oops!

If you put signs up for your garage sale, be sure to write down where you put them, so you can find them again to take down when the yard sale is over.

Make a vow to immediately take whatever doesn't sell to a local charity when the sale is over. Don't even *think* about letting it back into the house!

Clean with the Pros

One day I watched a professional cleaning company scrub my whole house, clean my carpets, and wash all my windows in less than five hours with only two people. It suddenly dawned on me that if I wanted to learn how to clean, these folks probably know all the secrets.

I discovered that they used different tools and cleaning products than the average homeowner does. I also discovered that these tools and cleaning solutions (as well as manuals and videos on professional cleaning methods) are available to any homeowner through janitorial supply houses and mail-order companies. I could clean like a pro, too!

Tool Time!

Let's start with tools. Most of us use our arms and backs to do the housework. We spend time on our hands and knees scrubbing floors, clean windows endlessly with paper towels and blue sprays, and probably have several different cleaners for every job in the house.

Professionals use only a few well-made tools and simple cleaning solutions that can be used full-strength or diluted, depending on what's needed for a particular job. You'll need a disinfectant cleaner, a neutral (not alkaline or acidic) all-purpose cleaner, a heavy-duty cleaner and degreaser (with high pH), and an ammonia- or alcohol-based glass cleaner for small windows, mirrors, appliances, and tiles. You may also need a phosphoric acid-based cleaner if you have hard-water deposits on bathroom fixtures (although I find applying white distilled vinegar usually does the job). These can be purchased in quantity, transferred to spray bottles (available from variety stores, hardware stores, or wholesale clubs), and diluted according to directions. Make sure you label the contents.

You'll need some wax remover and wax for your floors (many professionals recommend using wax even on so-called "no-wax" floors), and a good wood polish for your furniture. A wax coating protects floors from dents and dings. It's also safer: A layer of wax creates resistance and actually helps prevent slips and falls.

I bought an interchangeable mop/scrubber system from a professional cleaning supply mail-order catalog. It consists of one pole with a strong plastic swivel head with Velcro on one side. It accepts a variety of scrubbers, a dust mop head, a damp mop head, and a wax applicator head. I have less to store, and all I have to do is put on the head I need for the job.

Orderly Pursuits

If one goal of yours (it's one of mine!) is to reduce the artificial chemicals in your environment, you can use simple, natural homemade formulas to get and keep your home sparkling clean. Learn how from Annie Berthold-Bond's book *Better Basics for the Home: Simple Solutions for Less Toxic Living* and *Clean House, Clean Planet: Clean Your House for Pennies a Day the Safe, Nontoxic Way* by Karen Logan.

Get yourself a professional squeegee for cleaning windows and a bucket that's wide enough to accept your mop or whatever you need to plunge into it (an oval shape is even better). Buy good quality sponges (again, go with the pros) and cleaning cloths. Add a good wet mop and two brooms—a smaller angle broom and a heavier push broom for outdoor cleanup—and you've got a pretty good cleaning arsenal.

You'll also want some rubber gloves to protect your hands, some paper towels, and an old toothbrush for tough-to-reach places.

Where Do They Get That Stuff?

In the resource guide at the back of this book, I've listed some mail-order companies where you can get the items I've mentioned. You can also look in your local Yellow

Pages under "Janitorial Equipment & Supplies." Ads will often say "open to the public," but if you're not sure, phone ahead and ask. You may also be able to rent equipment like floor waxers, heavy-duty vacuums, and carpet cleaners/extractors. Although some of these are available for purchase on the consumer market, they're usually not as powerful and don't hold up as well. Besides, they take up too much space, considering how infrequently you'll use them.

Cleaning on Schedule

I've learned that it takes a minimum amount of effort a little each day to keep a home and its contents clean, and that the same job is back-breaking if it's allowed to go undone for months at a time. You'll do yourself a favor if you break up your cleaning and maintenance into daily, weekly, twice-weekly, monthly, semiannual, and annual chores. Some of this will be dictated by the level of cleanliness that satisfies you and how busy your schedule is. I don't always stick to my schedule, but this is the one I try to follow:

Everyday Duties

These few tasks, done on a daily basis, keep the house humming and save hours later on:

- Swish the toilets.

- Straighten up. I usually try to do this as I go and again each evening before retiring for the night.

- Do dishes after each meal. If for some reason I can't finish doing them right away, I rinse them or at least let them soak in a dishpan full of warm water and detergent. Never go to bed with a sink full of dishes. It just starts your day out wrong!

- Wipe counters and range tops. Generally a neutral cleaner (soap and water) is enough. As with any cleaning job, leave on the cleaning solution a few minutes, so it has time to do the work. Most people wipe the solution away too soon and end up using too much "elbow grease."

- Make beds. A comforter alleviates the need for a bedspread. Just straighten the sheets, fluff up the pillows, smooth out the comforter, and the bed's made!

Tickler Files
"Housekeeping ain't no joke."
—Louisa May Alcott

- Straighten cushions and throw pillows.

- Dump kitchen garbage.

- Clean up any spots or spills as they're made.

- Hang up clean clothes and put dirty clothes in bins.

- Go through and dispose of all mail and reading material. Either toss it, put it in appropriate slots, or pass it on.

- Cruise the yard and put away any tools or toys. Throw away any litter.

Twice-a-Week Tasks

Two tasks are essentials—vacuuming most-used areas and doing laundry (wash, dry, fold, hang, mend, and iron). Twice a week is a guideline. I let the level of laundry in my sorted laundry bins be the trigger. If it's at the top, it's a load. If you live alone and don't have pets or entertain much, you may not need to do certain tasks as often. If, however, your house is like Grand Central Station and the Bronx Zoo rolled into one, twice a week might not be often enough.

Once-a-Week Work

Keep up with these tasks weekly and, with regular daily tasks thrown in, your home will always look presentable. You can put off heavier cleaning and still have a fairly clean house if you stick with this list. If it doesn't need doing this week, skip it until next week.

 Orderly Pursuits

There's a wealth of home maintenance tips on the World Wide Web. Just point your web browser to the *Hometime* home page (connected to the popular PBS television show) at hometime. com/hmpg.htm for tips, checklists, and even videos you can order.

- Vacuum entire house.

- Sweep and damp mop floors, including bathroom.

- Dust furniture surfaces.

- Clean TV screen.

- Change sheets.

- Spot-clean walls, doors, and so on. Look for fingerprints and spatters.

- Clean mirrors and any door glass that's mucked up with fingerprints or pet nose prints.

- Clean sinks, showers, and tubs.

- Wipe out microwave.

- Clean outside and inside of toilets. Use a delimer for hard water rings, or pumice stone if you have a serious buildup, but if you swish daily, chances are you won't.

- Dump all trash cans. The day before garbage pickup is usually a good time.

- Vacuum door mats. If you don't have mats inside and outside all your doors, get them, and keep them clean. They're your first line of defense against dirt and can greatly reduce the cleanup time needed inside.

- Shake smaller rugs. Rugs in the kitchen will probably need to be shaken more often, perhaps even daily.

- Sweep outside entryways, patios, and porches.

Monthly Majors

These are heavier tasks that go deeper than regular daily and weekly cleaning. I find it best to rotate these chores by room, running through the list over the course of a week (remember the power of 15 minutes?) for one room a week.

- Dust or vacuum all high and low areas. Don't forget the woodwork and catch the cobwebs.

- Vacuum upholstery, drapes, and blinds.

- Vacuum carpet edges and air vents. Don't forget the grate under the refrigerator and the clothes dryer vent and door.

- Clean carpet if needed, paying special attention to any spots and high-traffic areas.

- Wax floors if needed.

- Clean out refrigerator (treat your refrigerator like another closet!).

- Clean kitchen cabinet doors, appliance fronts, and tops.

- Clean laundry appliances.

- Wash and disinfect trash containers.

- Wash and dry doormats.

- Wash easy-to-reach windows if needed.
- Sweep garage and walkways.

Quarterly Reports

These tasks have some high quarterly earnings. You protect your furniture and save money on heating and cooling costs.

- Polish furniture and wood cabinets.
- Check and clean or change furnace/central air-conditioning filters. Check your manual if you're not sure how, or ask your service technician to show you.
- Check the hoses on your washing machine for cracks or holes and make sure connections are secure.

Semiannual Clearance

I like to schedule these in the spring and fall, since some of them help prepare for the change in seasons.

- Clean oven.
- Degrease stove hood and exhaust fan.
- Turn mattresses.
- Dust tops of tall furniture and rafters.
- Clean rain gutters and down spouts. Also check for leaks and caulk or refit if necessary. Pay attention to window wells, too, and make sure they're free of dirt and debris.
- Wash hard-to-reach windows or have them done professionally. If you choose to do it yourself, a squeegee with a long extension (and washing pad attachment) will make the job easier.
- Inspect for carpenter ants, termites, and other household pests. Call an exterminator if necessary.

> **Amazing Space**
>
> Put away summer/winter sports equipment after doing regular maintenance and repairs. Don't let the stuff from the previous season clutter up much-valued *prime real estate*, but get it into *secondary storage* as soon as it's no longer "in play."

Annual Alignments

I suggest doing many of these tasks before winter sets in, since they're preventative or can cut costs significantly during the coldest months. Think how much peace of mind you'll have knowing everything's shipshape before winter winds howl and snows swirl.

◆ Check weather stripping around doors and windows, making sure there's an air-tight seal. Reapply caulking along exterior trim if necessary.

◆ Prune back shrubs and tree branches from house and windows.

◆ Have chimneys and flues inspected and cleaned as necessary.

◆ Roll out the refrigerator and vacuum the coils.

◆ Have the furnace inspected and cleaned.

◆ Change batteries in your smoke detectors. Check fire extinguishers and make sure they're charged.

◆ Check roof for leaks, both outside and in. Use a flashlight on a rainy day in the attic to look for drips or water marks. Use a pair of binoculars to observe the roof from outside. If necessary, replace missing roofing material or have it done by an expert.

◆ Touch up interior and exterior paint.

◆ In cold climates, before winter sets in, drain outdoor plumbing and store hoses.

I schedule my longer-range chores into my planner/organizer and assign months for seasonal tasks. That way I'm less likely to forget or put them off.

As you're doing your regular chores (daily, weekly, monthly, or whatever), be sure to jot down bigger projects on your Master To-Do List in your planner/organizer, so you can schedule them later.

Clean from the outside in and from the top of a room to the bottom. As you clean, keep your basic organization principles in mind, such as "group like objects together" and "store it nearest to where you use it."

Orderly Pursuits

A wealth of information and even some services may be available from your local government cooperative or agricultural extension service. Check your phone book under "Cooperative or Agricultural Extension" in the state or county pages, or check with county offices or your state university system.

Remember that keeping up is much easier than catching up. Do a little each day and clean up messes when you make them.

Organize the Stuff You Clean With

Where do you keep your cleaning supplies? Under the sink? In the broom closet? In the garage? In the basement? All over the place? Bet you have lots of goo and gunk in there you haven't used for years!

It sure is a lot more pleasant to tackle the unpleasant job of cleaning when you don't have to fight with mops, brooms, bottles, and pails just to get started. So, let's unstuff your cleaning stuff!

The first step is to bring all your cleaning supplies and tools from hither and yon, so you can see what you have. Pare down to only what you need and nothing more (if you're not sure, refer back to the section on cleaning earlier in this chapter). Get rid of duplicates. Consolidate wherever possible.

A broom closet is a wonderful thing to have, but many homes aren't built to include one. Perhaps there's a coat closet or other storage area that can be outfitted as one. You can also create a broom or "cleaning" closet by buying one of those free-standing cabinets made out of heavy plastic, laminated fiberboard, or wood. Just make sure it's sturdy and has room for everything you need to store. It helps if there are hooks or brackets to hang the mop, broom, dust brush, and whatever other tools you can get up off the shelves. Check to see if there's enough room for the vacuum cleaner, as well. Hang the hoses, and put the attachments in a bag and hang that.

Keep your supplies near the places you clean the most. Mine are located near the kitchen and family room, since those are the busiest areas. Supplies are in boxes, grouped for specific tasks, and the most used ones are in a caddie that can be carted from room to room. If your house or apartment has more than one story, it may be helpful to duplicate some commonly used cleaning supplies, like window cleaner, all-purpose cleanser, and sponges, so you don't have to carry them up and down stairs. They could be stored under the sink in a bathroom in a bucket or caddie. Just keep the duplication of supplies to a bare minimum, for clutter's sake!

Lovely Linens

An often-neglected area of most houses is the linen closet. Towels get pulled out, fitted sheets don't fit, and cloth napkins get lost in the corners somewhere. First, pull everything out of your linen closet and sort. Take out any holiday linens and put them in a pile. Then separate seasonal linens, like winter flannel sheets, from regular sheets and pillow cases.

In our house, since we have beds of three sizes—king, double, and twin—I further sort according to size. I also sort towels by size— washcloths, hand towels, and bath towels. Keep napkins together. Fold tablecloths or hang (a towel rack or two on the back of the linen closet door works nicely for this).

Add a sachet to each shelf and your linens will be easy to find *and* smell nice!

Oops!

Avoid putting bathroom and personal care products in the linen closet. If they fall over and leak, you could have a real mess and stained linens. If you *must* keep these items with your linens, make sure they occupy their own shelf or group them together in a plastic leak-proof container.

Do You Feng Shui?

Sometimes I like to consider whether the placement of furniture and other things in my home has any meaning, or any effect on how we feel. I notice that when I re-arrange things, certain floor plans seem to work better than others. This is usually because of creating better traffic flow, allowing light to work in the room better, or simply placing things in a more convenient pattern. But there may be more subtle reasons why one arrangement seems to be more pleasing than another.

The ancient Chinese art of Feng Shui (pronounced *fung shway*) has recently taken the West by storm. Meaning (literally) Wind-Water, Feng Shui tells us to pay attention to the energy in a home, as well as the physical stuff in it. Feng Shui is founded on the principle that all things are alive and connected, therefore emitting energy, called ch'i. Feng Shui practitioners consider a building's relationship with the environment surrounding it, the building itself, how people interact with the structure, and how time affects all of these. It's about understanding the relationships between nature and ourselves so we can live in harmony with our environment, rather than against it. In essence, Feng Shui postulates that what we surround ourselves with, we become.

As you unstuff and organize your shelter, your home, it might be fun to consider some of these things and strive for balance and harmony in your home decor. There are "rules" that practitioners of Feng Shui live by, and "cures" for existing conditions in a home that can't be changed. You may not want to apply anything that strict to your life, but I do believe there are some useful principles. Here are some for you to play with:

◆ Avoid sharp angles and favor rounded edges.

◆ Avoid too much light or too much darkness.

◆ Incorporate natural elements wherever possible.

◆ If things seem stagnant, change them. Move furniture. Change drapes and curtains. Put away some accessories and bring out new ones. Roll up the rugs or add some new ones.

◆ Pay attention to the artwork on your walls and the messages or feelings it sends.

◆ Use some warm colors in every room to represent the element of fire. Use red, but use it sparingly. Use candles or light a fire in a room to invoke the element.

◆ Bring running water into the house in the form of a fish tank or fountain. Both the sound and the appearance of water has a calming effect. But don't let your leaky faucets drain away your wealth or health. These, according to the rules of Feng Shui, must be fixed immediately!

Orderly Pursuits

If you'd like to know more about Feng Shui, you might like to read further with: *The Western Guide to Feng Shui: Creating Balance, Harmony, and Prosperity in Your Environment* by Terah Kathryn Collins; and *The Complete Idiot's Guide to Feng Shui* by Elizabeth Moran and Val Biktashev.

◆ Consider adding plants, but use round-leafed plants for a softer feeling.

◆ Add sound through the use of wind chimes. In order to hear them, you may have to buy your teenager a set of earphones for his stereo!

◆ Eliminate clutter as much as possible. This blocks the flow of positive energy in a room.

◆ Don't locate your desk so you sit with your back to the door. This creates nervous energy, negative ch'i. Similarly, locate the bed so you can see someone entering the bedroom.

Clearing the Decks for Safety

How safe is your home? If you haven't done a safety check in the last year, go through your house, room by room, as you did in the beginning of this chapter, using the following checklist (you may want to photocopy it and take notes in the margins):

◆ Smoke detectors are installed (at least one on every floor) and batteries have been checked in the last 90 days. Batteries have been replaced in the last six months. Carbon monoxide detectors are installed where needed. The grillwork of your smoke detectors has been vacuumed regularly.

◆ A well-stocked first-aid kit is available and within easy reach. All items are in good condition and items used have been replaced.

◆ Emergency phone numbers for fire, police, ambulance, doctor, poison control center, and a helpful neighbor are on *every* phone. (Don't rely on the "memory" feature of your telephone. It may not operate in a power failure.) All family members know where the list is on each phone and understand when to call. Teach children when and how to use 911.

◆ There is a phone by the bed and at least one that is easily accessible from the floor in case of a fall or other emergency where you can't get up to reach a wall phone.

◆ Bathtubs and showers have nonskid mats or strips to prevent slipping. Grab bars are installed for anyone who might have trouble getting in and out of the bathtub or shower.

◆ Nightlights are plugged into key outlets to light the way to the bathroom or other important areas at night.

◆ Ground fault circuit interrupters (GFCI) are installed in the bathroom to prevent electric shock from small appliances. Small appliances are unplugged when not being used.

◆ Lamps or light switches are easily reached from each bed.

◆ Smoking in bed is never allowed in your home. All sources of fire (such as smoking materials, candles, heaters, and hot plates) are located away from beds, bedding, furniture, drapes, or other flammable materials.

◆ Safety precautions regarding electric blankets are observed, according to the manufacturer's instructions. (Don't tuck electric blankets in under mattress and avoid putting anything, including pets, on top of the blanket when in use. Use similar cautions with heating pads.)

◆ Electrical cords don't present a hazard to children or pets. All lamp, extension, and telephone cords are out of the flow of traffic. There is no furniture resting on cords, and none are under rugs or carpeting.

◆ All damaged or frayed cords have been replaced.

Oops!

Be sure that medicines and household products are stored properly, clearly labeled, and out of children's reach. If a child ingests any of these, call your regional poison control center immediately and follow their advice.

◆ Cords attached to walls or baseboards are attached safely, not with nails or staples that can damage cords and cause a fire or shock.

◆ All cords carry their proper load. (Check ratings labeled on the cord and appliances attached to it.)

◆ Electrical outlets and switches have been checked and none are warm or hot when touched. If any are unusually warm, remove all cords and call an electrician to check the wiring immediately.

◆ All light bulbs are the correct size and type for the application. Check ratings on lamps or fixtures.

◆ Lighting throughout the home is adequate to activities. Especially in the kitchen, there is bright enough light (either electrical or natural light) to see adequately, preventing cuts and burns. Areas where there is glare have been corrected by using frosted light bulbs and shades or globes. Glare from outside light is controlled through curtains and blinds.

◆ Fuse box or circuit-breaker box is easily accessible. If fuses are used, they are the correct size for the circuit.

◆ All rugs and runners are slip-resistant. If double-sided adhesive tape has been used to affix rugs, make sure to check to see if new tape needs to be applied. Check rubber backing, as well, which tends to deteriorate as it's washed.

◆ The hot water heater thermostat is set to 120°F or below.

Amazing Space
Always keep a sturdy stool around the house that's easy to grab. This way, you can make use of high storage space without making things inaccessible. And you won't be tempted to stand on chairs, boxes, or other unstable items to get something out of reach.

◆ All flammable and volatile materials are tightly capped and away from any ignition sources, such as heaters, furnaces, water heaters, stoves, or other appliances. Gasoline, kerosene, and other flammable liquids are stored out of your living area and are clearly labeled in nonglass safety containers.

◆ Small stoves and space heaters are located where they can't be toppled and away from furniture, drapes, and other flammable materials. Any three-pronged plug is being used in a three-pronged outlet.

◆ You have read and understand the installation and operating instructions for any kerosene, gas, or LP gas space heaters, use the correct fuel, and have provided proper ventilation.

◆ Wood-burning stoves and fireplaces are properly installed and maintained. All flammable materials are kept away. Check with the fire department if you're not sure your stove or fireplace has been installed according to code. Have a licensed professional clean the chimney regularly and make sure it's free of leaves or other debris.

◆ There is syrup of ipecac in your home, in case you are advised to induce vomiting.

◆ There are special child-resistant closures on drawers or cabinets containing potentially harmful substances. Don't forget to include cosmetics in this category. Do this even if you don't have children currently living in the home but have children who come to visit.

◆ There are no medicines or chemicals in containers normally used for food.

◆ When cooking, family members know to keep pot handles turned inward. If small children are around, use back burners.

◆ All dish towels, potholders, plastic utensils, or other flammable materials are kept away from the stove. Family members know that cooking with long, loose sleeves can be dangerous.

◆ Kitchen ventilation systems and exhaust fans are clean and operating properly.

◆ Swimming or wading pool has been properly enclosed and has an automatic "childproof" gate.

◆ Handrails along stairways are fastened securely and run the whole length of the flight of stairs.

Orderly Pursuits

Check the Internet for numerous specialized safety checklists for the elderly, infants, and children. Or contact local resources on parenting and aging, as well as your county cooperative extension office, and ask if they have brochures or flyers available on this subject.

◆ Stair treads that are worn have been replaced. Loose carpeting on stairs has been made secure. Smooth textures have been replaced with rough ones, including rough texture paint. All steps are the same height and size. If step edges are difficult to see, they have been painted white or bright yellow.

◆ Nothing is stored on steps, even temporarily.

◆ The house number is prominently displayed, not obscured by any trees or bushes, and can be easily seen from the street.

♦ You have devised an emergency exit plan and backup plan in case you and your family need to evacuate the house. You have chosen a place to meet outside your home, so you can be sure everyone has escaped. You've practiced the plan regularly.

♦ All passageways, stairs, hallways, and doors are clear and well lit.

This is by no means a complete list, but it's a general guide. If you have elderly people, babies, or small children in your home, you'll need to take special precautions for their health and safety.

I recommend doing a home safety check at least once a year; twice is even better. This just means taking out your list and walking through the house to make sure everything's still safe and secure. A good time to do this is in the fall and in the spring. Put it on your calendar along with your regular maintenance chores.

Preparing for the Worst: Creating a Disaster Plan

Disasters come in many forms. They can be natural ones like hurricanes, floods, or earthquakes, or personal ones, such as the loss of a job, a disabling accident, or illness. Having a disaster plan, including food and water storage and alternative ways to heat and light your home, can make a big difference and may even ensure the survival of you and your family members.

> **CAUTION** **Oops!**
>
> It's easy to become complacent and to put off preparing for a disaster. Most people find it hard to imagine it can ever happen to them. Don't fall into this trap! Pretend that you know a disaster is coming and prepare as if it were real. Set a date and a time limit to have your basic preparations done. It may save your life or the life of someone you love!

What are the likely disasters you might encounter in your area? If you live in an earthquake area, your preparations will look different than if your greatest threat is a flood. Typical natural disasters are floods, tornadoes, severe storms, fires, and earthquakes. But other disasters, too, can require you to evacuate your home or to live without power or water for an extended period of time. These include hazardous materials accidents, aircraft, rail, or highway accidents, ruptured dams, or others too numerous to mention or predict.

Learn what types of disasters are most likely to happen in your area, and get information on how to specifically prepare for each one. Know what your community's warning signals sound like and what you should do if you hear them.

There's no risk in being prepared, and every risk in not being prepared. The Red Cross recommends keeping enough supplies to take care of yourself and your family for at least three days. Their checklist for a Disaster Supplies Kit (also known as the 72-hour kit) includes the following:

◆ A three-day supply of water and food that won't spoil. The rule of thumb for water is one gallon per person per day, more in hotter climates.

◆ A change of clothing and footwear for each person.

◆ A blanket or sleeping bag for each person.

◆ A first-aid kit, including prescription medications.

◆ Emergency tools, such as a battery-powered radio, flashlight, and plenty of extra batteries.

◆ An extra set of car keys, a credit card, and some cash or traveler's checks.

◆ Sanitation supplies.

◆ Special supplies for infants, children, elderly, or disabled family members.

◆ An extra pair of eyeglasses.

◆ Family documents kept in a waterproof container.

A smaller version of the above kit should be kept in each vehicle. Make sure you have made provisions for your pets, as well.

You should also know how to turn off the main electrical breaker to the house, turn off the water, and shut off the gas. Teach other family members how to do this, as well, and make sure any tools needed are kept near the gas and water shutoff valves. Turn off the gas only if you are told to do so or suspect that the lines are damaged, since it will take a professional to turn it back on. Keep fire extinguishers on each level of the home, and make sure everyone knows how to use them. Check to make sure they're still charged (there's usually a gauge that will tell you), and replace them or have them recharged when necessary.

Orderly Pursuits

For more detailed information on how to prepare for an emergency, request the free publications *Are You Ready? Your Family Disaster Supplies Kit* and *Emergency Food and Water Supplies* from the Federal Emergency Management Agency (FEMA), P.O. Box 70274, Washington, D.C. 20024. Or check out their website at www.fema.gov/fema/.

Have two places to meet that everyone in your family knows by heart: one just outside your house, to ensure everyone has evacuated in an emergency, and one outside your neighborhood, in case you can't return home. The Red Cross also recommends having an out-of-state friend or family member to be your "family contact." Each family member should "call in" to let him know where he is. Make up a card with this information, laminate it, and insist family members carry it in their wallets at all times.

Ask your workplace and your children's schools or day-care center if they have a disaster plan. Familiarize yourself with it. If you find out they don't have one, insist that they develop one right away.

Make sure your insurance coverage is adequate and up-to-date. Encourage family members to carry cards indicating their blood types and any known allergies. It's not a bad idea to have at least one family member who has taken a Red Cross first aid and CPR class.

Some agencies recommend having up to three months of food and water stored, in case of more severe emergencies. Again, there's no risk to doing this, and in the best case you are simply assured of extra food in the event you can't get out of the house to shop, you lose your job, or you suffer a temporary financial setback. Rotate your food and water so that it's replaced with fresh every six months.

The Least You Need to Know

- Assessing your existing home environment will help you organize further and minimize cleaning efforts. As you do your inventory, you can also make note of any special projects that need to be done or items you need to purchase.

- Using professional cleaning tools and supplies will simplify your housecleaning, save you money, and make you more effective.

- A cleaning calendar, broken up into daily, weekly, twice-weekly, monthly, quarterly, semiannual, and annual chores and added to your planner/organizer, will help ensure that you keep up.

- It's important to maintain your home inside and out to save yourself costly repairs and extra work. There are many sources for information on how to do simple home maintenance and repairs yourself.

- Organizing your home includes making sure it's safe and your family is prepared for emergencies.

Part 4

Money and All That Stuff

Money isn't everything, but when there isn't enough to pay the bills, it can certainly seem that way. And then there's the question of what's in store for the future, from as little as a year away when the IRS comes knocking, all the way to retirement.

The next two chapters will guide you through an organization plan for the financial side of your life. First, you'll take stock of where you are now and find out how to get control over your current finances. Then in Chapter 14, you'll prepare to meet the future with financial confidence.

Chapter 14

Winning the Money Wars: Guerrilla Budgeting

In This Chapter

◆ Assessing your current financial condition and preparing a realistic budget

◆ Repairing damaged credit and staying out of debt

◆ Getting help out of financial chaos

◆ Avoiding credit card fraud

◆ Surviving the holidays without plunging into debt

◆ Discovering the benefits of frugal living

Organizing your financial life is worthwhile both from a cost/benefit standpoint and as a boon to your sense of well-being and control. In fact, once you get your finances organized, many other areas of your life will seem to skyrocket to new heights overnight. I can't emphasize enough how important this is.

In this chapter, I'll take you through the first steps: taking stock, setting up a budget, cutting costs, and repairing credit. You may not need to do all of these, but if you're like many Americans, you've neglected most of them.

Afraid to find out the truth? Don't worry, there's help here even if you're in serious debt or have a compulsive spending problem.

Facing Facts About Finances

Let me ask you a question. What are your financial goals, and are you meeting them right now? If your answer is something like, "To be able to find the checkbook," then obviously it's time to take serious action. Whether you're dodging creditors and trying to stretch a paycheck, or wondering how you're going to put the kids through college, the first step is to find out where you are now and make a plan for where you want to be.

Budgeting Baby Steps

Here are the first steps you need to take to set up a budget:

♦ Gather together your monthly bills (*all* of them) and put them in a pile. Weed out any duplicates and be sure you have the very latest statements.

♦ On a piece of paper, write down each payee on a separate line with the amount owed next to it. Add up your total amount of debt. Don't just include minimum payments on your credit cards, but the entire balance. Include the entire balance of any loan you have, including a mortgage. If you're not sure of the balances on your loans, call the lender and find out.

♦ Write down any other debts not represented by your monthly bills (for example, a loan from a friend or family member).

Orderly Pursuits

If you're looking for a step-by-step financial management system that's integrated into your overall life organization plan, invest in the book *Your Money or Your Life: Transforming Your Relationship with Money and Achieving Financial Independence* by Joe Dominguez and Vicki Robin. This book can change your life!

♦ In another column, write down the amounts of the fixed bills again, but this time, only include the minimum payments on your credit cards and your regular monthly loan and mortgage payments. Add this column up. You should have now two figures, one representing your total debt and the other representing your debt for the current month. If you're behind on any payments, add those back payments to the second figure.

♦ Now add up all your assets, with one line for each item and the amount written next to it. Include bank account balances, cash, and any paychecks or other payments that haven't yet been deposited, plus any investments, CDs, savings bonds, IRAs, 401(k) plans, life insurance policies, and the like. Add to this the estimated current value of your home, cars, and any other major asset, like a boat, second home, or valuables. Do *not* include any future payments, such as bonuses or commissions that are not definite or that have not yet been earned. Look only at net income (after taxes), not gross.

◆ Do a second calculation of only your liquid assets—all cash you could easily lay your hands on without any penalties or fees.

◆ Do a third calculation, this time of your total yearly income. You can do a gross income statement or a net income statement. I prefer to use a gross figure and include in the budget all deductions that might come out of a paycheck (401[k], automatic savings, FICA, Social Security, etc.) in a budget. That way you see where all your money is coming from and where it's going. The gross income system would also work best if you're self-employed. Also include in your year's income statement any anticipated bonuses or commissions.

◆ Arrange to get a copy of your credit report. As we discussed in an earlier chapter, the three major credit bureaus are Equifax, Experian, and Trans Union. To order your credit report, contact them at:

Equifax; (800) 685-1111; www.econsumer.equifax.com

Experian, National Consumer Assistance Center; (888) 397-3742; www.experian.com/

TransUnion Corporation, P.O. Box 2000, Chester, PA 19022; (800) 888-4213; www.transunion.com

All three have online ordering capability. Just follow instructions on their websites.

Looking at your cash on hand and immediate monthly debt, you obviously need to have more in the plus column than the minus column. If that's not the case, then you need to look at some of your other assets and see what you can access to pay your bills for this month. If that's not possible, you somehow have to generate enough cash to cover your bills.

Oops!

While you are preparing a profile of your financial status, it is absolutely *key* not to withdraw and try to ignore the situation. As difficult as it may be to face reality, this is your chance to get valuable information and use it to improve your financial outlook.

Difficult Decisions

You *must* make an honest assessment of exactly where you are and find a way to work your way out of your immediate debt. If you're not standing on the financial precipice, you can skip this section and move on to the budgeting section. But if you're in a financial crisis, can you:

- Work a second job for a short time to get yourself on a more even keel, while at the same time reducing spending (with a clear budget you can follow)? Do you have a skill you can temporarily use to create some income?

- Sell something of value that will take care of the immediate crisis?

- Consolidate your debt into one payment at a lower interest rate? Make sure you can afford one lump payment a month as opposed to making smaller payments spread throughout the month.

- Declare a moratorium on spending (other than fixed expenses) until you get yourself on track? Try using up the food you have in the house, cutting out all entertainment (read a book), packing a lunch instead of eating out, and walking to work. Challenge yourself to be a tightwad.

- Is there any temporary assistance you might qualify for?

You know what has to be done if you have more bills than income. It's really pretty simple. You either need to increase your income or reduce your spending. And while we're on the subject of spending, what kind of spender are you?

- Do you continue spending on credit, even though you're unable to pay off your current credit card debt?

- Do you spend inordinate amounts of time shopping or thinking about shopping?

> **Amazing Space**
>
> While you are getting your finances in order, separate essential from nonessential expenses and see how many nonessentials you can do completely without— at least until you get yourself out of the woods.

- Do you shop to avoid pressure, to escape or fantasize, to increase your self-esteem, or to feel more secure?

- Do others regularly make comments about your excessive spending, or do you spend money you don't have on things you don't need?

If you answered yes to any of these questions, you may need some help. Go back to Chapter 4, for resources to help get control of your spending.

Back on Track: Creating a Household Budget

Once you're out of the fire and back in the frying pan, you need to figure out how you got into the heat in the first place. Go through your checkbook, your credit card statements, and any receipts you have, to gather a picture of what you've spent over the last few months. Include no fewer than three months; six would be even better.

What Are the Details?

Down the left side of a piece of lined paper, write out the following categories:

♦ **Housing,** which should be broken down into mortgage (or rent), maintenance, homeowner's insurance, and utilities.

♦ **Auto,** which should be broken down into car payments, maintenance, fuel, and auto insurance.

♦ **Medical and dental** (include each member of the family), with a separate category for medical expenses and insurance.

♦ **Clothing,** broken down for each member of the family, including dry-cleaning.

♦ **Food,** which includes both groceries and meals out. You should break these down separately.

♦ **Child care,** if applicable.

♦ **Education,** if applicable.

♦ **Interest** on credit cards and other debt, as well as regular monthly credit card and loan payments.

♦ **Life and disability insurance payments.** If these are already deducted from your paycheck, look at your pay stubs for the correct amounts and put them in the appropriate category.

♦ **Taxes,** including federal withholding, Social Security, and state income taxes. Make a separate category for real estate taxes.

Amazing Space
Keeping your finances simple cuts down on clutter and paperwork. Set up a financial center where you manage your other household affairs, keep bill-paying supplies and financial files handy, give yourself a comfortable chair, and turn on some soothing music. Make your weekly financial chores as pleasant as possible!

- ◆ **Entertainment,** including cable or satellite TV bills and video rentals.

- ◆ **Gifts,** including holidays.

- ◆ **Miscellaneous,** which might include cash expenditures like lunches, newspapers, cigarettes, and so on.

- ◆ **Charitable contributions.**

- ◆ **Savings,** including any automatically deducted 401(k) savings plans.

Across the top of the paper, put each month you're going to be calculating and draw lines down to make a grid. Now, write down the total you spent in each category during each month. Be consistent about putting expenses in the same category each time.

Now calculate the monthly average for these categories. In some categories you can make projections for the year simply by multiplying the average by the number of months left in the year. Some categories may need to be adjusted, however, for seasonal variation. For instance, you may find most of your "Gift" category spending is concentrated in the months before Christmas. So if you've calculated a six-month picture that includes the holiday months, you probably don't need to double that amount to get a 12-month projection. You might only need to add another third or less of that figure for the remaining six months of the year.

Add up all your expenses for a grand total, and as a final part of the process, compare your expenditures with your total income.

What Do the Details Tell You?

Where do you stand? Are there areas, such as food or entertainment, that are way out of whack? Are you paying higher mortgage or rent payments than you can afford? Are utility bills, especially phone bills, too high?

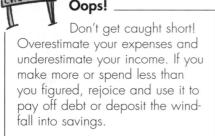

Oops!

Don't get caught short! Overestimate your expenses and underestimate your income. If you make more or spend less than you figured, rejoice and use it to pay off debt or deposit the windfall into savings.

If facing the facts means you can see that you're living too high on the hog for your income, you have some decisions to make. Again, it's a matter of stuff versus time. Some people would rather work more hours or find a better job so they can make more money and enjoy the lifestyle they want. Others would rather have more time to themselves and choose voluntary simplicity, either saving money for the things they want or simply doing without. But the facts are clear—you need to either cut expenses or increase income. Otherwise, you're headed for disaster.

In addition to the obvious areas where expenditures are too high, take a look at the less obvious areas where you can save money. Have you done some comparison shopping for insurance rates lately? Perhaps you can lower your monthly payments. Have you looked at mortgage or car loan rates lately? Would a refinance at a lower rate help your situation?

If you've done your assessment and realize you should have more money than you do, then you probably have a spending leak you're not aware of. The cure for this problem is to keep a spending diary for a few weeks. In your planner/organizer, write down every penny you spend, recording the date, what was bought, and how much was spent. Look for patterns and categories you may have missed.

From this exercise, you can now develop a budget. Transfer your categories to another sheet and transfer fixed expenses. Next, decide on cost control measures and come up with realistic figures you can adhere to each month for variable expenses, and put down those amounts on your budget sheet.

If after a couple of months you still can't seem to control your budget, make yourself stick to a cash system. If you haven't done so already, do away with all credit cards (you may want to consider a debit card, however, only for emergencies), and even stop using your checking account for a while. Put all money into a savings account and pay all your fixed expenses with cash or money orders. Whatever's left is what you have to live on. This takes discipline, but it can really help get you on the right track. If a cash system is the only way you can make ends meet, then stick to it for a while. In the meantime, you may want to take emotional stock, too. What is it about you and money, anyway?

This is your chance to figure out your relationship with money and get it right. You may find that when you begin organizing your life, you end up changing your life in deeper, more meaningful ways than you ever imagined.

> **Orderly Pursuits**
>
> If you're looking for ways to cut costs, join the ranks of the tightwads and frugal living advocates. Check out *Living More with Less* by Doris Janzen Longacre (Herald Press, 1980); and Mary Hunt's The Cheapskate Monthly at www.cheapskatemonthly.com.

Budget Review

In the beginning, it's probably a good idea to review your budget each month after you pay your bills (more often, if necessary). This holds you to a monthly standard, and you'll know immediately whether you're going over or under what you estimated. If you decided you needed to cut costs in certain areas, you'll see how your efforts have panned out—and if you succeeded, you'll be motivated to continue the trend.

Once you achieve some monthly financial discipline, I recommend building a quarterly review into your schedule. Make sure to put the date in your planner/organizer so you don't forget. It's a good idea to hold yourself accountable on a regular basis. You can correct any problems before they turn into disasters, and if you're ahead of the game, you can channel resources into savings and investments.

When you get out of debt and tame your financial tigers, you'll be amazed at the energy you'll regain and the extra time you'll have. The more you owe, the more enslaved you are, and the more time you spend trying to catch up. Free yourself of the burden and worry of debt.

Computer Finance Tactics

There are several good computer software programs designed to help you manage your finances. For more than 10 years I have used Quicken from Intuit, which is one of the most popular. The best packages are set up in checkbook format. You can either hand-write checks and simply record deposits and withdrawals in your computer, print checks directly from the program, or pay bills electronically online, using a modem and a telephone connection.

There are many benefits of using a computer program for managing your finances:

- ◆ Balancing the checkbook takes less time.

- ◆ All accounts are searchable and integrated, so you can find things faster when you need to track an item down.

- ◆ Online paying of bills is cheaper per transaction than the cost of a stamp and envelope, and it eliminates having to write a check.

- ◆ You can set up, modify, and monitor your budget, right in your computer program.

- ◆ Tracking investments is easier.

- ◆ Online banking, featured in the top programs, allows you to make funds transfers and get up-to-date balances without leaving home, any time of the night or day.

- ◆ When tax time rolls around, you can pull things together faster by assigning categories to all your transactions as you enter them.

Some additional features, depending on the program, are the ability to set up a debt reduction program, do mortgage comparisons, develop overall family financial plans, keep a home inventory, and get online stock quotes.

You do need to enter the information, however, and that takes time. The initial setup, where you enter all your financial information to get started, can take many hours, but the benefits in terms of knowing where your money goes and saving time in the long run makes the effort worth it. I suggest setting aside time once a week to enter your information so it doesn't pile up. Fridays are my time in the office to do paperwork, file, catch up on correspondence, and handle various odds and ends. I add to that paying the week's bills and entering my deposits and the checks I've written into my personal finance software.

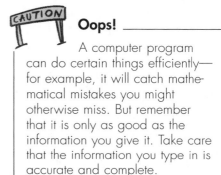

Oops!

A computer program can do certain things efficiently—for example, it will catch mathematical mistakes you might otherwise miss. But remember that it is only as good as the information you give it. Take care that the information you type in is accurate and complete.

Don't forget to back up periodically, as well. I do this on Fridays, along with all my other maintenance chores; but whenever you do it, do it *regularly*.

You'll need to decide whether or not using personal finance software is for you. Ask someone to give you a demonstration. Talk to people who use it, and get their feedback. If you decide to use a manual system, do just that—use a *system*, and use it faithfully. The important thing is to keep track of where your money goes and stick to your budget. Whatever tools best help you do that are the ones to use.

Don't Let Santa Blow Your Budget!

Every year when the holidays roll around, families brace themselves for the ensuing debt. And they often spend much of the following year climbing out. This doesn't have to be the case ever again, if you make a pact with yourself and your family *right now!*

The vast majority of families don't make a holiday budget. Without a plan, disaster is far more likely. When you make up your overall family budget, don't forget to include holiday spending.

There are at least two good strategies for handling holiday spending so that it doesn't put you into debt. One is to put a portion in savings just for the holidays each month, and use only that money when shopping time comes. This means *no* credit. What you've saved is what you can spend.

A second strategy is to budget a small amount for gift buying throughout the year and do your shopping a little at a time, taking advantage of sales and the less frenzied shopping environment. Catalogs and online stores can also help, and although shipping can add to the overall cost of the item, keeping you out of the stores may mean less money spent in the end.

Some families set up a gift exchange early in the year, drawing names so each family member only needs to shop for one person. The benefits are obvious—there's only one person to shop for, so you can get just the right gift, and the financial pressure is removed. Or you can set a cap on spending for each gift—not to exceed, say, $10. This can present a fun challenge, as each person tries to outdo the other for less. It also makes it easy to budget.

Or consider alternatives to traditional store-bought gifts. Make something instead. I like to make what I call "consumables," which are items that are used up and don't remain as clutter after the holidays. Food items, bath salts, potpourri, and homemade toiletries are a few suggestions. We also give holiday coupons, which entitle the bearer to any one of a number of services to be redeemed at a later date. These could be for baby-sitting, a massage, a car wash, a day running errands, preparing a meal, cleaning—use your imagination! Or how about a pair of tickets and your time? One year we gave contributions to a worthy cause in each relative's name. This works well for the people on your list who have *everything*. Throughout the year, they usually received a newsletter or regular updates, and nothing had to be returned because it was the wrong size or a duplicate!

Oops!

Beware of "pay later" or "skip a payment" offers from credit companies. The interest still accumulates, so read the fine print. The same warning applies to "checks" you may be sent in the mail. These are actually loan applications, often with very high interest rates.

Credit CPR

Even though you may now have a handle on your budget and you've got your expenses down, what do you do if you've ruined your credit?

There are some definite steps you can take to repair damaged credit. You've already taken the most important one—you've done an honest inventory of your financial situation, set up a budget, and begun to get yourself out of debt.

Here are the next basic steps for repairing your credit:

♦ Find out how bad it is. You should have already requested your credit report from the major credit reporting agencies mentioned earlier in this chapter. If you haven't, do it now. You can't see what has to be done until you know where you stand.

♦ Contact your local credit bureau, which is basically a credit reporting agency that may cover only a single state or county. If you're not sure whom to call, check your local Yellow Pages under Credit Reporting Agencies. Call them all.

♦ Look for any inaccuracies or missing accounts on your report once you receive it. You may request an investigation of anything that's incorrect or incomplete. You can also have out-of-date information removed by writing a letter to the credit reporting agency. You are also entitled to tell your side of the story in any credit dispute that is on your record by sending a letter to be added to your file.

♦ Make sure you follow up on any changes and request a copy of your updated file to make sure the changes were made.

♦ Reduce the number of credit cards you carry. One is usually enough. Two might be helpful if you own your own business, to keep expenses separate.

♦ Return all unwanted credit cards to the issuing company. Just cutting them up means they're still on your credit file. Ask the company to close the account and send you a letter of verification stating you requested the account be closed.

♦ Leave credit cards at home unless you're making a planned and budgeted purchase.

♦ Only charge items you're able to pay cash for. Remember to calculate into the cost the interest charges if you don't pay your credit card bill right away. Imagine what that interest money would earn you if it was invested at an 8 percent return. Investing $250 a month at that rate would grow to almost $600,000 in 35 years.

♦ Buy yourself a copy of Robin Leonard's *Money Troubles: Legal Strategies to Cope with Your Debts*, and read it!

Orderly Pursuits

Ordinarily you have to pay for copies of your credit reports. If you have recently been turned down for a loan or credit card, however, you can get a free copy from the agency that reported your credit, as long as you act quickly. Send the agency a copy of the credit denial letter with your written request to see your report.

◆ Make sure your credit file includes any positive account histories that might be missing. Try to build a positive credit history once you're financially healthy by borrowing small amounts using a secured credit card or bank passbook as collateral, or by finding a cosigner. Be diligent about making payments in full and on time.

How to Avoid Credit Fraud

Credit fraud costs everybody money, even if it never happens to you. Credit card companies cover the cost of fraud through higher fees and interest rates, and it's a growing problem.

Types of Credit Fraud

There are different kinds of credit fraud, some more easily detected than others. The most common is the lost or stolen credit card, which can be stopped simply by reporting the loss or theft to the issuing company. But some fraud can occur even when you have possession of your card. Criminals steal account numbers through a variety of methods, including telephone or Internet scams, looking over your shoulder and copying the information from your card when you're not looking, or "dumpster diving"—taking information from receipts or account statements you've thrown in the trash.

A more serious form of fraud is "identity theft," where a criminal uses your name and Social Security number to take over existing credit accounts and/or start new ones in your name.

Avoiding Fraud

How do you prevent this kind of fraud? Well, getting yourself organized as you have, following the steps in this chapter, will go a long way toward keeping you out of harm's way. You're more aware of what's happening with your accounts, you've gotten your credit reports, and you've cut down the number of credit cards you have. These are all steps to preventing credit fraud. Some other tips are:

◆ Treat your credit cards the same way you would cash.

◆ Don't carry your Social Security card, birth certificate, or passport with you on a regular basis. That way, if your purse or wallet is stolen, you'll minimize the information a criminal has.

- Sign your credit cards as soon as you get them. (As an added safeguard, next to your signature on your credit card write with a permanent maker "Ask for photo ID.")

- Know the billing dates of your credit cards and call the issuing company if the bill is late. It may mean someone has diverted your bill to a different address.

- Read your statements carefully each month and check for charges you didn't make. Report them immediately. Each month I enter my credit card purchases under individual categories in my finance software for tax purposes, so I'm on top of my statements and can detect any irregularities.

- Don't give anyone credit card or any other personal information over the phone or online, unless you initiated the communication.

- Get a shredder and use it. Shred all preapproved credit card offers, receipts, and any other documents that indicate your credit card number.

- Get a credit report once a year and check it for errors.

Another credit ploy to be avoided is so-called "credit doctors" or "credit repair" companies. They charge a fee for something you can easily do yourself, and some are actually conducting scams, promising to expunge negative but accurate credit information from your record (this is not legally possible). Instead, contact the National Foundation for Credit Counseling at (800) 388-2227 (or at their website at www.nfcc.org/), and get the name of the local member agency near you.

Tickler Files

"Through want of enterprise and faith men are where they are, buying and selling, and spending their lives like serfs."
—Henry David Thoreau

Frugal Living Is Fun!

Getting your financial life in order is crucial to organizing the rest of your life. You now know where you stand, you know where you're going, and you have a plan. One benefit to having a financial reckoning may be less noticeable. You may actually have embarked on a lifestyle change, a frugal way of living, and you may find you like it much better that way.

The frugal living/simple living movement (yes, I think we can call it a movement—just look at the number of websites and books on the subject!) is here to stay, and is a logical reaction to the "buy-more, do-more, enjoy-less" direction of much of today's consumerist society. As Joe Dominguez and Vicki Robin put it so well in their book *Your Money or Your Life:* "If you live for having it all, what you have is never enough. In an environment of more is better, 'enough' is like the horizon, always receding." So create financial freedom by living within your means and wanting what you have.

The Least You Need to Know

- To organize your finances, start by determining exactly what your assets and liabilities are.

- Designing a realistic budget will keep you on track.

- If your credit is damaged, you can take some simple steps to repair it on your own.

- Nonprofit agencies can help you with debt counseling or financial planning; beware of quick-fix "credit doctors."

- Debt elimination can be the beginning of a healthier (and happier) financial lifestyle.

Tax Tactics and Advanced Money Maneuvers

In This Chapter

- Getting a head start on April 15
- What records to keep and for how long
- Organizing your insurance information
- Preparing your will
- Tricks to organize yourself into saving
- Choosing a financial planner and accountant

If your tax, insurance, will, and investment records are in a jumble, you're playing a high-stakes procrastination game. As you saw in the previous chapter, a little sober reflection and a solid plan can get your household budget straightened out. In this chapter, you're going for the longer view and looking at your future; how well you prepare for it will determine whether it's rosy or not. You'll also put your affairs in order so if anything happens to you, the people you care about won't be burdened by any lack of preparation or disorganization on your part. Think of it as a gift, both to yourself and to those who survive you.

There are benefits to financial planning in the here and now, as well. Because you're on top of things, you'll be able to sleep well at night. Moreover, you'll have the information you need to take advantage of financial opportunities and adjust your plan if the winds of change dictate. The disorganized person doesn't know what's happening and leaves everything to luck or providence. You, of course, know better than that!

The Tax Man Cometh

Are you one of those people who files for an extension every year because you just can't get your records together or even face preparing your forms? Do you always have that nagging feeling you might have been able to pay less or get back more if you'd been more together?

Well, you're going to fix that right now. First of all, let's review a bit. In Chapter 6, we organized your household financial records. If you haven't done that already, *do it now!* This is the first step in getting ready for tax time, this year and in years to come. If you're thinking of buying a personal finance software program, do it now and take the time to enter your information.

Orderly Pursuits

If you're a computer maven, consider getting a program called Personal RecordKeeper, available for Windows or Macintosh from Nolo Pressat www.nolo.com. Personal RecordKeeper is a predesigned database program that tells you everything you need to keep and even where to store it!

It will take longer to prepare your tax return if your financial records are incomplete or scattered hither and yon. If you have a professional prepare your taxes, it'll cost you more, the more he has to pull together. So, I'll say it again: Get your regular financial files complete wherever your life management center is set up, and keep them up-to-date. Doing a little bit each week or month (however often you pay bills) will make tax preparation relatively simple. Now that you're on a budget, you should have an idea of what's ahead. When tax time arrives, it's a good time to evaluate your budget and see whether you're on target.

The Not-So-Tender Tax Traps

Here are some common mistakes taxpayers make that can be the indirect result of keeping poor records.

- ◆ **Forgetting or not budgeting for a tax-deferred retirement plan contribution.** According to the Institute of Certified Financial Planners, 34 percent of eligible workers don't participate in 401(k) plans offered at the workplace. If you're self-employed, you need to look into an individual retirement account (IRA) or a simplified employee pension (SEP) plan and see if you should make a contribution to one of these. If you're not sure, you may need to talk to a financial planner or accountant.

◆ **Having too much withholding deducted from your paycheck.** Why make a tax-free loan to the government when you could be saving or investing that money (or paying off your debt)? If you get a large refund each year, go to your employer and fill out a new W-4.

◆ **Overlooking deductions.** Again, this is where good records can save you money. Did you take all your medical deductions? How about mileage, phone calls, parking, and postage relating to charitable activities? The best way to find these hidden deductions is by going over your planner/organizer. If it's well-kept, it will be a record of your day-to-day life over the past year and will tell you where you went, whom you saw, and what phone calls you made.

 **Oops!**

Don't forget to claim deductions carried over from previous years. Have your previous years' tax returns handy and make sure you've included all losses, depreciations, and so on.

Tax Records Demystified

Once you've filed your return, what do you keep and what do you toss? Good question. Here's a simple list of what you should keep:

◆ Receipts for deductible expenses.

◆ Canceled checks for deductible expenses.

◆ Canceled checks for any estimated tax payments, if you're self-employed.

◆ Automobile mileage logs.

◆ Any other proof of deductible expenses, like your daily calendar sheets with notations of business appointments, and so on.

◆ W-2 forms.

◆ Interest income statements.

◆ Investment income statements.

Amazing Space
Instead of keeping canceled checks in a box, organized by month, you may find it handier to staple them to the invoices of deductible expenses.

- 1099 statements.

- Records of charitable contributions.

- Records of all medical expenses, as well as any medical insurance payments you may have received.

- Records of any other deductions, such as mortgage interest, real-estate taxes, or tax preparation fees.

- A copy of your annual tax-return form.

The only time I was audited, my detailed daily records proved my case. Keep your planner/organizer pages for the year with that year's tax information. They can help you recreate events in the event of an audit.

These items all go in whatever container you use to store each year's tax information. There are corrugated cardboard boxes available from mail-order office supply houses like Quill. (You can reach them at [800] 789-1331 or www.quillcorp.com.) I find the ones made for checks and vouchers to be just the right size to keep a year's worth of tax information, but you may need something bigger, or perhaps can manage with something more compact. Whatever you use, make sure the containers are uniform so they can be stacked easily. If you store your tax records in a location that's prone to dampness, use plastic containers that are tightly sealed. And, of course, *label them!*

Remember, tax time isn't just another excuse to start piling up all that *stuff* again! Use the same criteria you used for all your paper in Chapter 6. If it's a duplicate of information you have or could easily obtain elsewhere, if it isn't truly related to taxes, and you wouldn't need it in an audit, toss it!

These tossable items include:

Oops! _____

Don't rely on your memory! If you had anything unusual on a return, like a discrepancy between your declared income and the sum of your 1099 forms, write a note to include in that year's file box about how you came up with your calculations. You'll never remember three years down the road.

- Old bank statements. If your bank returns your canceled checks, you don't need to keep previous years' bank statements. If not, keep only those from the current year and six previous years.

- Loan books for loans you've already repaid.

- Tax-related receipts that are more than seven years old.

- Canceled checks for nontax-related items like food, spare cash, dry-cleaning, or haircuts.

Keep all your canceled checks, receipts, and paid bills until you've had a chance to tally them for the month and check the totals against your budget. If you do this each month, you'll have a handle on where the money's going and be able to decide quickly if you need to adjust your spending, bring in some more cash, or put some money in savings or investments.

How Long Is Long Enough?

How long do you keep your boxes full of tax information? The common wisdom is that you should keep your current year's return plus those from the six previous years. Generally speaking, the IRS can audit up to three years from your due date or the date you finally filed if you were late. However, if auditors suspect a problem with a return, they can go back six years.

Laws on tax audits vary from state to state, so you must also check with your local tax authorities. And, by the way, the "records" that you keep include electronic records, if you do your cash management or taxes on computer. I recommend keeping a backup disk off-site and updating it regularly.

Once you're clear on both federal and state requirements, go back and weed out the previous year's records so you have the essentials, transfer them all to uniform boxes, and label them. Get rid of anything older than six years, except the documents you should hold out and keep longer, which are listed next.

> **Amazing Space**
>
> Toss the oldest year's records when you store the newest ones. Just empty the oldest box, relabel (use pencil, so you can erase), and put in the newest information. You may, however, want to hang on to just the tax forms longer than six years. They take up little space and give you an ongoing record of your financial history.

And While You're at It: More Records to Keep

Besides backup information for taxes, there are additional financial records you should have files for and keep. These should be stored in your regular file cabinet, the one you have at your life management center, or at least somewhere you can easily get at them. First, there are medical records. Keep a file for each person for each year and put in receipts for treatment and prescriptions chronologically, as well as statements from the insurance company. At the very least, keep indefinitely a record of illnesses and injuries, and the doctors who treated them.

In files you store separate from your individual year's tax returns, you should keep:

◆ **Profit-and-loss statements,** if you own your own business. These you should probably keep indefinitely. You may need them to apply for a loan, analyze your business direction, or appraise the market value of your business should you decide to sell.

◆ **Personnel records.** Again, this one's for business owners. You need to keep employee records for seven years after an individual has left the company.

Orderly Pursuits

To get the skinny on what federal tax information to keep and how long, log onto www.irs.gov, then download the PDF file for IRS Publication number 552, "Recordkeeping for Individuals." It's *free and no long waits on the telephone!*

◆ **Payment records** for all equipment you depreciate on your return. You should keep these for seven years after the last return on which the equipment (such as a computer or fax machine) is listed.

◆ **Pension records.** Keep your 401(k), IRA, or SEP records in a separate file and hang onto them until you retire and are happily spending the money. Keep both the plan documents and the statements, at least the annual ones.

◆ **Investment records.** If you're investing money that's not tax-deferred in stocks or mutual funds, keep records of all your transactions so you can create a basis for those assets when you sell them. If your annual statement shows all your transactions for the past 12 months, you can keep that and toss the monthly or quarterly statements. If not, you need to keep them all.

◆ **Data about your home,** if you own one. This includes bills, canceled checks, and invoices for any improvements you make. When you sell, you can reduce the tax due on your profit by deducting the cost of permanent home improvements.

◆ **Receipts for high-ticket purchases** like expensive jewelry, antiques, and artwork. You may need these as proof of value in case they're lost or stolen and you need to file a claim. The best place for these might be with your Home Inventory file (we'll discuss this in the following section on insurance), in a separate Valuables file or, if you have a lot of valuables, in separate files by category.

Hard-to-replace original documents, such as birth certificates, cemetery deeds, marriage papers, and the like should be kept in a safety deposit box, but only if your state law doesn't require the box to be sealed upon the owner's death. In that case, you may want to consider keeping a fireproof safe on your own premises or having your lawyer keep them.

Get the Most from Your Insurance

Being disorganized can cost you money when you need to file insurance claims. When you did your budget, you may have found you were short on cash. Did you overlook unfiled medical insurance claims? If someone broke into your house, could you document what was taken and its value? Do you know whether your auto insurance covers a cracked windshield?

Setting Up

If you haven't already done it, set up files for each of the different types of insurance you have. For most people that'll be four files: Health, Auto, Life, and Homeowner's or Renter's insurance. If you're self-employed, you might need to add a file for business disability income and/or liability insurance.

Some people recommend storing life insurance policies in your safety deposit box. I think, however, that if they aren't stored in the home, they can easily be forgotten in case of emergency: out of sight, out of mind. Besides, you can get replacement copies of your policy from your insurance company, and if you have an emergency, you'll probably need it to refer to right away. If you have a fireproof box or safe, keep your policies there rather than in your safety deposit box.

I'd suggest putting your basic policy information for all of your types of insurance in your planner/organizer on one sheet. Include the type of insurance, the insurer, the policy number, deductible amount, agent information or number to call to make a claim, the dates the policy is in force, the key provisions of the policy, and anything you might find useful in an emergency.

Orderly Pursuits

For a comprehensive glossary of insurance terms, check out the list online at www.insure.com/glossary.cfm.

Always Read the Fine Print

Now, gather up your policies and read them. I don't want to hear all that moaning and groaning! This is for your own good. Just go through each policy and make some quick notes on what your coverage includes, plus any exceptions. How big a deductible do you have? Does your homeowner's policy cover water or wind damage? How about vandalism? If your home is completely destroyed, does your coverage provide for guaranteed replacement cost? Ask similar questions for your auto, health, and other insurance policies.

Be critical. Ask questions about what the policy says and means. Imagine different scenarios that could occur and whether you'd be covered. If you're confused and need something explained, call your insurance agent and go over the information until you're satisfied you understand it. You need to know what you have before you can evaluate it. Even if you decide you can't afford better coverage, at least you know where you stand, and you may want to plan on upgrading in the future.

If you haven't evaluated your insurance coverage lately, you'll want to make sure it meets your current needs. If there have been any substantial changes, like the birth of a child or a marriage, you'll need to revamp your coverage. Now that you know what you have, make a few phone calls and see if you can get better rates or better coverage for the same rate. Be sure to ask if you're entitled to any discounts. Some homeowner's policies have discounts for non-smokers and seniors. Health insurance discounts vary from company to company. Auto policies have discounts for safe drivers with no accidents or tickets over an extended period of time.

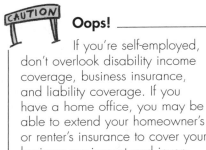

Oops!

If you're self-employed, don't overlook disability income coverage, business insurance, and liability coverage. If you have a home office, you may be able to extend your homeowner's or renter's insurance to cover your business equipment and inventory, but more often than not, you'll need a separate business policy.

Opinions vary on how much life insurance you should buy, and what kind. I'm not an insurance specialist, so I can't advise you. When you go over your total insurance situation, you should inform yourself about life insurance and assess whether or not you ought to carry it, how much, and what type.

Stake Your Claim!

The next thing you need to review is the claims procedure. Do you have all the forms you need? Do you have all the information you might need to make a claim? For homeowner's insurance claims, this means knowing what you have (or had before it was stolen or damaged). Aha! Now you understand why we talked about doing a home inventory in Chapter 13. If you haven't done it yet, put it on your schedule and do it as soon as possible.

Pull out your medical bills and see if you've neglected to file any claims. Find in your policy (or ask your agent) how far back you can make claims, and submit as far back as you're allowed. Even if you don't get any money back, you'll at least have everything applied toward your deductible for future medical expenses that you're entitled to. If your doctor or hospital doesn't file claims for you, make sure from now on that you place claims to be made in your Action/To-Do file, kept at your life management center. That way, you won't forget.

The basic message I'm trying to get across is: Know where you stand, take advantage of everything you're entitled to, and be prepared to document any future claims you could conceivably have to make. By having your insurance materials filed so you can find them, reading your policies, making any claims you've failed to make, and completing your home inventory, you'll have made the most important steps toward getting that part of your life organized.

Having a Will Gives You a Way

Experts estimate that 70 percent of Americans die with no will. So, let me ask you—do you have one? If your answer is no, chances are you have your reasons. Which one of these has the ring of truth for you?

- I'm too young.
- I don't own enough.
- Everyone knows who gets what.
- It costs too much.
- I don't have the time.
- It's hard to find a good lawyer.
- I don't like making these kinds of decisions.

Guess what? None of these excuses cuts it. As long as you're an adult and have some assets that would need to be divided up if you died, you need a will.

Be advised that if you don't have a will, the state decides what happens to your assets and belongings, and it may decide in a way you wouldn't want. By the way, if you're married, don't assume that everything goes to your spouse. It may end up being divided equally between your spouse and your children, and even your parents.

Orderly Pursuits

Good books and software programs available for writing your own will include *Nolo's Simple Will Book* and *Quick & Legal Will Book;* and Quicken Lawyer 2002, Personal Deluxe, (Nolo for Windows or Mac; call [800] 728-3555 or visit www.nolo. com).

Initial Considerations

In organizing your thoughts to write your will, you'll need to ask yourself some questions beforehand:

◆ What specific property do you have that you would like to go to certain individuals and who are they? If those people die before you do, would you like your bequest to go to their heirs, to someone else, or to an organization or charity?

This is another good reason to do your home inventory, as recommended in Chapter 13. You can refer to it now and select those items of value, monetary or sentimental, that you'd like specific people to have.

◆ Do you need to name a guardian to care for your children? If you have someone in mind, have you discussed it with him or her? Would that person also manage your children's money and property? If not, who would?

◆ Who will be the personal representative (called an *executor* in some states) for your estate? Have you discussed it with them?

◆ Are there any debts that would need to be paid off, and are there specific assets you would like used to make those payments?

◆ Are there assets your personal representative should use to pay off estate and inheritance taxes and probate expenses?

◆ Is there anyone (person or organization) you'd like to have whatever's left from your estate after specific instructions have been carried out?

These are just a few things you should think over (and discuss with your spouse, if you're married) before meeting with an estate lawyer or sitting down to write your own will. You may want to consider transferring property by means other than a will. This saves on probate fees and taxes. Some of these ways are:

◆ Gifts

◆ Living trusts

◆ Joint tenancy

◆ Pay-on-death bank accounts

◆ Marital trusts

◆ Life insurance

CAUTION

Oops!

Will-writing software, books, or kits may be adequate if your needs are simple. If you have considerable assets, children under the age of 18, or other special conditions, you should probably seek the advice of a lawyer who specializes in estate planning. It couldn't hurt to do a draft first, though.

You should discuss these options with a knowledgeable estate planner and find out whether any of them would benefit you in your current situation.

A word about where to store the original copy of your will. Some people recommend storing it in your safety deposit box, but that may be a problem if, as mentioned earlier, your state law requires your box to be sealed upon your death. Find out, and if your state does seal upon death, have your lawyer or a close member of the family or executor keep it.

Other Issues

While we're on the subject of wills, you might want to consider preparing a living will. This is another document that explains what you want done about life-prolonging medical care in the event you have a terminal illness and you can't speak for yourself. This can be coupled with a durable health care power of attorney, also known as a health care proxy, which gives someone you choose the ability to make all health care decisions for you. Together, these are called your advance directive. Laws concerning living wills vary from state to state, especially with regard to state proxy requirements, health care during pregnancy, and witnessing and notarizing requirements.

Another document you may want to prepare is a durable power of attorney, which gives someone you choose the power to make financial decisions for you in case you become mentally incapacitated. You can make this power fairly limited or very broad in scope. That's up to you.

When preparing your will, either by yourself or with an attorney, the question that should be uppermost in your mind is, what if? When dealing with money, be careful of giving fixed amounts. Rather, work with percentages. Who knows how much you'll be worth when you die?

Figure on reviewing your will every three years once you work it out. It probably wouldn't hurt to read it over once a year, when you do all your other year-end tasks such as taxes. You're less likely to forget if you make it part of a yearly ritual.

Orderly Pursuits

You can get help writing many of the documents referred to here by requesting a free form with instructions from Partnership for Caring. Call (800) 989-9455 for further information, or visit their website at www. partnershipforcaring.org. Their national office is at 1620 Eye Street NW, Suite 202, Washington, DC 20006.

Other times you'll want to review your will are:

- If you get married or remarried

- If you have a child

- Whenever your financial situation changes markedly, as in the case of an inheritance or winning the lottery (lucky you!)

- If you get a divorce

- If you retire

- If your spouse dies

Saving for a Rainy Day

Besides a will, you should give some thought to developing a general financial plan. You may feel you don't have enough assets right now to even think about such a thing, but as soon as you start to accumulate even a little in savings, you'll want to put those funds where they'll earn the highest returns. That immediately puts you in need of some financial planning.

There are plenty of reputable firms that can help you set up a plan, and you can start yourself on a simple stock investment plan. There are even investment clubs around the country (or online, for that matter) through which you can invest small amounts each month and learn about investing together. You can also join the National Association of Investors Corporation (NAIC) as an individual (most investment clubs belong to this organization as well) and learn all about investing in stocks on your own. Just call the NAIC at (877) 275-6242 for more information, or check out their website at www.better-investing.org/.

Whether you're working with a financial adviser or making investments on your own, you need to have both short-term and long-term goals clearly in mind. A short-term goal might be a vacation or a new car; more long-term goals are children's education and your retirement. Once you determine these, you can better choose investments that will help you achieve your goals.

Another factor to consider is your tolerance for risk. If you tend to be very conservative and tolerate very little risk, it may take you longer to reach your goals. This takes some soul-searching and an honest evaluation of your temperament. Usually a mixture of conservative and more aggressive investments is recommended.

Since you did a household budget in Chapter 14, you know where your money is going and how much you can realistically set aside for saving and investment. This should be done before you pay bills. Either have your savings automatically deducted from your paycheck or "pay yourself first," meaning write yourself a check and deposit it in your savings or investment account the very first thing. This becomes your "Do Not Touch" fund and can either help you make a major purchase down the road or protect you from a disaster.

The next step is making sure what you put away is earning money for you, not merely keeping pace with inflation or, worse, losing value over time. If you have an investment plan at work, you'll want to go over it with your financial adviser and compare it with what you can do on your own. You may be able to get a better rate of return on something other than what your company offers. Sometimes 401(k) or 403(b) savings plans allow (or require) you to make one or more investment choices within your account. You'll want to base these choices on sound fundamental principles and make sure they're compatible with your financial goals.

If you decide to work with a professional planner, you'll want to use his or her time to your best advantage. Having your financial records in order and your budget in place, as you've done in previous chapters, will help you do that. A good financial planner will help you put all of this into an overall plan for the future, and will review it with you annually.

Do You Need a Financial Planner?

How do you know if you need a financial planner? Well, if you're achieving your financial goals, have no money worries, are rarely confused about investing, and have plenty of time to manage your investments, you probably don't need one! Most of us don't fall into that category, however, including me. I tried planning my own finances for a while, but I decided later to hire Mike, a professional planner, and this was a good decision. Even if you *do* have time to manage your own investments, you still might want to consider a financial planner, if only to do a "tune-up" now and then, and to provide you with a second opinion on key decisions.

Studies show that, on average, people who work with a financial planner do considerably better than people who don't. I'm convinced! Since we started working with Mike six years ago, we've been able to move to a nicer home *and* increase our investment portfolio by well above average.

There are independent financial planners and those who work for financial services companies, and there are pros and cons to each. The independent isn't selling any particular product, so might be more objective in choosing investment vehicles for you. On the other hand, the planner who works for a financial services company has a lot of resources available that the independent might not. Mike works for one of the large corporations, but he frequently recommends investments outside his company's offerings. He wants us to make money. If *we* make money, *he* makes money.

A good financial planner analyzes how changes in financial conditions affect you personally. He or she understands your goals and knows how to diversify your investments to protect you from changing market conditions.

But how do you choose a financial planner? Here are some things to look for and ask about:

- ◆ Is the planner with a reputable company?

- ◆ Have you heard recommendations from others concerning his or her performance?

- ◆ What kind of background and credentials does the planner have? How long has he or she been in the business?

- ◆ What degrees, licenses, certificates, and registrations does the planner have?

- ◆ What services does the company provide?

- ◆ What is the overall financial management philosophy?

- ◆ What fees can you expect and what do you get for them?

- ◆ How often will your portfolio be reviewed?

Interview several financial planners and make your decision based on how they answer these questions and whether or not you feel comfortable with them. Mike is like a partner; he's someone we share our hopes, dreams, and fears with. We feel free to ask questions of him when we're confused. He listens and has the answers that make sense to us.

We liked the services Mike performed for us so much that we got referrals for planners from the same company for our children where they lived. The financial plan included helping them each put together a budget and evaluate their current job benefits. Some began while they were in debt and had no savings. Happily, none of them are still in that position today, and we believe working with a financial planner got them on the road to getting out of debt and starting to save and invest.

Do You Need an Accountant?

Whether or not you need an accountant is based on a different set of factors. If your tax returns are simple and you don't own your own business, you may be able to handle things yourself, or simply use a tax preparer. But if you feel your tax-related tasks are too complicated to handle on your own, hiring an accountant is probably the solution. And don't think of an accountant simply as a glorified tax preparer. Think of her as a tax planner as well. She is part of your financial planning team. And don't wait until just before taxes are due to hire an accountant. You'll need time to get to know each other and to devise a tax strategy for the future.

Besides tax planning and preparation, an accountant can help you evaluate and install accounting systems for a new business, help you decide on a structure for a new business, help improve profitability of an existing business, help get financing or restructure existing financing, give advice on mergers and acquisitions, design employee compensation and benefits plans, and make sure your business is in compliance with government regulations.

How do you choose an accountant? If you know little about accounting, you'll need someone who can get down to basics and explain things so you'll understand. Be aware that the more you can learn on your own and the more organized you are, the more money you'll save. Some things you'll want to know are:

- How much experience does she have? How about experience in your particular type of business? In your initial conversation, does she seem to understand *your* business? If you have a home-based business, how well does she understand the home office deduction?

- What billing procedures are used? Can you get an estimate?

- Will the accountant you're interviewing be doing the work, or will a staff member be doing it instead?

- Can you get a list of references? Are any of those references for businesses like yours or related to yours?

- Is the accountant willing to seek outside expert services, if necessary?

Even if you're not in your own business, you may want to consider an accountant, especially if you're managing an estate, own rental properties, or simply have fairly complicated finances. Your financial planner can help you decide if you need an accountant, as well.

The Least You Need to Know

◆ You'll save time and money by keeping accurate and complete financial records.

◆ Most tax-related documents should be saved for six years; some should be saved indefinitely.

◆ A thorough review of your insurance policies may mean found money, either in unfiled claims or by finding better coverage for less money.

◆ Keeping a summary of your insurance policies in your planner/organizer can be invaluable in an emergency.

◆ Everyone needs a will, even if it's a simple one you prepare yourself using will-preparation software or a published kit.

◆ It's never too early to think about financial planning and investing. There are many resources for investing intelligently on your own, but hiring a professional financial planner is also worth looking into.

Part 5

Getting People Involved

By now you might be experiencing some resistance or downright hostility from the people around you. After all, you've been a lovable slob all this time and people have gotten used to you that way. Now all of a sudden you're on this organization kick, and your family and co-workers might not know what to make of it.

Be patient. Help is on the way. In this section, you'll learn how to make your transition from messy to marvelous easier for the people around you, and maybe get them to be part of the team. You'll also learn when and how to call in the cavalry and get some outside help.

Chapter 16

Healing Trends: Organizing for Health and Fitness

In This Chapter

◆ Using your organizing skills to get and stay fit and healthy

◆ Making sure you don't forget doctor and dentist appointments

◆ Organizing health information to prepare for emergencies

◆ Simplifying insurance forms filing and getting your full medical tax deductions

◆ Providing time and space for your emotional and spiritual health

We've all heard the saying "If you don't have your health, you don't have anything." Well, it's true. Ask most anyone who's suffering from a chronic disease, and she'll tell you she'd give up anything to be healthy. So what's the most important thing we can do to stay "in the pink"? Use preventative medicine! Although there are some things we can't control or foresee, there's so much we can do to ensure our health and well-being. And now that you have some basic organization and time management skills under your belt, there's no excuse for putting your health on the back burner.

A Healthy Dose of Organization

"Can my health really benefit from being organized?" My answer is that your health *depends* on your being organized! I read somewhere that "if you're too busy to stay in shape, you're too busy," and I agree. How you manage your time, what you allow to take priority, and how much stress you have in your life could help determine how fit and healthy you are.

Not sure where you stand with regard to your health? Well, let's apply the basic principles and processes of organization to your health and see what happens.

Take Stock of Where You Are

Taking stock of your health is pretty easy. You know what to do. Step on the scale and consult a weight chart if you're not sure what you should weigh. If you know you need to lose weight, then admit it here and now. Get your blood pressure checked, and while you're at it, get a complete physical (throw in a visit to the eye doctor and the dentist, too, if it's been a while). Learn how to check your heart rate and what it should be (your doctor can help you with this, and you can find the information in any number of books on health and fitness). Decide whether you're getting enough sleep and eating the right foods. Take a look at the amount of exercise you're getting, and be honest about whether you're really taking care of your body. Look the truth in the eye!

 Oops!

Don't let your family be caught without the information they need in case of an emergency or when a question arises. Keep a good medical reference guide handy. There are several good ones available; one popular one is the *Harvard Medical School Family Health Guide* edited by Anthony L. Komaroff, M.D.

Set Realistic Goals

If your doctor tells you your blood pressure is high, then the goal is clear. You need to make whatever lifestyle changes are necessary to bring it down a little at a time. If you know you need to lose a few pounds, that's one of your goals. If you need to lose a lot of weight, take a manageable amount and make that your first goal. If you don't get enough exercise, then make building regular exercise into your daily life a priority. Write your goals down, and make them as specific as possible. Wherever possible, make them *measurable* so you can hold yourself accountable!

Decide on Actions to Achieve Your Goals

Actions are the things you're willing to do to get what you say you want. They reflect the big picture. If you need to bring your blood pressure down, for example, some of your actions might be: lose weight, get more exercise, and learn to manage stress. In the next stage you'll decide what steps you need to take to support those actions.

Divide Major Actions into Manageable Steps

Once you've figured out what major actions to take, wherever you can, subdivide activities into daily and weekly steps you can take right now. What changes do you need to make to meet your goals? How can you make those changes as satisfying and fun as possible?

If, for instance, you need to get more exercise, what activities really give you pleasure? Which ones are you most likely to stick with? Why decide you're going to take up running when it's martial arts you really enjoy? What kind of support would you need to lose weight? Would having a buddy or group to work with be the most enjoyable to you? If you're eating unhealthy snacks, what healthy foods could you substitute that you enjoy? Make one of your actions a purge of those unhealthy foods from your pantry, and add to your To-Do list a shopping trip to replace them with yummy and healthy goodies.

Put These Steps into Your Overall Plan

Write down in your planner/organizer the specific steps you've decided to take. Make appointments with yourself to exercise. Make an appointment at a future date to have your blood pressure rechecked. Make an appointment to attend the next weight-loss program meeting, if that's what you've determined you need. Or keep a daily food diary to get a handle on where you're spending unnecessary calories. Tell the people who care about you to be supportive and even "in your face" about your goals, if that's effective for you. Get whatever help you need. Commit to having what you say you want.

Orderly Pursuits

For a chart of healthy blood pressure ranges and information about the effects of high blood pressure, check the Patient Health First website sponsored by Aventis Pharmaceuticals at www. patienthealthfirst.com/sitemap. htm. To determine the ideal weight for your height, check out the Desirable Weights Chart prepared by Metropolitan Life Insurance Company at the Public Employees Health Program site. Find this downloadable PDF file at www.pehp.org/phc/ healthtracks/pdf/section6/ obese.pdf.

Evaluate Your Progress

Regularly measure your success. Take your physical measurements once a month to evaluate the effects of your weight-loss and/or exercise program. Get regular checkups if there's a medical problem you're working on. Check off on your calendar the times you exercised this week and for how long. Keep track of this information so you can chart your progress. Make a fanfare of doing this if it engages your spirit. Ritualize it—make it as big as you want to! Play the Olympic theme as you disrobe and step onto the scale. Put on the soundtrack from *Rocky* each time you take your measurements. Have a progress chart on the bathroom mirror or in your planner/organizer if you're too shy to publish the results just yet. I don't care! Whatever works! Have fun with it.

Reward Yourself and Move On

When you complete each step toward a goal, give yourself a pat on the back, but also give yourself a tangible reward. Consult your rewards list for ideas. If you haven't made one yet, do it now! Make sure you have both large- and small-scale rewards. Having a major reward in mind for when you reach your final goal is great, but you need smaller incentives to keep going. Buying a bottle of special bath oil to commemorate a 10-pound weight loss, or treating yourself to some new exercise clothes as a reward for sticking to your routine for a month, will spur you on to greater successes. Enjoy, then quickly pick a new goal and move forward.

If you believe you're fit and healthy, if you get regular exercise and have regular medical checkups with a "clean bill of health," then move on to the next topic in this book. But if you can't honestly say you fall in that category, if there's room for improvement, then get organized to support your new goals regarding your health.

Finding Time to Get Fit

One of the most common excuses offered for failing to get in shape is "I don't have the time." Well, you *know* you're not going to get away with that here! If you're committed to being fit and healthy, there are no valid excuses. Even with disabilities and various physical limitations, you can always do *something*. Something leads to more and more somethings, and pretty soon you're getting fit.

You've learned that the only reason to "get organized" is so you can have the things in your life that you most want. So, the first thing to do is evaluate your motives and honestly decide if you want a healthier lifestyle.

Sometimes all it takes is a new approach—some ideas for making it easier to create new habits. Here's a list of ideas to help you set up a healthier lifestyle. Take what most applies to the things you need to change, and add them to your master list in your planner/organizer, or schedule them *now*.

◆ Decide on the form of aerobic exercise you find most pleasurable, make sure the tools you need are functional and easily available, and schedule at least 30 minutes three times a week. For example: If you like using an exercise machine, put it next to your home office or in front of the TV. If you enjoy exercise tapes, make sure there's ample space to exercise by the TV, and store the tapes right next to it. Ease the way to sticking to your schedule.

◆ Consider joining a convenient gym or a nearby aerobics class. Perhaps you find you get a better workout when you do a class than when you're by yourself. If you know that you're more motivated exercising with others, then make that your priority. Some people find that taking a class gets them started, and then they can take off on their own. Plus, they get the added bonus of learning how to do the moves correctly.

◆ Get your bicycle, or any other equipment you plan to use for your fitness program, in tip-top shape. You've been going through the house sorting things into categories, including the *Fix It* category. Put your exercise equipment at the top of that list, if it needs repair. Make sure you have the necessary tools to begin and stick to your program, and put them in a convenient place.

◆ The form of aerobic exercise that most turns you on is the one you're most likely to stick to. Don't let the lack of clothing or functional equipment stop

> **Picture This**
>
> Close your eyes and visualize what a healthier you might look and feel like. What can you do in your fantasy that you can't do now? Notice what resistant feelings come up about it. What obstacles do you think you might have to surmount? Once you settle the issues with yourself and make a commitment, you'll find the time and the will.

Orderly Pursuits

Looking for exercise videos? The best catalog I've seen is from Collage Video. You can call them at (800) 433-6769, write to 5390 Main St. NE, Minneapolis, MN 55421, or visit their website at www.collagevideo.com. For everything imaginable to do with fitness and nutrition, check out the Internet Fitness Resource website at www.netsweat.com.

you. Consider used equipment if finances are tight. (Just make sure it's in good working order. You don't need another thing to fix.)

♦ Fitness can help you in your relationships, too. How? One way to find more time for someone you care about is to exercise together! Besides, when you have a fitness buddy, you're far more likely to stick to your plan.

♦ I'm the type of person who doesn't like to exercise unless I feel I'm accomplishing something. For me, bike riding, a self-defense class, yard work, or learning a sport or skill holds my interest better than exercising in front of the TV. If you're the same way, choose a lifetime pursuit that gives you that satisfied feeling and holds your interest.

♦ Don't overlook organizing for exercise at work. Would having an extra pair of walking shoes, a Walkman, and a fitness audio tape (or motivational tape or upbeat music) in your desk drawer make you more likely to go walking on your lunch hour? You bet it would!

♦ If you're avoiding exercise because you're not getting enough sleep and find yourself too tired, handle that problem first. Remove things from your bedroom that might distract you from sleeping. Reading, telephone conversations, and TV can be stimulating enough to keep you awake. Make your sleeping area a place conducive to sleep. Having it orderly and clean helps as well. Sleep needs vary from person to person, but a minimum of seven hours is usually best.

> **Amazing Space**
>
> Even people with super busy schedules can fit exercise into their routine. Walk or ride a bike to work. Walk to lunch. Take the stairs instead of the elevator. Park a good distance away from the office, allow some extra time, and walk. Use this same trick at shopping malls or any time you run errands.

Locate your phone and answering machine where they won't disturb your sleep. If you can't put them in another room, turn down the volume or turn off the ringing mechanism before retiring at night. Don't forget to turn it up in the morning!

♦ Before you begin any exercise program, you should consult a doctor. With your planner/organizer in hand, schedule doctor, dentist, eye doctor, and any other health-related appointments you've been putting off. Then decide on a yearly event to tie your visits to every year.

I find that scheduling appointments around my birthday ensures I never forget. If finances require you to spread them out over the year, picking special days of the year still isn't a bad idea. Be creative—like choosing the week of Valentine's Day to have your yearly physical and heart check.

- Check in with yourself regularly. Weigh yourself weekly or monthly. Take your measurements. Calculate your heart rate. Get a home blood pressure machine and take your blood pressure if that's something you need to watch. Take responsibility for your health, and give yourself the tools and information you need to track your progress.

- Decide on a food plan that's balanced and based on sound scientific research, and adapt it to your lifestyle. Consult your doctor first, if you're not sure which one to choose.

- Get rid of foods that don't support your eating program, and stock up on those that do. Purge your pantry, your refrigerator, and other places you store food. Make sure you include in your next shopping trip healthy snacks like fresh and dried fruits, low-fat microwave popcorn, raw veggies for dipping in a low-calorie dip, herb teas, and flavored mineral water or seltzer.

- Pull out the recipes (or find some new ones) that are in synch with your eating plan. Make up menus for a week or two using them. You'll be less tempted to go off your program if you already have meals planned. Make up batches of healthy soups, grains, and cut up veggies, so when you're hungry they're easy to fix in a hurry.

 Oops!

Do you have a tendency to forget doctor's appointments? Then take advantage of office reminders, if your doctor or dentist provides them. Ask to be called the day before. If you have computer software with an audible reminder feature, put it in there, too. Wherever you can build in redundancy, do it.

Amazing Space

When you reward yourself, try to make your reward something that won't sabotage your health objectives (*not* a hot fudge sundae, for example) and won't add clutter to your life. How about a self-nurturing experience instead, like a massage or a visit to a favorite place?

- Photocopy suggestions for healthy eating out at restaurants, and keep them in your planner/organizer, wallet, or purse. When you're looking at the menu and are overwhelmed with temptation, having a list might keep you in check.

- Reward yourself regularly for sticking to your eating and exercise program.

The simple principle I've been hammering home since we started—*the fundamental purpose of organizing is to support you in your goals*—can help you move toward a more healthy lifestyle. Use all the tricks you've learned so far, and make them work "to your health!"

Managing the Medical Morass

Are you deluged with receipts, insurance forms, and other medical records that never seem to be there when you need them? Do you neglect making insurance claims because the paperwork is just too much of a hassle? Let's tackle organizing your family's health next. Devoting one good weekend's worth of time is probably all you need to get this area "rosy."

Gathering Information

Keeping accurate medical records is an important part of taking care of the health of you and your family. I suggest having a family health center, where you keep a well-stocked first-aid kit, any prescription medicines (out of children's reach and locked up, if necessary), over-the-counter medications used most often, and a complete record of everything about your family's health. A three-ring binder works well for this. You can use sheet protectors to keep your pages clean. Set up dividers for each member of the family. Here are some of the lists you should have in your binder:

♦ Emergency contacts: doctor's names, specialties, and phone numbers, as well as phone numbers of relatives and friends you might call in an emergency.

♦ Prescribed medication being taken, categorized by family member. Include purpose, dose, instructions, counter-indications, doctor, and date prescribed.

Orderly Pursuits

If you want to use a pre-designed medical records book, consider *Healthmate Medical Planner: A Practical Guide for Taking Control of Your Health and Having Your Medical Records Always Available—Even When Your Doctor Isn't* by Kathleen Deremer; and *Your Child's Medical Journal: Keeping Track of Your Child's Personal Health History from Conception Through Adulthood* by Sharon Larsen.

♦ Over-the-counter medication taken regularly, categorized by family member.

♦ Any allergies to medication, foods, insects, and pollens.

♦ All diagnosed illnesses.

♦ Surgeries for each family member, including dates, doctor, and hospital where the surgery was performed. Include the same information for any hospitalizations.

♦ History of any pregnancies.

♦ Insurance information, including phone and ID numbers. Include a copy of your insurance form, which can be photocopied, if necessary.

◆ Blood work and x-rays. Include when and where they were taken and what type. Know and record everyone's blood type.

◆ The name of your preferred hospital along with emergency information.

◆ All your family doctors, including dentist and eye doctor, along with their address and phone number. Also list their specialty.

◆ A record of your last eye exam, along with a copy of your prescription if you wear glasses or contact lenses.

◆ A record of your last dental exam.

◆ Immunization records, including last flu shot, most recent tetanus, pneumonia, and hormone injections.

◆ Dates of childhood diseases for each member of the family.

◆ Family medical history. If you have a relative who has or had diabetes, epilepsy, stroke, heart disease, glaucoma, cancer, asthma, or a genetic disorder, include that in your family's history.

◆ Manuals and information on any special devices like a pacemaker or hearing aid.

If you don't have all of this information, make an effort to get it from the appropriate health care professionals. You may need to write some letters or make some phone calls if you've moved or changed doctors over the years. Do your best to fill in everything you can to give a complete medical history of each person in your family. If you kept a baby book for your children, some of the information may be there.

Update your family medical records each time you have an appointment. When you go on vacation, take your Family Medical Records binder with you, or at least have most of the significant information in your planner/organizer and take that. If you leave your kids with a baby-sitter or send your child off on vacation with another family, make it available to them. At least copy the child's information so the temporary caregiver knows everything he or she needs to know about your child's health in case of an emergency. Whenever you move or change doctors, having this information is invaluable for remembering the details you need to pass on to your new physician. In an emergency, when you're flustered or too ill to communicate well, having everything written down can mean the difference between life and death.

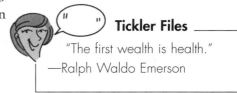

Tickler Files

"The first wealth is health."
—Ralph Waldo Emerson

Other Considerations

There are several computer programs on the market for keeping these records, but keeping your records in a simple database or word processing program will give you the ability to update them easily each time you or a family member makes a doctor or dentist visit. You'll want to have a scaled-down version of this information (the most pertinent in an emergency) in your planner/organizer and in each family member's wallet. You'll also want a current printout in your binder, regardless, so anyone can access this important lifesaving information.

If you're caring for someone with an acute illness, you'll want to have separate records to track the progress of the disease. A friend of mine provides home care for her husband who has multiple sclerosis. Her doctor keeps a copy of her reports each time they make a visit, because they're so thorough and helpful. I know she gets the highest quality care for her husband, because she's so involved in seeing to it that he gets it!

Look over your insurance forms carefully, and make sure you understand how to fill them out and where to send them. Keep them in the folder with your medical insurance information and bills. If you're not sure how the claims process works, make an appointment with your agent, and have him or her explain it to you until you understand. This is part of what they should do to earn their commission.

Orderly Pursuits

Health-Minder software for Windows is one program specially designed for tracking your family's medical records, plus your medical expenses, insurance claims, child growth and development, diet and exercise, and even pet health records. Visit their website at www.health-minder.com for all the information and a free trial offer.

To make the most of your health care professionals, it helps to be an informed consumer, just as you would strive to be in any other area of your life. Today there are many resources to help consumers be aware, including reference books and free online databases on prescription and over-the-counter medications, disease prevention, and general medical knowledge. Know the drugs you're taking and their side effects. Look up terminology, if you're not sure. Ask questions and do your homework. You're responsible for your own health and well-being, as well as your own health care.

Downtime/Recreation

Perhaps you're working too much overtime and never have time to play golf like you used to. Or maybe you love to read, but never have the time anymore. Or do you think about playing tennis, but whenever you have the time, your racket needs to be restrung, or even worse, you can't remember where it is? Maybe you need to get some new watercolor paints or dig out that sweater you started to knit and never finished. Besides tending to your physical health, you need to pay attention to your mental health as well. Play definitely helps keep us healthy!

By now you're getting the hang of this organization thing, so how do you see it fitting into this part of your life? Can you come up with your own list of actions to take to make sure you have the time, tools, and order you need to "play"?

To help you get started, here's my list of things you might do:

◆ Make a list of all the things you enjoy doing during your downtime. Number them, putting the one you find most pleasurable first and the rest in descending order.

◆ Make sure the equipment or tools you need to do the activities on your list are in good working order and are easily accessible (using the "keep-it-where-you-use-it" principle). If things need to be fixed or replaced, add that to your Master List, or even better, to your Daily To-Do List, and get it done right away.

◆ Call about court availability, class schedules, meeting times, or get whatever information you need so you can take action on your goals. Have the phone numbers in your planner/organizer if this is information you have to check on regularly.

◆ Schedule time this week to play. This one is its own reward!

◆ If competition is a form of play to you, sign up for a match, a race, a contest, or whatever. Prepare yourself, practice, compete, and enjoy it, whatever the results.

◆ If you would enjoy an activity with an important person in your life—a romantic partner or spouse, a child, a friend, a favorite family member—invite him along. If spending time alone is a priority, then do that. You know what you need!

Whatever you do, make sure you give yourself time to play regularly—every day, if you can. And be careful not to turn play into work. The end result should be an energized feeling, as well as a relaxed feeling. Funny, but they go hand in hand.

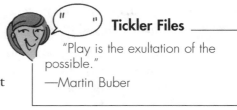

Tickler Files

"Play is the exultation of the possible."

—Martin Buber

Feeding the Soul

Next I want you to ask yourself this question: "How can I organize to support my spiritual goals?"

Now, *spiritual* means different things to different people. For you it may mean actually communicating with or studying about your God. It may mean certain kinds of reading, meditation, or simply communing with nature. It may mean attending organized religious services or simply creating your own "sacred space." Whatever it is for you, it needs to be part of the plan. If you don't include it, you won't organize for it. If you don't organize for it, you probably won't do it, and you'll be the lesser for it.

Organizing for the spiritual side of your life may be as simple as making a place for quiet contemplation, meditation, or study. It may mean scheduling some volunteer work or making time for gardening or music. These can be simply hobbies or, in a very real sense, "spiritual experiences," depending on how you feel about them and the place they hold in your life. Just keep your spiritual side in mind when you work your plan, and remember that if you're well nurtured in every aspect, the rest of your relationships, and indeed the rest of your life, will fall into place in a much more harmonious way.

Orderly Pursuits

If you'd like some creative ideas for setting up your own special place for worship, meditation, or simple contemplation, you'll enjoy *Altars Made Easy: A Complete Guide to Creating Your Own Sacred Space* by Peg Streep. To view your home as a sanctuary for your spirit and a place to renew your soul, read *Sacred Space: Clearing and Enhancing the Energy of Your Home* by Denise Linn.

The Least You Need to Know

◆ By including your health in your overall life plan, you'll be more likely to become and stay healthy.

◆ Organizing your home (and office) and having the right tools to support you in your health and fitness goals is another important step to achieving them.

◆ To make the most of the professionals who care for your health, and to protect yourself and your family in an emergency, having complete and organized family medical records is a must.

◆ Caring for your mental, emotional, and spiritual needs is just as important for your overall health as physical health care.

Chapter **17**

Nobody Said This Would Be Easy

In This Chapter

◆ Listening to what other people want and need

◆ Communicating your system to others

◆ Identifying problem areas and negotiating solutions

◆ Accepting limitations and resolving issues of control

What kind of reaction are you getting at home to the changes you're making? At work? How have you been behaving? Have you become an evangelical organizer, pointing out other people's lack of order? Are you keeping these changes to yourself, leaving everyone unable to figure out where you put things that aren't where they used to be? Are you beginning to see some chronic problems in your household or workplace that you didn't see before? Is there someone at home or at work whose habits conflict with your desire to get organized? Or, now that you're getting organized, do people suddenly want you to organize *them?*

If some of these challenges are cropping up, believe me, you're on the right track. It means you're making progress. Any time you move out of your comfort zone and start taking action, challenges will appear. You may even meet serious resistance. All that's as it should be. You may just need to stand back and take a longer view of your behavior right now and make some minor adjustments. Maybe you need to take some time to communicate, negotiate, and enlist the people in your life in your mission.

If They Don't Know, They Can't Do It

The most common mistake newly converted unstuffers and organizers make is to fail to explain to people what they're doing. In your enthusiasm, you may simply have overlooked this. Maybe you weren't sure you'd succeed. Or maybe you thought they'd laugh at you.

In the beginning, it may not be a bad idea to keep things to yourself. If you've attempted this many times before and failed, people just may not have the confidence that *this* time you mean it! No need to set yourself up to be undermined or criticized. But chances are, people have already noticed a change. They've watched you get on top of your paperwork, organize your time better, and keep your work flowing when it used to pile up. They see you managing things at home, getting control of your finances, and making plans for the future. Heck, your whole attitude has changed!

But they may not know *why* things have changed. They may not even trust the changes. They don't realize you've experienced a major shift in the way you see the world, a *paradigm shift*, and are committed to having your life be more directed, more effective, and more satisfying.

Oops!

Just because your new orderly, more goal-centered life brings you happiness doesn't mean that everyone shares the feeling. Pay attention to the reactions of others, keep the lines of communication open, and beware of the "zealot syndrome." Besides, other people learn best by example, not "preaching the gospel."

It is hoped you involved other people as you tackled individual organization projects outlined in this book. When you revamped the finances, you talked it over with your partner and your kids. If you found while taking stock that your financial picture was truly bleak, you called your creditors, explained that you intended to pay, and asked them to work with you. If you reorganized your filing system at work or changed the way you sorted your mail, you let your secretary or your boss know.

These are just basic courtesies, fundamental communication that goes a long way to having people in your court. If you haven't been communicating in these ways, start now.

For some, the change they see in you will be welcome. For others, it may not be. At one time I was a temporary office worker at an international corporation. As a long-term "temp," I had no ax to grind, no promotion or raise to seek; I was simply trying to make things work efficiently for my often-traveling boss, an executive vice president. I streamlined files, set up a better telephone-message system, and found that by computerizing some operations I could get through the work he left me in half the time it took the former secretary. Other secretaries in the department began to sabotage my efforts, and even pointedly told me to "cool it." Once I convinced them I wasn't angling for a full-time job and would keep the improvements to myself, I got a lot less flack, and I learned a lesson in team-building.

Change causes all sorts of discomfort for people, for a variety of reasons in a variety of ways. Some may resent change because they feel it points out their own failings. It may mean they have to learn something new or adjust to a new system, and they may resist. Don't worry about the reactions in other people. Expect them. Accept them. Be compassionate. And know that consistent behavior on your part can eventually change attitudes.

Listen Up!

Once you explain what you're trying to do, make sure you allow a lot of room for feedback. Hear what other people have to say. Be conscious of other people's needs. When I started to get serious about organizing our home and home businesses, my husband stood in the doorway of his home shop/office with arms outstretched and said, "You're not getting in here!" I heard him, and to this day I don't touch that room. That's his "inner sanctum," and he arranges it however he wants. (But I don't dust or vacuum there either. That's his job!) He was perfectly willing to make changes in the common areas of the house, and of course I could arrange my own office and affairs the way I wanted, but he needed some turf all his own that could be however he wanted it to be.

Listening doesn't mean patronizing. It means listening until you understand. It means giving someone your full attention. It means putting aside your point of view and fully experiencing another's. It means checking periodically to see if you understand what the person is saying and not injecting your own insights and information. It's so easy to say something like "I know exactly what you mean! Why, when I—" That's not listening—it's using what another person is trying to share with you as a springboard for talking about yourself.

At first, you might feel that making concessions to the needs of those around you reduces your efficiency. With more experience, however, you'll discover that by finding ways to integrate your needs with the needs of others, you're actually creating an environment that will sustain your unstuffed life.

Instead, after the person stops speaking, rephrase what you think you heard and ask if you understand correctly.

Some people talk about learning to compromise, but I prefer learning to *synergize*. This is a process where the sum of the parts is always greater than the whole. If you have worked it out that the laundry gets done on Tuesday and Friday nights, but the family just wants to collapse and watch TV on Friday night, then be with them Friday night and agree to do the laundry in the morning.

Work Within Your Sphere

Stephen Covey tells us to concentrate on our "Circle of Influence." The well-known Serenity Prayer suggests we ask for the wisdom to know the difference between what we can change and what we can't. The Beatles simply said, "Let it be."

The first place you can effect change is within yourself. Work with yourself and the things you have control over. Perhaps you were always late, unprepared, and constantly in an uproar, but now things have changed for the better. If you maintain these changes, making them habits, people will eventually come to trust them. Continue to work in the areas where you've begun to make strides. Remind yourself of your goals and work on your plan. Stick to the basic principles we've gone over. Continue to take small, regular steps toward fulfilling your mission in life. Use your new skills to improve your life and the lives of the people around you. People will most likely come around!

What About the Kids?

One of the greatest gifts you can give your kids is to teach them organization and time management skills. You'll help them excel in school, accomplish their career goals, manage their own households, flourish financially, and even get the most out of their relationships. The fact that you're taking steps to get your own life in order means you're developing the greatest teaching tool of all, your own example.

Very young children can learn to help out at home. Even babies seem to do better in an orderly home with something of a routine. Toddlers can learn to pick up their toys at night and adhere to a schedule. Standing on a chair, little ones can even "help" you do the dishes. You can set the table together. Not only are you teaching your child responsibility and the skills they need to get along in the world, these are also wonderful opportunities to teach things like vocabulary and concepts of space, time, temperature, size, texture, and more. Other skills they can learn are fine motor coordination and how to take direction and listen.

By labeling things in large printed letters, children can begin to learn to read. Silverware can be counted as they put it away.

This means working *with* the child. A task may take longer at first, but you're not only teaching, you're spending quality time with your child, becoming closer and sharing experiences. Don't expect too much, don't criticize, and don't push. Make it fun. By being inventive and making it enjoyable for your child, you'll have a better time yourself.

> **Amazing Space**
>
> Want your children to take the time to make their beds? Make it simple by using just a fitted bottom sheet and a comforter or sleeping bag. All they have to do is smooth the sheet, straighten the comforter, and fluff up the pillow, and they're done. Even a small child can manage this one!

Getting Kids Involved

Provide tools that make it easy for a child to help: a small broom or snow shovel, garden tools that fit a smaller hand, a stool, lower shelves, an apron or smock, and baskets or carts to haul things and put them away.

The older the child, the more he or she can grow in responsibility. If you have more than one child in your household, give each one chores according to his or her ability. And each child should be responsible to you, not to each other, since this causes friction—and besides, you're the one assigning the chores in the first place.

Have a family meeting to discuss how everybody can pitch in. Make sure everyone knows what's expected and how to do the job. As much as possible, let children choose their own method or process for accomplishing a task. See to it that the proper tools are available and easily reached. Make chores simple and clearly defined. Don't expect a child to work too long or with vague instructions.

We used to put a chart on the refrigerator door. When a chore was done, the girls got a gold star. Certain jobs everyone had to do for themselves. (Oh, by the way, Mommy was on the chart, too!) As much as possible, each girl got to choose the nonpersonal chores she liked best, and the rest were rotated. Some jobs were daily, like putting away toys, picking up clothes and putting them in the laundry bins, clearing the table, and so on. Other jobs were weekly, usually scheduled for Saturday mornings.

Periodically we changed the chart, adding chores or simply changing the way it looked. Gold stars turned into more long-term rewards, like going to see a movie or a special outing. Sometimes the system would start to break down and we'd have to work on it again, but mostly it worked.

Give lots of praise. Notice the little things. Put up a banner. Pin an "I'm Number One" button on a hard-working child for the day. Go on a picnic or a special day trip.

Expect that sometimes your child will resist or test the system. Stick to the rules, and be consistent. Allow some flexibility, but don't let the system break down. Deal with each instance individually. Be nurturing, but firm. If they don't do a job, don't do it for them. Be willing to follow through, even punishing if necessary. The deal I made with the girls was, "No TV until the chores are done." Sometimes, there was no TV.

Make sure there are spaces for things and those spaces are easy to reach. Label them, so nobody forgets where things belong. Choose organizers that just *beg* to be used. Make sure the kids have a large trash can to encourage throwing things out. Give them space for doing homework and keeping their papers. Teach them the basic principles of organization as you work together by grouping like things together, putting things closest to where they'll be used, labeling, alphabetizing, and even setting up a simple filing system with older children.

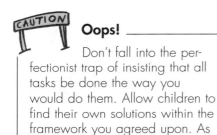

Oops!

Don't fall into the perfectionist trap of insisting that all tasks be done the way you would do them. Allow children to find their own solutions within the framework you agreed upon. As long as the results are there, heap on the praise!

If you work and run a household, you can't afford *not* to teach your kids how to help with the housework. They should, *at the very least*, be able to take care of their own toys, groom and dress themselves, make their beds, and keep their rooms clean.

Tips for Toys and Tasks

One way to make this easier for both of you is to "unstuff their stuff"! Pare down the number of toys, games, and clothes, and you'll be amazed how much easier it is to keep up. Besides giving you the necessary help, you're teaching them skills they'll find invaluable as adults.

It's sometimes difficult to get children to part with their "stuff." They're possessive (not unlike most adults), and it's difficult for them to see the benefits of paring down and getting organized. But once they have the experience of order, they tend to like it. To start them on the right road, here are some tips:

◆ Give children a place to keep their treasures, school papers, and artwork. Nice heavy cardboard chests are available just for that purpose, or you can use one of those plastic drawer units placed on a closet shelf. Make a deal that when it's full they need to go through it, weed it out, and make space for new things.

◆ Don't ask them to throw out toys they've lost interest in or outgrown; ask them to recycle them. Make them a part of giving toys to the less fortunate. Visit the hospital or shelter where their former valuables are going so they have a clear picture of the good they're doing.

◆ Make sorting and cleaning fun. Use the labeled boxes you made for your unstuffing. Have cleanup hats, aprons, and rubber gloves just for the occasion. Scale down tools like sponges, mops, and brooms so they can participate easily.

◆ Rotate toys periodically so that those of current interest are handy and those they're less enthusiastic about go in less-accessible storage. Agree that when the "old" ones come back out after a designated period of time, if the kids are still not interested in them, they go in the *Pass On* box and get recycled to charity.

Your Spouse Is Not Your Child—Really!

Beware of treating your spouse like one of your kids. He or she is your adult partner and deserves to be treated as such. If your partner seems to be sabotaging your efforts to get organized, you need to work out some control issues. Does he or she understand what you're trying to do? Have you consulted your partner before making changes? Was he or she a part of the important decisions?

You could say mine is a fairly traditional household. Most of the running of the household falls to me. My husband is perfectly willing to help, he just likes to be told what to do. He's not one to take it upon himself to see something that needs doing and just do it. There are good and bad parts to that. The bad part is that I'm responsible for seeing that everything gets done. That's also the good part. By being responsible, I'm also in control. It gets done my way, and I can organize things the way I want. I just need to remember to ask for help and I'll get it.

What's the situation in your household? Does your spouse like to be the organizer? Does he or she prefer to leave that to you? Is it more of a team effort? Can you split tasks by preference? Could you focus on certain problem areas? What changes would have the most immediate impact for both of you?

Don't forget to communicate clearly what's important to you. Make sure your spouse "gets" your commitment and understands your goals. Ask for cooperation and input.

Oops! _____

Your partner may be threatened by the changes you're making. He or she may be afraid of losing you or fear the relationship will change. Reassure your partner by doing special things to remind him or her how much you care. Remember, you're partners, not adversaries!

Orderly Pursuits _____

Collect in a folder all the things you need to talk to a team member about. Add a sheet of paper to jot down ideas, and share them on a regular basis, whether at meetings, through phone calls or memos, or whenever you're in contact. This will keep you from forgetting to discuss important points, or just remind you to say "well done!"

Your spouse may accept your offer, decline, or make a counteroffer. If he accepts, great! You've got a partner and the support you need. If he declines, respect that, but let him know you're going to work on the things within your control. If he has a different plan, you can synergize and still move forward.

What if your spouse is simply messy? Perhaps you can give the "offending" partner a place where he can be just that—as messy as he wants! The deal is, he keeps the mess confined to one area—preferably somewhere out of the way!

If you live with a packrat, the important thing is not to nag or take it personally. It's about him, not you, even if it sometimes seems like deliberate provocation. Recognize there's a deep psychological need at play here. It may be a need to feel thrifty and smart, or a need for security spawned by an emotionally and/or financially deprived childhood. It may be a sentimental attachment to the past due to events that you may not know about.

Don't attack; just be an example and express the good feelings you experience as you make your way toward order and simplicity in your own life. Try to help your partner fulfill these needs in other ways. And most of all, be patient.

Caution: Work Zone!

Handling challenges at work isn't so different from handling those at home. Sure, you can't tell a colleague to clean up his room or brush his teeth (too bad), but the basic principles of delegating (that's what you were doing at home, didn't you know?) are the same. Many people think of "delegating" as "sloughing off" or passing the buck. But if it's done right, it's more like building a team. At work, as at home, you have to work with the people around you, gain their cooperation, and depend on their input.

Here's a list of some basic steps to follow to delegate effectively:

◆ Meet regularly with the people you want as part of your team.

- Pay attention to the people you're working with. Make sure they hear you and understand what you expect from them. Leave *how* something gets done up to the individual. The more freedom they have to choose the method, the more they'll take ownership of the task.

- Identify resources. Make yourself one of them.

- Give a minimum of guidelines, but give advance warning of pitfalls.

- Agree on realistic deadlines and standards of performance. Have people evaluate *themselves* at the agreed-upon time.

- Be clear about what the rewards will be when the job is accomplished—and the consequences if it's not.

- Say "please" and "thank you." Pay attention to simple courtesy and manners.

Roommates and Other Strangers

When you decide to organize your life, sharing your space with someone who's not a family member or partner can pose some different challenges. I mean, when the two of you moved in together you were a slob, so what happened? Well, maybe the change hasn't been that dramatic, but still it's a change that you decided you wanted to make. But your roommate may be happy with things the way they were!

Again, communication is the key. Hopefully, you and your roommate respect each other's values, goals, and desires and can talk about your feelings. That's where to start. Just as you worked out how to handle visitors to the dorm room or apartment, who takes out the garbage, and how loud the music can be, you need to discuss your excitement about "getting organized." Recognize that this is a personal decision, something you've decided to do for yourself, and that your roommate may feel his or her level of organization is just fine.

Your roommate may want to work on this, too. But then again, maybe not. If that's the case, work on your own space, your own habits, your own life. And refrain from being critical or acting superior as you make strides toward your goals. Things will go more smoothly if you respect differences and let your progress speak for itself.

There will probably be areas where you'll need to make compromises, especially where you share space. Concentrate first on the areas that are yours exclusively, and slowly work on enlisting your roommate's help and enthusiasm about unstuffing and organizing common areas. You may also find that, although the other person doesn't want to get involved, they don't mind if you want to do the work! If it will make things better for you, then why not "just do it"?

Don't Take Yourself Too Seriously

Lighten up! Admit you've been a slob or a ditz or both, but you're trying to do better. Don't become an ogre or a taskmaster. I don't care whether someone is a professional organizer or just someone like me who works hard at being organized—none of us are perfect. The idea is not to become a machine enforcing a completely orderly world where every spill is eradicated immediately, there's never a dirty dish in the sink, no piece of paper ever lands on any surface for longer than half a second, and no hair is ever out of place. If that's being organized, I wouldn't want it either!

What you're aiming for is more time, less stress, streamlined methods for the "must-do" tasks, and doing more of the things you really want to do in life. If you get the basics handled, you can concentrate on the really good stuff! "Organized" does not mean "neat." Organized is not necessarily pretty. Organized is not spotless. Organized is a level of order that allows you to function efficiently and be in control. That level of order is different for each of us. The object is to notice what's going on, change what's not working, make and implement a plan, then reevaluate it periodically, adjusting it according to what you've learned.

Picture This

Go back and revisit the "ideal day" picture you created in Chapter 1. Knowing what you know now, imagine getting up in the morning in your newly organized bedroom; walking into your newly organized, pared-down, fully functioning closet; eating a leisurely breakfast with a quick cleanup in your newly organized kitchen; and climbing into your newly organized car.

Be more specific than you were the first time. Allow yourself to feel pleasure about the things you've accomplished. Make a mental note of things you'd still like to attend to. Pat yourself on the back. How does this picture differ from the first one?

I've made lots of suggestions to you so far. Some of them come from my own experience. Some of them were offered by others, I tried them, and they worked. Others I mentioned because I know they work for other people, although they've never been particularly useful to me. It's up to you to find the formula that works best for you. Muster up your creativity and come up with new ideas of your own. Remember, it's your starship and you're the captain! Make it so.

Keep in mind that, as we'll discuss in later chapters, what works at one stage of your life may need some major adjustments at others. When I was a single parent with two growing daughters, my life looked a lot different than it does now that I'm remarried, my children are grown, and my husband and I both have home-based businesses. Sticking to the old ways wouldn't make sense. The principles don't change, but the methods and practice do. If you remember this and apply the basic principles, you can't go wrong. Getting organized isn't "once and for all"—it's part of your life's work!

If You Organize It, They Will Come

One final thing to remember: When it all comes out in the wash (as my mother and grandmother used to say), the only person's behavior you can control is your own. You're the one who wanted to get organized! Just because you made this decision and are taking action doesn't mean anyone else has to. You can have many areas of your life the way you want them, even if other people aren't very cooperative. You're responsible for yourself. Don't use other people as an excuse for not following through.

Amazingly, if you just go along, doing your thing, making the improvements that you want to for yourself, other people may start to make changes, too. They may see how much happier you seem—how you seem to be getting more done and enjoying life more. They may actually be reaping the benefits of your newfound organization. Maybe you have more time for things they've been wanting to do with you. As with so many things, the key ingredient is *time*. Give yourself time for this new way of life to become a part of you. Give other people time to adjust to the changes you're making.

The Least You Need to Know

- If you want to gain cooperation and even useful ideas, *communicate*.

- Listening is an important part of communication. Give people your undivided attention when you listen, and don't try to inject your own experience or thoughts.

- Children need to be taught basic organization skills to succeed in life. You can play an important role in giving them the gift of these skills.

- Delegating well means you're building a team, rather than just someone passing the buck.

- People don't appreciate a "preacher" or "taskmaster." Having a sense of humor is extremely important, especially being able to laugh at yourself.

- In the end, the only person you can change is yourself. Accept people for what they are and go forward with your plan.

Chapter 18

Calling in the Cavalry: Hiring Others

In This Chapter

◆ When to consider hiring someone else to do a job

◆ How to hire the right people and keep them doing their best for you

◆ Pitfalls to avoid when hiring professional help

◆ Benefits of hiring a professional organizer and how to get the most out of the experience

There may come a time when you throw up your hands and say, "I quit!" Maybe you've organized yourself to the hilt and you still can't get caught up. Perhaps you've tried to get cooperation from others but somehow ended up doing everything yourself. Or maybe there are some tasks no one wants to do, ever!

Solving the problem may be as simple as picking up the phone and dialing "Dirtbusters," but before you do, here are a few things to consider.

When Do You Hire a Pro?

There are some instances when you should definitely consider calling in a professional, rather than trying to do it yourself:

- **When there's a disaster.** We once had a torrential rainstorm that separated a gutter pipe and caused water to wash into a window frame and behind the wall in our living room. It stained the wall and soaked the rug. This is an obvious instance when it's a bright idea to call a professional. Even though the damage didn't exceed the deductible on our homeowner's insurance, we didn't have the equipment or the expertise to do the job right.

  In a disaster, time is of the essence. You have to drop everything and tend to it or further damage could result. If you happen to be a professional carpet cleaner, plumber, or carpenter, by all means feel free to handle the disaster cleanup yourself. But if you're not, this kind of work is best left to the experienced professional. Get a few estimates and get the job done quickly.

- **When you get behind.** I'm all in favor of sending out the laundry or having a cleaning company come in occasionally to get caught up. The boon to your psyche is immediate. You're suddenly back on track and can start working your plan again. Seasonal shifts might also make hiring out a good idea. Some years I have an outside cleaning service come in and help with spring cleaning. If I've kept up with washing windows and cleaning carpets, grand! But sometimes I don't get to those jobs, and bringing someone in to handle them makes me feel (and the house look) like a million bucks.

Oops!

If you're behind on a regular basis, something's wrong. Look at how you spend your time, whether your methods are efficient, whether you have the proper tools, and whether you're expecting too much. You may need to hire someone on a regular basis if you have everything else covered. Analyze the situation and be honest about what's really going on.

If you own your own business and generally handle most of the paperwork yourself, fine. But if it starts to pile up, consider hiring someone to get yourself on solid ground again. Other chores you may occasionally want to consider hiring out are yard work, running errands, dog grooming, and home maintenance chores like cleaning gutters or raking leaves. Go over your Master List of things to do and decide which ones would have the greatest impact on your life if you paid someone else to do them. Then go back and see what your budget allows.

◆ **When you really don't know how to do it.** I'm not a plumber—never was, never will be. I have lots of better things to do and you probably do, too. Leave things you don't know how to do to the people who do. Measure, too, the time, effort, and money (tools are expensive!) it would take to learn how to do something, versus the cost of paying a professional who's already experienced and has the necessary tools.

There are also times when hiring a one-time consultant makes sense. If you're not particularly talented in the home decorating department, it may be worth it to hire an interior decorator to guide you. This can save you considerable money and time in the long run, as well as saving you from decorating mistakes that you would have to live with. A computer consultant can be another worthwhile investment. Paying an expert for a few hours of time can save you many hours of frustration and trial-and-error. Look again at your Master To-Do List and decide if there are areas where professional help might move things along.

◆ **When you just don't have the time.** Work schedules coupled with long commutes may make hiring someone to do regular cleaning and other chores a must if you're going to have time for family, friends, or other things you enjoy. It's a matter of time vs. money, and setting priorities. Some people find it's not worth it to spend their hard-earned money to pay someone else to do chores. For others, the time saved is worth the money spent.

Some possibilities: cleaning, laundry, landscaping and yard work, errands, gift-buying services, business paperwork, and household paperwork like filling out insurance forms. Figure out what you make an hour and compare this with the cost of having a task done by someone else. It may make economic sense to hire the task out.

◆ **When you're at an impasse.** My friend Marcia's husband, John, fancies himself a "do-it-yourselfer." He means well, but somehow things around the house just never get done. Secretly, I believe John wants to be rescued from himself, but he just won't call someone else to come in and do the job. His procrastination was driving Marcia up the wall until a friend said, "Why don't you just hire somebody to do it and see what happens?" It wasn't a matter of money. It seemed to be more a matter of pride.

> **Amazing Space**
>
> If you decide to get a regular weekly cleaning service, find one that will let you work along with them. Once a week, while they do the heavy jobs, you can do your weekly chores. At least use the opportunity to get some things put away so you can get the most from your cleaning service while they're there.

Well, Marcia called a carpenter and got all those little unfinished jobs done. John heaved a sigh of relief and said, "Gosh, it feels so good to have all that taken care of!" Now, when John suggests he'll do it himself, Marcia simply says, "Why don't I have someone come in and do it this time, and next time you can do it if you want to." John doesn't protest. It's a funny little game they play, but things get done and John still has his pride.

♦ **When a professional's advice will hold more weight than yours.** It's amazing how someone can come in from outside the office or the household and say the same thing you've said for years, and suddenly it's a "great idea." Don't throw a fit, just be glad it's finally sunk in—even if you don't get the credit. Professional organizers repeatedly relate this phenomenon to me. They may say something their client has heard a thousand times; somehow, though, because it comes from The Expert, it holds more weight. So what? It's results we're after, right?

A professional cleaning service can get away with things you'd never be able to. Try touching the stuff on top of your teenager's dresser and you'd get your head handed to you. When "the cleaning lady" does it, nobody complains; in fact, the kids may even put the stuff away *before* she comes!

♦ **When it's a job you (and everyone else) simply hate to do.** Let's face it. There are some things you just don't like doing. That's why you procrastinate. You know they need to be done, but you just can't find a way to make them palatable. Long before I met my husband, he used to do all his own automotive maintenance. At the time, he couldn't afford to have someone else change the oil or tune up the motor. On bitterly cold New England winter mornings, he would get up early and tinker with the car so he could get to work. He swore that when he became more successful he would never work on a car again. Since I've known him, he's been pretty much true to his word. It's perfectly okay to choose not to do something you hate and hire someone else to do it for you.

Orderly Pursuits

Look for free services to help you save time and get organized. Did you know that many large department stores have free wardrobe consultants? They'll tailor clothes to your size and color and style preferences. Ask about free home decorating consulting at furniture and home decor stores, too.

♦ **When you want to reward yourself.** Earlier I told you to make up a rewards list. Several things on my list involve hiring someone to do something for me. Maybe it's a manicure or a facial. I sometimes treat myself by taking the car to a car wash, rather than washing it in my driveway. For more money, you can have your car detailed, where they do all the little extras and even give it that "new car" smell!

Make a list of tasks you'd truly enjoy getting done for yourself, tasks you'd consider a reward. Add them to the rewards list you keep in your planner/organizer. Then give yourself a gift whenever you need a boost or want to say "well done!" This list can be helpful for thinking of gifts for others in your life, as well.

How to Hire Happily and Avoid Getting Ripped Off

One reason people put off hiring out certain jobs is they're afraid they might not pick the right professional to do it. There are a lot of unprofessional "professionals" out there who simply don't do a good job. How do you know you're getting the best one?

Here are five helpful hints for hiring anyone, from a key employee to the cleaning lady. Follow them, and 9 times out of 10 you'll hire the right person.

1. **Know the job you're hiring them for.** It helps if you actually know how to do the job you're hiring someone for. If you don't, the person you're hiring should be able to explain exactly what the job entails and how they're going to accomplish it. If they can't or won't explain it, go on to the next person.

2. **Do your research.** Check the Yellow Pages and get a list of the people in your area who specialize in a particular service. Then call your Better Business Bureau to see if they've had any complaints lodged against them. Ask people you know and trust for recommendations. Ask for references and check them out.

   This is such an obvious step, and yet people often ignore it and choose a professional without getting any background information.

3. **Interview the prospective "employee."** Before you offer someone the job, make sure you interview them. Make a list of questions before you call to make the appointment. Ask if they're bonded, if that's appropriate. Do they have the necessary licenses or insurance? How long have they been in business? What methods, equipment, or cleaning products do they use? What preparation will you have to do? Is there anything they won't do? Many smaller cleaning services do not do windows or carpet cleaning, for example. Do

Amazing Space
Besides emergency repairs, some of the most common services people hire others to do are housecleaning, gardening, carpet cleaning, window washing, pet grooming, laundry, cooking, home maintenance, personal shopping, gift-buying, reminder services, financial planning, and record-keeping. Which ones make the most sense for you?

you get the feeling they want your business, or are they put off by your questions? If they don't want your business, find someone who does.

4. **Communicate clearly the results you want.** Make sure you're on the same wavelength and that the job you need done is the job you hire to be done. Get a contract or letter of agreement if at all possible.

   Most cleaning services will want you to sign a contract at the outset. If yours doesn't, write a list of what you want done each week and give them a copy. Be sure to cover regular jobs and things you want done periodically, with a schedule for getting them done.

5. **Don't accept shoddy work.** Hold the professional accountable, and work with him until the job is done to your satisfaction. You have a right to get what you're paying for, so make sure you do. If necessary, withhold payment until the job is done properly. If, on the other hand, you're pleasantly surprised with more than you expected, let the person know, and perhaps even give him a bonus. Let him know you'll use him again and recommend him to your friends and neighbors. We all like to know when we've done well.

Don't Clean for the Cleaning Lady

When you hire someone, it's his job to perform the work. Let go. This can be especially hard if you hire out a job you've done yourself for a long time. Remember, you're the customer, and you're not entering a popularity contest.

Oops!

Don't hover over the cleaning staff. Be available to answer questions, of course, but don't stick your nose in where it's not needed. The next time the worker should see you is when the job is done and you're ready to evaluate it and hand over a check. If you don't trust someone to do the job right, why did you hire him in the first place?

If you called in a cleaning service because the house is dirty and you don't have time (or the desire) to clean it, they expect the house to be dirty. Let people do their job.

Do make sure you know what the cleaning service is specifically going to do, and how much you're paying for individual tasks. Ask what their routine tasks (basic fee) include. Usually, included in a basic cleaning are: dusting and polishing of furniture; dusting open shelves, ceiling fans, air vents, baseboards, window sills, and miniblinds; cleaning mirrors and picture glass, cleaning and towel drying of bathroom tile, shower doors, commodes, sinks, counter tops, and open shelves; cleaning the top, burners, and front of stove; cleaning the top, front, and sides of the refrigerator; damp mopping floors; and vacuuming all carpeted areas.

Don't assume, however! Most dissatisfaction comes from the customer not communicating properly what they expect, and the service not explaining clearly what their basic fee includes. Make a list, and check it before handing them the check.

Many tasks are usually not included in the basic deal, including cleaning inside the refrigerator, cleaning the oven and under the stove top, damp wiping baseboards, window sills, door facings, and frames, cleaning up the fireplace, oiling and polishing kitchen cabinets, and vacuuming or cleaning upholstered furniture. Of course, you can still get them done—for a price. If you want carpets cleaned, windows washed, floors stripped and waxed, and outside decks, porches, or furniture cleaned, you need to make this clear and find out what each task will cost.

If you decide you don't want to pay to have these specialized jobs done, doing some of them yourself either before or right after a commercial cleaning job will add value to what you've just had done. For instance, you may want to vacuum, shampoo, and rotate the cushions on upholstered furniture just before the cleaning service comes in and steam cleans the carpets. Schedule outside services at a time when you can make the most of them.

Maybe You Just Need to Move!

"Maybe you need to move." Shocking idea, isn't it? But don't dismiss it too quickly. Are you still living in a four-bedroom house even though the kids are grown? Do you have a lawn you hate to keep, and a big garden, even though you don't like gardening? Maybe you just need to wise up, dump the old homestead, and move to a place that's easier to take care of.

What kind of maintenance does your home require? Do you live in a climate that requires a lot of extra work to keep up a house? Do you have to live there? Could you move to a planned community or condominium where much of the outside work is done as part of the regular monthly fee? Give it some thought. It's not for everyone, but it could be for you.

Orderly Pursuits

If you're considering simplifying your yard work, hiring a landscaper might make sense, if only for a consultation on how you can change your yard from high-maintenance to easy care. For suggestions on how to reduce the work in your yard, consult *The Free-Spirited Garden: Gorgeous Gardens That Flourish Naturally* by Susan McClure. You'll know what you're talking about when you speak with the landscaper!

If not a move, how about making some changes to cut down the work? Aluminum siding and simpler landscaping might be just the ticket. Just getting rid of certain plants might cut your garden maintenance in half. When a neighbor of mine moved in, she had all the rosebushes torn out and replaced with low-maintenance shrubbery. Although she enjoyed roses, she wasn't willing to fertilize, prune, feed, spray, and clip them each year.

How about replacing plants that take a lot of care with native plants that are adapted to the environment you live in? These usually require less watering, fertilizing, and general care than plants that aren't naturally suited to a particular climate or soil. I've seen people replace a lawn with a field of wildflowers that doesn't need to be mowed, or simply let part of their property overgrow to merge back into the surrounding woodland. Simplify, and you'll save time (and money, too).

You're Hired, Kid

Should you hire your kids? This is a sticky question. Only you can tell if this is a worthwhile arrangement. First of all, I don't believe in paying kids for things they should do anyway. After all, they live there, too! However, if there are bigger jobs that older kids could handle and you want to offer to pay them, that's up to you. *Offer* is the operative word here. If they don't want to do it, then that's the end of it.

By the way, I don't consider mowing the lawn a job worthy of extra pay. If you give your children a regular allowance, fine, but I've never liked the idea of tying that allowance to specific jobs. The subject of an allowance is separate from the chores a child or teenager is expected to do to maintain the house.

Now, if we're talking major work like rototilling, washing windows, or digging a ditch, then compensation makes sense. And all the principles of good delegating apply!

The Benefits of Bartering

The barter system is ancient. Before we used currency, humans bartered or traded for everything. The concept has made a comeback in recent years, and it can be a creative, inexpensive way to get things done. For example, my husband is a leather craftsman. He paid for his last eye exam and pair of glasses with a beautifully hand-carved leather item, custom-made for our eye doctor. Not a single cent changed hands. For him, it was a matter of time and some inexpensive materials, but it reflected a skill the eye doctor doesn't have. In exchange, my husband received a service that requires a special skill. An even trade.

This may be an excellent solution in many areas. You can exchange child care for cleaning services, sewing for home repairs—whatever you can think of. Just make sure you exchange products or services of equal value. It's also advisable that you get an agreement in writing and work out the tax consequences.

It's common when bartering to trade for full value. So, even if you would normally give your friend Sue a discount on your hourly accounting fee, if you barter with her, swap your full amount for her full amount.

> **Oops!**
> Don't try to hide the dollar value of what you receive as part of a barter arrangement. You must report it as income on your federal income tax. Be sure you know what your state income tax requirements are, as well. Order IRS Publication number 525, "Taxable and Non-Taxable Income," for details on federal tax requirements at www.irs.gov.

When Do You Need a Professional to Organize You?

No matter how organized you are (or think you are), you can almost always benefit from at least a few hours with a professional organizer. Why? Because a professional organizer does this day in and day out. Believe me, they've seen just about everything, and they've solved problems in ways you and I haven't even dreamed of.

I see several good reasons for hiring a professional:

♦ **You can't solve a particular problem no matter what you do.** I already told you about my problem with missing papers and messages. I thought I'd tried everything, yet I overlooked two simple solutions that were inexpensive and easy to implement. My professional organizer solved the problem in a minute.

If you can, get the lion's share of the work done yourself and bring in a professional for the few things you just can't seem to get a handle on; that's the ideal situation.

♦ **You're almost a hopeless case.** Okay, you've read this book (and many others, I'd wager) and you just can't seem to get it together. You can always hire a professional to work with until you get your problem licked. This won't be cheap, mind you, but it may be the only way to go—you're desperate! A good professional will work with you on one area at a time—just like we did in this book. You'll get a list of things to do before the next session and then pick up where you left off. You can concentrate on one area or keep going until you've done it all. That depends on you and your pocketbook. Consider this "organization therapy."

Orderly Pursuits

To get in touch with the National Association of Professional Organizers (NAPO), call their Information and Referral Hotline at (512) 206-0151; fax them at (512) 454-3036; or write to P.O. Box 140647, Austin, TX 78714. Their website is www. napo.net/. NAPO publishes an annual membership directory and a brochure titled "What Is a Professional Organizer?"

♦ **You need to nudge others and haven't been able to do it yourself.** As mentioned earlier, sometimes people can take direction from an outsider better than from someone they know. You may see the problem clearly, but a professional will know all the tricks for getting cooperation and getting the job done. Besides, when someone's paying for the advice, sometimes they're more likely to use it!

♦ **You need a "jump-start."** If getting organized seems overwhelming and you aren't able to get going, a professional can be just the push you need. A professional organizer can sit down with you and help you break the whole up into manageable chunks, setting priorities and following up with you over time.

♦ **You need help to stay on track.** It could be you've done a mammoth job of unstuffing, organizing the heck out of your life, but things seem to be going back to the "old way." Maybe what you need is a periodic checkup! Share your goals with your professional organizer and ask to be called for a quarterly checkup session (or more often if needed). You and your organizer can refine your systems, pull you back to your goals and priorities when you get sidetracked, and set up better maintenance schedules.

♦ **You've experienced a major lifestyle change.** Perhaps you've gone out on your own and have moved your office into your home. Or maybe you've been a stay-at-home mother and have just reentered the workforce. Any time you experience a major lifestyle shift, organization systems that worked before may suddenly not fit anymore. A professional organizer can help you adapt and revamp for the way you live now.

How do you find a professional organizer? Follow the same procedures for hiring someone that I outlined earlier in this chapter. As a jumping-off point, I recommend contacting the National Association of Professional Organizers (NAPO). This is a nonprofit organization that has annual meetings for organization professionals where they exchange innovative ideas and solutions for problems. There are also many local chapters located around the country.

You can hire a professional organizer to help you with your home, your business, or both. Some specialize in one or the other, so be sure to ask. If you are computer-based, you'll probably want a professional with computer expertise.

Don't be afraid to ask about qualifications or experience. If you're doing some heavy-duty revamping of complicated business systems in your organization, you want someone with the ability to handle such an in-depth project.

> **Amazing Space**
>
> One effective way to use this book along with a professional organizer is to take one unstuffing/organization project I've outlined and tackle it yourself. If you feel you need additional help, bring in a professional to augment that particular project. You'll save money and get the best from your organizer!

Ask up front about pay schedules. Many organizers charge by the hour, but some charge by the project and will give you an estimate. They may even have a "frequent visitor's plan," whereby you get a discount for a longer-term arrangement. Be sure to ask about travel pay as well. This may be a considerable expense if your organizer is traveling some distance.

A good professional organizer will call after a session to see how you're coming along, and you'll probably want to schedule a checkup after you have a chance to work with the new system.

Another thing to ask about is whether you or your organizer will provide supplies. You'll have to pay for them either way, but your organizer may mark them up—or they may get them for you at a discount. Ask about his or her policy and compare prices.

Some professional organizers do a lot more than just organize you. Some have personal shopping services, where they get your sizes and shop for clothes, then bring them to your home where you try them on. You pay for what you keep, and your organizer returns the rest.

Others have gift-reminder and buying services. You give them information about birthdays, anniversaries, and anything else you want to be reminded of, and they'll even send a gift and a card for you at the appropriate time. This is too impersonal for my taste, but may be just what you've been looking for.

Still other professional organizers are image consultants. They work with businessmen and -women to improve their professional images, helping them choose clothing, accessories, hairstyle, and makeup to create the best impression. They may even work with people in the public eye and coach them on public speaking or for radio and television appearances.

There's no shame in admitting something is over your head or you just could use some help. Whether it's a specific task that a professional could remove from your To-Do list or an organization overhaul, weigh the pros and cons. Then farm out whatever your budget (and psyche) can handle.

Picture This

Close your eyes and imagine you had unlimited time and money to work with a professional to help you organize your life. What areas would you tackle that you haven't dared to so far? If you didn't have to do the work, what would give you the most pleasure to just snap your fingers and have it all "handled"? Can you take a piece of that fantasy, perhaps just one phase or step, and give it to a professional to help you with it?

The Least You Need to Know

- There are many reasons to bring in an outside service or expert to help you.

- If you follow some specific steps before making the final decision to hire someone, you'll maximize your chances of having a mutually beneficial experience.

- It's common for people to have trouble letting someone else do tasks they've normally done. Let the person do his job, then sit back and enjoy the results.

- You may not need to hire professionals to help with the work; you may simply need to cut back on the work. Moving into less demanding quarters or making some time- and work-saving home improvements could be a solution.

- Alternatives to hiring an outside contractor may be to hire your kids or to barter services.

- There are many benefits to hiring a professional organizer, and one of the best ways to use one is to do as much as you can on your own and then consult a professional for specific areas where you need help.

Part 6

Now That You're Organized, Let's Keep It That Way!

Congratulations! You've come a long way. You've got the essentials in your life unstuffed and organized. Now you need to know how to maintain your new systems, figure out how to fix them if they start breaking down, and be able to adjust what you've learned for your particular lifestyle and the different stages of your life. What works today may need some tweaking or even total revamping tomorrow. The next two chapters will address these issues and help you kick yourself up another notch.

Chapter 19

Minimum Maintenance

In This Chapter

- Strategies for keeping your life management machinery in optimum working order
- Moving to the next level and putting your life in high gear
- Avoiding pitfalls that cause backsliding
- Dealing with system breakdowns

Once you do the major reorganizing projects I've outlined in this book, all that's left is to maintain the systems you adapted for yourself and enjoy your newfound free time. The key to maintenance is simple—do a little each day, *every* day.

This chapter will help you solidify the progress you've made and look for ways to move to an even higher level. Don't panic if your efforts seem to erode or even come unraveled. You'll learn some practical ways to get back on track and keep it from happening in the future.

Here's the Bottom Line

We've covered a lot of ground together, so you may feel a little overwhelmed. Ask yourself, "Have I tried to do everything at once?"

If the answer is yes, stop! Take stock! There's an easy remedy: Remember my advice on setting priorities. Focus your time and resources on the areas that cause you the most grief, confusion, money, time, or stress. That's where the dividends will be the greatest. What's *your* bottom line? Do you desperately need to get your finances on an even keel or everything else will soon fall apart? Then do that first. Are your disorganization and inefficiency in certain areas causing real problems with your "significant other," housemates, or co-workers? Then working on those areas may be your first priority.

Decide on the basics that make your life work (or not), and do them no matter what. The basics for most people would be:

- Getting bills paid on time. Getting out of debt.

- Having the dishes done every day.

- Doing the weekly grocery shopping.

- Making sure you get adequate rest, nutrition, and exercise.

- Having your house tolerably clean, so you feel comfortable coming home to it.

- Doing the weekly wash.

- Getting to work on time and keeping up with your assignments.

- Keeping track of appointments.

- Maintaining your automobile (if that's your main mode of transportation).

Oops!

Taking care of yourself isn't for later. It's definitely a part of "minimum maintenance." Without the captain, the ship loses direction. Make sure you're part of the "bottom line."

The systems I've outlined for these areas should handle them for you in a hurry. Have in mind an absolute minimum level of order that you won't go below, and stick to it. That's your *bottom line*. You can always do better, but maintaining this bottom line organization will give you a good foundation on which to build.

Get Regular Tune-Ups for a Smoother Ride

Just like maintaining your automobile, maintaining your organization systems takes regular checkups and even periodic replacement of parts. Here are some regular maintenance tasks to keep everything humming:

- Add to your Master List the projects you didn't get to while you were working with this book. You've been concentrating on high-priority tasks and major life systems, but you probably came across tasks and projects you know need to get done at some time. Get them in front of you so you can schedule them for the future.

- Schedule regular maintenance days. Have a Closet-Maintenance Day, a File-Maintenance Day, a Car-Maintenance Day, a Food-and-Kitchen-Maintenance Day, and a Financial-Maintenance Day. If it only takes half a day, treat yourself to an afternoon off.

- Make up checklists for maintaining various areas of your life, and make copies. For example, a food and household supplies inventory list. Or how about a spring cleanup list for the outdoors? Why reinvent the wheel each time when you can save the time and energy for other things?

When you set out on your maintenance mission, look carefully at the new systems you've created and ask yourself these questions:

- How's my system working?

- If it's not working well, where and how is it breaking down?

- If it's working pretty well, is there anything I can do to improve it?

- Have I learned any new tips, methods, or ideas to try? Have I found any new storage solutions or organization products that might work better?

- Are there any ways I can streamline this system, make it more efficient, or save additional time?

- Is there any way I can make my system more aesthetically pleasing? For example, I have some cardboard organizers that I know do the trick. My next step is to find or make something more durable and nicer to look at. The idea is working, but I can still improve on the way it looks.

Amazing Space
New products are constantly being developed as more people take organizing their lives seriously. Browse hardware, business supply, crafts, and department stores for new, space-saving ideas. Write down the measurements of problem areas in your planner/organizer in case you see something that might work.

Making and keeping appointments with yourself for evaluating and planning is essential to maintaining your organization systems. If you pick a regular time slot, it will become a habit—something you actually look forward to. For me, planning time is Sunday evenings. I curl up with the three Cs (a cat, a comforter, and a cup of tea), get out my planner/organizer, and do everything from reminding myself of my mission statement, goals, and plans, to deciding on the week's menus and making out a shopping list. Find a time that works for you and make an enjoyable event of it.

Continue to reward yourself for the strides you're making. Praise yourself. You'll discover that the rewards of the changes themselves are self-reinforcing. Cooking in a kitchen that's efficient, orderly, and clean makes it more fun to cook. Opening the garage door and seeing everything in its place, in working order, and well-maintained is a reward in itself. Every time it takes me one step and five seconds to retrieve an account number or balance, I get this smug, self-satisfied grin on my face. It works that way—honest!

Taking It a Step Further

Here are some more "tune-up" ideas:

♦ Make a list of self-improvement or inspirational books to read, seminars you'd like to attend, or audio- or videotapes you'd like to purchase or borrow. Use them regularly. Reinforce your new habits and build on them by feeding your conscious and unconscious mind with positive messages.

♦ Set up a "brain trust" or resource network of positive, organized, motivated achievers. When you "unstuffed" your relationships, you eliminated those that dragged you down. Build new ones with people whose goals are to constantly improve themselves and make their lives and the lives of those around them better. Tap this network when you're looking for new ideas, and share ones you've found that work.

♦ Keep writing down your goals. In fact, try keeping a journal as well, so you can express your thoughts on your self-improvement journey and, later, look back and see how far you've come.

♦ Ask "Why not?" instead of "Why?"

♦ Continue to develop yourself and look for ways to contribute to the lives of other people. If you need something, give it away. In other words, if you need understanding, give understanding. If you need love, give love. There's more power in this than you may realize.

♦ If you're having a problem with something, study people who have solved the problem effectively. Find models for success.

♦ Meet regularly with the people in your life. Make sure you listen.

♦ If you find a system that works, see if you can apply it to some other area of your life. You may need to adapt it somewhat, but see if you can standardize it in some way.

Orderly Pursuits _____

Make a list of resources that you know you can count on, and keep it in your planner/organizer. Include companies that sell supplies you use most often and their toll-free numbers or websites; dependable people you can call to hire for various tasks; organized friends you can brainstorm with; books you refer to regularly. Whenever you're stumped or things don't seem to be working quite right, turn to your resource list for help.

If you pay attention every day to honing your life management skills, the results will be enormous. Organization and simplification give you a feeling of control and self-confidence. From there, you can accomplish anything.

Lists, Schedules, and Files Revisited

You're probably tired of hearing it, but I'm going to say these three things one more time. If you missed them before or they didn't sink in, now you have no excuse!

1. **Lists are your friends.** Your Master List is one of your most powerful tools. It keeps you from forgetting things you must do and helps you get in touch with your real desires. Lists hold you accountable, and they let you see all you accomplish as you check off the items. Eventually, some things will become automatic and you may not need a list (like your daily cleaning list, for example). But keep it handy in your planner/organizer anyway, so you can check up on yourself periodically and see if you're beginning to slide. If you are, you can use the checklist again for accountability.

2. **Schedule, schedule, schedule!** Make appointments to do things on your list. Make appointments with the key people in your life. Make appointments with yourself. Don't just put it on the list, set a time to *do it*.

 Tickler Files _____

"Our remedies oft in ourselves do lie, / which we ascribe to heaven."

—William Shakespeare

3. **Set up efficient files and purge them regularly.** A good filing system keeps the mounds of paper in your life moving. Once it's filed it's out of the way, and you can retrieve it when you need it. By purging regularly, you keep those files fresh and useful.

   If you haven't finished setting up or revamping your files, this should probably be a high priority. If they need purging, do it promptly. You'll create space and you'll be on top of what's there.

If Things Start Breaking Down

It's not unusual to experience some amount of breakdown, even if you worked hard to get things in order and you thought you had it licked. Don't despair, and don't pack it in. Just step back. Ask yourself, "What's happening here?"

You may be trying to do too much at once. Do one thing well and completely. Once you master that, move on to the next. Choose the problem area that came up during some of our visualization exercises and work on that first. You'll see an immediate impact.

> ### Picture This
>
> Review your day yesterday. Close your eyes and see it in as much detail as you can, exactly as it happened, from morning until you laid your head down at night. Where did problems come up? Is there a pattern? How could you have solved or prevented those problems with what you now know about organization? Write down what you discover, and set aside time this week to concentrate on these areas.

The area that kept coming up for me when I first committed to getting myself organized was our household finances and records. It loomed over me, aggravated me daily, and caused resentment. When I finally said, "Look, I'm going to make this work, and I'm going to make it as easy on myself as possible," things immediately got better.

I organized our financial files, got on a regular bill-paying schedule, computerized with financial management software and electronic bill-paying, rounded up all our back tax information and transferred it to uniform boxes, hired a financial planner to help me develop an investment plan, and set up a flow system for incoming bills, checks, and financial statements.

Concentrating on this one area had an enormous effect on my disposition, sense of control, and ability to lay my hands on anything financial in seconds; it actually made tasks I dreaded—like bill-paying—almost enjoyable. After my success in that one huge problem area (yours might be a totally different one), I was so charged with energy I was almost self-propelled. Choose what most annoys you or gets in your way. The rewards you'll experience will get you moving again.

Don't forget to delegate, either by getting people to take more responsibility at home or at work, or by hiring out some work. The latter solution may only be temporary, until you get organized in that area. Or you may find that you'd rather concentrate on other things, so it's worth it to pay someone else to do it. If things are breaking down, it may mean other people aren't pulling their weight.

Remember, it takes 21 days to make a habit. Are you giving yourself enough time? You may be expecting too much, too soon. You didn't get disorganized overnight, and it will take longer than one day to fix it.

Here are a few tricks I use to get back on track when things seem to be slipping:

- Make appointments that will force you to focus. If you're losing control of your finances, call up your financial planner to do a portfolio or budget review. If the house looks like a pig pen, make an appointment for a cleaning service to come in. You'll have to straighten up at least a little bit before the service can do their work.

- Entertain. Really, this works! Invite your mother-in-law or your boss (or just imagine you have). Imagine them going through every room in your house. Imagine them going through your closets, your files, your kitchen, your garage. If you're single, invite a date over. Before that special someone gets there, the floor and countertops will be clean enough to eat off of!

- Get an estimate for a cross-country move. When you get the estimated cost of moving all that junk, you'll start unstuffing your house like you wouldn't believe. Just imagine packing it all, too!

Oops!

When obstacles appear, you may be tempted to give up and go back to the old way. Resist the urge to abandon what you're doing altogether just because some of it isn't working right now. Rewrite the plan, don't scrap it!

Terminating Time Wasters, Overcoming Organization Ogres

If you're not getting where you want to be as fast as you expected, you may be the victim of one of these adversaries:

Falling into the television trap. Analyze your TV-watching habits. It's easy to mindlessly sit in front of the tube to "relax," but it will rob you of precious time with very little return. Choose your TV programs carefully and put them on your schedule. Don't just sit down in your easy chair and zap the remote. Use your VCR to record programs to watch *what* you want *when* you want.

Succumbing to interruptions. You may undermine yourself by allowing too many interruptions. Of course, not all interruptions can be avoided, but many can. Don't just accept them—control them. Set aside a period of time that you don't take any phone calls. Let the answering machine do its job. If people drop in, tell them you have an appointment (you do—with yourself) or that you're on a deadline and will see them when you're done.

Procrastinating. Do a procrastination checkup. Go back to Chapter 3 and review the section on procrastination. Keep giving yourself the message, "Do it now!"

Not having a plan. You may have done a great job of identifying your goals, but failed to work out a manageable plan, breaking things into smaller chunks and adding them to your schedule. Goal-setting is an important step, but it doesn't go far enough. Set aside time to plan, if that's what's hanging you up.

Reaccumulating stuff. Keeping your life from becoming overrun by "stuff" is an ongoing process. If your system worked great for a while and then started to bog down, you may have fallen into the acquisition trap again. Do a clutter inventory and pare down right away. Stop allowing junk to come into your life (including junk relationships), and get rid of what already has. Remember, too, if you buy something that's better than what you had, don't keep the old one.

Making things too complicated. Simple is better. You may have packed away umpteen widgets in neat little boxes with color-coded cards to tell you where everything is, cross-referenced and dated. The chances you'll keep up such a complicated system are slim. If you stick with the KISS system (Keep It Simple, Sweetie), it'll be less likely to break down.

Giving up too soon. If your system doesn't work the first time you try it, you may be tempted to scrap it entirely and give it up. Not so fast! It may just need some fine-tuning or some simple repetition to get it up and running.

Resting on your laurels. I said to reward yourself, but I didn't say you could stop there! Enjoy your successes, do something nice for yourself, and move on. Continually ask, "What's next?"

> **Amazing Space**
>
> Ask your friends and family to stop giving you stuff as gifts. Tell them you'd rather they spend time with you, contribute to a worthy cause in your name, or create an experience for you. Share with them how hard you've worked to unstuff your life and how much you're enjoying your newfound space.

Being too much of a perfectionist. Have you become an organization zealot? Are you spending too much time doing everything perfectly instead of just getting it done? Somewhere between a neatnik and a slob is a functional, comfortable level of order we can all strive for. You can always go back and do it better, if and when you have the time, but personally, I'd rather be out walking in the sunshine or spending time with my husband! Organization is a tool to master, not our master.

Failing to include yourself in your maintenance plan. If you leave yourself out, everything will break down. Make sure you renew yourself in the four basic areas: physical (exercise, rest, nutrition), mental (reading, learning, organizing, and planning), social/emotional (relationships), and spiritual (prayer, meditation, nature, creative expression). Make sure you include activities each week to fine-tune, maintain, and improve all four areas. Seek a balance.

Can Your Computer Keep You Organized?

If you have a home computer, you may be underestimating it as a tool to help you maintain your organization systems. One of the best ways a computer can help is as a reminder tool. There are plenty of software packages out there for scheduling appointments. Even if you don't use a program for your day-to-day ones, program it for major maintenance reminders. My organization software has the ability to create audio reminders. These are little alarms that sound when it's time to do something important. I use this feature to reinforce maintenance chores that may be easy to forget, like quarterly file purging, early tax preparation, or regular oil changes; I also use it for birthdays and anniversaries. Maybe this can work for you!

If a paper-based system you're currently using for some task doesn't seem to be working well, maybe there's a computer program that does it better. Stay on the lookout for any tools that might help keep you on track. There are new ways of accomplishing things via computer being developed all the time. You can now vote on stock proxies, buy and send gifts, track packages, look up phone numbers and addresses, send greeting cards, and even file your tax returns online. Many of these services are free. Why not take advantage of them?

Oops!

Computer-based solutions are not always the most time- or cost-efficient. They're also not always the most mobile or adaptable. Before you make a major changeover to a computer program, consider the low-tech solutions as well as the high-tech.

Some programs require some heavy setup—like recipe, personal record-keeping, or financial software—but once the initial data is entered, they're quick and easy to maintain. Weigh the investment in time and money needed for setting up a program against the time, money, and/or clutter savings in the long term.

Aesthetics Essentials

My first aim in writing this book was to help you get things functioning more smoothly in your life. Once that happens, you can move to the next step, which is making what already works more beautiful. Order in itself is beautiful, in my opinion, and once you have a basic level of order and simplicity in your life, you can then turn your attention to making it even more aesthetically pleasing.

You can use the free time that results from being organized to pay more attention to details, including aesthetics. I have two rules, however. First, if something looks nice but fails to do the job I created it for, I opt for the less attractive tool that works. And, second, if it isn't functional, it goes—unless it truly adds pleasure and beauty to my life.

I've tried lots of household paper-sorting systems, including ones made of wicker and other decorative materials, but the one that works best for me is a horizontal cardboard cubby system that fits on a shelf. Someday, I may have a more attractive wooden one made, but until then, I'll take my ugly organizer over the decorator ones anytime!

There are lots of little ways, however, to add some beauty to otherwise mundane aspects of daily existence. Here are a few:

◆ Once you get your closet organized, decorate the inside with colored hangers, attractive boxes, and picture postcards or posters on the unobstructed wall space. Change them periodically when the spirit moves you.

- Put fresh flowers on the breakfast table regularly and maybe a single bloom on your nightstand next to your bed.

- Cover recipe binders with wallpaper scraps or coated gift paper.

- Add scented sachets to your closet and drawers.

- Have a pretty, well-stocked basket of stationery within easy reach, and postcards, note cards, stamps, and an elegant letter opener that you can grab when you have a few minutes to do your personal correspondence.

Orderly Pursuits

Alexandra Stoddard has made a study of adding beauty to everyday rituals and spaces. For some inspiring ideas, try reading her books *Living a Beautiful Life: 500 Ways to Add Elegance, Order, Beauty, and Joy to Every Day of Your Life*, and *Living Beautiful Together*.

You Have a Dream!

Being organized doesn't mean becoming a drudge. On the contrary, it should mean you're pounds lighter, experiencing a freedom you've probably never known.

If you find yourself burdened, a slave to your schedule, then you've lost sight of the purpose of getting organized—to fulfill the mission you said you wanted in life! Go back to the beginning and take another look. Review Chapter 2. Redo some of the exercises. If you need to, get some additional help with developing a mission statement and formulating your goals.

As I've mentioned before, I strongly recommend Stephen Covey's book *The 7 Habits of Effective People* and any of Anthony Robbins's books or self-improvement tapes. Many other excellent books, audiotapes, and videotapes are on the market, as well as seminars, that cover these topics. Doing this groundwork will make the difference between being a drudge and a dynamo! Tapping into your real desires and passions can't help but infuse your efforts with zest and energy.

Make sure you allow yourself time and space to wish and dream. Exercise your visualization muscles. There are good books and tapes on developing and using visualization techniques, as well. These techniques are enjoyable, since they activate the unconscious, invigorate the imagination, and teach you how to employ your fantasies to help you identify what you really care about in life. I've listed several tools and how to obtain them in the resource guide at the back of this book.

Getting organized around your true desires for a fulfilled and joyous life is fun. If it's not, you're doing it wrong! Give yourself the time and space to embark on this important exploration—it will fuel everything you do.

Let the Seasons Tell the Time

Since first developing my own organization plans and implementing them, I've learned a trick that has added a new dimension to tasks that need doing every year: Key them to the seasons. This is how our ancestors made sure things got done on time! I find it adds a wonderful rhythm to life, when what I do works along with the changes in nature.

Winter is a time for turning inward. There's not much that can be done outside, so I can focus more on the house's inner workings. This is when my life centers more around the hearth and my own goals and dreams. It's a time for taking stock and planning. Chores such as cleaning out drawers and closets seem perfect for this time of year. Detail work, like mending and sewing, takes precedence.

Spring means clearing out. There's a reason why our mothers and grandmothers called it "spring cleaning." That's the season when the earth is waking up and activity will begin to heighten and move outdoors. What better time to unstuff, have a yard sale, and get the family car in shape?

In summer, we can shed our heavy clothes, live more in the fresh air, and schedule tasks like painting and refurbishing for a time when windows can remain open and cleanup is easier.

The fall, harvest time, is a time for reaping the rewards of our industry, making preparations for the coming cold weather. This is a good time to survey your disaster preparedness, food storage, and batteries.

Make Maintenance a Celebration

I can't encourage you enough to make organizing your life and maintaining your organization systems joyous and celebratory. Growing a happy life is something to celebrate! Add silly rituals, songs, rhymes, readings, music, and dance to your celebrations. Add whatever trappings make them fun. Make up your own holidays to both celebrate and serve as a reminder, or key them to our mysterious past, if you like.

Each February, for example, I celebrate Candlemas (or Imbolc, if you prefer its Celtic name), an ancient holiday that has since been transmuted into Groundhog Day, which reminds us of the longer days to come with the spring. I air out the house (whatever the temperature), imagine any stale influences taking flight out the windows, take an inventory of my spices and pantry staples, light every candle we own, and welcome the coming of the light and green of spring.

All holiday decorations and seasonal cooking utensils are carefully put away in long-term storage. I begin collecting all the statements, documents, and receipts for taxes. I drool over seed catalogs. The actual celebration of this event when the date appears on the calendar adds a depth and a richness to it that grows in meaning each year.

Whatever your nationality or religious faith, look for ways to integrate daily tasks into larger events and celebrations. Find out what seasonal tasks were associated with these dates and adapt them to your own. At least try it. You may like it!

Orderly Pursuits

Want to learn more about seasonal celebrations? Find a copy of *Mrs. Sharp's Traditions: Nostalgic Suggestions for Re-Creating the Family Celebrations and Seasonal Pastimes of the Victorian Home* by Sarah Ban Breathnach for a perspective on the old-fashioned way of observing seasonal changes.

The Least You Need to Know

◆ Finding your "bottom line" and maintaining it is the best foundation for keeping your life organized.

◆ Lists, schedules, and an efficient filing system are the fundamental tools for maintaining an organized life.

◆ If your organization plan starts to break down, there are specific steps you can take to identify problem areas and get yourself back on track.

◆ If your system is functioning well, you can add beauty to everyday spaces and rituals.

◆ Giving yourself time and space to fantasize, visualize, wish, and dream is crucial to successfully building and perpetuating order and high performance.

Chapter 20

Organization Styles for Different Lifestyles

In This Chapter

◆ How to adapt your basic organization plan to your current lifestyle

◆ The importance of changing your plan for changes in lifestyle

◆ Resources for the special needs of frequent travelers

◆ Tips for single parents, caregivers, singles, widows, and widowers

The basic organization principles I've given you in this book apply regardless of your age, living situation, or financial status. Whether you're a student or a retiree, live alone or have a large family, getting organized will make your life better.

In this chapter, however, we'll look at how you can adapt these basic principles to your specific lifestyle and status, concentrating on the areas of food, clothing, shelter, people, money, and work.

All by Yourself

According to the latest U.S. Census information, men and women are marrying later than ever before, and one in every nine adults lives alone.

If you have the house or apartment all to yourself, it's easier to implement an organization plan that works for you. You don't have other people to mess it up! You may live alone by choice; you may be a student living on your own for the first time, or a professional seriously pursuing a career; you may be divorced or widowed. Whatever your reasons, being single presents its own organization challenges, whether you're beginning your adult life or are well into adulthood.

Young and Single

If you're young and single, chances are you have a fairly social lifestyle at this stage of your life. You may not eat at home very often. You're more likely to rent a house or apartment than own your own home, and you may move several times before settling in one place.

Although you may not yet be building equity in a home, it's important that you begin budgeting now, so you can keep a close watch on where your money goes and plan for emergencies. Now is also a good time to think about the future with a small investment fund. If you're not sure of the best way to begin investing, speak to a financial planner or educate yourself through an investment club or seminar.

Start organizing your work records now. Keep employment information and reviews in your files. Think ahead about references for future employment. If you're a student, your professors will be among your first references, so keep them in mind. Organizing to find a job might be a top issue soon, if it's not already. Now's the time to think about that resumé and begin collecting the information you'll need to write a good one.

Orderly Pursuits

For helpful tips on cooking, you can head for your computer, the bookstore, the TV, or the video store. Check out *Going Solo in the Kitchen* by Jane Doerfer, and *Serves One: Super Meals for Solo Cooks* by Toni Lydecker. You can join the Cooking for One or Two Recipe Club on-line at www.kitchenlink.com/msgbrd/board_16/tklcc.html.

Although you may be inclined to eat out a lot, with some simple kitchen tools and basic ingredients you can create meals that are more nourishing and easier on the budget than eating out or "ordering in." It's easy to get into the junk food habit when you live alone, but it's expensive and doesn't promote good health. Even if you only cook for one, treat yourself like a guest. Sit at the table, not in front of the TV. Put on some dinner music and set the table. Enjoy a good, wholesome meal you prepared yourself.

Go back to Chapter 11 and review the information on bulk cooking, quick cooking, and Crock-Pot cooking. Experiment to see which methods work best for you. If you're simply not in the mood to cook after a hard day at work or school, try cooking only a couple of times a week and freezing single portions for other days. Soups and stews work well, as do many pasta sauces and casseroles.

You can often find good used cookware at garage sales and thrift stores. Whatever you can't find there, purchase from reputable companies and try to buy the best quality you can afford. Here's a short list of the basics:

◆ Ten- or twelve-inch nonstick skillet

◆ One- and two-quart saucepans with lids

◆ Five-quart Dutch oven with lid

◆ Eight- or ten-inch high-carbon, stainless-steel chef's knife

◆ Three-inch paring knife

◆ Sharpening steel and whetstone for sharpening knives

◆ Large cutting board (plastic or wood)

◆ Wooden spoons of various sizes

◆ Slotted spoon

◆ Ladle

◆ Plastic spatula for nonstick cookware

◆ Rubber spatulas, large and small, for scraping out bowls

◆ Tongs

◆ Set of measuring spoons and measuring cups

◆ Two-cup glass measuring cup

◆ Mixing bowls in various sizes

◆ Grater

◆ Baking/roaster pan

◆ Large strainer or colander

◆ Can opener

◆ Corkscrew and bottle opener

◆ Oven mitts and trivets

◆ Kitchen towels

Oops!

Not only do manual can openers work better than electric ones and take up less space, they'll come in handy when the electricity is out or you don't have an outlet handy.

Orderly Pursuits

There's a great book called *Where's Mom Now That I Need Her? Surviving Away from Home* by Betty Rae Frandsen, Kathryn J. Frandsen, and Kent P. Frandsen. It explains basic food preparation, simple first aid, laundry and clothing repair, stain removal, and lots more basic survival information for starting out on your own.

♦ Kitchen shears

♦ Vegetable peeler

♦ Microwave-safe storage containers

♦ Jar and bottle opener

Of course, you'll add to your collection as you cook more or if you decide to bake, but these are the basics. Add one good, basic cookbook like *Joy of Cooking*, the *Fanny Farmer Cookbook*, or the *Better Homes and Gardens New Cookbook*, and you're all set.

You're probably doing your laundry out, but since you're only one person, the weekly trip to the Laundromat shouldn't be too taxing. Take advantage of off-peak hours, but don't compromise your safety. Dinnertime is usually a good time for doing laundry and grocery shopping.

Since you're just starting out, you can unstuff and avoid the acquisition trap now. Make careful selections, and buy quality things. It's better to buy quality used things than new, cheaper ones of inferior quality. When selecting furniture, remember that you'll likely be moving it several times. Stay away from massive pieces that need special handling or may not fit through the door or up the stairs of your next apartment.

Older and Single

If you're older and single, you also have control of your environment and destiny, but you're at a different stage in life than the "young single." You may be living alone as an intentional lifestyle, or you may be divorced or widowed and have no children at home.

One great challenge for you could be balancing alone time with social activities. It may mean forcing yourself to get out and be with other people. If you have a career, you'll have more opportunities to socialize, but if you're no longer in the workforce, you may have to make a conscious effort to involve yourself outside the home.

Add some activities to explore to your Master List. Using your planner/organizer to schedule specific activities will remind you of your social needs. Join a discussion group, take up a hobby, volunteer, or get involved in your community. There are lots of opportunities to meet new people and contribute your skills and experience.

A starting point for finding out what's out there is The Singles Mall on the World Wide Web. The URL is www.singlesmall.com/sm2.html. It has links to many resources, products, and services (including groups in various states) for singles of all ages and situations. There's even an inventive list of things to do when you have "nothing to do."

Statistics show that women make up the largest number of those surviving a spouse. Many women haven't had responsibility for the finances during their married years, so developing money management skills becomes crucial once they're on their own. If you're in this situation and haven't done so yet, taking stock of your finances should be your number-one priority. If you and your husband had a financial plan, it needs to be revised for your new circumstances.

> **Amazing Space**
>
> If you're alone due to the death of a spouse, one delicate issue is getting rid of things belonging to the departed. It's hard to say when is the best time to pack up your spouse's belongings and pass them on, but at some point it will make sense. If you need support, have someone go through the process with you.

A book specifically aimed at widows and divorcees that can get you on the right track is *After He's Gone: A Guide for Widowed and Divorced Women* by Barbara Tom Jowell and Donnette Schwisow.

Now that you're cooking for only one person, you can cut down the ingredients for your favorite recipes or make the same amount and freeze the rest for a later meal. Make sure you don't give in to the "why bother?" syndrome when contemplating a meal just for yourself.

My recently widowed friend Edith, who loves to cook, decided she missed cooking for other people more than she realized. She now regularly invites friends over for dinner. Everyone pitches in with ingredients, but she does the cooking. Guests help with the cleanup, too. This gives Edith great pleasure and stimulating evening conversation. She eats more nutritious meals than she would if she was only preparing food for herself. And her guests don't have to cook that night! A good deal all around. Don't be afraid to try offbeat ideas. They're often the ones that work the best.

Single-Income, Dual-Parent Families

Some couples feel the sacrifices they must make to have one parent home at all times are worth it. One partner may give up his or her income altogether, or each may have a part-time arrangement so they can share child-care responsibilities. I think that this trend will grow even more in the coming years.

For couples embracing this lifestyle, organization issues focus around thrift and scheduling child care. Time management issues are different. With reduced income, the family is choosing a quality of emotional life over material things. Careful budgeting, cooking from scratch, and even having a vegetable garden and sewing some of the family's clothes might be part of the plan. Children can be brought into these activities and, in fact, taught valuable self-reliance skills. If children understand the reasons for the tradeoffs and are made a part of the process, they'll be more willing to cooperate.

A writer friend of mine, Steve, and his wife, Leslie, decided they both wanted to be highly involved in the daily life of their new baby. Leslie is a school-teacher, and Steve was a technical writer. Steve left his job to become a home-based freelance writer, while Leslie kept her teaching job. Together, their two present incomes equal roughly half of what they were making when both worked full time.

During the summer, Leslie takes over the child-care duties so Steve can develop his writing business. During the school year, Steve has to juggle caring for the baby with getting his work done. He can handle some of it at night and on weekends, but when deadlines loom, he sometimes needs help.

One solution is in-home child care, where the parent is still available, and the baby-sitter tends to the child's needs while the at-home parent works. Another is a trade situation, where several at-home parents trade off caring for each other's children one day a week.

If one parent takes on the role of at-home child care provider, it's important that the other spend time with the children and give the at-home parent some

Orderly Pursuits

Subscribe to "The Dollar Stretcher," a free online newsletter that's delivered to your e-mail address, by sending an e-mail message to gary@stretcher.com with "subscribe" in the subject and your e-mail address in the body of the message. This cyber newsletter is filled with useful suggestions for those trying to get by with less.

Oops!

Because they tend to be very career-oriented, DINKS can sometimes forget how important it is to pay attention to their primary relationship. Over time, they may grow apart. Make sure if you fall into this lifestyle category you see to it there's adequate focus on your significant other, not just your own personal ambitions.

private time. Negotiating these times, as well as the cleaning duties, are key issues. It's all too easy to assume that the at-home parent is responsible for cooking, child care, and keeping the house clean. No fair! Those duties should be shared. How they're divided up needs to be negotiated and jobs scheduled.

Dual-Income Couples

For DINKS (dual-income, no kids), meshing schedules and sharing housework are the key organization issues.

The only time available for maintaining both the house and the relationship is evenings, weekends, and vacation time, so it's important that both partners share their schedules and commit to certain chores around the house. This group can often benefit from hiring outside help, and they're more likely to have the income to do it. Doing housework chores together is another solution, building some fun and communication into what needs to be done anyway.

Another time for sharing and reconnecting is during the preparation and enjoyment of the evening meal. Make these times special by planning menus and perhaps doing some food preparation ahead of time (refer to Chapter 11 for meal preparation strategies), so you can concentrate on making mealtime unhassled and relaxing. Light some candles, use those fancy cloth napkins, hold hands, and talk!

Dual-Income Families

Organization issues for families where both parents work are likely to revolve around child care and work-related topics. The working couple knows that spending time with the children needs to be one of the highest priorities, but it can be tricky. Balancing the personal need for renewal and "downtime" against the needs of the children isn't easy. And, again, who does the housework? All too often it's the working woman who ends up trying to do it all. No fair, guys!

Planning and scheduling come to the rescue here. So does finding ways to get things done and spending time with the kids at the same

> **Amazing Space**
>
> Like other families, dual-income families need to look at accumulating money for college tuition, so financial planning and careful budgeting are high priorities. Since time for managing investments is most likely hard to come by, finding a good financial planner is crucial. Review Chapters 14 and 15 to get your finances in shape for now and the future.

time. Who says washing the car has to mean time away from the family? It can mean a fantastic water fight and a cleaning session at the same time. Even the dog may get a bath.

If you're clear about your mission in life, and you write down your goals, develop a plan, and work on it each day, you'll raise great kids (a worthy life mission) and get ahead in your career. It doesn't just happen by accident.

Single Parents

The adult of a single-parent family has to do it all. There simply is no one else (or so it seems). It's a tough place to be. I know—I've been there. If you become a single parent through divorce, besides all the challenges you face, you may hear from outsiders and the media that your home is "broken." Well, I never accepted that, and neither should you!

Sure, it's best for kids to grow up in a healthy two-parent household, but when you're going it alone, there's no reason not to have a great family! Just recently I read a list of ways that single-parent families have unique strengths. I thought I'd paraphrase some of them for you:

- Just because a family has two parents doesn't mean it's healthy or happy. If there was an unhealthy situation before, a single-parent situation is vastly superior. Now the children may have an opportunity to bond with both parents separately, without the discord that existed before.

- Single parents have more flexibility in planning time with their children. They don't have the regular demands and distractions of another adult. When the children are with each parent, they can have exclusive attention and the individual parent may be more attuned to their emotional needs.

- Single-parent households can be more interdependent. Single parents depend more heavily on cooperation from each family member, and children are more likely to pitch in voluntarily. I'm convinced my children are the responsible adults they are today largely because they learned responsibility early. They felt needed and rose to the occasion.

- Children in single-parent households are often exposed to a wider range of experiences. Rather than getting a baby-sitter (which I couldn't afford), I took my children to college classes with me, to work on my college newspaper, to the library, and on field trips. When I organized the company Christmas party, they were the elves.

♦ In divorced families, children can experience two totally different spheres. They get a wider view of life, and besides, they get two birthday parties and two Christmases!

Of course, single parents have their work cut out for them, as well. Certain standards may have to be lowered, especially those surrounding housework. But order and organization are even more important in a single-parent household. Since there's so little time, things need to be streamlined to operate as efficiently as possible.

The once-a-week food preparation method worked best for me when I was a single parent with young children. I shopped and cleaned on Saturday while the children were with their father, and cooked the week's meals on Sunday afternoon. The children knew what was scheduled for when, so even if I got home late they could get things started. If the meal was frozen, I took it out to thaw in the morning before I went to work. We had good, wholesome, home-cooked meals that were within my budget, without having to cook after a long day at the office. The Crock-Pot came in handy, too.

Two of the biggest issues for the single parent are making sure that children aren't alone when they come home from school and that there's always someone available in an emergency. Some school systems have after-school programs for "latchkey kids." If you don't live in an area with support programs for single parents, you may want to consider relocating. You can't do this alone, and it helps to live in a community where you can get some help. Look to church groups and single-parent organizations as well.

For emergencies, the best system is to have several people who can cover for you in case you can't be reached. Line up relatives, friends, or neighbors you can trust in advance. You'll also need to cover the times the children are sick and you have to go to work. A redundant system with several backups is the way to keep things covered no matter what.

Orderly Pursuits

The National Organization of Single Mothers can be reached at P.O. Box 68, Midland, NC 28107; (704) 888-KIDS; www.singlemother.org. This organization helps new members form or join local support groups and publishes "SingleMOTHER," a bimonthly newsletter offering information and advice, plus tips that can save single mothers time and money.

Amazing Space

Although it's not something we naturally want to discuss, it would be a good idea to feel your children out about what they would want if you couldn't be there to take care of them. Choose a time carefully to broach the subject, reassure them that nothing's wrong, but tell them you want to make certain that no matter what the future brings, they're always taken care of. Take their wishes into consideration when choosing a guardian.

It helps to work for a company that is profamily. You should never have to choose between your job and the well-being of your child. There are organizations that rate companies in these areas. Do some research (start with your local research librarian). When you go job hunting, have this objective clear in your mind. You're more likely to find what you want if you firmly plant the idea in your mind before you start looking.

On the financial front, you'll need to provide for your children in case something happens to you. Get all the benefits you're entitled to at your workplace and through the local, state, and federal governments, whether you're divorced or widowed. Think through what you want done with and for your children if you die or become seriously ill. Name a guardian who will have immediate access to all your financial information. Organize it the way I outlined in Chapters 14 and 15, and show the person you choose how you have it set up. Be sure to include any special information about the children that this person may need to know, like medical history or special needs.

The Empty Nest

I can personally address the empty nest change in lifestyle, since I'm smack dab in the middle of it! When the fledglings fly from the nest, Mom and Dad can be anywhere from their 40s (if they started a family early) to well into their 70s. The issues for empty-nesters are somewhat different depending on age and financial status, but certain things crop up regardless of when your little birdies fly the coop.

Orderly Pursuits

It's sometimes difficult to be balanced in our approach to our children. On the one hand, we want to make them feel that they're loved and can always come home if they need to. On the other, we want them to be independent and self-sufficient, solving their own problems and forging their own future. Strive to create this balance—both offering support and letting go.

One such issue is deciding when to take over the kids' rooms. This can be more trouble than you might think. When my oldest daughter left for college, I immediately moved my office into her bedroom. I had been using the dining room, but there was too much activity there for me to work effectively, and I couldn't keep my papers in order. Rachel was crushed. I was looking at it from a totally practical standpoint; her reaction was purely emotional. I never intended to make her feel she wasn't welcome (I had a bed fixed up in the family room downstairs), but that's how she felt. What can I say? I goofed! It's a good idea to find out from your kids how they feel about using their old space *before* you make changes.

On the other hand, don't become a storage facility for your grown kids. As soon as they're on their own and settled semipermanently, they need to decide what to take, what to toss, and what they'd like you to hang on to. Keep the last category to a minimum. I'm keeping some furniture that's been in the family for more than 100 years until the girls are more permanently settled, but I just recently divided up their childhood storybooks and passed them on so they can share them with their own children someday. Strike a balance between keeping a place for your grown children and moving on to the next stage in your lives.

Make sure you reevaluate your finances. Most likely your children will have their own benefits at work and you'll be able to make some changes there. As a gift to each child, we arranged for them to have a professional financial planner where they live draw up a complete financial plan for them, while we did the same for ourselves. We also set up custodial accounts for each of our granddaughters. Rather than contributing more clutter to your children's lives, why not give them something they can really use?

Caregivers and Extended Families

Having an ill, disabled, or aged family member in a household creates several crucial organization issues. Laying out the home in an efficient manner is essential to saving steps for caregivers and making it easier for a loved one to care for him- or herself as much as possible.

Much has been written on this topic, and contacting one of the various organizations that addresses your particular situation would be an excellent idea.

You may need to rethink how you store things and how you shop. Perhaps smaller sizes would make it easier for a disabled or aged family member to prepare meals. Many ingredients come prechopped or preprepared, making it less labor-intensive to put together a dish. Lower shelving might help, or simply relocating essentials to an area within easy reach. Some simple aids might contribute to independence.

 Orderly Pursuits

To find a caregiver support group, contact the American Self-Help Clearinghouse at www.mentalhelp.net/selfhelp/. They'll give you information on self-help organization chapters in your area, or send you to the headquarters of a national organization that addresses your needs.

In some cases you may need a home health-care aide to assist you, even if only temporarily. Contact your local social services agency and ask for referrals. A professional might know simple techniques to make things easier or be able to point you toward helpful equipment and tools.

The role of caregiver needn't fall to one member of the family alone. Everyone can be involved, sharing scheduled time and responsibilities. Even small children can give the primary caregiver a hand, and older children can provide much-needed relief.

These days, extended families often include adult children living at home. If older children come back home to live, it shouldn't be on the same basis it was when they were children. They are now housemates, and they need to understand that right from the get go. Negotiate their household share of the cooking, shopping, cleaning, and financial requirements. Expect them to behave like adults, and resist the temptation to treat them like they're young children again. It's also a good idea to have a defined period of time for this arrangement. Is it for six months? A year? Don't wait until they've moved in to discuss these things. Get things out in the open from the start.

You'll need to work out storage arrangements, too. If they have furniture, where will you put it? You'll have to make room, they'll have to find a solution, or someone will have to pay for rental of a storage facility. Will you be eating together, or will your adult child be responsible for his or her own meals? If the latter, will they be shopping for their own groceries? Do they understand they'll be cleaning up after themselves? What about laundry? Discuss these issues up front, to avoid misunderstandings and hurt feelings later.

> **Amazing Space**
>
> Ideally, in a dual custody situation, chores assigned to a child in one household should also be assigned in the other. This will reduce the feeling of disruption in a child's life and will also help both households keep working efficiently. Both parents need to work together to create consistency, and see that one doesn't undermine the discipline efforts of the other.

Blended Families and Dual Custody Arrangements

With more than half of all marriages ending in divorce and many divorced partners remarrying, new solutions have evolved to handle parenting by more than one set of adults. These arrangements can work if everyone involved keeps their main priority in mind: the welfare of the children. Beyond this, organizing for smooth transitions from one residence to the other is imperative.

In some cases, there are as many as five sets of children involved in the blending of families: the divorced couple's, each of their new spouse's kids, and children from the two new unions. The challenges are enormous, but are being met by real people every day.

My friend Katie and her husband have a dual custody arrangement with Katie's children. Both she and her ex-husband live in the same area, so the kids attend the same schools and activities, they just go home to a different house every other week. Certain basics are duplicated in each household, and personal areas are designated for each child to call his own. Certainly, this arrangement would not work for everyone, but when adults put their efforts into cooperating and promoting their children's welfare, it's amazing how well children adapt.

For some helpful resources for blended families, refer to the resource guide.

Scheduling regular "family conferences" is crucial to keeping communication flowing and resolving logistical issues before they get out of hand. If a child is being disciplined in one household for unacceptable behavior, the adults in the second household need to know what's going on and, hopefully, support those efforts.

The Road Warrior

I covered the needs of the home-based worker at length in Chapter 9, but one lifestyle we only touched on was that of the "road warrior" or frequent traveler.

Whether you're self-employed or working for someone else, your job may involve a great deal of travel. This lifestyle brings up a whole host of special organization issues. To name a few:

Who handles things while you're away? If someone's holding down the fort at home and/or at work, you may naturally be tempted to dump everything on him or her. How fair is that? You need to be organized to handle your daily tasks on the road. If you normally pay the bills, consider an electronic bill-paying service and computer cash-management program on your laptop (with built-in modem, of course), which makes handling this stuff on the road pretty easy. If this won't work, see if your bank has an automatic bill-paying service. If it doesn't, you may want to look for a new bank. Look for other ways you can take care of the same responsibilities while you're traveling that you do when you're at home.

Oops! _____
Don't forget to designate someone to keep extra keys if you live alone, so they can get into your home or apartment in an emergency, and so *you* can get in your home if you lose your keys. Trusted neighbors are ideal, especially if they're home during the day.

Orderly Pursuits

Three good books to help you learn the ropes of serious business travel are *The Unofficial Business Traveler's Pocket Guide* by Christopher J. McGinnis; *The Business Traveler's Survival Guide, How to Get Work Done While on the Road* by June Langhoff; and *Keeping Your Family Close: When Frequent Travel Pulls You Apart* by Elizabeth M. Hoekstra.

What happens in an emergency? Have people and services lined up for everything that might go wrong, from a flooded basement to a sick pet.

What if people need to get in touch? A detailed itinerary with accurate information about where you'll be at all times is crucial. Be sure to include phone numbers. If things change en route, be sure to amend the itinerary as soon as you know. Leave this information with all the key people back on the home front.

I've been a "road warrior" myself at various times, and I know many other writers and business people who spend a lot of time in planes, trains, and automobiles. Here are a few tips I've put together from my own "road show":

Portable everything! Consider bulk, weight, and durability in things like luggage, clothing, computer equipment, and personal appliances. Look for small-sized toiletries, too, and small containers you can transfer things into. Make frequent use of resealable plastic bags for individual items that can leak.

Exercise. Select accommodations where you can walk safely, or ones that have exercise facilities indoors. Schedule time in your planner/organizer just as if you were at home. You'll feel better, and it's a great stress reliever!

Eat a balanced diet. Stay away from fast-food places and try to eat balanced meals that aren't too rich. Ask the locals to recommend places that fit the bill. Take your vitamins! If I'm going to be in one place for a few days, I often get meals from my favorite take-out: the grocery store! Fruits and vegetables can be kept on ice from the hotel or motels. Some cooked, chilled shrimp, with cocktail sauce and a salad make a delicious, light meal that's easy to put together in a hotel room. My husband and I, tiring of rich restaurant food, have often made a repast of fruit, cheese, and hearty bread.

Pack light. Most experienced, heavy-duty travelers recommend packing everything into your carry-on luggage. If you can't get it into two manageable bags, don't take it. That way you don't have to wait in line for your baggage or run the risk of losing it between stops. If you're away for a long time, you can use hotel laundry services or a Laundromat. If you know you'll accumulate stuff on the road, like brochures or conference materials, pack it up and ship it home.

Stay in touch. Make regular calls if someone at home is taking care of things. Tell them how much you appreciate their help and support. If you're maintaining a relationship, communication is essential. Most people I know with heavy travel schedules who are in a relationship call home at least once a day. This gives the one at home base the opportunity to involve you in important decisions, and gives you a feeling of connectedness, even if you can't remember which city you woke up in this morning.

Dress for travel success. Invest in lightweight, easy-to-care-for, mix-and-match separates. Women actually have it easier in this area, since male business travelers generally have to cope with suits. Many clothes travel best rolled rather than laid flat. Make sure to wear only comfortable shoes.

Don't bring it home. Restrain yourself from bringing home clutter from your travels, either for yourself or as souvenirs for those who stayed behind. E-mail often. Write long, love-filled letters. Share your feelings. Tell them you miss them and what you love about them. Those things are better than souvenirs any day!

Picture This

Take some time to think about your present lifestyle. Has it changed recently? What are the positive things about your particular situation? What are the unique challenges that might be helped with planning and organizing? Are finances the greatest area of concern? Or does finding time for intimacy need more of your attention? If you could change one thing about your current lifestyle, what would that be?

Be sure to detox from your trip as soon as you can. Listen first to what's gone on at home, then tell your tales from the hinterlands.

Whatever your particular circumstances, an organization plan can be adapted to suit them. It's not a "one-size-fits-all" world. Know the specific challenges and advantages of your lifestyle, and create a plan that works best for you.

The Least You Need to Know

- ◆ You can adapt the basic principles of organization to every lifestyle.

- ◆ You can organize for the way you live now and for future changes by changing emphasis and priorities.

- ◆ Key activities for adapting your organization plan are negotiating, scheduling, and planning.

- ◆ Whatever your situation, strive for balance between the physical, mental, emotional, and spiritual.

Part 7

Now for the Fun Stuff!

Organize to have fun? Why, that's a sacrilege, you say! It's against the very nature of fun! But you'd be wrong.

Organizing your fun times means you have more of them and they'll be closer to the way you dreamed they'd be. Think of this kind of organization as orchestration. Your fun times are a symphony and you're the conductor controlling all the instruments, the dynamics, the interpretation, and the tempo.

With good orchestration, your fun times will be better than ever!

Chapter 21

Road Show: Making the Most of Your Vacation

In This Chapter

- Packing for trouble-free travel
- Preparing yourself to travel safely
- Traveling happily with kids
- Organizing for international travel and going off the beaten track
- Choosing and using a travel agent

A vacation is something we don't get to take very often. We work, plan, save, and have high expectations for every moment of the trip. Now the time has come—two weeks in Hawaii, a camping trip out West, a cruise to the Caribbean, or perhaps just a long weekend getaway. How can you make sure your trip will be everything you want it to be? Organize it, of course!

In this chapter, you'll get the inside scoop on how to save yourself time, money, and aggravation by planning your next vacation, plus you'll get some important tips on how to protect yourself, your kids, and your belongings when you're traveling. And this time, you'll learn better ways to remember your trip than bringing home all those useless souvenirs!

Travel Agents: Is This Trip Really Necessary?

Decide early whether you're going to use a travel agent or make your own arrangements. The travel agent industry has undergone a huge change in the last few years, especially since the terrorist attacks on U.S. soil. But things were changing before that. The major airlines have reduced the commissions they pay to travel agents, while more and more people have learned they can book flights, cruises, hotel rooms, and rental cars using online services or simply dialing the phone. If you have the time and inclination, you can easily act as your own travel agent and it's getting easier every day.

Agent Advantages

There are, however, still advantages to using a travel agent. Here are some of the benefits:

◆ Because the professional travel agent's time is spent becoming familiar with travel products, trends, and venues, they have a broad picture of what's available and what might suit your vacation vision.

◆ Travel agents get notification of special promotions that you generally wouldn't know about. Through experience they can determine whether the promotion is really a good deal or just a gimmick. The cheapest is not always the best.

◆ An agent will know if any changes in your schedule might mean better air fares. If you buy direct from the airline, they'll only quote you the rates for the times you ask. Agents also are notified of fare changes on a regular basis and may be able to get a better fare, even after you've initially booked your tickets.

◆ Agents have access to heavily discounted airline tickets sold through consolidators. (These were not generally sold direct to the passenger, although now some consolidators that sell direct are appearing on the web.)

Picture This
Having trouble deciding where you want to go and what you want to do on your vacation? Ask your inner self! Close your eyes and pretend you have all the time in the world, have no budget limitations, and can go anywhere you want. What would that look like? What activities would you be engaged in? Would you be in a resort or roughing it in the wild? Is it in the mountains or at the shore? You may not be able to reproduce your "ultimate vacation" in real life, but your visualization should give you some valuable clues to your heart's desires.

◆ Sometimes larger travel agencies buy bulk tickets from airlines at bargain prices. This happens when an airline doesn't think it can fill the seats. The savings are passed on to the agency's customers.

◆ Travel agents also get complimentary tickets from time to time, which they can sell if they want at whatever price they choose. These are promotional tickets and are for standby. You might want to let your agent know if this is something you'd be interested in.

◆ An agent can help with terminology and other questions you might have about penalties and restrictions. They'll be able to advise you about trip insurance and other practical matters.

◆ Because agents are usually widely traveled themselves, they can make specific suggestions about where to stay, what to see, and the best time to go, based on personal experience.

◆ By going to an agent, you can take advantage of one-stop shopping, saving time and wear and tear on you. He or she has all the information and options available at one time. (Although, again, some of the online travel services have become closer to "one-stop" shopping outlets as well.)

◆ Usually an agent has more clout than the consumer when there's a problem or you need special arrangements. She can also be an important advocate if something goes wrong.

◆ If you work regularly with an agent, she gets to know your preferences, disposition, and interests, and can make vacation recommendations tailored just for you. It's the personal, "human" touch that makes lots of people more comfortable going to a travel agent than dealing with an online travel service or handling the arrangements themselves by phone.

But There Are Disadvantages, Too

There are some distinct disadvantages to using a travel agent, however. Or perhaps we should say "cautions." Travel agents are paid a very small hourly wage, making their money on commissions. So it's to their advantage to sell at the highest prices possible. The more cost to you, the higher their commission. Conversely, if they find you the cheapest fares, you'll come back and they'll make more money in the long run, but you may want to keep an eye on your agent, especially at first, to make sure she's getting you the best possible rates.

You may want to ask your agent if she has received bonus commissions from airlines. This may mean the agent is booking tickets with one particular airline, without looking around for the best possible fares for customers. These bonuses are paid as an incentive, after an agent reaches a certain number of ticket sales with a particular airline.

> **Oops!**
>
> There are two main causes of problems with travel agents: The agent is unqualified, or the customer hasn't effectively communicated her wants and preferences. These can be avoided if you take the time to find a reputable, qualified professional, and make clear (put it in writing) what you want before any money is exchanged.

The online services are now just about as complete as a large travel agency in what they offer. Websites like Travelocity.com, Expedia.com, and Orbitz.com include cruises, tours, car rentals, hotel and motel reservations, and more. Part of knowing which method is best for you is knowing yourself. Do you like trusting someone else to do the legwork to find the best deal for you, or do you like to investigate for yourself? What is your skill level on the Internet? Which takes the most time?

It might be worth an experiment with your next trip to both see a travel agent and do some of your own research on the Internet. Compare results, prices, and details. Keep track of how much time each took. Obtaining this information should go a long way toward helping you decide which is the most efficient tool for you.

Ask Your Agent

If you do decide to use a travel agent, choose one carefully. You'll need to choose your agent the same way you would any other professional. Here's a list of questions to ask:

- How much experience does the particular agent have? Is this a part-time job or a full-time career?

- What's her background?

- How long has the agency she works for been in business?

- If you have particular vacation interests, you want to ask if the agent has any particular specialties. For example, if you're a skier, you wouldn't want a cruise specialist. You'd want to ask if any of the agents are skiers, how many ski bookings they do annually, and whether they've been on familiarization trips to particular resorts and ski areas. Or if you're a diver or a nature buff, then you'd want to talk to an agent who shares those interests.

- Is the agent a member of either the American Society of Travel Agents (ASTA) or the Association of Retail Travel Agents (ARTA)? These are the two major professional associations for travel agents. ASTA members are supposed to adhere to a code of professional conduct, and ASTA even offers an agency/consumer mediation and arbitration service.

- If the agent isn't a member of ASTA or ARTA, ask if he's a certified travel counselor (CTC). This means he has at least five years' experience and has completed a two-year graduate-level program offered by the Institute of Certified Travel Agents.

- Some agencies play favorites with particular airlines, because they have incentive programs to reward ticket sales. Ask how many airlines your agent will be checking. You'll want at least three comparisons.

- Does the agency use CRSs (Computer Reservations Systems)? How many? Larger agencies use as many as five to get the best fare comparisons and keep abreast of any last-minute changes in availability. Does their computer system rank flights according to fare?

- Does the agency have relationships with preferred suppliers? Are they companies you like doing business with?

- Does the agency work with airline or hotel consolidators? This could save you a bundle, especially on international travel.

- Is there a 24-hour, toll-free emergency number in case you have a problem in an unfamiliar location?

Before making a final decision, interview a travel agent you're thinking of using. You might ask questions about a place you've visited and know well, and see what kind of responses you get. You might also ask the agent to price a vacation package for you and then comparison shop using the same package. Look at service as well as price. Get recommendations from people who enjoy traveling the same way you do, and whose tastes are similar to yours. Ask for the name of a specific agent, since not all the agents in a particular agency may be as good.

Orderly Pursuits

Knowing what's available first will only make you a better consumer, even if you use a travel agent. There are some excellent travel sites on the web, and I always like to check on flight availability and fares even if I decide to use an agent. The ones I use the most are Expedia.com and Travelocity.com, but there are others that family and friends favor.

Other Issues

Be aware that some travel agencies are primarily geared toward the business traveler. You may want to look for one that specializes in leisure travel. They usually have the best information on cruises, popular vacation destinations, and specialized travel such as eco-tourism or adventuring.

To get the most from your travel agent, make sure you share as much information as possible. Let her know you are flexible about days of the week and flight times, if that's the case. If you're looking for the cheapest fare possible, make that clear and be willing to put yourself out. The cheapest fare may be the red-eye flight on a little known airline with no amenities.

Make known your travel preferences, such as which airline seat and what kind of food you prefer. You'll want to pass on your frequent flyer numbers, as well.

Decide what kind of relationship you want with your travel agent. You might prefer a personal relationship in which your agent is a travel counselor who makes recommendations, offers tips, and informs you of special events and packages she thinks you might like. Or you might prefer to use your agent as a clerk who follows your instructions and makes reservations. Either is fine as long as you're clear about what you want.

Going It on Your Own

Those of us in the do-it-yourself travel crowd rely heavily on online computer resources. I'm not an expert, but in just a couple of hours of research on the Internet, I found some handy resources for just about every aspect of travel. I've gathered some of the best below:

- ◆ All the major airlines have their own websites. These include:

    America West: www.americawest.com

    American: www.aa.com

    Continental: www.flycontinental.com

    Delta: www.delta-air.com

    JetBlue: www.jetblue.com

    Northwest: www.nwa.com

    Southwest: www.iflyswa.com

    United: www.ual.com

    USAirways: www.usairways.com

♦ Most hotels and motels have their own websites where you can check availability and rates and make reservations. Just pick a search engine and put in the hotel name to locate the home page. Another site with information on hotels and flights in one place is Travel Web at www.travelweb.com.

♦ For a free hotel reservation service covering all major U.S. cities, try Budget HotelFinders at www.bookahotel.com.

♦ TravelNow.com Global Reservations lets you make reservations for 40,000 hotels in 5,000 cities on the web. They're at www.travelnow.com.

♦ There are lots of bed-and-breakfast directories available online, some with photos and detailed information. Check out AA Bed And Breakfast Directory at www.aa-bedandbreakfasts.com or Bed and Breakfast Inns of North America at cimarron.net/index.html.

♦ Major car-rental companies have their own websites. If you're looking for all of them in one place, try BreezeNet's Guide to Airport Rental Cars at www.bnm.com/rcars.htm. This is for companies with airport service only.

♦ If you can't find a travel agent you like in your hometown, you may want to use one of the online travel agents. You get the best of both worlds—all the services of a big travel agency, plus the convenience of business online. Some sites to check out are: www.trip.com, www.travelocity.com, and www.expedia.msn.com. Some features you might like are fare comparison search engines, up-to-the-minute arrival and departure information, saved itineraries, and tracking of your personal frequent flyer accounts.

♦ If you're traveling by car, check out the Mapquest website at www.mapquest.com. You can submit your point of origin and your destination, and it will generate driving directions, distances, and driving times.

Oops!

You know the old saying, "If it sounds too good to be true, it usually is." This is especially true when it comes to discount airline tickets. Be sure you're dealing with a reputable company and that you understand any restrictions. The low price may only apply to a one-way fare, standby, or particular time frame.

Amazing Space

Instead of taking lots of little pieces of paper with you where you've noted confirmation numbers and other pertinent travel information, consolidate it all on one sheet in your planner/organizer. Include airline, hotel, and car rental (plus who you talked to, if that's helpful), confirmation numbers, check-in and check-out times, and any directions you might need.

♦ Are you the outdoors type? You may find your perfect vacation on the Great Outdoor Recreation Page (GORP) at www.gorp.com. If you're into hostelling, check out the Internet Guide to Hostelling at www.hostels.com.

♦ Join general travel discussions online to learn traveling "secrets" and get first-hand accounts from those who've already been where you're hoping to go. There are newsgroups for travel type (rec.travel.cruises), destinations (rec.travel.usa-canada), and activity (rec.travel.budget.backpack), plus one for products and services (rec.travel.marketplace). Also look for e-mail lists covering your favorite travel subjects.

Travel, in General

Whether you're using a travel agent or making arrangements yourself, you can avoid most vacation nightmares with some extra planning. Here are some things you can do to make sure your transportation, accommodations, and meals meet your expectations and budget:

♦ Once you choose your destination, have a written itinerary with all the information in one place. You don't necessarily have to stick to it, but it helps to have an idea of what you're planning to do. I keep mine in my planner/organizer and make a copy for the folks at home so they can reach me in case of an emergency. Make sure to leave one with the house- or pet-sitter, and anyone else who may need to reach you.

♦ Always call ahead and confirm everything. One week ahead is good. The night before or even that morning is advisable for airline reservations. If you're traveling from city to city, you might want to call just before you leave one for another. The objective is "no surprises" and the maximum mount of notice to make other arrangements if something falls through. Check on special travel advisories and anti-terrorism measures. In these times, you need to keep your ears open and double-check!

Oops!

If your flight is canceled for some reason, don't run to the airline counter like everyone else. Pick up the phone and call the airline reservation system. You'll get the same service without standing in line.

♦ Get to know the concierge at the hotel or the desk clerk at the motel. Ask about restaurants, places to go, and anything else you're interested in.

◆ If you're traveling by plane, take the earliest flight you can manage and try to fly Tuesdays through Thursdays or on Sunday morning. These are the times that are least crowded and when you'll experience the fewest delays.

◆ Seats up front on airlines are best for getting overhead storage space and getting off once you're there. Aisle seats are best for getting up and stretching or going to the restroom without having to climb over people.

Pared-Down Packing

Now that you've got your travel arrangements made, the next thing to tackle is what to take. The old school of seasoned travelers recommended packing light and keeping all your luggage as carry-on, but times have changed and many things are no longer allowed in the cabin. There are also new restrictions to the number of carry-on bags (currently one, rather than two) and their size. It's best to check with the airline before you pack. Even if you're not a road warrior, it's a good idea to study those who travel for a living. They can show us the way to keep our infrequent trips from becoming standout nightmares.

When traveling by air, getting everything into the number of carry-on bags allotted (and meeting the size requirement, of course) can be difficult, but it's worth the advance planning and the self-discipline of traveling light. You'll save yourself time waiting for luggage and the inconvenience of lost baggage.

Some regular travelers like a "travel pack" style of luggage. These work as both soft-sided luggage and as a backpack. You don't have to deal with those little wheels getting caught as you try to roll your suitcase or struggle with a collapsible luggage cart. With your travel pack on your back, your hands are free to open doors, handle money, read maps, or hold on to handrails. Several companies make good versions of these, and two of the best are Eagle Creek (www.eaglecreek.com) and REI (www.rei.com). They range in price from under $100 to well over $200, with zippered compartments to hide shoulder straps when you're using them as more conventional luggage.

> **Orderly Pursuits**
>
> For some neat travel luggage and accessories geared specifically for women, call (800) 280-4775 or log on to www.christinecolumbus.com to get your free catalog from Christine Columbus. One product that could help keep you safe is the Arm Alarm, which you put on your wrist. You can trip the alarm, which emits an ear-piercing 120 decibels. The catalog also offers a take-along photoelectric smoke alarm/intrusion sensor for added hotel-room security.

Garment bags can be used for packing suits or fancy dresses, but they're really a pain to carry for any distance. You can sometimes carry them on board and hang them up front in the airplane in a special compartment with a bar for hanging; but these fill up quickly, and you may end up cramming the bag in the overhead compartment. I prefer packing a regular bag or carry-on and pressing these items when I arrive. Most hotels have an iron and ironing board they can lend you, or you can pay for their pressing service.

How to Pack

The best way to pack depends on your priorities. If you're traveling in a more formal mode, you'll be carrying more difficult-to-care-for clothes and will want to keep them as unwrinkled as possible. In this case, you might want to carry a garment bag, where clothes can be laid flat, using tissue paper to keep things from crushing. Hang each item individually, with plastic casings from the dry cleaners pulled over them. If you need some, your dry cleaner will probably be happy to oblige. Make sure to hang up your clothes as soon as you arrive.

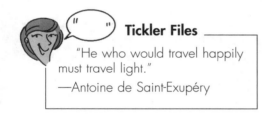

Tickler Files

"He who would travel happily must travel light."

—Antoine de Saint-Exupéry

Layer clothes on hangers so they provide natural cushioning for one another. You can use softer clothes, like sweaters, to hang in between blouses and jackets. Make sure you smooth out each layer before you hang the next one over it.

You can also layer clothes when folding them in a flat suitcase, crisscrossing easily wrinkled clothes with softer knits and "sandwiching" them in half-folds.

If you're traveling with mostly casual clothes, I've found that rolling works best. I carry easy-care knits or gauzy fabrics that are *supposed* to be wrinkled. Broomstick skirts, for example, can literally be tied up in knots. Just lightly roll each item, putting the heaviest items on the bottom, lightest on the top. If you're using soft-sided luggage or a duffel bag, make sure you fill all the corners, or else things will slide around. Use underwear and socks to fill in. Drop your bag a few times (zippered, of course) and reopen, to see where there are any other nooks and crannies to fill.

Always pack things that can leak in separate resealable plastic bags and then in a single plastic toiletry bag. Never pack things that can break or leak with your clothes. Put them in a separate carry-on instead. Changes in air pressure on plane flights and just being knocked around can cause leaks. Remember to leave some room in travel-size bottles so they don't burst with changes in pressure.

Take everything you can't live without in your carry-on, as well as any valuables. Things like medicines, credit cards, cash and traveler's checks, keys, jewelry, electronic devices, cameras, business and travel documents, and eyeglasses or contacts should remain with you at all times. Make sure you have some basic toiletries and a set of clothes in case your checked luggage is delayed. But be sure to be informed about new tightened restrictions on things like nail files, pocket knives, even knitting needles and tweezers. If in doubt, put it in your checked baggage!

What to Pack

Besides your clothes, here's a list of the absolute basics you need to take:

- Toothbrush and toothpaste.

- Razor.

- Hair-care stuff. I just need a brush, shampoo, conditioner, and some elastics, barrettes, and bobby pins, since I have long hair and let it dry naturally. Sure beats lugging that hair dryer and curling iron everywhere! Short hair styles can have the same advantage. If you don't have either, you'll want to take the equipment you'll need—the smaller the better.

- Makeup. Keep this to a minimum.

- Sun protection.

- An umbrella and folding raincoat. These come in very compact sizes and are a must, even (or especially) where they swear it never rains!

- A small travel alarm or a watch with an alarm.

- Important phone numbers and personal information. Just grab your planner/organizer. It should have everything you need, plus you can keep up with your planning and goal-setting activities while you're waiting for your flights.

- Small flashlight.

- Plug adapters (if you're traveling outside the country).

Orderly Pursuits

A great catalog to send for is from Bon Voyage! Travel Books and Maps. Write them at 2069 W. Bullard Ave., Fresno, CA 93711, call (800) 995-9716, e-mail them at info@bon-voyage-travel.com, or log on to their website at www.bon-voyage.travel.com. There's everything for the traveler, from gear to guides, maps to mini-umbrellas, and a store to visit in Fresno if you're ever there.

◆ Earplugs. These are useful not only when you arrive at your destination, but also on the plane, bus, car, or train.

◆ Moisturizer. This is for the skin, but also should be considered for the inside of the nose (a saline spray works best). If you've ever traveled to drier climates or higher altitudes, you'll know what I'm talking about. Also bring along some lip balm. Keep these in your carry-on or in your purse, jacket pocket, or fanny pack.

Orderly Pursuits

If you're a frequent traveler, keep a permanent toiletries bag set up with mini supplies of all the stuff you use regularly. When your next trip comes around, your pre-packed bag is ready to go!

◆ Emergency medical kit. I just use a cosmetic bag to hold a small sampling of aspirin or similar pain-killer, cold remedy, antacid, Band-Aids, and gum for relieving ear pressure on flights or during altitude changes. Bring Dramamine (or some crystalized ginger, for a natural remedy) if you or anyone else is prone to air or car sickness, and antibacterial ointment.

◆ Passport, driver's license, or other photo ID. Don't take your passport if you don't need it!

Picture This

Play out your trip in your mind ahead of time. See yourself en route, then getting to your destination. What's the climate like? What kinds of activities are you involved in? See yourself at night and in the daytime, in your hotel and out sightseeing. What are you wearing? What kind of shoes, hat, clothing? Would a lightweight backpack be practical? A fanny pack? Make your picture as detailed as you can (you've thoroughly researched your destination, right?), then write down what you'll need to bring.

A Word About Clothing

Clothing always represents a special challenge whenever you are preparing to travel. Here are several things to keep in mind:

◆ Pack what you think is enough underwear for your trip, then add two extras. If you're on a long trip, you might want to pack one week's worth and hand wash some or visit the Laundromat. A capful of shampoo makes a fine hand-washing soap in a motel sink!

◆ Layers are best. Make sure you're prepared for colder weather. Even in the desert, nights can be chilly, and when it's overcast you'll be glad you have something warm to snuggle in. Wear your heavier clothing on the plane, if you can.

◆ If things get wrinkled, hanging them in a bathroom while you take a shower helps. There are also compact steamers available.

◆ Stick with only a few compatible colors to mix and match. Black travels best.

◆ Avoid jeans. They're bulky to pack or to hand wash, and they take a long time to dry. If you must have a pair, wear them on the plane (or train or bus) and wear them again on the return trip.

◆ Try to take as few pairs of shoes as possible, and wear your bulkiest ones, like tennis shoes, on the plane, bus, or in the car.

◆ Bring something washable for your feet, like flip-flops or thongs. You can wear them in the shower if it's not up to snuff, as well as in the rain in warm weather.

◆ Make sure you have a sweater in your carry-on. Airplane cabins are usually cold.

Organization and preparation can mean the difference between a really good time and a disappointing vacation. Take the time to think things through and do your homework.

Casting Your Travel Safety Net

You can plan and pack carefully and still have your vacation spoiled by one person's ill intentions or simple bad luck. Prepare in advance for any situation that *doesn't* go as planned, and make sure you leave no openings for an enterprising thief to capitalize upon. Here are good tips:

◆ Identify your luggage inside and out. Use a business address or P.O. box if you have one. Also include your destination information so you can be contacted en route.

◆ If you're traveling by plane and get to the airport very early, wait to check your baggage. It's more likely to be overlooked or tampered with while it waits in the baggage holding area.

◆ Keep all valuables in your carry-on bag.

◆ Be aware of your surroundings. I think in terms of the white/yellow/orange/red principle of awareness taught in self-defense and firearm-safety classes. You

> **CAUTION**
>
> **Oops!**
> Never let your luggage out of sight at an airport or other mass transportation terminal. You're not only protecting yourself from theft, but also from being tricked into carrying drugs or other prohibited items.

should never be in "white" (totally self-absorbed and oblivious to what's going on around you) in public. Stay in "yellow" (alert, watching for signs of trouble, taking in your surroundings) at all times and be prepared to move into "orange" (flight/high alert) or "red" (confrontation/self-defense) quickly and without hesitation, should the need arise.

◆ Carry money, traveler's checks, credit cards, and passport around your neck in a special pouch, then tucked in your shirt. There's even a "water safe," which is a waterproof neck pouch suspended from a cord, ending the problem of what to do with your valuables when you're at the beach. You may want to consider a "redundant" system, where you carry money in a neck pouch, a money belt, and a pants pocket, so that the theft of one won't leave you completely high and dry.

◆ Stay "low-profile" in your dress and your luggage. Fancy luggage is attractive to thieves. Use luggage that can be locked, but be aware that this is not necessarily going to foil unscrupulous baggage handlers or thieves.

◆ A prime target for thieves in airports and bus and train stations these days is the laptop computer. Be sure to keep yours with you and install a security program, so that even if it's stolen, thieves won't have access to your files.

Be on the lookout for thieves working in pairs or teams. It's an old ploy. Two or more people create a distraction, and another grabs the goods. I use a laptop carry bag that has a shoulder strap and is fairly lightweight, so I can carry it across my back by putting the strap over my neck and resting it on the opposite shoulder from where I carry the bag.

> **Amazing Space**
>
> Be sure to carry a water bottle (some hook to a fanny pack or have a "holster belt" of their own that you can wear around your waist), and bring bottled water, if water quality may be a problem. This is especially important when traveling by air. Airplane cabins are often dry. Drink bottled or canned water en route and at your destination. Avoid caffeine and alcohol. They contribute to dehydration.

◆ Don't leave your carry-on luggage on the plane during a stopover. You can't be sure that it'll be there when you get back or that someone won't tamper with it.

◆ Keep a list of everything you have packed in luggage you'll be checking, in case you need to make a claim. When you travel by air, you won't be reimbursed for stolen valuables like cameras, electronic equipment, jewelry, or cash by the airline, so carry them with you.

If you need to make a claim, you'll probably need receipts or proofs of purchase, so keep these in a safe place. Best of all, carry your valuables with you!

- Carry a small amount of food, such as some dried fruit, crackers, or trail mix (dried fruit, nuts, and chocolate chips or M&M's). That keeps you covered if the airline food isn't very appetizing or you get delayed and need a snack. This can be very important if you're prone to fluctuations in blood sugar levels.

- When traveling by car, be sure to keep your doors locked at all times, including in traffic. Be observant, especially at rest stops, where statistics show criminals often lurk. Know the traffic laws in states you'll be traveling to (AAA guides have this information). Be sure your automobile has been thoroughly serviced and tires are safe before you leave. Don't leave valuables like cell phones and cameras visible—you're just inviting disaster. Keep your gas tank full. Don't wait until it's near empty to stop for a fill-up—you could get stranded. We usually go by the half-tank rule. When it's down to half a tank, we stop for gas. This gets you to take more frequent breaks, as well.

- Keep a flashlight, first-aid kit, emergency kit, fire extinguisher, and flares in your car at all times.

- Always accompany children to rest rooms, souvenir shops, and snack bars.

- A number of companies offer backseat organizers with lots of roomy pockets for car and travel paraphernalia like ice scrapers, tour books, and maps. Make sure you can lay your hands easily on your car's manual and a flashlight. A pad and pencil for writing down directions is good to have within reach, and it's not a bad idea to have a tire gauge along, too.

- Check the commuter survival kit you usu- ally keep in your car (see Chapter 9), and make sure it's well stocked. Add any extras that would be helpful on a longer trip, like a neck pillow, window cleaner, paper towels, and some bug and tar remover. Some auto clubs, like AAA, have a list of what auto travelers should carry, and some even carry ready-made kits you can buy.

Orderly Pursuits

The University of Wash- ington Medical Center has a Travel Medicine Service free on the World Wide Web. It alerts travelers to diseases in various countries and vaccinations that should be got- ten before leaving. The URL is depts.washington.edu/travmed. U.S. State Department travel warnings can be viewed at travel.state.gov/travel_warnings. html.

Off the Beaten Track: Specialty Travel

If you're looking for an unusual travel experience, consider giving your vacation a personal theme. I'm not the sit-on-the-beach type. Never have been. My favorite vacations have been pursuing our interests in history, architecture, and nature. If this is your idea of a good time, too, there are many resources to help you find the perfect alternative.

Get back to nature with Earthwise Journeys. They'll guide you to vacations that center around archaeology, ecology, wildlife studies, teaching, and community development. You can visit their website at www.teleport.com/~earthwyz/. Or check out Ecovolunteer at www.ecovolunteer.org/. You can also contact the Ecotourism Society at P.O. Box 755, North Bennington, VT 05257; (802) 447-2121. Their website is www.ecotourism.org.

If you'd like to make the world your classroom, try one of Earthwatch Institute International's expeditions. My daughter did one on an island off the coast of Puerto Rico, helping with sea turtle research, when she was still in high school. It was a deciding factor in her choice of careers. Contact Earthwatch at 3 Clock Tower Place, Suite 100, Maynard, MA 01754; (800) 776-0188; www.earthwatch.org.

If you like excitement, then you may be a candidate for adventure travel. You can experience everything from the white water of the Colorado to the rigors of dog sledding or working a cattle drive. For some ideas sure to thrill the most jaded traveler, contact American Wilderness Experience, P.O. Box 1486, Boulder, CO 80306; (800) 444-0099; info@awetrips.com.

Heritage travel is a general category that's become very popular in the industry over recent years. It covers trips that have a historical theme and may include searching for your ancestral roots. Follow the trail that Lewis and Clark did, for example, as they explored the continent. Visit the website at www. lewis-and-clark.org, and use Julie Fanselow's book *Traveling the Lewis and Clark Trail* as your guide.

> ### Amazing Space
>
> Planning an "alternative" vacation requires more initiative on your part. Most travel agents know little about these innovative choices. You may also have highly specialized needs when it comes to packing your suitcase. You'll need to rely heavily on the organization sponsoring the trip to learn what to bring and how to prepare.

Pick a theme, any theme, and gear your travel to that. If your interest is historic airplanes, then you can plan your vacation around the country's many air museums and exhibitions. If you're a literature buff, perhaps a visit to the homes of America's most revered authors may suit your fancy. Think out of the box for your next vacation. Whatever your interests, there are resources to help you plan a trip around them.

The Family Circus: Traveling with Kids

Traveling with children requires additional preparation. It's not just a matter of keeping them out of your hair; travel is a sterling opportunity to help them learn and discover more about their world. It's a time to build language and observation skills, plus a terrific chance to deepen your relationship.

First, you need to know your child. Does he get carsick? What are his optimum napping and eating times? What are his interests and how can you build them into your vacation?

This is a *family* vacation, not an adult vacation, and the rewards and challenges are different. It's an opportunity to see the world through a child's eyes. Give them time and room to experience it, and make the effort to share it with them.

On the Road

Many parents find traveling with kids by car allows them the greatest flexibility and, of course, is more likely to fit the family budget. But packing a bunch of people of varying ages and temperaments into a small moving box and expecting them to live in peace for eight hours at a stretch is asking too much. If your family car is a compact, consider renting a larger car or van for the trip, especially if the trip is going to be a long one. A minivan has lots of seats, allowing you to separate kids if need be.

And don't always sit with both adults up front and the kids squabbling in the back. Take turns sitting in back with the kids, and give a child the place of honor up front with the driver. The parent assigned to rear duty now has a great opportunity to get involved in games or observe scenery with the kids, and the driver might even ask the younger passenger up front to watch for signs or do some map-reading.

Stop often. That's the best thing about traveling by car—you get to choose when, where, and how often you take a break. Every two hours is a good guideline, even if it's only for 15 minutes or so. Take time to use the facilities, get a snack, stretch, and walk around. Look around you, and give the kids time to take it in, too.

Oops!

Try to stick as close as possible to your child's normal routine, even though you're traveling. Stay away from too many junk food snacks and sugary soft drinks. See that your child gets adequate sleep. There's nothing worse (for you *and* the child) than a sick child away from home.

That's Entertainment

Provide things for the kids to entertain themselves with. This goes for all kinds of travel, not just by automobile. Bring puzzles and coloring books, games, and toys. Let them choose what to bring. Play observation games like Spot the License Plate (more exotic ones get more points), Alphabet (finding objects on the road in alphabetical order), or "I See Something (color)," a guessing game even very young children can play.

Orderly Pursuits

Reading about your destination, before and during the trip, helps make traveling more interesting for everyone. If you're going to a historic location, don't overlook reading about what happened there in the past. And don't limit yourself to human history—we often bring field guides for birds and flowers, so we can "play detective" and identify unfamiliar species.

Encourage older kids to keep a travel diary or journal. They can illustrate it and maybe paste in souvenirs. There's even a prepublished one called *Travel Bug: A Travel Journal for Kids 7 to 14*, by Linda Schwartz (illustrated by Bev Armstrong). A travel treasure box is another good idea. They can take home only what they can fit in the box!

Safety First!

Take extra safety precautions. It's a good idea to have identification badges on smaller children with name, address, and phone information. Teach your children basic rules of safety, including what to do if they're lost. Go over (again) all the precautions about talking to strangers. Some good books and videos are available on the subject. I'm even an advocate of child harnesses or wrist connectors for small children. You may get some disapproving looks, but I'd rather hang on to my child than worry about what other people think. Dressing them in bright colors that are easy to spot is another smart idea.

Don't Forget

Here are some more sound words of advice about kids and travel:

◆ Get detachable shades for backseat windows to shield children from the sun while riding in the car. Just make sure they don't block the driver's view. Remove them for sightseeing.

◆ Choose motels or hotels with a pool, playground, or game room. Some even have programs just for kids. Try to arrive in the late afternoon, so kids have a chance to play for a while before settling down to a meal and then bed.

- Train travel allows kids to move around, get snacks, make new friends, and use the bathroom whenever they need to. It's not cheap, but check the fares for children. They usually go half-price.

- When making plans for reservations, be sure to give the airline the ages of your kids, and ask it to arrange seating accordingly. Children, for example, can't be seated next to exit doors.

- Always bring snacks and a sandwich onboard during a flight with children. You can't count on meals coming when they're hungry, and there can always be a delay. Some juice boxes, raisins, fruit, and crackers are good to have on hand.

- Most of all, chill out. Don't have too many expectations about family togetherness, and keep rules and restrictions to a minimum. Splurge where you can, and let the kids have special privileges, like staying up late or having a favorite meal or snack.

> **CAUTION**
>
> **Oops!** ___
>
> Time baby's bottles for during takeoff and landing, and bring gum for older children. Young children and infants can't "pop" their ears, so taking precautions will help avoid painful ear pressure.

Finally, refer to the resource guide at the back of this book for a good list of travel books for and about kids.

Going Away Without Leaving Home

Want to feel like you had a vacation, without the cost or bother of actually going on one? Take a minivacation close to home! With our busy schedule, we find getting away for weeks at a time difficult. But each year we try to schedule several short one-day getaways, sometimes using our own home as our "bed-and-breakfast." Try these ideas for planning your home-bred vacation:

- Go to your local chamber of commerce, tourist office, or visitor's bureau and find out what's available. Act like a tourist in your own town. There's probably more in your backyard than you ever imagined.

- Check the Yellow Pages for the nearest state park, and call ahead to see if there are any special activities scheduled in the near future. You can get information about national parks in your area by calling the National Park Service in your state (see the State pages of your phone book) or visiting them on the Internet.

For information about National Park Service publications, type in www.nps.gov.

Orderly Pursuits

For more information on hiking and camping opportunities in your area, contact these organizations: The American Hiking Society, 1422 Fenwick Lane, Silver Springs, MD 20910, (301) 565-6704, www.americanhiking.org; The Sierra Club main office in San Francisco, (415) 977-5500; www.sierraclub.org; The Appalachian Mountain Club, (603) 466-2721; www.outdoors.org.

◆ Create a file called Day Trips, and as you come across articles, brochures, or ideas for weekend getaways or daylong adventures, place them in this file. Then when you get the urge, pull out your file and go!

◆ Take day trips to museums, zoos, aquariums, botanical gardens, local farms, and orchards. Some corporations even have interesting free tours. You might want to develop a theme for your wanderings, like nineteenth-century American living or local flora and fauna.

◆ Pitch the tent with the kids in the backyard (or just put your sleeping bags out under the stars), and let the answering machine take any phone calls. The nice thing is, if you need an extra blanket, you just have to go "next door" and get one.

◆ Go on a picnic for the day. Start off early in the morning, and pack an old-fashioned picnic basket. Use real silverware, china (I pack some pretty, heavy glass plates I got at a factory closeout store for 99¢), and linens (food just tastes better that way!). You can roll utensils for each person up in a cloth napkin, and tie with a ribbon for an extra elegant touch. Add thermoses of drinks, finger foods you've prepared the night before or picked up at a gourmet deli, a heavy blanket to lounge on, and a good book you've been meaning to read, or your fishing pole.

Sentimental Journeys Without Silly Souvenirs

Just because you went on vacation doesn't give you a clutter license! Why is it that what seemed so important "to remember the trip by" when we bought it winds up as junk once we get it home?

Don't bring this stuff home. Please. Resist the tourist acquisition trap. Consider these suggestions for remembering your trip and not adding to the junk:

- Keep a travel journal. You can even buy one with a beautiful tooled leather cover and replaceable unlined refills for later trips.

- Purchase a videotape or book to learn more about where you've been, rather than a lot of dumb souvenirs.

- Take pictures, and then select the best ones and put them in your album right after you get home. Throw the bad ones away!

- Pay close attention and savor the experience. The memories and learning are what travel is really all about. If you're busy shopping and taking pictures, you miss the real essence of the experience.

Travel is one of the most important ways we broaden our experience and explore new things. Planning and organizing a trip helps us make the most of these exciting opportunities and concentrate on the "good stuff!" Take the time before, during, and after your vacation to prepare and keep clutter to a minimum. You'll find things go a lot smoother, and your back and shoulders will thank you!

The Least You Need to Know

- Advance planning and organization will help you have the best vacation possible.

- Packing light is a good idea, however you're traveling. If you can keep your luggage to only two bags, you'll be doing yourself a favor.

- Think about safety and observe simple precautions. Always be alert and in "yellow," never in "white."

- Restrain yourself and bring home a minimal amount of stuff from your trip. Rely on your memories, a few photos, and perhaps a travel diary as souvenirs.

Chapter 22

Getting It Together in the Great Outdoors

In This Chapter

- Making the most of your garage space for storage and activity
- Ideas for organizing lawn and garden equipment, tools, and sports equipment
- Outfitting the home workshop
- Basic car care

There are areas of our homes that tend to be neglected when it comes to organization planning, because we don't really consider them part of the living area. The garage, the basement, the yard, and the attic are spaces that are "outside" our daily perusal. We'll deal primarily with the garage in this chapter, but many of the ideas and resources I've presented here can be adapted to other areas as well.

Organizing and making better use of these "outside" spaces can go a long way toward helping us make the best use of our living space. They work with all our other plans to maintain our shelter, get more exercise, have more fun, and fix things that need minor repairs. These "hidden spaces" need organizing, too!

Gourmet Garages: For More Than the Car!

Two questions: Is it impossible to get your car into your garage? If not, is it a challenge that requires an engineering degree or the soul of a daredevil? If the answer to either question is yes, this chapter is for you.

First and foremost, the garage is a house for your car. If it's so cluttered you can't use it to house the family automobile, then you know it's time to hop to it and unstuff! Not only will reclaiming the garage make your car happy (and look nicer longer), it can affect your mood practically every day. Think about it: For many of us, this is the last room we see as we leave the house in the morning for work and the first place to greet us when we come home. We may go through the garage several times each day.

> **Amazing Space**
>
> The garage is a tremendous resource for freeing up your living area. Think about it as a large, open space that's dry, easily accessible to the outside, and handy to the house. It's easy to ventilate—you just open the garage door! And there's probably access to water, either inside the garage itself or just outside. Use your garage to its full potential!

The garage is also an extremely useful space for permanent storage, family activities, and temporary events. A garage is a place where surfaces allow us to make a mess and still easily clean it up, a place to play and work that's unlike any in the rest of the home.

Climate has a lot to do with how useful a garage can actually be. In humid climates, storage of certain materials in a garage may be restricted because of the damage moisture can do to things like paper and fabric. In warmer, dry climates, the garage can be used more like a room, which can be both a blessing and a curse. It can easily become a catchall for all the stuff you've avoided getting rid of. If your climate tends to be humid, you'll have to pay special attention to storage containers and materials.

Unstuff the Place!

You've got the unstuffing routine down pretty well by now. Do the same thing you've done with the rest of your house to get rid of junk that is broken, no longer used, or used so infrequently you can probably share it with someone else. You can use the box system or simply make piles, but the categories are the same: *Trash, Pass On, Put Away, Mystery,* and *Fix It.* You'll want someplace to group recyclables as well.

Decide whether you have the time and commitment to tackle the whole job of cleaning the garage in one fell swoop (having some family helpers makes it less daunting). It's great if you can set aside a full weekend; one day to do the unstuffing and sorting, a second day to hunt down storage materials and containers, and put things in their place. But if you can't see yourself tackling it all at once, clear a sorting area and begin with one section at a time.

Sorting It Out

As you begin to sort, repeatedly ask yourself how long it's been since you've used a particular item and how serious it would be if you lived without it. Also look for rarely used equipment and tools it would be cost- and space-effective to borrow or rent. If you have a neighbor or friend who would make better use of a particular item, offer to give it to them with the condition that you can borrow it back the few times you might need it.

Once you've sorted into your boxes or piles, take out the trash (or if there's more than your garbage company will take in one trip, make a visit to the dump). Move the recycling to the curbside bin or take it to the recycling center. Next, deliver to its destination stuff that needs to be given to charity, directly to other folks you know, or given to family members.

What you're left with are items that need to be put away or fixed, and items you'll make a decision about later (the *Mystery* items). Make this last category as small as you can. It's really just a way of putting off the decision and you'll have to face it sooner or later, so try to decide now. But if you come across something that stops you in your tracks and keeps you from moving on, put it in the *Mystery* pile and revisit it later.

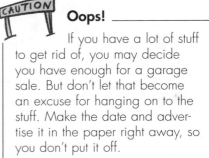

Oops!

If you have a lot of stuff to get rid of, you may decide you have enough for a garage sale. But don't let that become an excuse for hanging on to the stuff. Make the date and advertise it in the paper right away, so you don't put it off.

What stays needs to be sorted again. If you group like things together, you'll probably come up with more things to get rid of, because you'll realize you've already got others just like it. Get rid of duplicates and keep the best. Use any available containers to help you sort. Jars, baskets, boxes, food storage containers, and grocery bags can all be temporary sorting bins.

This is something kids can easily do, even young ones. Sit a seven-year-old down with a box of hardware and have him separate into like shapes. Help him distinguish between a nail and a screw, a nut and a bolt. He'll learn something and help you, too!

Here are some of the major categories of stuff you might find in your garage that can be appropriately sorted and stored there.

Seasonal/holiday decorations and equipment

Sports equipment

Car-washing supplies

Hardware and tools

Gardening supplies and tools

Hobby supplies and tools

Camping supplies and equipment

Bulk paper and canned items

Home repair and maintenance supplies

Electrical supplies

Tapes and adhesives

Bedding and off-season clothing

Long-term files and other papers

Compare this list with what's actually in your garage. Add anything that's specific to your activities or lifestyle. Since we run two businesses from our home, for example, our garage also needs to house boxes and shipping materials. Some of the writing files I need to retain, but don't refer to often, are in a four-drawer file cabinet in our dry Arizona garage.

 **Oops!** _____

Be aware of extreme temperatures in your garage (put a thermometer there and check it often). Extreme heat and cold can make it the wrong place to store paints, crafts supplies, or garden products. Read the labels for ideal storage temperatures. A basement or inside storage location may be better.

Super Centers

How well are things currently stored in your garage? Is there moisture damage? Are critters like insects or rodents chewing away at your precious possessions? Would better storage containers make a difference? Do you need to get some traps or have a pest control service come in? Are you using the space available for storage in the best way?

If you can manage it, clear everything out of the garage that's left and start from scratch. Try and view it as a room. It might help to make a floor plan, taking measurements and roughing it out on graph paper. Take into account the space you'll need for the cars. As you plan out how you're going to use the remaining space, think of the uses your family makes of the garage and create "centers" wherever possible. Some possible centers you might consider:

- Recycling center
- Gardening center
- Workshop and repair center
- Car-care center
- Sports center
- Camping center
- Outdoor furniture and accessories center
- Hobby center
- Shoe- and boot-care center
- Bulk and emergency storage center

> **Amazing Space**
>
> If there really isn't any room in your garage, consider whether you can add a shed or small outbuilding on your property to store large equipment like the lawnmower, snow blower, and wheelbarrow, as well as flammable substances. Make sure it can be locked and is thoroughly protected from the elements.

Giving careful consideration to actual uses will help you decide which storage solutions you'll need. It will also make it easier to locate various things. You'll want the bulk paper products near the door to the house, for example, but the outdoor furniture and bicycles need to be closer to the garage door, since they're actually used outside. Observe the same principles you did when you planned your indoor space, including traffic flow and storage priority (*prime real estate*, *secondary*, and the *deep freeze*).

There are also things you can do to the physical structure of the garage to make it more usable. If it doesn't have finished walls, you can put up dry wall, but if you use plywood instead, you can hang things more easily—even heavy things. Or perhaps consider finishing only part of it—along one wall, for instance—and using the unfinished spaces between studs to store garden and other long-handled tools and equipment. Consider painting the walls. It makes the garage look cleaner, but more importantly, white paint will mean better light reflection. Use a primer and a couple of coats of white paint if it's never been painted before.

Roll up all hoses, cords, wires, ropes, and string. Fasten and hang. Hang or group smaller ones together in a labeled container.

You can also paint the floor. You'll need a concrete paint or clear seal. You'll need to get it clean first, and get up any oil spills and other stains. You can use paint thinner or mineral spirits and work it into the stain, pour on kitty litter, and let it set overnight; then sweep it up to get rid of oily stains. Wash the floor down with degreaser, rinse, and then paint or seal. Follow the product directions.

If you've got the inclination and money to do some slightly more ambitious renovations to the garage area, my choice would be adding a utility sink. Another renovation that increases usefulness is putting in plenty of electrical outlets.

We keep a folding banquet table in the garage for use as a "staging area" during any projects like shipping, bulk shopping, certain work projects, or hobby projects. When we don't need it, we fold it and store it against the wall. A set of sawhorses and a sturdy piece of plywood can be used to create a similar work surface when and where you need it.

Oops!

If the fuse box or circuit breaker box is in the garage, make sure you allow for easy access. Never block doors or windows.

Make sure you sweep and dust the garage regularly. The garage is often the first line of defense in the war on dirt in the house, since it's often the place we enter the house from. Be sure to put mats at entrances from outside into garage and from the garage into house, and clean them often. Provide a place to leave soiled shoes and clothes, as well.

Storage Shopping List for the Garage

Once you've unstuffed the garage, sorted what's left, and made any improvements on the physical structure and decor of your new room, the next step is to make a list of the storage products and hardware you'll need to establish each of your activity centers. As you make your list, consider these garage storage solutions:

◆ **Plastic boxes in various sizes and shapes.** Plastic shoe boxes are a good size for hand tools, crafts supplies, seasonal decorations, and larger hardware. Uniform box sizes help make the most of shelf space because you can space shelves closer together.

◆ **Shelving.** Design shelves around what you store most often. Consider products that allow you to change shelving configuration as needs change.

- **Hooks and clamps** for hanging things overhead or on the walls. Heavier hooks, like those made to hold ladders, can also be used to hang up bicycles or a wheelbarrow. Hooks or racks suspended from the ceiling need to be put into the joists.

- **Pegboard.** A pegboard system is extremely flexible. You can get hardware for shelves and move them when your needs change. Make sure the pegboard is screwed into the studs, so it doesn't pull down with heavier items. Go from floor to ceiling in at least one area.

- **Plastic and metal trash cans.** These can be used to store pet foods, fertilizers, soil, sand, kitty litter, and any other dry materials you want to keep that way. If wall space is at a premium, you can use them to stand up long-handled tools and some lighter-weight building materials. Use a can to store clean rags and towels.

- **Coffee cans, glass jars, and plastic food containers.** When it comes to storing large quantities of small objects like hardware and hobby supplies, there's nothing like the old standbys. If you don't drink coffee, get a friend to save her coffee cans for you. You'll need to label anything you can't see through, so make sure you have plenty of labels and markers handy.

- **Cigar boxes.** The local tobacconist should be able to supply you with a steady supply of wooden cigar boxes. These come in all shapes and sizes and are great for storing both hardware and crafts materials. Best part is, they're free!

Orderly Pursuits

For ideas on storage to build or buy for your garage, attic, or basement, check out *Creating Storage: Hidden Storage and Rescued Space in the Garage, Attic, or Basement* from the editors of Sunset Publishing Corporation, and *Complete Home Storage* from the same publisher. Both books are excellent home storage primers.

Amazing Space

For storing small objects, don't forget glass jars with tops screwed to the underside of a shelf. These hold small hardware and make it easy to see the contents.

- **Netting.** An old hammock or flexible netting made specifically for storage is useful for suspending things like sports equipment, beach balls, and pool toys.

Your garage is going to be mostly for *secondary* and *deep freeze* storage. You're using the *prime real estate* inside your home for things you use on a regular basis. Put the things you use more than once a year at arm's length, within easy reach so you can get to them right when you need them. Stuff you use rarely can go in more difficult-to-reach higher spots or behind other things. Especially make use of areas near the ceiling and overhead.

Give Yourself a Shop

If you don't have a workbench, you may want to designate a space and either purchase or build one. For tools, you may want to use a toolbox or chest, but consider a rolling cart if you do a lot of tinkering on your car or work on hobbies that require you to spread out. Check industrial supply houses, automotive supply stores, and catalogs for some possibilities.

> **Orderly Pursuits**
>
> To create the ultimate workshop, you'll find all the ideas you'll need in the book *The Home Workshop Planner: A Guide to Planning, Setting Up, Equipping, and Using Your Own Home Workshop* from the editors of Wood Publications. Although specifically aimed at woodworkers, this book will help any home do-it-yourselfer build the workshop or his or her dreams.

You should have a fire extinguisher and a smoke alarm in the garage, even if you don't work there very often. If you're going to do anything like painting or gluing, you'll need to allow for adequate ventilation. During the months when you can't keep the garage door open, you may need a ventilating fan for getting toxic fumes out of the area.

Setting Up Shop

Before you actually get your shop storage organized, decide which tools you use most often and make them easy to access. Pegboard is one solution, and it can be put up right over your workbench. Some people advocate drawing a silhouette around each tool once you've got it placed where you want it, to encourage putting each one back where it belongs. Since I'm someone who moves from one activity to another at different times of the year or when the spirit strikes me, I reorganize my tools each time I start a new project, so that arrangement probably wouldn't be flexible enough for me.

> **Oops!**
>
> Always make sure you have enough room to work safely. Cramped spaces can be dangerous. Bring the job out into the driveway if you need more space. Wear "eyes" and "ears" (eye and ear protection) whenever working with power tools and even some hand tools. Make sure to take steps to protect children and pets while you're working.

If it's rusted, if you don't know what it went with, or if you don't know what it is or what it's used for, get rid of it. Sort hardware by type (screw, nail, nut, bolt) and then subdivide if necessary (sheet metal screws, wood screws). Take the time to sort, contain, and label (or, as I said earlier in this book, get a kid to do it!).

Every household should have a toolbox or tool kit of some kind. And they should be hand tools, not power tools. Sure, power tools have their place and can be added once your basic tool kit is outfitted, but you need a set of good quality hand tools, especially in the event of an emergency like a storm that knocks the power out. Think about the jobs you most often do around the house and start there. You'll need to drive screws and nails, remove nails, measure, paint, and drill a hole.

What kind of toolbox should you have? Plastics now are rugged and more resistant to extremes in temperature. They're lighter than metal and don't rust, which makes them a better choice than metal most of the time. Or you may want to try a heavy-gauge canvas carrier with pockets for individual tools for your basic kit.

Orderly Pursuits

Get yourself a good, basic home repair manual. One excellent one is *Basic Home Repairs* by the editors of Sunset Publishing Corporation. You can also find a wealth of information on projects, tools, and storage from the Home and Garden Television website at www.hgtv.com/.

Buy the best-quality tools and tool box you can afford. You'll have them a long time, and they'll always do the job if they're of good quality. Make sure power tools are scaled to your size. They can be dangerous if you can't hold them properly. Before you use any power tool, always read the directions! Store manuals and instructions in your household file or an accordion file for all manuals and Warranties. Ask the salesman to show you how it works, if you're not sure. Bring it back and ask again if, when you go to use it, you're stumped.

Even hand tools need to be used properly or you can do damage or hurt your yourself. Again, if you're not sure, get a more experienced do-it-yourselfer to show you how.

Tool Checklist

Here are some basic tool categories and specific suggestions for you to build your basic tool collection for most household jobs:

Hammers

One large claw hammer (16 ounces)

Smaller hammer

Rubber hammer

Magnetic upholstery hammer

Pliers

Channel lock

Needle nose

Vice grip

Hardware

Finishing nails

Standard nails

Wall anchors

Cup hooks

Picture-hanging hardware

Bolts

Wing nuts

Screwdrivers

Flat

Phillips head

Insulated

Wrenches

Hex

Allen

Crescent

Adjustable crescent

Measuring implements

Tape measure

Straight edge

Yardstick

Combination square

Level

Power tools

Electric drill/screwdriver, cordless

Sander

Jigsaw

Circular saw

Soldering iron

Dremel tool

Screw eyes

Thumbtacks

C clamps

Spring clamps

Tapes and glues

Duct tape

Electrical tape

Teflon tape

Masking tape

All-purpose white glue

Epoxy

Saws

Standard

Miter

Coping

Hacksaw

Miscellaneous

Wire stripper and cutter

Metal snips

Chisels

Utility knife

Razor scraper

Putty knives

Hand drill and drill bits, including a spade drill bit for larger holes

Assorted sandpapers

Assorted wires; braided picture wire, copper, and galvanized

Paint brushes and roller set

Paint scrapers

Wire brushes for cleaning

Awl

X-Acto knife

Kevlar gloves

Safety goggles

Dust mask

Rasps and files

You don't need to buy all these tools at once, nor will you necessarily need them all. But having a good basic toolbox filled with high-quality tools will make it easier to keep things around the house in good repair and might even lead to your tackling some challenging and rewarding do-it-yourself projects.

Car Care for the Connoisseur

The garage is primarily, after all, the place you keep your car. Keeping it in the garage protects its finish from the oxidizing rays of the sun and damaging elements like weather, bird droppings, and tree sap. It's only fitting your garage should also have a center for keeping your car clean and beautiful. If you don't want to wash your car yourself, then make regular appointments to take it to a car wash, and don't neglect it. Make sure the car wash is the "brushless" kind, but be aware that even those can do damage to your car's finish if the rotating fabric they use to do the cleaning isn't clean.

The kindest method for keeping your car clean is a hand wash, and nobody will give it the time and effort you can, even if you can find a commercial hand car wash. So, if I've convinced you do it yourself (or at least convinced you to bribe your kids), then organize your car-care tools and supplies to make it easy.

Wash your car (or any other vehicles) every few weeks, and wax it twice a year (how about at tax time and just before Thanksgiving, or any other six-month interval you are likely to remember?). Be aware that asking about formulas for washing cars is a lot like asking a fisherman which

Oops!

For safety's sake, make sure to check if the garage door reverses. Put a wood block under it and bring it down to see if it automatically goes back up when it hits. Maintain your automatic door carefully. Lubricate, tighten, and replace parts.

bait is best—it depends on the fisherman! Usually a mild soap is all you need. I like to use a little bit of dishwasher detergent to soften the water. Use tepid water, not hot—you don't want to remove the wax.

Have a bucket; some natural sponges; a small can of kerosene to dissolve road tar, bird droppings, bugs, and tree sap; some old towels (cotton diapers also work well) to dry the car; glass cleaner; paper towels; upholstery or leather cleaner; and whatever wax products you like to use (carnauba is considered best by many professionals). Keep these supplies all together and easy to get to. When it's time to wash the car, all you need to bring is the hose and a vacuum cleaner.

> **Amazing Space**
>
> Hang a ball on a string from the garage ceiling to touch the windshield of each vehicle being housed in the garage, so you know the ideal spot to park the car. If it's a tight fit or the garage is shallow, use old tires hung up at the proper height to protect your car from bumping the garage wall. Paint a white or yellow line if it would help position the car in the garage.

Vacuum the car's upholstery thoroughly, and spot clean if necessary. Empty ashtrays and change holders. Check any storage bins and pockets. Wash windows on both sides (in the shade), and air out the vehicle by opening all the windows and doors. I have a small aromatherapy diffuser that plugs into the cigarette lighter. This can be filled with any essential oil you choose to give the car a fresh, natural scent that may even improve your mood or help heal you!

Make sure your emergency kit is stocked and in good order (see Chapter 9 for how to put together a commuter survival kit). Each time you wash the car is a good time to evaluate whether your car needs any repair or servicing. When was the last time you took it in for an oil change? Check fluid levels. Replenish windshield washer fluid. Check the spare tire and jack.

Grow Smart: Setting Up a Garden Center

If you're an avid gardener like me, you'll need lots of room for supplies and tools. But even if all you do is maintain a simple, low-maintenance yard, you'll need some basic things to do the job, and a place to store them.

Most garden implements can be stored in the garage, but certain substances may be best stored in a shed that's not attached to the house, and should be under lock and key. I try to use only nontoxic fertilizers and insect control methods, but once in a while the only solution is a mild poison. Weed out old sprays, powders, and poisons, and dispose of outdated ones properly.

Most long-handled garden tools hang nicely on the wall. You can stagger them up and down (like shoes in a shoe box—one with handle up, the next with handle down) to fit them closer together and make the best use of available space. Pegboard is a good storage solution, or there are several rack systems you can buy that hold tools with clamps, pegs, or brackets. If you don't have enough wall space to hang tools, use a heavy metal garbage can and set them in the can, handles down. Use a garden caddy for smaller tools or sort by type in boxes and label.

Have an area set aside for caring for your garden tools and equipment. At the end of each day you garden, wipe off dirt and moisture. Every couple of months, sharpen, grease hinges, repair or replace split or broken handles, and replace missing parts.

Oops!

Proper disposal of hazardous household products and chemicals is extremely important to protect your local water supply. To find out how and where to take them in your area, contact your city or town, your garbage disposal company, or your cooperative extension service. Excellent guidelines are available through the North Carolina Cooperative Extension Service at www.bae.ncsu.edu/ programs/extension/publicat/ wqwm/he368_3.html. The publication number is HE 368-3.

When fall cleanup or spring planting comes around, we consider the garage our "staging area." All the appropriate tools for cleaning gutters, touching up paint, planting bulbs, cleaning up debris, or whatever, are assembled and either laid out on the floor or arranged on our folding table. We make a list of what's needed to complete the job and do our shopping, and when we return home we're ready to roll!

Be a Sport!

Another common garage storage challenge is dealing with the various sports equipment members of the family use at different times of the year. Any garage might house a portable basketball hoop, baseball paraphernalia, soccer balls, skis and poles, bicycles, exercise equipment, and more. If you find yourself overwhelmed by the ghosts of sports enthusiasms past, weed out stuff from activities you or your family members no longer engage in. If junior doesn't play baseball anymore, but is heavy into soccer, ditch the former slugger's gear.

There are special storage systems for specific sports gear—ski racks, fishing gear storage systems, netting to hold balls and gloves, and bicycle brackets, but most can be adapted from inexpensive hardware for general use. Fishing poles lie nicely, horizontally suspended from two pegs or hooks. A fishnet hangs from pegboard on a hook.

Ladder hooks screwed into studs hold up bicycles off the floor. Skis can be put with bottoms together and tips turned upward, then suspended between two pegs put close together. Ski poles can each rest between two pegs. Look around at commercial storage solutions and see how they can be imitated.

Periodically revisit your sports equipment storage center and honestly evaluate whether you're still "into" each activity. If not, pass the equipment on. There are now outlets for secondhand sports equipment that might be eager to have yours—they might even give you cash or a trade-in discount for new equipment for your current sports passion.

I Can Use the Garage for That?

Now that your garage looks like a million bucks, think about some unconventional uses for that glorious new "room." Did you ever think of entertaining in the garage? I mean, how many other spots in your home could really accommodate a dance floor? Move out the cars, give the floor a clean sweep and a rinse, decorate and get creative with the lighting, set up a sound system, and you've got a dance!

Or how about gathering evergreens and floral supplies and staging a holiday wreath-making party? Add a Crock-Pot with some spiced cider, play some holiday music on the boom box, and you'll get in the holiday spirit in no time.

Picture This

Close your eyes and imagine a large open, covered space with nothing in it—your garage! Imagine you had unlimited resources and time to transform it into anything your heart desires. What might that be? A tropical setting complete with palm trees and parrots? A proper English ballroom with chandeliers and a long banquet table dressed in fine linens? A bowling alley? Don't laugh! With some ingenuity and creativity, this often overlooked space could be the foundation of your next party or family gathering—use a theme to make it fabulous!

When I was a child, the boy next door was one of the few kids on the block to have an automatic garage door. The neighborhood kids all got together and, Andy Hardy–style, started a theater group. We used Arnold's garage door as our "curtain" and the garage as our stage. We sold tickets, provided refreshments, and set up seating in the driveway. There were several summers that our "theater" kept us busy and provided hours and hours of fun. Each year the productions got more elaborate. Nobody said "I'm bored" during the summer at Arnold's house!

Do you do a lot of entertaining for large groups? If you have the room, you may want to use part of the garage for an extra refrigerator or stove. First make sure the wiring is adequate, but having another oven when you're creating a sit-down dinner for 25, or an extra refrigerator for beverages and do-ahead dishes, is a true boon for the avid entertainer.

If you're involved as a community volunteer, some tables and chairs set up in the garage will provide a large space for doing a bulk mailing or making posters or signs for an event. We use ours periodically to do shipping for our businesses.

Think creatively about your garage space. Make it work to enhance your activities and as a tool to make the most of the outdoors. Don't overlook the other "forgotten" spaces in your home, as well. The basement and the attic may offer new frontiers for your cherished activities if you'll only look at the space in a new way.

The Least You Need to Know

◆ As with other spaces in your life, the first step to making efficient use of your garage space is to unstuff it.

◆ Viewing the garage as a room, and planning it accordingly, will help guide you to make the most of it for family activities and storage.

◆ Activity centers are one effective way of organizing what you store.

◆ Safety is important in the garage. Pay attention to the storage of hazardous materials and dangerous tools. Dispose of toxic products properly.

◆ Consider unconventional uses for your garage space.

23

Let the Good Times Roll!: Planning the Perfect Party

In This Chapter

- ◆ Using organization and planning techniques for a great party every time

- ◆ Ways to cut party preparation time down by planning ahead and using premade elements

- ◆ Managing guest lists, equipment, food preparation, space, time, and traffic flow

- ◆ Tips for handling weekend guests

- ◆ When and how to hire a caterer

Some people seem to have been born to the Royal Order of Great Hosts. They're somehow blessed with an aptitude for entertaining, which for them seems effortless and fun. When faced with some catastrophe like a boorish guest or a hurricane, these creatures are totally unfazed and somehow manage to make the event into something enjoyable.

What makes a confident, relaxed host? Study some carefully and you're likely to find they're well organized, practical, intuitive, and open to a challenge.

Planning for Party Success

Advance planning and list-making are the two most important keys to giving a successful party, no matter what kind, formal or casual. These basic organization techniques (you've had lots of practice perfecting them by now!) can do much to eliminate chaos and help you be relaxed and in control. If you're having a good time, so will everyone else.

I usually plan a party on a legal pad or in a spiral-bound notebook, and I make several lists. Once I've decided on the menu, I make a grocery list. Don't forget to check your staples. This prevents problems such as running out of sugar and having to dash out for it at the last minute.

You could make another list for equipment, decorations, and dishes you'll need. This is especially important for a larger party. Make sure to include things like a coffee urn, plates, silverware, platters and serving bowls, serving utensils, and linens.

Try not to buy things just for this one occasion; this will only add to seldom-used clutter. See if you can borrow from a friend, or you could rent. You may need some help with additional refrigerator or freezer space, as well, so you'll want to line that up.

> **Amazing Space**
>
> Making the master grocery list suggested in Chapter 11 makes checking staples easy. Before the party, just glance over the list and add anything you're low on to your party shopping list.

Still another list is a To-Do list specifically for the event with a schedule of when to do each task. By using this list, there will be no rushing around at the end, and you can use that time instead to pamper yourself and look your best. You may want to organize this list as a timeline or "countdown to lift-off" for the event.

What Kind of Party?

There are basically four kinds of parties:

1. **An open house,** where guests can drop in between certain hours, but time is not specified.

2. **A cocktail party,** which revolves around beverages (alcoholic and nonalcoholic) and smaller finger foods.

3. **A coffee and dessert party,** centering on a variety of sweeter dishes, coffee, and tea.

4. **The dinner party,** which can be either a sit-down affair or a serve-yourself buffet. Sometimes guests cook part of the meal along with the host. This type of party can be centered around any meal—breakfast, brunch, lunch, or supper.

Which one you choose will be based on time, budget, the nature of the occasion, and what strikes your fancy, energy, and ambition.

Choosing a Date

Once you decide to have a party and what kind, you need to decide the best day and time. Choose a date that gives you ample time to prepare. If you work a full-time, five-day week, Friday night doesn't give you much leeway. It can work, however, if you choose food that can all be prepared ahead of time and work on it a few nights in advance.

Saturday's the classic "party night," and for that reason often competes with other activities. Make sure you give plenty of notice (two to three weeks) so you're sure to have a good turnout.

Some people like Sunday afternoon or early evening for a nice, relaxing time. I especially enjoy Sunday brunches. I can prepare the day before, the housework is all done, and everyone's gone early enough that I can get the house cleaned up for the week ahead and have Sunday evening to myself.

In many circles, Thursday night has become the "new night out." With work looming in the morning, scheduling a party on this night usually ensures people will leave before the wee hours and the party will be fairly subdued.

Allow plenty of time if you're planning a gathering for key holiday weekends. Forget the weeks before and after Christmas, unless you get your invitations out early. Be aware of important sports events. There's nothing like planning a Sunday afternoon party and finding out no one can come because the Super Bowl is on!

 Tickler Files

"A balanced guest list of mixed elements is to a successful party what the seasoning is to a culinary triumph."

—Letitia Baldridge

Planning the Best Guest List

Sometimes you want a party filled with familiar faces—maybe it's even a family gathering. But now and then, you may want or need to plan a party for business associates or acquaintances who are less familiar to you or to each other. Here are some basics for putting together a good group:

◆ Don't go for a homogeneous group. Invite people with different occupations, from different backgrounds and age groups.

◆ When introducing guests, explain their connection to you to get the conversation going. If you know one guest shares an interest or business with another, introduce them to each other first.

Oops!

Make sure guests know whether the party includes kids. Nothing's worse for everyone, including the child, if you get your wires crossed. If you're including kids, provide activities to entertain them, plus food they'll like.

◆ If your personal and professional circles tend to center around people of similar ages and backgrounds, consider co-hosting your gathering with a friend to broaden the list and assemble a more diverse group. You'll also have someone to help plan the party!

◆ If it's a sit-down affair, separate couples, and put compatible strangers next to each other if at all possible.

◆ If you're looking for a certain number of people, have some alternates you can invite if your first round of invitations yields several who can't make it.

You Are Cordially Invited

Invitations help set the stage and can actually be used to smooth the way to a successful party. Consider written and mailed invitations. This can cut down on time spent on the phone and gives your guests a piece of paper they can refer to with all the pertinent details. You can even send along written directions and/or a map if your place is difficult to find, or guests haven't been there before.

Whether you issue your invitations by mail or phone (or electronic mail), the obvious information to include is the date, time, and location (make it clear if it's indoors or out); the reason for the party and the type (breakfast, brunch, lunch, cocktails, dinner, dessert, late supper, open house); a request to RSVP with your phone number and any special instructions as to dress (formal, semiformal, casual, costume); whether bringing a guest is appropriate (I then address it John Doe and Guest); and whether children are invited ("Children Welcome" or "Adults Only" usually does the trick).

For very formal occasions, sending invitations three to four weeks in advance is a good idea, but for more casual parties, a week or two is sufficient. Then there are those impromptu gatherings (often the best, in my opinion) when you decide to celebrate an occasion only a few days hence or even that very day. These serendipitous occasions require a different approach, obviously, and the invitation may be nothing more than a verbal one with a follow-up phone call with details and directions.

A word about RSVPs: I've taken to contacting those who don't respond, in spite of an "RSVP" on the invitation, simply because I need to know how many are coming for seating arrangements or estimating quantities of food. Make an effort not to embarrass the invitee who's been remiss, even though it would have been nice of her to let you know her plans. She may have forgotten or may just not be as organized as you!

> **Amazing Space**
>
> Use postcards for invitations if the information is short and sweet. It's quicker, easier, *and* cheaper!

Planning the Food

There are scads of books and magazine articles on party food and the ideal entertaining fare. I'll leave the details up to you. Here are some general things about party food planning that I've learned over the years or gleaned from experts, including caterers and professional party planners:

♦ Stick with classic dishes, not fussy food. You may get more ambitious if you have the time and the inclination, but generally, prepare things you know how to do well. Simpler food is also more likely to appeal to a greater number of your guests.

♦ Prepare everything you can the day before. Desserts can be done ahead of time, especially if you choose a cake, pie, or pudding. All you might need to add is a final topping or garnish. Rice, pasta, and potato dishes also lend themselves to advance preparation, at least in part.

 **Oops!**

Go easy on the hors d'oeuvres at a dinner party. If you serve too much food before dinner or it's too rich, no one will have room for the main meal. Have a limited time for cocktails and hors d'oeuvres, then usher people to the table or open the buffet.

♦ Avoid fragile food that needs to be handled carefully (like a soufflé) or stored in the refrigerator with nothing touching it (like meringue pie or a Jell-O mold). Look instead for foods that fit easily into plastic storage containers or stack in casserole dishes.

Amazing Space

For parties, one way to apply the techniques you learned from bulk cooking (Chapter 10) is to compare recipes and see if you can double up on tasks for several dishes. Chop all the onions, peppers, or parsley at the same time, for example.

♦ Avoid foods that are time-consuming to prepare, unless you really have the time. Be realistic about the time you have. Check recipe preparation times and make sure you account for them in your written planning schedule.

♦ Consider the keeping times of foods when scheduling their preparation. If you're making a rice and seafood dish, for example, you can make the rice well ahead and reheat, while you'll want to buy and cook the fish the same day you'll be serving it.

♦ If you're chilling foods to put out for a hot buffet, make sure to allow time for them to come to room temperature or to reheat, if necessary.

♦ Err on the side of generosity. Having too little food can really dampen the party spirit, and you can always freeze the extra or send people home with leftovers. And make sure you and your family like what you've prepared. You may be eating it for the next day or two!

♦ If you choose to fix something that has to be made just before serving, do what they do on the cooking shows—have everything premeasured in little cups or bowls and prepare anything else you can ahead of time.

♦ If you're having an outdoor party, play it safe. Bacteria can grow quickly, especially in warmer temperatures. Keep foods either cold or hot (heating destroys bacteria) and keep utensils and preparation surfaces clean.

♦ You'll want to keep foods served outdoors fresh and good-looking, too. Provide shade. Hot, direct sunlight quickly heats up and dries out foods. Use umbrellas, roof overhangs, shadow from buildings, or greenery to provide shade.

♦ Include some low-fat and vegetarian dishes, since food preferences vary widely. I usually have two desserts, one for the calorie-, fat-, and sugar-watchers, and one for those lucky folks who don't need to be concerned.

♦ Keep a rein on the alcohol. That's easier to do at a sit-down dinner, but at a cocktail party, open house, or buffet where you may have a bar set up, it could be a bit trickier. One way to handle it is to have one person assigned to fixing drinks, instead of an "open" bar.

Do-Ahead Entertaining

In Chapter 11, you learned some great methods for taking the load off of weekly meal preparation. Why not adapt some of them to entertaining? Certain hors d'oeuvres can be made ahead and frozen to be used any time you feel like having a few guests over. Make meatballs, quiches, cheese- or meat-filled pastries, or pizzas in bite-sized portions, and freeze. Even dips and spreads can be frozen ahead (guacamole freezes well!). If you're not sure, make a small batch and experiment with freezing and thawing. There are also some helpful cookbooks to help you learn to use your freezer to its full party potential.

For dessert and coffee parties, choose desserts that you can do ahead and keep in the refrigerator or freeze and thaw. Pies and cheesecakes usually freeze well. Even meringue or cream pies can be completely baked, frozen uncovered for one or two hours until firm, and then wrapped, labeled, and frozen further. Cookie doughs can be made ahead, rolled into logs, sealed, and frozen, too. Just thaw the log, slice, and bake.

Besides having the hors d'oeuvres made ahead for a cocktail party, you can make up drink mixes (sans alcohol) and freeze those, too. Strawberry daiquiris, margaritas, and other fruit drink mixes can be whipped up in the blender and frozen in containers for party night. Make all your setups, and slice lemons and limes ahead of time, so you're not doing it at the last minute.

Orderly Pursuits

Don't want to add another cookbook to the shelf? Check out some great do-ahead recipes on the Busy Cooks website at The Mining Company, www.busycooks.about.com. For other ideas, check out www.ichef.com.

If you use the bulk cooking method outlined in Chapter 11, you can add a party to the plan, cook most of it ahead, and freeze it. This will not only save you time, but will make the most of bulk buying and save you money. We've done a french bread pizza party, for example, buying the bread, making a big batch of homemade tomato sauce, and even dividing up the fixings in individual resealable freezer bags (cheese, pepperoni, sausage, peppers), then putting them all in the freezer. The morning of the party, everything is taken out to thaw, and when guests arrive we assemble the pizzas and put them in the oven. Great for a Friday night party when we have to work all day. Just add your party plans into your once-a-month cooking shopping list.

Short-Order Get-Togethers

Impromptu gatherings can be pulled off easily, too, even if you don't have a stash in the freezer. In fact, you can decide to have a party during the day and pull it together by the time you get home from work! Short-order entertaining makes use of premade foods available from a variety of sources—the grocery store, the corner deli, the wholesale club, your local bakery, and area eateries that have take-out.

Assemble an elegant wine and cheese party in record time, with just a stop to the grocery store for crudités, breads, fruit, and deli meats, then a stop at the local liquor store for an assortment of wines. Just a slice of salami spread with herbed cream cheese and folded over makes a delicious megaquick finger food. Try a specialty deli for some unusual salads and spreads. Our local health food market has a wonderful variety of healthy and adventurous salads to choose from, and so does our Italian deli. Add jars of marinated artichoke hearts and marinated mushrooms, make some quick spreads in the food processor (try cream cheese and crabmeat or pitted green and black olives, olive oil, lemon juice, and some garlic). If you want a luxurious touch, buy some precooked frozen shrimp and thaw quickly under cold running water. Add some cocktail sauce for dipping.

The trick here is presentation. Put everything into attractive dishes and trash the supermarket packaging. It'll look like you spent hours preparing!

> ### Amazing Space
>
> Keep ingredients for last-minute garnishes and enhancing premade dishes on hand in the pantry and the fridge and freezer. I usually try to have a supply of various chopped nuts, dried fruits, shredded coconut, cans of mushrooms, artichoke hearts, chile and jalapeno peppers, bamboo shoots and water chestnuts, and soups for sauces in the pantry. Frozen cooked shrimp and an assortment of vegetables come in handy for a quick appetizer or additions to soups or salads. Chopped dehydrated onions and lots of different dried herbs and spices come in handy, too.

The short-order entertaining concept works great for dessert and coffee parties, too. Buy fresh berries, whipped cream, and sponge cake or pastry shells for a quick but fancy-looking dessert. Buy assorted cookies and pastries at the bakery, brew tea in a pretty teapot, and put on the coffee. If you add some fresh flowers from the grocery store florist and your extra-nice dishes and linens, you've got an elegant gathering.

Even dinner parties can be put together on the fly. The idea is to buy the basics ready-made and then add your own touches. These days, chickens roasted on the spit are available at any large grocery store. Add a special sauce, glaze or gravy, garnish attractively, and you've got the main course. Use frozen vegetables, but add toasted almond slivers, green onions, bacon bits, or other "extras" to make them special. Instead of potatoes, cut frozen corn on the cob into smaller pieces and toss with melted butter and pepper.

Parties where guests do the cooking are another short-order idea. Remember the fondue parties from the '60s? Well, dust off that fondue pot and skewers! It's fun and takes practically no preparation. All you'll need are the pots (figure on one pot per four people). Just about everybody's got one of these in their basement gathering dust. Ask around. Check thrift stores and yard sales. Make sure you have enough long-handled forks for dipping and some Sterno (if the pots aren't electric) to provide the heat.

You can prepare the traditional cheese fondue, with bread cut in cubes and presented in a basket for dipping. This is pretty rich, so provide some light accompaniments like a salad, cut-up vegetables, olives, or a pickle assortment. You can also provide meat, which is cooked in oil and then dipped in a variety of condiments and sauces. Even dessert can be a fondue. Melt chocolate and provide fresh fruit and sponge cake cubes for dipping. Cleanup after a fondue party is minimal, since everyone's eating out of the same pot!

Another group-cooking idea is a taco party. Just provide the shells, fillings, and trimmings, and watch the fun begin. All of these can be found prepared at a grocery store salad bar, on the shelves, or in jars or cans. You'll have to brown the chopped meat and add seasonings for the meat filling, but that's a quick task.

"Assemble your own pizza" or "cook your own omelet" parties work well, too. Or how about "top your own pasta"? Just make sure you keep the number of guests small, so everyone can move around and cook his meal. For cooking omelets, extra cooking stations can be created by using plug-in electric burners or frying pans. The ingredients can be picked up already chopped and sliced at any good grocery store salad bar. Add some cubed ham and pregrated cheese, and you're all set.

Oops!

Be sure to sound out guests you may not know all that well, if the party you've planned is going to revolve around food and cooking. If you're putting on a medieval feast complete with roasting a suckling pig and you learn your guest is a born-again vegetarian, things could get a bit awkward.

Parties where guests cook are great for introducing new people. The party itself becomes the ice-breaker, since everyone's participating. It can also add new life to get-togethers with old friends.

Potluck Means More Parties!

Another way to make light work of a party is to have a potluck. You know the drill. Everyone makes a dish and brings it. With everyone pitching in, you'll feel like having more frequent get-togethers. It's also a lot easier on the budget.

Here's where a theme adds some interest. We recently attended a soup potluck and it was delightful. Each couple brought a batch of their favorite soup, and the hosts provided various breads and rolls, beverages, and dessert. Simple, quick, and delicious. Make sure you have plenty of outlets and extension cords available for those dishes that need to be kept warm.

Try a short-order potluck for the fastest party on the planet. Everyone stops off at the deli, take-out eatery, wholesale club, or supermarket and brings a prepared dish. Assign specific types of foods, so you don't get too many of one thing and none of another. Pick a theme (such as Chinese, Thai, Italian, Mexican, seafood, small pizzas, finger foods, deli) to tie it all together.

Presentation Is Everything

Even take-out food can make a party if the presentation's right. How food is served and garnished, plus things like flowers, lighting, and music, all serve to create the atmosphere of a party. Here are some tips for making your presentation count:

- ◆ Consider handwritten place cards at a sit-down dinner party. Hand-lettered tent cards near buffet dishes add a touch of class and prevent your having to answer "What's this dish?" for the umpteenth time. This also saves on waste, since people know not to take what they don't like. Include key ingredients on the card.

- ◆ Decorate with lots of flowers, store-bought or from the garden. Nothing's more spectacular than nature. If you have a garden, use its fruits generously. My favorites are trimmings from the holly bush for the holiday table, and tiny thyme or lavender blossoms or mint leaves from my herb garden in the summer. Look for natural grasses and any foliage cuttings that might add a special look.

- ◆ Try using a basket of fruits and vegetables as a centerpiece. Pick some with great color and combine them with some of the more exotic varieties, such as artichokes, persimmons, or prickly pears.

◆ Pick a theme. Beef stew becomes a "peasant dinner" with a hearty bread and a pudding for dessert. Use "harvest" decorations. Historic themes work well. A medieval feast can be alarmingly simple. Use stout mugs, goblets, and chunky plates to eat from, individual salts—and, remember, no forks! You can often find primitive wooden bowls, plates, and goblets at thrift stores. Sterilize in water with a little bleach and then rub with some olive oil to condition the wood.

> **Amazing Space**
>
> To increase the impact of candle-light, put candles next to a mirror or on mirrored tiles.

Other theme ideas include: "Devil or angel?" Serve foods like ambrosia, angel and devil's food cake, and hotter-than-hell chili. Label everything to get your point across. The decorating ideas are endless. How about a "beat-the-blahs" beach party in February? Tell everyone to dress for the beach. Turn the heat up. Use tropical and summer props, music, and foods.

◆ Use candles to create a mood. Consider low white candles in votive glasses or mismatched candlesticks—tall with short, glass with metal. Be imaginative. A word to the wise: Avoid heavily scented candles on the dinner table. It can really detract from the "good food" smells. After all, you didn't slave in the kitchen all day for them not to notice!

◆ Look for unconventional vases like teapots, creamers, and pitchers from your china cabinet, weathered garden urns, old tin pails, and cache pots. Wrap less appealing containers in fabric (velvet, damask, or satin are nice choices for the holidays), then tie the mouth of the container with some ribbon.

◆ Create individual arrangements for guests by filling a liqueur glass or even a pretty juice glass with a single blossom or sprig of greens.

◆ Think about the music at your event. If you have a theme, key the music to that. Think about what kind of atmosphere you're trying to create—boisterous, subdued, elegant, ethnic, festive—and find music that goes along. If you've got room for dancing, have plenty of dance music on hand. Live music is always special. Is there a good musician in your crowd who enjoys playing to an appreciative

Orderly Pursuits

Learn how to fold napkins in scores of creative ways. Check out the book *The Simple Art of Napkin Folding: 94 Fancy Folds for Every Tabletop Occasion* by Linda Hetzer.

Oops!

When you're planning a theme party, don't go overboard with permanent purchases; consider borrowing or buying and donating when you're done. After all, when the luau's over, when will you ever use all those skewers or grass skirts again?

audience? By all means, send him or her an invitation and encourage a performance by providing space for instruments! Have some simple "play-along" percussion instruments for guests to join in the fun.

- Something as simple as napkins can set the mood. Have a Western party and use inexpensive bandannas as napkins. Napkins are easy to make if you're handy with a sewing machine. You can choose fabric that fits perfectly with your theme or party decor.

All the Right Stuff

You'll need all sorts of "equipment" for your party, some of which you may not ordinarily have on hand. Consider borrowing what you need or even getting it at a thrift shop, and then returning it or passing it on when you're done.

Here are a few more words about "gearing up" for your party:

- Weigh looks against convenience, the work involved against cost. Especially with a large crowd, you'll probably be better off leaning toward convenience—unless, of course, you have plenty of help. You may want to use disposable plastic glasses and utensils, paper plates, and napkins. For a sit-down Thanksgiving dinner I had one year for 21 people, I bought pretty but inexpensive (99¢ each!) glass plates at a discount store to supplement my own everyday dishware. I borrowed silverware from a friend. It meant an extra dishwasher load, but no disposables. Much more elegant, too.

- Improvise. If you don't have platters, use regular dinner plates for serving. Try mixing bowls or casserole dishes as serving bowls. A cutting board can be used as a hot plate, and a large decorative basket can be used for serving bread. Linen dish towels can be used as napkins, and their generous size may be welcome at a meal that's, well, shall we say "sloppy" to eat.

- You may want to rent or buy electric warmer trays to keep foods hot. A dish set in a larger bowl filled with ice can be used to keep foods cold.

- Another rental item you may want to consider is a coffee urn. I have one of these, and I'm the lend-lease business that my friends turn to when they're having a party. But I entertain quite a bit. Don't buy one, though, if you don't entertain often enough to make it worth the bother to store. You can usually rent them in different sizes. An alternative is to borrow a couple of smaller coffee makers. You'll probably want at least two anyway, for regular and decaf.

♦ What do you do with all those coats? If you've got a nice, big coat closet, great. You could put them on the bed, but that looks awful and can cause a lot of confusion with people leaving at different times. Consider renting a lightweight collapsible rack from a party-supply house. They usually include plenty of hangers and cost under $20 to rent (plus a refundable deposit).

♦ Make sure there are plenty of guest towels in the bathrooms.

♦ For outdoor parties or even indoor buffets, have plenty of baskets or bags for litter. Also have baskets or pans in which to deposit used utensils, plates, and glasses that need washing. Cleanup is easier, and the entertaining area stays clear for other activities.

Picture This
Still nervous? Close your eyes and think about your favorite parties. What made them so special? I'll bet it was the guests having fun and the charming host. Rehearse your party visually beforehand. Imagine people mingling. Imagine preparing the menu. Walk it through. Create a scene where everything is going smoothly and everyone's having a fantastic time, especially you!

Managing Space, Traffic, and Cleanup

One real party dampener is a poor layout and use of space. Here are a few suggestions for keeping things moving smoothly:

♦ Set up a fix-it-yourself bar far from the buffet and other heavy traffic areas, especially doorways. If there's enough space, set it away from the wall so people can access it from both sides. You can use an occasional table or card table for your setup. If you don't have room for a bar, then don't try to cram one in. Limit drinks to champagne—or, for a smaller budget, white wine. Don't forget sparkling cider and seltzer for those who don't drink alcohol.

♦ Don't set up a bar or coffee service in the kitchen. You'll be dodging guests every time you need to get into the refrigerator or use the sink.

♦ Take a fresh look at the space you are planning to use. Rooms can be rearranged temporarily. Think about where everyone will sit. Rent or borrow chairs if you need to. Remove furniture if it will improve traffic flow or provide space for a performer or dance floor.

◆ You may want to consider serving all easy-to-handle finger foods if space is at a premium and you want folks to mingle more freely. All they'll need to worry about is their plate, cup, and napkin ... no utensils to balance or drop.

◆ Consider hiring servers for hors d'oeuvres. It keeps traffic problems to a minimum, since everyone stays in one place and the food is brought to them.

◆ Plan for parking. If you can, get your own car out of the driveway (maybe you can park at a neighbor's?), and let people know in the invitation if there are any special parking instructions.

◆ Try to clean stains and spills as they happen, without making anyone feel bad. Some just won't come out if they dry. Expect them and be prepared.

Oops!

Avoid red wine for a buffet or cocktail party where people will be walking around with drinks in their hands. If it spills, it can make a stain that's tough to get out, especially if it dries.

◆ Check the waste receptacles periodically and put in fresh garbage bags. Use oversized bags, as people tend to pile things on, and it's easier to pack them down if you've got some extra room at the top.

◆ After the party's over, clear away clutter first. If you're not up to doing the dishes, at least scrape and soak them in soapy water overnight. Sweep, wash the floor, and spot-clean the carpets and walls the next day.

Child's Play: Planning Great Parties for Kids

Children's parties can be fun for everyone, including the parents, but it takes preparation and planning, with lots of emphasis on the children's participation. Whether it's a birthday celebration, a Halloween party, or a Valentine tea party, children at just about any age can be a part of the decision-making, decorating, food preparation, and activity planning. Parties give your child a chance to develop organization and planning skills, as well as to try out social skills, such as how to be a good host, take turns, introduce friends, and observe the house rules while having a good time.

Children can make the invitations with construction paper and crayons or on a computer, if you have one. There are simple programs just for this purpose. Once they're printed out, your child can color and fold them and help address the envelopes. It's best to mail them, rather than have your child give them out at school and run the risk of their not reaching their destination. Kids have a knack for forgetting to tell their parents important things! You'll want to follow up with a phone call to the children's parents.

Themes help make parties even more fun. Try dinosaurs, "tea," outer space, jungle animals, dressing up, angels, race cars, a time in history (medieval, Renaissance, Western, or Victorian are always fun)—anything that strikes your child's fancy—for his or her next party. If it's a seasonal party or your child enjoys certain activities associated with the season, build them into the party. Make it an apple festival (complete with a trip to the local orchard to pick apples) or a spring nature celebration, winter carnival, or summer pool party.

> **Amazing Space**
>
> After the party, put all your notes and the recipes that worked best into a file folder or party planning notebook for the future. Note what worked and what didn't for the next time. Keeping track of quantities per person and costs will help you budget, as well.

Be careful to gear the number of guests, the difficulty of the activities, and the duration of the party to the child's age. If you're not sure, ask the child's teacher for suggestions. One idea is to invite as many children as the child's age. Two guests for a two-year-old's party is just about right, and so on. If you're planning a party around an outing, be sure to have enough adults to help for the number of kids in your charge. One adult for every three or four children is a good minimum. If you're going on an outing and bringing food, choose food that's easy to transport and handle, such as juices and cupcakes.

The food can become part of the party's activities. Make cupcakes, for example, and ice them with plain butter-cream icing. Then let children decorate with sprinkles, candy dots, and tubes of decorative icing. This gives them a fun thing to do and saves you time to boot. Children can create their own place mats as a party activity. Give them sheets of construction paper, stickers, magazine cut-outs, and crayons, then cover with clear self-stick shelf paper. These mats can be wiped off and taken home when the party's over. For an "outer space" theme party, for example, have plenty of astronomical stickers, stars, and science magazines to cut up—maybe glue and glitter, too.

Orderly Pursuits

If you're looking for more party ideas, here are some books to help you: *The Kids' Pick-a-Party Book: 50 Fun Party Themes for Kids, Ages 2 to 16* by Peggy Warner; *Einstein's Science Parties: Easy Parties for Curious Kids* by Shar Levine and Allison Grafton; and *The Ultimate Sleep-Over Book* by Kayte Kuch.

Don't forget to plan some games (adults enjoy these, too). For neat ideas, check out *The Best Birthday Party Game Book* by Bruce Lansky.

A Few Guests for the Weekend

When we invite friends to spend the weekend with us, we often learn a lot—both about them and about ourselves. You may know friends for years, but you never really know them until they are guests in your home.

This is a special kind of entertaining, and when it's done well, it can be an especially enjoyable experience for both guest and host. Here are a few things to keep in mind if you're entertaining guests for the weekend:

- As with all entertaining, preparation is the key. Make sure you have enough bedding, towels, toothpaste, and soap ready.

- Check with your guests about any special dietary requirements ahead of time, before you go shopping.

- When guests arrive, give them time to get settled and then offer them a cool drink and a snack. Ask them when they'd like to eat the next scheduled meal.

- Have something prepared for the first night that's easy to do ahead and just pop in the oven. I usually make something like lasagna or a meat and vegetable casserole. I'll even cook it partially and then put it in to finish cooking a few minutes before dinner is planned.

- Make an effort to share the interests of your house guests. You'll discover new things, and they'll feel right at home. When a friend and her husband came to visit for a few days, I discovered she had become very interested in New Age topics and Native American folklore and medicine. When we visited nearby Sedona, Arizona, I suggested she and I join a tour specifically aimed toward her interest. It's something I wouldn't have done on my own, but I enjoyed it immensely, and it gave me new insight into an old friend.

- A comfortable bed is an absolute bottom-line must. The only way to be sure your guest bed is sleep-worthy (and your guests might not tell you if it isn't) is to take it for a test-sleep. Spend a night in your own guest room or on the fold-out couch. That's only fair! Besides the bed, make sure there's enough drawer and closet space, extra pillows and blankets, and a way to block out light.

- Some extra touches for the guest room? How about writing paper and pens, a folding umbrella, brochures on local sights, some recent magazines, and a few well-chosen books. Some personal-size toiletries in the bathroom are nice. I even put together a "guest basket" sometimes. Make sure there's fresh soap.

- Ask about waking hours early on. If guests are early risers and want to hit the hiking trail by 5:30 A.M. but you're not joining them, you can get things ready

for them in the kitchen so they can handle their own breakfast (muffins or
quiche work well). Set the timer on the
coffeemaker to have it brewing when
their alarm goes off. Or you can set your
alarm to rise with them, then hit the hay
again as soon as they've hit the woods.

◆ Some guests are self-sufficient, others
need to be entertained. Learn what kind
yours are and plan accordingly.

◆ If there are any cardinal rules in your
house, like removing shoes or not smoking, make sure guests know at the outset.
After all, it's your house!

> **CAUTION**
>
> **Oops!**
>
> Don't leave your guests
> in the dark. If there are any idio-
> syncrasies in your house, such as
> the plumbing, things guests need
> to know about light switches,
> comings and goings, pets, or
> dressing requirements for planned
> events, write them down and go
> over them when your guests have
> had a little time to get comfort-
> able.

Do I Need a Caterer?

Having a party catered is the most expensive way to entertain, but it's definitely the
most relaxing. Basically, you just make sure the house is clean, dress for the occasion,
and show up! Your budget will be the major factor in determining whether you
should hire a caterer, but if it's personal service and pampering you want at your own
party, then catering is the way to go.

When my first book was published, I had a "birth of the book" party that was catered.
I felt it was a once-in-a-lifetime occasion, and I wanted to be free to take in all the
attention and enjoy the moment. Since the book was on Victorian weddings, we had a
fancy Victorian tea party. It wasn't outrageously expensive. Beverages were a variety of
English teas, champagne, and wine, which made it simple and elegant.

You'll want to shop around for the best caterer. Make decisions about the type of
party you want, the number of guests, date, time, type of food and decor, and approximate budget. Be aware of the caterer's specialties or personal tastes, so you can match
the caterer to the event. When you choose the one you like, it will probably take
three meetings in person or by phone to iron out the details. Ask for references, *and
check them out*. Ask for a certificate of insurance along with an estimate. Ask, as well,
who will be in charge the day of the event. Will the owner be there himself or will
someone else be handling it?

Make sure both you and the caterer are clear about each and every element of the party. Who provides the liquor, mixers, ice, glassware, flowers, decor, linens, and serving dishes? If you want to use some of your serving pieces, let the caterer know so there are no problems with size or shape.

Amazing Space
If you can't afford to have an entire party catered, you may be able to hire a portion of it out. Consider hiring a bartender to handle the drinks or someone to cater the cocktail hour and help serve the dinner.

If you want the catering staff to dress a certain way, you need to let them know. Our "tea party" staff was dressed in pink-striped Gibson Girl blouses with lace aprons, to complement the Victorian theme, but this was part of their regular service. If yours is a black-tie party, the staff will need to dress accordingly.

You'll want to have a contract. It should include final costs, what charges there will be for special services and overtime, plus a clause stating that the house will be left exactly as it was found.

Make sure you make room in your refrigerator, if the caterer's going to need it, and put out any serving pieces you want them to use. Then go take a sumptuous bubble bath or a nap. You're all done!

The Least You Need to Know

♦ Using lists and schedules will help you plan a perfect party. When the party's over, you can save these and note for the next time what worked and what didn't.

♦ Presentation is (almost) everything and can turn even the simplest food and humblest setting into something special.

♦ You don't need to let a party be an excuse for accumulating junk you'll never use again. Borrow, rent, or buy at a thrift store, and return when you're done.

♦ Use do-ahead dishes, short-order ingredients, and potlucks to have impromptu parties more often.

♦ A few simple preparations will make weekend house guests comfortable. Let them in on any special household routines or idiosyncrasies.

♦ Hire a caterer if your budget allows and enjoy feeling pampered and relaxed at your own party.

Chapter 24

Ready for Prime Time: Planning Weddings and Reunions

In This Chapter

◆ How to plan important events like the pros do

◆ Organizing and scheduling for weddings

◆ Special tips for family and high school reunions

◆ Remembering once-in-a-lifetime events in creative ways

This chapter is about the really big events in your life. When you're in charge of planning a wedding, a silver or golden anniversary party, a milestone birthday party, or a family or class reunion, the sheer scope of it can be overwhelming. The realization that this occasion comes only once in a lifetime adds to both the excitement and the pressure.

Here's where your organization skills will help you survive and make everything turn out right. You've had lots of practice every day managing your own life with your newfound skills. Now you're going to use them to carry you through planning and executing a major life event with style and confidence.

The Big Ones

What are the big events coming up in your life? Are you likely to be involved in helping to plan a child's wedding? Do you have parents with birthday or anniversary milestones coming up? Do you cringe at the thought? These are the joyous occasions, the meaningful celebrations in our lives and are not to be avoided, but embraced. You've learned a lot about organizing your own life. Now it's time to *share!*

Take Your Cues from the Pros

So how do professional events and wedding planners do it? How do they keep all the details from slipping through the cracks? Study them and you'll learn these secrets:

- **Standardize.** Wherever possible, use forms, checklists, and manuals. Seek out ones that have been devised by others and adapt them to your own event.

- **Keep up with what's new.** You may have experience planning a wedding—20 years ago! Check into new tools to help you do your legwork. There are now computer software programs, videos, guidebooks, and television shows that probably weren't around then.

- **Stick with what works.** As much as things may have changed, certain methods are still "tried-and-true." Professionals know how to blend the new with the time-tested.

- **Find good people and treat them well.** Professional events planners and wedding consultants have lists of people they hire on a regular basis. They know these vendors can be counted on, time after time, to do an excellent job. You'll need to develop your list through research and references. Once you find an excellent caterer, for example, do everything you can to help them do their job.

- **Delegate.** You were first introduced to the delegating process in Chapter 9, when we discussed your work life. Wherever possible, hand tasks over to others to do and let them do them. Results are what count, even if their process looks a lot different than yours.

- **Interview, visit, and try it yourself.** Don't just take someone's word for it. Speak to everyone in person, visit their shop or office, and if at all possible try products and services before choosing them for the big event.

◆ **Rehearse, rehearse, rehearse!** Go over the details again and again. Try on the dress, walk through the hall, or read and reread the vows: Leave nothing to chance if you can help it.

◆ **Use your imagination.** In the planning process, use your innate creativity and ability to visualize possibilities. When trying to come up with a solution to a problem, don't restrict yourself—you can always tone it down. Look to unusual sources for inspiration—a movie, a song, a work of art, or a work of literature. Be bold.

> **Amazing Space**
>
> Take a tip from the pros and *keep it all in one place.* Set up a file box, a three-ring binder, or a card file to keep track of everything. Make whatever method you choose mobile, so you can take it with you when you visit vendors or look at sites.

◆ **Improvise.** When you come up against a problem, look for ways you can rework your original idea. Something not available? Substitute something else. Again, consider resources that are out of the ordinary. If the florist doesn't have it, maybe the nursery does!

> **Picture This**
>
> Close your eyes and visualize the event you're planning. Start with the general atmosphere, then focus on details. Where is it taking place? In a grand ballroom? On a beach? Who's there? What are people wearing? What time of year is it? How does it sound? Try on several different "movies" to see which one suits your fancy the most. Is it a "vintage" setting? Rustic? Formal? Casual? Is there a particular ethnic theme that comes to mind? Write down all your thoughts, and refer to this exercise as you begin to plan your event. See how others react to your different scenarios.

Being Your Own CEO

You've learned how to think like the pros do, so let's take it a step further. You're now president and CEO of your own company. Your product? The Big Event!

Pretend you're in business for six months or a year, while you're planning the big party, the reunion, or the wedding. Perhaps you have a co-president—hopefully you do, especially if you're planning a wedding! Or maybe you have some other corporate officers that can help you with specific jobs, like a treasurer or communications director. You hire and fire and track performance, you work up a budget, you advertise the "product," you package it, and everybody ultimately reaps the rewards.

The main areas of your corporation are most likely to be:

Finance: You'll need a budget and a way to track expenditures. Nail down all sources of cash and call them in before you get too far along in the planning process. If you're working with several people on the event, find the person best suited to handle the money and give them authority to pull in the reins, if need be.

Human Resources: Someone has to be in charge of the people involved. This means interviewing, hiring, and if necessary, firing and finding someone else. It helps to have plenty of time set aside for finding the right people and communicating to them exactly what you want done.

Research and Development: This is a large part of any planning process. What's available? When is it available? What are the restrictions? Who's in charge? What's the cost? Somebody needs to handle the nuts and bolts of assembling information for consideration, weighing different possibilities, and then following up on decisions.

Sales and Marketing: Communication is a vital part of ensuring the success of any major undertaking. The way you get the word out, and the excitement you create—that's what makes the day! Let people know what's going to be happening and why. Make sure you get across the sentiment, the spirit of the event. Look for dramatic ways of delivering your message (we'll talk more about invitations and programs later in the chapter).

Manufacturing: This is the actual labor involved in orchestrating the event. Who's going to pick up the invitations from the printer, lick the stamps, and take the envelopes to the post office? Who picks up the extra chairs?

Oops! _____

Just as if you were running a real corporation, you shouldn't delegate tasks to others and assume everything is being done. Trust your "employees," encourage them, and motivate them, but oversee them, as well. Make time for regular reporting and evaluation. Ultimately, the responsibility is yours!

I hope you are not responsible for the whole she-bang. It's better if you have help, unless you really can afford the time to devote to nothing else but this for several months. If you don't have anyone to help you, do consider hiring a wedding consultant, reunion manager, or events planner. It's worth the extra money to be able to keep your sanity and get some help, plus you'll often recoup the cost in savings in other areas!

Also consider a theme for your event. A theme ties everything together, from location and food to decor and music. It can be a historical period, an interest or sport, the time of year, a family tradition, or just a concept or phrase that has meaning to those involved. A theme brings out the creativity in people, and it gives them a structure, a unifying principle to hang their hat on. See if a theme is something that will work for you.

Wedding Bells in Harmony

Of all the events the average person will ever plan, a wedding is probably the most important and complicated. There's always a lot of pressure placed on a once-in-a-lifetime event, but perhaps the uniting of two people has an added dimension, that of joining two families, two histories.

If you can plan a big wedding, you can plan anything. You're not just planning an event but a series of events, which include the rehearsal dinner and the honeymoon. You'll have more individuals to deal with, and need to concern yourself with more individual components than with the average event. Besides that, you'll be handling certain legal and financial arrangements, as you or the people you're helping begin a new life.

Because wedding planning has been given so much attention, the resources available are also extensive. However, you can actually adapt them to planning any large event, simply by subtracting those parts you don't need and adding things unique to your particular occasion.

One of the essential tools for planning a wedding is developing a timetable or count-down schedule for everything you need to do from the moment you decide to have the event in the first place. In my opinion, this is worth doing for any major "happening."

My friend Hazel Bowman is a professional wedding consultant and special events planner. Hazel has been involved in planning everything from small gatherings to large weddings, and way beyond—she's planned super-events and galas for the likes of Michael Jordan! Hazel is an organization marvel, and she uses standardized checklists and calendars wherever possible to plan all her events. Here I'll share one of her check-lists: her "Bridal Countdown" for planning a wedding. Consider how you can adapt this for your own wedding or any other event you find yourself in charge of.

Tickler Files

"Blest is the bride the sun shines on."

—Old English proverb

Oops!

Don't let yourself get too bogged down by all the work and details involved in planning a wedding. Your survival requires a sense of humor—regular giggles and the occasional guffaw are mandatory. If you want a laugh, view this site *before* you buy the wedding gown, but *after* you've looked at plenty of bridal magazines: www.visi.com/~dheaton/bride/the_bride_wore.html.

Hazel Bowman's Bridal Countdown

AS SOON AS POSSIBLE:

- Decide on the number of guests from your own guest list, your parent's guest list, and the groom's family and guests.

- Establish an overall wedding budget.

- Determine the formality and style of your wedding and reception.

- Ask selected family members and friends who are to be part of the wedding party.

NINE TO TWELVE MONTHS BEFORE THE WEDDING:

- Decide on your wedding date and time.

- Reserve ceremony and reception sites.

- Secure clergy, rabbi, or magistrate.

- Investigate and determine caterer. Review menu possibilities before making final decision.

- Book entertainment (musicians for ceremony and reception).

SIX TO EIGHT MONTHS BEFORE THE WEDDING:

- Purchase bridal gown and attendants' outfits. Mothers should also be shopping for their dresses at this time.

- Confirm florist.

- Confirm photographer and/or videographer.

- Confirm baker.

- Select your bridal registry.

- Shop for wedding rings.

- Select a hotel conveniently located to ceremony and reception sites and arrange to block out the number of rooms out-of-town guests will need.

THREE TO FIVE MONTHS BEFORE THE WEDDING:

- Order wedding invitations, announcements, and informals.

- Ensure fiancé makes reservations for honeymoon plans.

- Apply for or renew passport, if applicable, for honeymoon. Make appointment with doctor if inoculations are required.

- Arrange fittings for bride and her attendant's outfits to avoid last-minute attire problems.

- Make sure groom and his attendants purchase or reserve wedding attire.

Orderly Pursuits

Several software programs are available to help you plan your wedding. Locate shareware programs at www.shareware.com, choose your operating system, and type "wedding." For commercial software, use any major search engine and type in "wedding software" or "wedding planning software." I've listed some in the resource guide appendix.

Amazing Space

At least two months in advance, schedule the wedding rehearsal date and time and advise all rehearsal participants. Friends and relatives from out of town will appreciate early notice.

TWO MONTHS BEFORE THE WEDDING:

- Address and mail all wedding invitations. Rule of thumb: Out-of-state invitations are sent six to eight weeks in advance; in-state invitations are sent four to six weeks in advance.

- Book and pay for attendants' hotel accommodations.

- Have your wedding portrait taken if you're having a formal sitting.

- Make a list of documents that will require a name change, such as Social Security card, bank accounts, and credit cards.

- Determine what state laws require for getting married. Some require blood tests and physical examinations.

- Confirm transportation to and from ceremony and reception sites.

ONE MONTH BEFORE THE WEDDING:

- Send newspapers your formal engagement announcement with a print of your favorite photo. If you're planning on having an engagement portrait done, you'll need to do it early enough to have a print for the papers.

- Schedule final fitting for groom's and bride's attire. Ensure entire bridal outfit is in order—shoes dyed, jewelry selected, and any special accessories ready (such as garter belt, "something old, something new").

- Plan honeymoon wardrobe.

- Make sure all attendants have ordered their accessories.

- Purchase and wrap bride's and groom's attendant gifts.

- Change beneficiaries, if applicable, on insurance policies, trusts, and other financial documents.

- Instruct attorney to create prenuptial agreement, if desired, and have it executed.

- Instruct attorney to prepare will, if desired.

Orderly Pursuits

Easy Wedding Planner, Organizer & Keepsake by Elizabeth Llulch is a comprehensive, well-thought-out guide full of checklists and tips. For all the basics, you can also count on *The Complete Idiot's Guide to the Perfect Wedding* by Teddy Lenderman.

- Finalize music selections for ceremony and reception.

- Finalize photography or videotaping details. Advise photographers of restrictions of ceremony and/or reception sites.

- Provide photographer or videographer the list of shots you definitely want taken during pre-wedding, ceremony, and reception stages.

- Advise out-of-town guests of rooms blocked for hotel accommodations.

- Secure any special things you will need, like candles, guest book, and cake knife.

- Make appointments with hairstylist, manicurist, and cosmetologist.

ONE WEEK BEFORE THE WEDDING:

- Coordinate RSVPs.

- Do seating arrangements and place cards for bridal table (always), optional for parents' tables and guests' tables.

◆ Double-check and confirm all servicers and suppliers, times and date, reaffirming any last-minute changes.

◆ Provide final head count to caterer and reconfirm menu selections.

◆ Provide hotel with hospitality baskets that include maps of the area and information about local sights for out-of-town guests.

◆ Remind wedding rehearsal participants of time, date, and location of rehearsal and rehearsal dinner.

◆ Obtain marriage license.

◆ Secure wedding rings.

◆ Write and send change-of-address cards.

> **Amazing Space**
>
> Planning a wedding is another great time to employ a three-ring binder and a small file box. Use plastic sheet protectors to hold odds and ends in the binder. If you end up with lots of brochures and literature, you may want to set up file folders by topic and keep them in a portable file box. Make your binder pretty by covering it with contact paper or attractive wallpaper. Later, it will become a keepsake. Mine has!

Consider developing individual checklists for different aspects of the planning process. You could have one for each component, such as a checklist for the location, for the caterer, and for the florist. Whenever possible, incorporate your research into a checklist or list of questions to ask.

So, enjoy your wedding knowing you've got everything organized from the start. And may your days together be filled with smart planning and smooth sailing from now on!

Assembling the Clan (or Class) Without Chaos

Has your high school or college graduating class ever had a reunion? No? Then maybe you should organize one! Or perhaps you've thought fondly of having a family reunion, but don't know where to start. Well, you start the same way you begin anything. You take the first step—planning it!

To get the ball rolling on a school reunion, find out if friends from your class would like to have a reunion, too. Ask some family members what they think of the idea of a clan reunion. Feel everybody out before you get too deep into the planning process, just in case there isn't a lot of enthusiasm for the idea. But don't give up too quickly: All it takes is two or three people to get things started. The process isn't unlike planning a wedding, except it's far less complicated, since there are fewer elements to pull together.

Revving Up the Reunion

As "reunion coordinator," your first step is to get things rolling by notifying the clan that, "We're all going to get together." This will probably take some time, since you've most likely lost touch with some family members or classmates. You'll need to do some detective work to track people down.

In the case of family members, you'll have to network from those you know to those you don't. For a class reunion, there are other resources available to begin to reach people who've moved away or even changed their names.

You'll want to begin a master list of people as you do your research. Include addresses and phone numbers and contact each one to see who else they may be able to lead you to. Check phone books (the library should have some out-of-town directories) and online free "people finder" locations to see what you can come up with. Of course, contact your school and let them know you're planning a class reunion. Some people have had good results from putting personal ads in the appropriate papers. Things have a way of mushrooming, and before you know it, people will start contacting *you!*

Orderly Pursuits

To aid you in creating the reunion everyone will remember, there are some books you can consult. Check out *High School Reunions: How to Plan Yours,* by Harry McKinzie, if you're planning a class reunion. For family reunions, find a copy of *Family Reunion Handbook: A Complete Guide for Reunion Planners,* by Thomas Ninkovich.

Make sure you keep track of the information you gather. Put it in a card file or binder, or type it into a database program. You may end up doing this again at a later date, so why reinvent the wheel?

The Delights of Delegating

Divide up tasks into major categories, and as you make contact with the various branches of the family or have a decent number of classmates together, set up teams to be in charge of a particular category. You'll need groups or individuals to handle:

◆ Money, including drawing up a budget, collecting money, and paying vendors

◆ Designing invitations, getting them printed and mailed, and following up

◆ Arranging for the food and following up

◆ Securing lodging for out-of-towners

◆ Researching and reserving an event location

◆ Providing entertainment and activities to break the ice and draw people out

◆ Finding, collecting, and displaying memorabilia

◆ Recording the event in some way— photographing it, videotaping it, or creating a scrapbook

Pick the people best suited to the job and capitalize on their interests!

> **Amazing Space**
>
> Find out if anyone has photographs, home movies, or videos of the clan. Make sure you have the equipment to show them at the event to take everybody back and add to the nostalgia. If anyone's done a family history, encourage them to share what they've gathered at the family reunion.

Where and When

You'll want to pick a date that has some special significance in the family or for your high school or college class. Be careful about holidays, though. They're popular, but can mean you'll have a harder time getting the location you want, and travel arrangements may be more difficult. Make sure you allow plenty of time, in any event. If people are traveling a long way, you may want to make the event more than one day, so provide for that if it makes sense.

Whatever location you choose, it'll have to be large enough for your group, which may expand over time as more people hear of it. A public place with lots of space, like a campground or park, can be ideal for the family. If you reserve a hall, make sure it has some flexibility, in case your class reunion starts to grow.

Once you have a list of prospects, you'll be ready to send out invitations. Make sure to include information about travel and lodging in the invitation, as well as a map, and make sure the contact information is clear. Also ask recipients to notify you promptly if they're aware of other appropriate guests you may want to include.

Come up with a "clock" similar to the bridal clock given earlier in this chapter. You'll need at least six months to plan a successful reunion, so start with six months and work all the way down to the day of the event. Try to include every detail.

Saving the Memories

Big-time events just cry to be recorded. I mean, who knows when it will ever happen again? One way is to purchase a quantity of disposable cameras (check out the wholesale clubs for the best prices), and hand them out to the shutterbugs in the group. Collect the cameras at the end of the event, and when they're developed, have the photos scanned into a computer and create a collage that can be duplicated and distributed to attendees. Make sure you include the cost in your initial budget.

You can have a videographer record the event and attendees can purchase copies. Or take photos, journal entries, and memorabilia and create a special scrapbook that you can share with relatives or classmates the next time you see them. Be sure to include quotes ("overheard") and stories that surfaced during the reunion. You might attempt to get each person to say something on tape, either video or audio, to use for your project.

Orderly Pursuits

If you decide you don't want to do your high school reunion yourself, you can hire a "reunion manager" to do it all for you. Find one near you by going to www.reunions.com. You'll learn what a professional can do for you and how to choose one, as well.

I think keeping a journal during the entire process, from planning to saying good-bye, could be a wonderful keepsake. Make sure to include your emotions, poignant anecdotes, and humorous notes in your entries. This could become part of your family history.

The Least You Need to Know

- When taking on the planning of a big event, learn as much as you can from the pros.

- Managing big events is like running a corporation. Divide up major areas and delegate wherever possible.

- Weddings and other special occasions run more smoothly when a timetable is used, working forward to the day of the event.

- Be sure to record the event in some way, such as by making a collage that can be cheaply reproduced for participants, or a scrapbook that can be shown at future events.

25

Wrap It Up: Holiday Planning Made Easy

In This Chapter

- ◆ Making your holiday schedule less hectic
- ◆ Creating a holiday season that's less about "stuff" and more about "fun"
- ◆ Tips on holiday gift-giving that save you time and keep you out of debt
- ◆ Conquering holiday storage problems

We all know the recipe for ruining the holiday season: Start with unreasonably high expectations, heap on a good dose of guilt and a dash of procrastination, let simmer with family differences and distances, try to do too much, then garnish with a little flu bug. No wonder you'd rather spend the holidays alone in Timbuktu!

If you've become a grinch, why not turn things around? Make this the year you truly look forward to the holidays with wide-eyed enthusiasm and delight.

Goal-Setting, Holiday Style

There are those words again: *goal-setting* and *planning*. Do the holidays have a way of just "happening" to you? When you don't focus early on how you want things to be, they can take on an unintended life of their own. But if you start out with clear intentions, you're more likely to create what you intend.

Granted, getting in touch with your inner desires when it comes to the holidays may not be as simple as it sounds. Holidays are fraught with emotional triggers and baggage that are often very complicated and not wholly clear. I think you'll agree, however, that it's easier to navigate a minefield when you know where the bombs are buried.

Creating a great holiday is a lot like orchestrating a great party. Imagine you're putting on a play or making a movie. There's a script, props, scenery, various players, and a director. Everyone's the director in their own holiday pageant, whether they know it or not. Why not accept the role and make the production your own?

Picture This
Close your eyes and imagine your ideal holiday. Imagine it the absolute best it could be. Start with Thanksgiving and make your "movie" go all the way through New Year's Day. Who would be there? What kind of food would be served? How are things decorated? What is your mood? Be free in your imaginings. This doesn't have to be like any holiday season you've ever known.
Write down the major elements of your "movie." If you imagined going out into the woods and cutting down your own Christmas tree, put that down. Keep your list close by. We're going to use it later.

Write Yourself a Book: Your Personal Holiday Planner

Some years ago I made a holiday binder that I now rely on every year to make our holidays bright. It's a standard-sized loose-leaf notebook, with colored dividers and lined three-hole-punched paper. My categories are Cards, Crafts, Decor, Food, and Gifts. I use it for Thanksgiving, Christmas, and New Year's planning each year. Other possible categories you might want to add are Parties, Menus, Lists, Songs, Traditions, Budget, or anything else you want to keep track of.

I have our Christmas card mailing list on a label program. Each year I revise it, making any necessary changes, additions, and deletions, then print it out on regular paper and add to my planner behind the Cards divider. I use that printout each year to make notations and then to revise my label program when card-sending time arrives.

Under Crafts, I keep directions for making decorations or ornaments that we especially liked that year or ones I'd like to try next year. I add notes that might be helpful. If I make ornaments to give away, I sometimes take photos and add them.

Decor contains ideas for decorations, inside and out. If I see something in a book or magazine, I photocopy it or tear it out and add it to my binder. I do the same for printouts from my Internet wanderings. If you create a decorating scheme you're especially pleased with, take a picture and put it in your binder so you can duplicate it the following year.

The Food category contains copies of our traditional family recipes, plus some new ones to try. I also have these recipes elsewhere, but I find that during the holiday rush it's nice to have them all in one place—a sort of personalized family holiday cookbook. I also keep menus and shopping lists (you can use plastic sheet protectors as "envelopes" to store these).

Under Gifts, I keep gift lists and any notes on what people might mention during the year that they'd like for Christmas or "someday." If you see an item in a catalog, you may want to make a note of it here. Having gift lists from the past reminds me what I've already given, so I don't duplicate.

You may want to have a shopping list page and a To-Do list for next year. When the season begins to draw near, that can become your head start. You may want to make a copy of the shopping list and keep it in your planner/organizer so you can buy stocking stuffers or even major gift items when you see exactly what you want, or when items are on sale.

The Holiday Book is your book and can be as elaborate or as simple as you want or need. You can have several volumes for various family celebrations. I think once you begin to "write" it, your Holiday Book will fast become indispensable.

> **CAUTION** **Oops!**
>
> One cause of holiday disappointment is family members having different priorities or emotional attachments to different traditions. Try the Ideal Holiday visualization (see the "Picture This" earlier in this chapter) with your family. Look for ways to fulfill some of each person's fantasy. Compromise on the rest.

Making a List and Checking It (at Least) Twice!

Referring back to the "Picture This" earlier in this chapter, use your visualization list to decide which holiday activities mean the most to you. It might be baking cookies, making Hanukkah goodies like donuts or latkes, having a tree-trimming party, going out caroling, or doing an extravagant job of decorating the house. What activities would give you the most pleasure? The greatest kick? Which would cause you the most pain or disappointment if you didn't do them?

Now decide on the top three or four and break them down into the main tasks needed to make them happen. Caroling might be as simple as finding a group that organizes such an event, getting the music together, practicing a few times, and putting the date on your calendar. The best time for advance planning is a couple of months before Thanksgiving, so you have time to really play with your ideas, reserve time on your schedule, and prepare ahead.

> ### Amazing Space
>
> Remember, when you delegate, things may not be done exactly the way you would do them. Especially at holiday time, standards and expectations can be impossibly high. Decide on the desired results and let whomever does the job do it his way. This will probably yield the best results, too.

Be realistic about your schedule, your budget, and your skills. Look for ways to get others involved and committed to helping with the work.

We generally have Thanksgiving and Christmas dinners at our house, with the children, who are now scattered all over the country, coming to visit us, so I know that shopping, cooking, and baking for two fairly large dinners is going to be part of my schedule. I also really like to do a tree-trimming party if it's at all possible. But with two large meals to plan for, I make that very simple and combine it with another activity I love, music.

Whatever events or activities you choose as your holiday centerpieces, make plans and throw yourself into them. The more energy and focus you give the things you care about, the more fulfilling the holidays will be.

Make up menus and gather recipes early. If your family's like mine, certain traditional favorites must be on the table, but it's fun to experiment with vegetables, appetizers, or desserts from year to year. By planning ahead, you may be able to stock up on some ingredients at bargain prices.

The same goes for your gift list. By having in mind what you're giving each person well in advance, you can shop here and there instead of putting in a few grueling days close to the holidays. I know, you've heard this advice many times before, but it really does make the season much more enjoyable if you shop ahead. And it's easier on the budget to spread out holiday buying over as wide a period as possible.

Finding Time to Get It All Done

First and foremost, realize that you *can't* get it all done! Just accept there will be things on your list that won't make it into reality. If you put your list in priority order, so what if the items on the bottom bite the dust? You did the things you wanted to do most.

Here are a few more tips for getting the important things done and having a top-notch holiday season this year and every year:

♦ Remind yourself who are the most important people in your life, and commit to pleasing them first. And remember, the most important person on that list is *you*.

♦ Sit down with your family and negotiate their share of the work. Make a list of holiday chores and let them choose those they'd most like to do. You won't get help if you don't ask.

♦ Hire some help. Sure, you want to do the good stuff yourself, but who says you can't hire someone to do the stuff nobody wants to do? My friend June has a cleaning service come in before the holidays and has her carpets done as well. She throws a big bash on Christmas Eve, and has the wine and champagne delivered. She always makes a few dishes herself, but she supplements her favorites with others from a caterer. This allows her to concentrate on the things she enjoys most.

♦ Consider hiring a baby-sitter while you do your shopping or, better yet, trade off a couple of days with other parents.

♦ Hit the mall as a family, with one parent taking the kids for the morning while the other shops solo. The whole family meets for lunch at the food court, then the kids switch and shop with the other parent.

♦ Learn to combat "the perfects." Instead of aiming for the perfect meal, the perfect tree, or the perfect gift, be present in the moment and make it wonderful as only you can.

> **Amazing Space**
>
> Watch *National Lampoon's Christmas Vacation* on video or TV at least once this holiday season. Sure, you can get teary-eyed over *It's a Wonderful Life* or *Miracle on 34th Street*, but when you need to come back to earth, let Chevy Chase add some (albeit exaggerated) humor to your holiday cheer.

♦ Don't beat yourself up. Don't tell yourself you've somehow failed because you didn't make cranberry relish. Don't berate yourself because you couldn't afford all the gifts the kids asked for. Don't whip yourself because Aunt Jane asks why you're still single this holiday season and tries to fix you up with the delivery man. Decide not to accept the guilt!

◆ Remember, a holiday isn't any one moment. It's larger than that.

Christmas in July (and Other Time-Savers)

For most of us, the holidays seem to creep up on us, and suddenly there's only a few weeks left to do everything. Well, get a real head start—in July! When the kids are home from school and that familiar chorus "I'm bored!" starts ringing through the house, tell them to get ready to celebrate the winter holidays. Put on Christmas music, don your Santa hat, and get out your Christmas planning binder. (This works for any holiday, by the way!) Assemble crafts materials, go through old magazines and holiday crafts books, try out new cookie recipes, or make up the family's gift lists. Are there any decorations that need repairs, spiffing up, or even replacement?

Dust off the holiday sheet music and make copies. Make a nice cover, bind them, and you're all ready for a musical gathering or caroling. Talk over party possibilities and begin planning decorations and menus. If you don't use them this year, they'll probably come in handy some other holiday season.

When you have "Christmas in July," there's time to experiment and an opportunity to perfect new skills so that gift-making can be relaxed and creative. It's like having a buried treasure put away for just the right moment!

You Shouldn't Have! Giving Great Gifts

For some people, the holiday season is one enormous Acquisition Trap. They spend too much, enjoy too little, and pay for it for the next six months. The holidays aren't about getting or having, they're about doing and being. This year, give things that won't add clutter to the lives of the people you love and won't bury you in debt.

Consider these ideas for greater gift-giving:

◆ Give something really useful that you know an individual wants or needs (even if it isn't what *you* want to get for them). You can even ask directly. If your favorite crafter really wants a glue gun or a band saw, then make that her gift.

◆ Give something consumable—a special liqueur, a monthly fruit or flower club, bath salts, or a homemade cheesecake. Make it yourself if you have the time.

- Make a donation to someone's favorite charity. If you don't know which one it is, but know he likes animals, adopt a wolf, a dolphin, or a manatee in his name.

- Give gifts that emphasize the tradition of the holiday, not the commercialism, such as homemade holiday treats and decorations. Don't put the focus only on the children, but also on the elders in your family and community.

- If you don't subscribe to the religious part of the holiday, but love the seasonal associations, make your gifts reflect the season and its symbols, with decorated evergreen arrangements or ivy topiaries for the winter holidays.

- Give something only you can give. Make a collection of meaningful photographs. Record an audio tape of you reading your favorite poems or a videotape of your locale if you're far away. Write a song. Draw a picture. How about compiling a family cookbook? Solicit contributions from everyone, type in the recipes on your computer, lay out the book, and then have it photocopied and bound. From now on, no one will be calling at the last minute for your famous crab dip recipe. *It'll be in the book!*

Orderly Pursuits

You can adopt a wolf through Wolf Haven International in Tenino, Washington. Their phone number is (360) 264-4695, and their website is www.wolfhaven.org/. Your gift will include a photo of your chosen wolf and a subscription to Wolf Haven's newsletter for the year.

- Give something that grows. Start bulbs that will come up during the dark winter months—an amaryllis, paperwhites, maybe a crocus. Include watering and planting instructions. Start some houseplants from cuttings of your own. Include care instructions.

- Give experiences instead of things: a balloon ride, a Jeep tour, a picnic, a massage, a day at the movies, a trip to a museum, tickets to the ballet, a concert, or sporting event—whatever will tickle the recipient's fancy.

- Give gift certificates to favorite stores, restaurants, or service providers. Or make your own gift certificates, customized for the people you're giving them to. You can offer baby-sitting, cleaning, hugs, afternoons together, foot massages, or a weekend getaway.

- Divide up the giving. In some families, each buys for one person by drawing his or her name from a grab bag. That way, the recipient can get something more substantial, and the giver only has one person to worry about.

◆ Set a limit on spending. One way is to use cash only—no credit cards. When you lavish gifts on your children and put yourself in debt, think: "Are these the lessons I really want to instill in my kids?"

CAUTION

Oops!

Some people hate practical gifts like appliances or tools. For the practical-present-hater, give something that's pure indulgence, like some sinfully rich chocolate or sumptuous bath oil. Note, too, the people on your list who thrive on practicality!

◆ Use mail-order catalogs or Internet shopping sites. They allow you to avoid the crowds, and make it easier to map out your spending.

◆ Put aside a few small gifts for serendipitous giving. Include a couple of items for adults and some for children. A book of holiday verses, a pretty box, some stationery, some crayons with a holiday coloring book, or some homemade gourmet coffee or hot chocolate mixes (I make these up in big batches) are all good things to stash away "just in case."

◆ Let the store (or mail-order company) do the gift wrapping and shipping. It's worth the extra couple of dollars so you won't be running to the post office at the last minute trying to make the deadline if you have gifts to mail.

◆ Give yourself a present! That's right. You deserve it. Wrap it up and put it under the tree.

Most of all, give of yourself. Give your attention, your listening ear, your love.

Stellar Strategies for Holiday Entertaining

Because the holidays are more hectic than most of the year, if you throw a party, you'll need to give it extra thought and planning.

You'll probably have to be creative with the calendar, since so many events are competing with each other at this time of year. Consider throwing a party just before or right after Thanksgiving—a sort of "launch the holidays" party. Combine Hanukkah and Christmas in an interfaith household, or celebrate Twelfth Night, a Medieval tradition that falls after Christmas. Or how about the week after Christmas, but before New Year's? Or perhaps the weekend after New Year's?

Open houses work well, because people have more flexibility to fit them into their schedules. It's often easier to merge your professional and personal worlds in this less formal setting. An open house works well for a tree-trimming party. Make sure to have the lights already strung before guests arrive. A potluck might work better for a menorah lighting, with guests arriving at a set time.

If you're just starting out on your own, have guests bring an ornament for the tree. It's a great way to start your own collection, and what your friends bring can be amazingly revealing. You can also provide a few simple materials for making ornaments.

Don't be afraid to do something different with your holiday entertaining. How about a cookie exchange party? Everyone brings a couple of dozen of his or her specialties, there's a quick sampling, and each guest ends up with an enticing array of goodies.

How about an ornament- and decoration-making workshop? I've done this for the past several years, and it's always a hit. I provide lots of crafts materials, a big newspaper-covered table, some crafts books and magazines, and plenty of finger foods and refreshments. Then we play!

> **Amazing Space**
>
> Don't forget to pay attention to presentation. It can turn the mundane into the spectacular. Sprinkle gold glitter or "confetti" over tablecloths before you lay down the silverware or serving dishes. Make use of evergreenery and seasonal fruits, berries, and nuts. Enhance candlelight with mirrors and inventive candleholders. Scan magazines and books for creative presentation ideas.

Do a historically oriented Christmas party. You might try a medieval, colonial, or Victorian theme. Slant the decorations, foods, music, and customs toward whatever historic direction you choose. If you have a costume that reflects the era, wear it to set the mood.

Cocktail parties work well, because they can be held early in the evening and guests can still fit in another engagement that night. Or consider a party for the other end of the meal. Dessert and champagne is elegant and relatively easy to do.

How about a Day-After-Christmas brunch? I'll bet you have enough leftovers to pull this one off without even hitting the supermarket!

Decorations can be traditional or modern, fussy or uncomplicated, depending on your taste. Take pictures of your most effective ones so you can duplicate them.

Finessing the Family Tug-of-War

"Whose house do we go to for Christmas (or Hanukkah) this year?" Is that a familiar question at your house around Thanksgiving? Or how about this variation: "Who gets the kids this year?"

Conflicts over who gets to host the family holiday celebration or, if you're divorced, who gets the kids on what days, can wreck even well-laid plans. If you're newly married or newly separated, I can understand this being an issue, but if it's a problem every November, this year I suggest you come up with an enduring solution.

Some couples spend Thanksgiving with one set of parents and Christmas with the other. Others alternate each year. Since Hanukkah is eight days long, there's plenty of opportunity for equal time. The same arrangement can be worked out between divorced couples. My ex-husband and I used to alternate Thanksgiving, and split Christmas Eve and Christmas Day. The kids and I made our celebration on Christmas Eve, and he usually took them for Christmas Day. As long as the children know what the plan is and all the kinks have been ironed out ahead of time, this can work quite smoothly.

The important thing is not to let it ride each year—come to an agreement as to how it's going to be on a regular basis. Then there are no surprises, and the one who's going to be without the children can make alternate plans. If you're going to be alone on Thanksgiving, Hanukkah, or Christmas, why not invite someone else who's going it solo to spend the holiday with you? Other singles are bound to be in the same boat, and if you're feeling a little self-pity, they're sure to understand.

Oops!

Trying to accommodate everyone's wishes will leave you angry and exhausted. You can't be everywhere and please everyone. Decide with your own family what's most important to each of you, and honor those things first. Even extended family and friends are less important. Gently make changes and assert your wishes, and don't back down.

If you'd rather not be with other people, plan a special trip. Book a room at an inn or B&B, sign up for a cruise, or stay in a rustic cabin and get away from it all. Whatever you do, prepare yourself and do something. Don't let it sneak up on you.

Just because the family's not together on a particular holiday doesn't mean you can't celebrate the spirit of the season together at a different time. Institute some creative family traditions that aren't just for a particular day. Make tree-trimming a regular event with specific rituals you repeat each year. Have an annual light-gazing tour or go window shopping. Volunteer each year to work at a soup kitchen or to go caroling at a local nursing home.

If You Must Travel

With extended families spread out from coast to coast, someone will probably have to travel at holiday times. Sometimes it's worth bringing the family to you (tickets become presents), but there are circumstances when this just isn't possible. If you're going to travel for the holidays, here are some ways to make it easier:

- Book flights and accommodations well ahead of time.

- Travel at odd hours to beat the rush.

- Ship gifts ahead so you don't have to carry them with you. Do the same thing on the return trip with the gifts you've received.

- Travel light, and prepare for changes in climate. We live in the Southwest, and if we're traveling back East in the winter, we need to arrange to borrow warmer clothing to wear while we're there. (I got rid of my down jacket years ago!)

- If you're driving, prepare for bad weather. Make sure you have emergency supplies like a flashlight, blankets, and flares, and watch the weather reports.

> **Amazing Space**
>
> Now that our children are spread far apart across the country and don't usually visit until Christmas, we've begun a tradition for Thanksgiving. We call it Orphan's Thanksgiving. Anyone in our circle of friends or neighbors who doesn't have a place to go for Thanksgiving can come to ours. We do it as a potluck, and move or add furniture as needed. One year we had 21 "orphans" for a sit-down Thanksgiving dinner! Everyone had a ball, hosts included.

Travel happily and be safe!

Holiday Storage Snags

What to do with all those bows, lights, ornaments, gift wrappings, and boxes? Well, first of all, if you have some you haven't used for the last three years, you know where they go! Once you unstuff, the next thing is to gather the proper storage materials so you don't end up having to replace things because they're crushed or broken.

I've used one of those divided ornament boxes for umpteen years now, and have never unpacked a broken or damaged ornament. They work great for those of a fairly uniform size, but some of the larger or unusually shaped ones need to be wrapped in tissue and put in a separate box.

Group all your holiday decorations and ornaments together, and label them clearly so they'll be easier to retrieve next year. They can be stored in less valuable *deep freeze* storage space, since it will be a whole year before you'll need them again.

Try to buy just enough wrapping paper so you won't store it a whole year. I use colored tissue for everything throughout the year and customize it with colored ribbon and stickers for the occasion. With the popularity of angels, you can use angel paper for a variety of special events. Glossy plain white, red, gold, or silver paper lends itself to any gift-giving purpose.

If you use all-occasion paper, make sure you don't store it with the holiday stuff, but somewhere more accessible, since you'll be using it throughout the year. Gift wrap organizers available from mail-order catalogs or in stores work quite well. You can also stand up rolls of paper in a wastebasket or deep bucket in the bottom of a closet. Ribbon, flat paper, gift cards, stickers, and rubber stamps (another way to customize gift wrap) can be stored in a flat box on a shelf, clearly marked. Another idea is to use one of those large, flat sweater storage boxes and store everything under a bed.

Other decorations such as artificial wreaths, garlands, menorahs, figurines, and banners should be put away carefully, protected with tissue or newspaper and a sturdy box, labeled, and put in a clean, dry place. Consider the effects that extreme temperatures, dampness, and dryness might have. I once stored a beautiful tree-top angel in the attic, not thinking about how hot it got up there in the summer. The next Christmas, our beautiful angel was a melted mess.

Special corrugated boxes for storing wreaths of various sizes work very well, or you can construct your own. Untangle lights before you put them away, and wrap them around stiff cardboard. Boxes designed especially for storing lights are also available through mail-order catalogs.

Don't get carried away keeping packing materials. Unless you ship regularly throughout the year, get rid of this stuff and buy (or start accumulating) new a couple of months before the holidays. Storing bubble wrap or Styrofoam peanuts for 12 months usually means it's unfit to use when you need it anyway. The same is true of boxes for shipping. Figure out how many you'll need and in what sizes for the gifts you have to ship, and be on the lookout closer to the holidays.

> **Amazing Space**
>
> If you find you've acquired more ornaments and decorations than you can use each year, share the ones you no longer use with a young person just starting out on her own or someone who's lost his belongings in a divorce or disaster. You'll lighten your load and help put the "happy" back into someone's holiday.

Finally, It's All Up to You

What I like most about the holiday season is the time it allows for reflection. It's a time of renewal and excitement about the year ahead. When else do we get to sip a glass of brandy, sit in front of a crackling fire, and contemplate the meaning of family? Whether it's a deeply religious holiday for you or more of a seasonal festival, why not make it a time to be thankful for our abundance and the natural beauty around us? Force the hubbub into submission and insist on a holiday filled with fellowship, appreciation, and joy. The holiday spirit is, after all, *your* spirit!

The Least You Need to Know

◆ Planning and scheduling are the keys to turning your holidays from madness to merriment.

◆ Sensible gift-giving means less clutter for the recipient and more enjoyment for the giver. Keep a careful watch for signs of the Acquisition Trap hidden in your holiday celebrations.

◆ Holiday entertaining requires choosing a date early or picking one that has less competition. Creative party ideas can forge new holiday traditions.

◆ Preparing for family issues ahead of time and negotiating standing arrangements can reduce holiday anxiety and conflict.

◆ Basic organization principles make storing holiday paraphernalia a simple chore.

◆ By controlling your focus and state of mind, you can make any holiday a happy one.

Divine Recreation: More Time for Pastimes

In This Chapter

- ◆ The difference between a hobby and an excuse for accumulating clutter
- ◆ Cures for the collector's blues
- ◆ How to keep your hobby from taking over the house
- ◆ Making pet ownership a pleasure, not a chore

How we spend our spare time is a revealing indicator of who we are. Many times our work doesn't give us an opportunity to use all our hidden talents, develop our interests, and indulge our creative fantasies. Hobbies can provide us with endless hours of pleasure and serious outlets for our creativity. Since many Americans will have several careers during their lifetimes, a spare-time passion can even develop into a career.

Whatever a hobby means to you, you'll want to make sure that you have time to pursue it, the materials you need are organized and in good condition, and you have the space to enjoy your leisure-time passions. This chapter is devoted to helping you spend more time with your hobbies and less time wishing you could.

Is It a Hobby or Just More Stuff?

There are hobbies and then, well, there are good intentions. Sometimes projects seem like something we'll enjoy and then we lose interest. Some so-called hobbies are simply excuses for accumulating and cluttering.

Make an honest assessment of your favorite pastimes—the ones you always turn to when you have some free time. Be honest, too, about the passing fancies that you haven't touched in years. Pass unfinished projects, supplies, and tools on to someone who will really enjoy them (and finish them). Concentrate on the ones you truly enjoy.

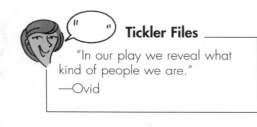

Tickler Files

"In our play we reveal what kind of people we are."
—Ovid

One reason hobbies may languish in the attic or the back of the closet is just that—they're so inaccessible they'd take too much trouble to dig out. Ferret out all those orphaned projects and gather them in one place. If finding them again piques your interest, put them where you'll be able to take them out at a moment's notice and see if they strike your fancy again. If not, pass them on.

Crafty Storage Ideas

Since a craft or hobby isn't something you're likely to do every day, you may not want it lying out where it can get soiled, pieces can get lost, or supplies might be chewed by the dog. Here are some general solutions to storing projects, tools, and supplies:

- ◆ See if there's a carry-all, case, or box that can house all you need to do your hobby. This can be grabbed any time and keeps everything together. One of my hobbies is quilting. I have a plastic project box that can hold everything except my larger quilt frame. I do, however, have one frame that comes apart and can be easily reassembled, made out of plastic PVC pipe that fits in my box. It's so portable, I've even quilted on an airplane!

- ◆ Use a rolling cart with drawers in various sizes. These come in a variety of sizes and can be found in the closet department of your favorite Kmart, Wal-Mart, Target, or art supply store. My daughter, a beader, has all her supplies in one of these carts, so she can pull it to her work area whenever she has a few moments to herself.

- ◆ Some projects lend themselves to a box or bin for storage. You'll usually want a lid to keep light, moisture, and inquisitive hands out, and pieces in. This works well for hobbies like embroidery and hand-sewing. You may want a special keeper for threads and needles that fits neatly in the box.

◆ If your hobby involves many small pieces (like beading, for example), you'll probably want compartmentalized storage boxes that close tightly.

Check hardware stores before you buy specialized boxes and chests from craft stores. The hardware variety is usually less expensive. So what if it's battleship gray or military green instead of pink, mauve, or turquoise? You can always get out the spray paint!

◆ Roll up artwork or any large flat project and store in a clean covered trash container. Make sure to label the container so that everyone knows it's not trash!

◆ Larger tools can go on hooks and clips mounted on a pegboard.

◆ Be careful when storing chemicals, glues, or paints. Read labels thoroughly, and follow storage directions. Observe shelf-life limits. Individual paints can be put in small resealable plastic bags and then stored. This will prevent any accidents or leaks from ruining shelves or other surfaces. Clean and store paint brushes properly.

◆ Use binders to keep instructions and printed directions for projects. Rip what you want out of crafts magazines, three-hole punch, and throw the rest away. Like recipes, there are only so many projects you can make, so be selective and realistic.

◆ Sewing patterns never fit back in their envelopes once they've been unfolded. If you use patterns more than once, set aside space in a file cabinet, put patterns in manila folders, large resealable plastic bags, or large envelopes, label, and file. Be sure to include instructions and the original envelope in the file, plus any notes you'd like to add.

> **Amazing Space**
>
> Some unexpected mail-order catalogs have inexpensive storage options easily adaptable to crafts and hobbies. Try marine, office, kitchen, closet, and scientific supply catalogs, and peruse them from a new vantage point—storage solutions! Also request catalogs for your particular hobby to find storage solutions specifically tailored to its tools and materials.

If your hobby is portable, keep your supplies in a living-room drawer, next to your favorite chair, or beside the bed—wherever you're most likely to spend time and think to pick up the project. I have my embroidery in an attractive hatbox that sits in the living room under the coffee table. While the family watches TV (something I don't really do much of), I can grab my project and still be a part of the action.

Sometimes your choice of hobbies, or the extent to which you can pursue them, is decided by the space you have available. I mean, if you live in a two-room apartment, is it really practical to start building model airplanes as a hobby?

CAUTION

Oops! _____

There's nothing worse than a space hog. I know one couple where he dominates the whole house with his hobbies, and she, a seamstress, has to use the kitchen table and pack up her projects every time they eat. No fair! Be sure you check with the other residents of your abode before you appropriate space for your hobby. And share! Didn't they teach you *anything* in kindergarten?

If you have a hobby that takes up a great deal of room, like model railroading, for example, you'll need a permanent designated area of the house to pursue it. Preferably this will be in a room with a door, where your works in progress can be closed off. I'll never forget the time the family cat decided to use the sandy soil on my father's train table as a cat box. Took a while to figure out those newly formed "hills" weren't what they appeared to be!

You'll have to negotiate for space to spread out if your hobby is that large. Perhaps turning a basement into a combination hobby area for several family members is a good compromise. Or maybe a section of the garage or the attic can be yours.

Here are some more ideas for making space for your crafts and hobbies:

Borrow. Look for solutions devised for other purposes that might suit your needs. A fishing tackle box, for example, might make a great rubber stamp hobby box, or a handy way to transport small beading or sewing projects. Cardboard shelf units used for sorting sales literature might make a good system for storing quilting fabric quarters by color or any other supplies that are flat and come in multiples. Folding banquet or card tables might make good work surfaces that can be put away when space is at a premium. Dish pans or kitty litter pans lined up on close shelves and labeled can hold fabric squares, paper scraps, tools—almost anything. If you were looking for a use for all that excess Tupperware, you've probably got one now.

Build. Sometimes the best idea is to build something to fit your needs. Whether it's a specialized work table, a shelf system, or a box frame with compartments to affix to the wall, making your own gives you the freedom to create something exactly suited to your requirements.

Adapt. Another choice is to take something that's almost right and make a few changes so that it's perfect for your particular projects. By adding inserts, dividers, or a different closure, or removing something, you can make it better suit your particular application. An unused coat closet, for example, can be divested of its clothes rod and fitted with shelves and drawer units to make it a crafts closet.

Recycle. Use old coffee cans, tins, oatmeal boxes, baby food jars, and cigar boxes to store your hobby supplies. You'll get free containers and keep them out of the landfill for a while.

> **Amazing Space**
>
> Locate the material for your hobby close to where you use it. You want to spend time enjoying your hobby, not looking for it.

Use basic organizing principles once you get the containers, shelves, and carrying cases you need:

- ◆ Group like things together. Group by type, subject, color, texture, or purpose—whatever makes sense.

- ◆ Consolidate and compress. Use smaller, compartmentalized containers if possible. Stack and layer. Keep things from spreading out.

- ◆ Label it! If it's not in a see-through container, make sure you label your supplies so you don't have to go through a dozen boxes before you find the right one.

Multimedia Mogul

If you're like most folks in our day and age, you have substantial numbers of CDs, audiotapes, and videotapes. If you're really a hard-core music lover, you probably still have your share of vinyl LPs, as well. Wondering what to do with all of these, and how to untangle all those cords their players create? Then listen up!

High-Tech Horror Show: Wires and Cords

Whatever your electronic poison—a personal computer, stereo system, home entertainment center, or just a TV and VCR—you'll inevitably have a tangle of cords and shared electrical outlets to deal with.

There are basically two types of products on the market for managing cords and wires. One type is a flexible tube, slit down one side. You open it up and insert each cord or wire individually, snaking it along shelves to catch each set from individual pieces of equipment, then guide down to where the electrical outlet is.

The second type of cord and wire management system is basically a Velcro strap that either gathers cords into bundles or "catches" them and sticks to various surfaces to hide them along baseboards, shelves, racks, or desks.

Another decision you'll have to make is how you want to display your electronic equipment. Do you want it out in the open or do you want it discreetly hidden behind closed doors? All of our equipment is black and sits on three black industrial wire shelving units. The setup fits the high-tech look of our family room entertainment wall.

If your equipment is somewhat smaller in scale, you might want to hide yours in a sideboard, armoire, or cupboard. You can have a unit custom made or you can adapt an existing one. Check out unpainted furniture places and used furniture shops, as well. Don't overlook yard sales and newspaper classifieds. Entertainment centers specifically designed for audio equipment, TVs, and VCRs can work. The better ones are quite pricey, however, and the less expensive ones can be flimsy. When shopping, don't forget to consider the weight of your components, size (take measurements and bring them with you), how you're going to manage cords, air circulation, and ease of access for use and cleaning.

Orderly Pursuits

Rip-Tie manufactures Velcro cord management products. Write them at P.O. Box 549, San Leandro, CA 94577, call (800) 348-7600, e-mail (info@riptie.com), or visit their website at www.riptie.com. Look for their CableCatch and CableWrap products.

Composing Your Music and Video Collection

Some people don't mind the look of CD towers and video storage units, but I think they look unsightly in the average living room. There are lots of options for camouflaging or completely hiding your musical and film media. You need to decide whether you want to store them so you can see them (some people feel it's part of their decor) or get them out of sight.

There are lots of racks and towers for storing these items in plain sight. But if you opt for getting them behind closed doors or drawers, look for pieces of furniture originally intended for other uses and retrofit them for music and movie storage.

Don't overlook the storage possibilities of drawers. We have an antique secretary with very shallow but long drawers. They're just the perfect size for audiotape storage and can hold a considerable collection. Drawers also keep your collection at a lower height, so they're easier to see and you don't have to reach up to get them.

Since tapes and CDs are fairly narrow, you can build custom shelving that makes use of shallow hidden spaces. Look behind doors or along walls. We made storage shelves that just fit the depth of our largest video cases. They line the wall in the guest room.

Often overnight guests appear from their room with a video request in hand! If a piece of furniture doesn't fit the bill, consider stacking boxes. Narrow shoe boxes are just about right for CDs. Larger ones might fit videos. There are also sturdy, attractive file boxes created just for CD and video storage.

If you're really challenged for space, consider ditching the jewel cases that CDs come in and moving to a scratchproof plastic sleeve system that holds both CD and liner notes. These come in flip-through album styles and individual sleeves designed for a file drawer unit. One caution on this design is to be careful of transporting CDs in these plastic sleeves where they're going to be exposed to heat or dirt. The plastic can melt more easily than the hard plastic of jewel cases and ruin your CDs.

Old-fashioned vinyl is fast becoming replaced by the new forms of digital media, but there are those who feel vinyl is still technically superior, or for sentimental reasons have a few LPs they want to hang on to. Always store vinyl albums vertically, never flat, since they're easy to warp. Keep them upright (use bookends, if needed). Acid-free and polyethylene sleeves are available to replace the inferior paper ones that often came with the original album.

Consider temperature and humidity when storing your electronic media. Ideally your air temperature will be constant, with a steady 40 percent to 60 percent humidity—which, by the way, is also ideal for musical instruments.

Most audiophiles consider audiotapes a more temporary medium. Tapes are subject to stretching, and audio quality just isn't up to CDs or even vinyl in good condition. I like to use audiotapes to customize my music listening and to make copies for use in areas where my CDs might get damaged, such as outdoors when I'm gardening or in the car.

It's also fun to make specialized collections for certain themes, occasions, or moods, and I have certain tapes I keep near the bathtub for those long, luxurious bubble baths I mentioned earlier. Tapes are also great for learning, and I have several collections that I go back to for practicing meditation or visualization techniques. I've made copies and keep the originals in a fairly climate- and humidity-controlled environment. But the truth is, tapes just wear out more quickly, and it's probably good to have the CD version of ones you especially like.

You'll need a labeling and filing system for your music and movie collection. We have our videos

> **Amazing Space**
>
> Take a few CDs, DVDs, and audio- and videotapes along with you when you shop to see how many will fit, and estimate what materials might be needed to adapt your flea market or unpainted furniture find.

organized by general categories and then alphabetically within those categories. This is especially helpful if you have a large collection, which we do. DVDs take up less room, but not everyone has purchased a DVD player as yet, and even those who have usually have both tape and disk technology and need to store both videotapes and DVDs. Periodically purge your collection. If you tape something and decide later you've seen it enough times or it's not a favorite, tape over it or pass it on. Give away music you no longer listen to. Or make a tape of the few cuts on the albums, tapes, or CDs you truly enjoy, and let the individual volumes go.

Oops!

The enemies of all electronic media are dust, fingerprints, dirt, moisture, and extremes in temperature. Think carefully about where you choose to store CDs, DVDs, tapes, and LPs, and use the right cleaning systems to maintain them. Don't forget to keep your electronic equipment clean as well.

Racks created just for the purpose of storing CDs are fine, but they do have some disadvantages, especially slotted racks. If you're trying to set up an alphabetical filing system, every time you get a new CD, you'll have to move each CD and reinsert it into a new slot. Kind of a pain.

If you have an especially large music and/or movie collection, you may need to go to a more complex filing system. You can use index cards if you want to go low-tech, or check into some of the computer programs designed for the purpose. These are essentially databases, and their advantage is that they allow you to search for titles based on key words, artists, labels, or even individual song titles, if you want to get that detailed.

Book Beat: Learning Your Library Lessons

To book lovers like my husband and me, a house is not a home without a substantial reading and reference library. When we met and married, between us we had thousands of books. We've pared down to old favorites and the most useful reference works, but we have a tendency to acquire new books on a regular basis. For us, managing our library is a major organization issue, as it is for lots of other readers and book aficionados.

The system that seems to work best for us is to organize our nonfiction books according to major activities, and then have the rest divided into history, philosophy and a few additional nonfiction topics. Fiction has its own separate section. Like most people, we don't have the space for a separate library room, so our books are spread throughout the house in logical groupings. Books related to movies and TV, cooking, gardening, and travel are in the guest room, where the videos are stored. Guests seem to enjoy perusing these volumes the most, and the shelf of local history and travel books makes a practical addition to this location.

My husband's Civil War, World War II, and American Western history collection is downstairs in his shop. Books related to my profession as a writer are on bookshelves in my office. Fiction, poetry, and crafts-related books have their own home in a series of book cases in my hobby area.

New books usually find their way into the bedroom first, and when I'm done reading them, I either decide to keep them and find an appropriate place, or pass them on for others to enjoy. Since I like our bedroom to be fairly uncluttered for a relaxed atmosphere for sleeping and dreaming, I keep this pile to a minimum. There's just a small stack on the floor by my bedside table, and there are no bookshelves. My husband has his own stack on the other side of the bed. We're considering a very small bookcase just for books we're getting ready to read. If you're a heavy reader, too, try several solutions until you come up with one that works. What you don't want is stacks of books everywhere or a storage system that has you looking for hours to find the book you need.

Try to categorize your own library and see where the most logical places might be to store particular groupings. Look for spaces that best suit the number of volumes in a particular category. If you're not sure what you have or suspect you have quite a few books you could pass on, do a major overhaul and gather all your books together into categorized stacks for redistribution.

> **Amazing Space**
>
> Books can be a decorative feature, as long as they don't become clutter. If you have an especially attractive leather-bound set, display it in a living room or study. A neat pile of splendid picture books looks attractive on a coffee table or occasional table. Small volumes of poetry can grace a small nook almost anywhere.

If you sometimes have visitors who need to wait in a foyer or living room, or if you have a client waiting room for your home business, have a stack of interesting books and magazines available to keep them occupied. Don't put any special favorites there, though, just in case one decides to walk away!

Don't forget to keep a list of books you've borrowed from others and books you've lent. A bulletin board is a good place for this, or you may want to have a sheet in your planner/organizer. I've lost so many treasured volumes through my habit of loaning favorites to others. I'm sure they don't intend to keep them, but over time they forget, and so do I. Then when I'm searching for a favorite book or one I've been meaning to read, I can't imagine where to begin looking to track it down. Don't forget to put your name inside your books so the borrower has no excuse for not returning them, like forgetting who he borrowed them from!

Keep books borrowed from someone else's library in one place, so they don't somehow get absorbed into your own library and become lost forever. These usually end up in my special bedroom stack for current reading, so I always know where they are. Put a sticky note on the inside front cover with the name of the person you borrowed it from, and you'll remember where to return it.

Dust books and bookshelves regularly. Once a year, take them off the shelves, dust, and vacuum. Make sure wherever you're storing them is free of dampness. If there's any chance they might get mildewed, put a dehumidifier in the room and monitor it. Don't squash books into shelves—you'll damage them. Most books like to be stored upright, but very large books are best stored on their sides individually. Special narrow shelves can be created for this, to minimize the space they take up. Don't stack too many books on top of one another.

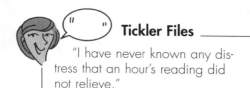

Tickler Files

"I have never known any distress that an hour's reading did not relieve."

—Baron de Montesquieu

When Collecting Is Your Hobby

All right, I admit it! Even though I'm anticlutter, I do have some collections of stuff that I really prize. I lean toward antique glassware and old photos, plus I have an antique fan collection. These things give me pleasure, but I must limit their size, and I use or display what I have.

It's easy for collections to get out of hand, though. I once knew someone who had a beer can and bottle collection. It started out innocently enough and then grew to engulf an entire basement, spilled into the living room, and even occupied a bedroom closet! Somehow things got entirely out of hand. Collections are like that.

Collection or Clutter?

Whatever your favorite collecting hobby, be it baseball cards or art glass, find some sort of special container or cabinet to house it in and use that container as a limit-setting device. My depression glass has its own cabinet, and when that's full, the size of the collection is determined.

If you've got a really special or rare collection, why not donate it to a museum related to your particular interest so other collectors can enjoy it? There's a museum for almost anything. Check with your reference librarian if you're not sure where there is one.

Why not use your collection? Although I wouldn't be pleased if I broke a piece of my depression glass, I gain the greatest pleasure from setting a table with it, not from keeping it in my china cabinet. If your collection is not substantially growing in value or you don't use it or gain pleasure from it regularly, consider giving it away.

Oops!

Beware of collections becoming just another acquisition trap. You'll know you're in trouble when your collection starts taking over the house and pushing other activities out of the way. Be aware of changes in your interests, as well. When a collection no longer gives you any pleasure and just collects dust, it's time to let it go.

Another suggestion is simply to pare down your collection. How about keeping only the rarest or most interesting examples? Narrow your collection to only one category or color. Or use the "trade up" principle. Keep only a certain number, and when you find something that's better than what you have, trade up—get rid of the lesser example and replace it with the better quality or more special one. Display your collection and make it a part of your decor.

Pet Care: Who Owns Whom?

You may not consider owning a pet a hobby, but I put it in this category because, in truth, having a pet is an "extra." I have to admit, though, a house without a cat or dog just isn't home to me.

Should You Get a Pet?

If you're going to take on the responsibility of giving a home to an animal, there are some things you should know and commit to beforehand:

Pets take time. It's not just the routine things like taking Fido for a walk or changing the litter in Fluffie's pan that takes time. Animals need attention, just like people. If you're not prepared to give it regular affection, exercise, and "quality time," then don't get a pet.

Pets need to be trained. To keep a pet from becoming a behavioral nightmare, you need to give it some training in the beginning. A dog must be housebroken, but that's really just a start. Some time and money spent at obedience school will be returned to you many times over in the future.

Pets need space and freedom. To be happy, an animal needs some space to roam and freedom to explore. Even if you live in an apartment, take your dog regularly to a park to run and play. If you own a cat and he's confined to an apartment, make sure your feline has plenty of space to roam inside and toys to entertain him. Rotate toys often, so your pet doesn't get bored.

Pets need grooming. Regular brushing, flea treatments, and bathing are necessary for your dog's health. Cats need brushing and flea treatments as well. (Bathing cats can be a bit dicey, but luckily, most cats take care of their basic cleanliness pretty well themselves.) Brushing will keep coats healthy and save cleanup on rugs and upholstery.

Pets need cleaning up after. Bowls should be washed regularly, and you'll need to treat stains promptly before they do more serious damage or breed germs. Kitty pans need regular washing and sterilizing.

Pets need proper food. Diet is important and will vary according to the animal's age and activity level. Special dietary considerations may be necessary if certain health conditions develop. Resist emptying table scraps into Fido's bowl. Much of what people eat isn't really best for dogs and cats (and maybe not for people, either!).

Pets need regular health care. You should spay or neuter and regularly vaccinate your adopted friend. You'll need to budget for these expenses and add regular vet appointments to your schedule each year.

> **Amazing Space**
>
> Sharing space with a pet means thinking out important issues like providing scratching areas for the feline set, managing pet hair, and ensuring that everyone gets a good night's sleep. Anticipate these issues and settle them right away. Research solutions and ask the advice of a veterinarian *before* you bring a pet home.

Pets require special arrangements when you travel. Whether you take your animal companion with you or travel without it, you'll have to make arrangements for its welfare.

Think seriously about your obligations as a pet owner. There's nothing wrong with admitting you simply don't have a lifestyle that makes keeping an animal as a pet a fair proposition. The decision to become a pet owner shouldn't be made selfishly. The animal's welfare should be as much a consideration as your desire to have the animal in your life.

Prevent Canine and Kitty Clutter

If you've decided pet ownership is for you, then you'll need to store all the goodies that go with your charge. Again, having everything in one centrally located place is the best idea.

- Put doggie's leash on a hook right by the door, along with the keys, flashlight, pooper scooper, raincoat, and umbrella.

- Keep a grooming brush next to your favorite easy chair. When kitty comes and jumps up into your lap, do her a favor by brushing her coat while you pet her.

- Have a caddy with flea treatment and bathing supplies all together. On bath day, just grab the caddy and hope the dog doesn't run the other way. A treat might help!

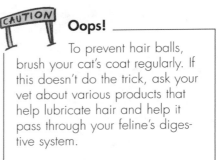

Oops!

To prevent hair balls, brush your cat's coat regularly. If this doesn't do the trick, ask your vet about various products that help lubricate hair and help it pass through your feline's digestive system.

- Store dry food in a sealed container, such as a small lidded trash can. This will prevent moisture, germs, and pests from attacking it and make it easier to scoop out. Store kitty litter in a similar container.

- Learn the basics of providing for your particular animal type and breed. Consult your veterinarian about any behavior problems right away, before they become more serious.

- If you're going to be away all day at work, consider having more than one pet so they can provide each other with company. Make sure they have adequate food, water, and sanitary facilities and spend plenty of time with them in the evening or on weekends.

- Piggyback your exercise routine with your dog's. By making a commitment to exercise him every day, you'll be doing yourself a favor, too. Write it in your planner/organizer so you don't welsh! Make sure whatever exercise you choose, it's something he can keep up with. Don't overdo it. If you're not sure what's "too much," consult your veterinarian.

Picture This

First, pat yourself on the back! You made it! Now close your eyes and go to your favorite place. I'll bet that place is now where you live all the time! Or at least the real world is beginning to look a lot more like the one you've been visualizing as you've gone through this book with me. Experience the rewards of having an organized life, one that matches the things you said you wanted in the beginning. Congratulations!

I've enjoyed making this journey with you, as I hope you have with me. Understand that making this life the way you want it to be is a do-it-yourself project that lasts a lifetime (and who knows, maybe an eternity?). But the journey is probably the point. Enjoy, and make each moment count.

The Least You Need to Know

- Finding space for hobbies closest to where you and your family spend time makes it more likely you'll complete projects you start.

- Basic organizing principles and tools can be used to organize hobby supplies, tools, instructions, and projects.

- Containers and carrying boxes can be adapted from other sources, such as catalogs and marine supply, office supply, and hardware stores.

- Organize electronic media attractively to make them easier to access and keep them safe from unfavorable conditions.

- Pets require a major commitment and deserve regular care, space, and attention.

Resource Guide

Here, all in one place, is a list of resources to help you develop your organization program. To make it even easier to find what you're looking for, I've grouped them by chapter. In some cases I have repeated sources that were mentioned in various chapters, just so you could have them in one handy guide.

Chapter 1: The Big Picture: Setting Goals

Books

The 7 Habits of Highly Effective People: Powerful Lessons in Personal Change by Stephen Covey, Simon & Schuster, 1990; ISBN 0671708635.

The Magic Lamp: Goal Setting for People Who Hate Setting Goals by Keith Ellis, Three Rivers Press, 1998; ISBN 060980166X.

Wishcraft: How to Get What You Really Want by Barbara Sher and Annie Gottlieb, Ballentine Books, 1986; ISBN 0345340892.

Software

GoalPro™ 5.0 is a product of Success Studios Corporation and you can download a free 30-day trial of the software at www.goalpro.com.

Chapter 2: It's All About "Stuff" and "Time"

Books

How Much Is Enough?: The Consumer Society and the Future of the Earth by Alan Durning, W.W. Norton & Co., 1992; ISBN 039330891X.

Voluntary Simplicity: Toward a Way of Life That Is Outwardly Simple, Inwardly Rich by Duane Elgin, Quill, 1993; ISBN 0688121195.

Newsletters

Creative Downscaling, Box 1884, Jonesboro, GA 30237-1884, (770) 471-9048, e-mail: kilgo@mindspring.com; $20/yr. for 10 issues.

Audio and Video Tapes

Affluenza and *Escape from Affluenza*, PBS programs available on VHS from The Simple Living Network, www.simpleliving.net/.

Chapter 3: Excuses! Excuses!

Books

First Things First: To Live, To Love, To Learn, To Leave a Legacy by Stephen R. Covey, A. Roger Merrill, and Rebecca R. Merrill, Fireside, 1996; ISBN 0684802031.

How to Get Control of Your Time and Your Life by Alan Lakein, New American Library, 1996; ISBN 0451167724.

Time Management from the Inside Out: The Foolproof System for Taking Control of Your Schedule and Your Life by Julie Morgenstern, Henry Holt, 2000; ISBN 0805064699.

Chapter 4: When Stuff Rules Your Life

Books

A Brilliant Madness: Living with Manic-Depressive Illness by Patty Duke with Gloria Hochman, Bantam, 1993; ISBN 0553560727.

An Unquiet Mind by Kay Redfield Jameson, Random House, 1993; ISBN 0679763309.

Born to Spend: How to Overcome Compulsive Spending by Gloria Arenson, Human Services Institute, 1991; ISBN 0830621555.

Can't Buy Me Love: Freedom from Compulsive Spending and Money Obsession by Sally Coleman and Nancy Hull-Mast, Fairview Press, 1995; ISBN 0925190462.

Credit, Cash and Co-Dependency: How the Way You Were Raised Affects Your Decisions About Money by Yvonne Kaye, Islewest Publishing, 1998; ISBN 1888461063.

Sink Reflections: Flylady's Babystep Guide to Overcoming CHAOS by Marla Cilley, Flylady Press, Inc., 2002; ISBN 0971855110.

The New Messies Manual: The Procrastinator's Guide to Good Housekeeping by Sandra Felton, Fleming H. Revell Co., 2000; ISBN 0800757262.

Organizations

Clutterers Anonymous
P.O. Box 91413
Los Angeles, CA 90009-1413
admin@clutterersanonymous.net
www.clutterersanonymous.net

Debtor's Anonymous
General Service Office
P.O. Box 920888
Needham, MA 02492-0009
(781) 453-2743
www.debtorsanonymous.org

Emotions Anonymous International
P.O. Box 4245
St. Paul, MN 55104-0245
(651) 647-9712
info@EmotionsAnonymous.org
www.emotionsanonymous.org

Messies Anonymous
5025 SW 114th Avenue
Miami, FL 33165
(800) MESS-AWAY (637-7292)
www.messies.com

National ADD Association
1788 Second Street, Suite 200
Highland Park, IL 60035
(847) 432-ADDA
mail@add.org
www.add.org

National Association of Professional Organizers
P.O. Box 140647
Austin, TX 78714
(512) 206-0151
www.napo.net
e-mail: napo@assnmgmt.com

National Depressive and Manic-Depressive Association
730 N. Franklin Street, Suite 501
Chicago, IL 60610-7204
(800) 826-3632
www.ndmda.org

Obsessive-Compulsive Anonymous
P.O. Box 215
New Hyde Park, NY 11040
(516) 739-0662
hometown.aol.com/west24th/index.html

Obsessive-Compulsive Foundation
337 Notch Hill Road
Branford, CT 06471
(203) 315-2190
info@ocfoundation.org
www.ocfoundation.org

The American Association for Chronic Fatigue Syndrome
515 Minor Avenue, Suite 18
Seattle, WA 98104
(206) 781-3544
info@aacfs.org
www.AACFS.org

Chapter 7: Creating a Command Center

Products

Day-Timer
Day-Timers, Inc.
One Willow Lane
East Texas, PA 18046
(800) 452-7398
www.daytimer.com/

DayRunner
DayRunner, Inc.
2760 W. Moore Avenue
Fullerton, CA 92833
(800) 643-9923
www.dayrunner.com/

FranklinCovey
2200 West Parkway Boulevard
Salt Lake City, UT 84119
(800) 819-1812
www.franklincovey.com/

Handspring Treo and Visor
Handspring
(888) 565-9393
www.handspring.com

Palm, Inc.
Corporate Headquarters
5470 Great America Parkway
Santa Clara, CA 95054
(800) 881-7256
www.palm.com

Chapter 8: People Who Need People: Interpersonal Systems

Books

Making Scrapbooks: Complete Guide to Preserving Your Treasured Memories by Vanessa-Ann, Sterling Publishing, 1998; ISBN 0806999012.

1001 More Ways to Be Romantic by Gregory Godek, Casablanca Press, 1992; ISBN 0962980323.

1001 Ways to Be Romantic by Gregory Godek, Casablanca Press, 1995; ISBN 1883518059.

Chapter 9: Work Systems: Getting Ahead Without Getting a Headache

Books

How to Take the Fog Out of Business Writing by Robert Gunning, Dartnell Corp., 1994; ISBN 0850132320.

The Three Boxes of Life and How to Get Out of Them: An Introduction to Life-Work Planning by Richard Nelson Bolles, Ten Speed Press, 1978; ISBN 0913668583.

What Color Is Your Parachute? by Richard Nelson Bolles, Ten Speed Press, 1998; ISBN 1580080081.

Working from Home: Everything You Need to Know About Living and Working Under the Same Roof by Paul and Sarah Edwards, J.P. Tarcher Inc., 1999; ISBN 0874779766.

Chapter 10: Methods for Your Morning Madness

Books

Beyond Soap, Water and Comb: A Man's Guide to Good Grooming and Fitness by Ed Marquand, Abbeville Press, 1999; ISBN 0789204452.

Color Me Beautiful's Looking Your Best: Color, Makeup, and Style by Mary Spillane and Christine Sherlock, Madison Books, 1995; ISBN 1568330375.

For Men Only: The Secrets of a Successful Image by Richard Derwald and Anthony Chiappone, Promethueus Books, 1995; ISBN 0879759100.

The Art of Makeup by Kevyn Aucoin, HarperCollins, 1996; ISBN 0062730428.

Chapter 11: Food Systems: Getting Your Daily Bread

Books

Fix-It and Forget-It Cookbook: Feasting with Your Slow Cooker by Dawn Ranck and Phyllis Good, Good Books, 2001; ISBN 1561483176.

Making the Best of Basics: Family Preparedness Handbook by James Talmage Stevens, Gold Leaf Press, 1997; ISBN 1882723252.

Once-a-Month Cooking: A Proven System for Spending Less Time in the Kitchen and Enjoying Delicious Homemade Meals Everyday by Mimi Wilson and Mary Beth Lagerborg, Broadman & Holman Publishers, 1999; ISBN 0805418350.

Products

Send for the Everything Rubbermaid Catalog by writing to Everything Rubbermaid, Mail Order Department, 115 South Market Street, Wooster, OH 44691. The company's more than 1,000 products are available in many department and hardware stores.

Call (800) 874-0008 for a locator service that can tell you which retailers carry ClosetMaid products. These include a paper rack, cup racks, wine glass racks, towel bars, plate and lid racks, slide-out cabinet, and over-the-door organizers, plus a Close Mesh Pantry Organizer.

Chapter 12: Clothing Systems: Easy Ways to Wash and Wear

Books

Don Aslett's Stainbuster's Bible: The Complete Guide to Spot Removal by Don Aslett, Penguin USA, 1990; ISBN 0452263859.

Short Kutz by Melanie Graham, Whitecap Books, 1992; ISBN 0801983525. This book tells you everything you want to know about repairing and maintaining your clothes.

Products

The Closet Factory. For information about the franchise nearest you and a free in-home consultation, call (800) 692-5673. This company not only designs custom closet solutions, but also pantries. Website: www.closetfactory.com.

ClosetMaid, "The Storage Authority" will send you catalogs and bulletins for their many storage racks, bins, and organizers. Write them at 650 SW 27th Avenue, Ocala, FL 34474 or call (800) 874-0008. Website: www.closetmaid.com.

The Container Store has catalogs for just about every room in your house. Call 1-888-CONTAIN (266-8246) to request yours. Website: www.containerstore.com

The Hold Everything catalog can be obtained by calling (800) 421-2264, or pointing your browser www.williams-sonomainc.com/com/hld/.

InterMetro Industries Corporation. Call (800) 441-2714 for a local dealer that sells these versatile modular shelving systems. Website: www.metro.com/.

Chapter 13: Shelter Systems: Giving Your Nest the Best

Books

Better Basics for the Home: Simple Solutions for Less Toxic Living by Annie Berthold-Bond, Three Rivers Press, 1999; ISBN 0609803255.

Clean House, Clean Planet: Clean Your House for Pennies a Day the Safe, Nontoxic Way by Karen Logan, Pocket Books, 1997; ISBN 0671535951.

The Cleaning Encyclopedia: Your A to Z Illustrated Guide to Cleaning like the Pros! by Don Aslett, Dell, 1993; ISBN 0440504813.

The Complete Idiot's Guide to Feng Shui by Elizabeth Moran and Val Biktashev, Alpha Books, 1999; ISBN 0028631056.

The Western Guide to Feng Shui: Creating Balance, Harmony, and Prosperity in Your Environment by Terah Kathryn Collins, Hay House, 1996; ISBN 1561703249.

Organizations

International Feng Shui Guild
P.O. Box 262152
Highlands Ranch, CO 80163
(303) 877-0142
e-mail: admin@fengshuiguild.com
www.fengshuiguild.com

Products

Many professional cleaning supply firms have mail-order catalogs. Check out Don Aslett's *Clean Report*, a combination newsletter and catalog for the cleaning professional and those who just want to clean like one. Call (800) 451-2402 to get on the mailing list.

Jeff Campbell's Clean Team Catalog comes from the author of *Speed Cleaning*. Contains books, cleaning tools, and supplies. Call (800) 990-CLEAN or write Jeff Campbell's Clean Team, 990 South Rogers Circle #5, Boca Raton, FL 33487-2848.

Chapter 14: Winning the Money Wars: Guerrilla Budgeting

Books

Cut Your Bills in Half: Thousands of Tips to Save Thousands of Dollars by Rodale Press Editors, Rodale Press, 1993; ISBN 0831718927.

Everyone's Money Book by Jordan E. Goodman and Sonny Bloch, Dearborn Financial Publishing, 1993; ISBN 0793107210.

How to Get Out of Debt, Stay Out of Debt and Live Prosperously by Jerrold Mundis, Bantam Books, 1990; ISBN 0553283960.

How to Want What You Have: Discovering the Magic and Grandeur of Ordinary Existence by Timothy Ray Miller, Avon Books, 1996; ISBN 0380726823.

Living More with Less by Doris Janzen Longacre, Herald Press, 1980; ISBN 0836119304.

Money Troubles: Legal Strategies to Cope with Your Debts by Robin Leonard, Nolo Press, 2001; ISBN 0873376404.

The Best of Cheapskate Monthly: Simple Tips for Living Lean in the '90s by Mary Hunt, St. Martin's Press, 1993; ISBN 0312950934.

The Cheapskate Monthly Money Makeover by Mary Hunt, St. Martin's Press, 1995; ISBN 0312954115.

The Complete Tightwad Gazette: Promoting Thrift as a Viable Alternative Lifestyle by Amy Dacyczyn, Random House, 1999; ISBN 0375752250.

The Tightwad Gazette II: Promoting Thrift as a Viable Alternative Lifestyle by Amy Dacyczyn, Villard Books, 1995; ISBN 0679750789.

The Tightwad Gazette III: Promoting Thrift as a Viable Alternative Lifestyle by Amy Dacyczyn, Villard Books, 1997; ISBN 0679777660.

Your Money or Your Life: Transforming Your Relationship with Money and Achieving Financial Independence by Joe Dominguez and Vicki Robin, Penguin USA, 1999; ISBN 0140286780.

Audio and Video Tapes

Transforming Your Relationship with Money and Achieving Financial Independence, an audiocassette/workbook course by Joe Dominguez of the book *Your Money or Your Life*. It includes four 70-minute audiocassettes and a 132-page workbook and is available from New Road Map Foundation, P.O. Box 15981, Seattle, WA 98115. Cost is $39.95.

Chapter 15: Tax Tactics and Advanced Money Maneuvers

Books

Nolo's Simple Will Book by attorney Denis Clifford, Nolo Press, 2001; ISBN 0873377125.

Quick and Legal Will Book by Denis Clifford, Nolo Press, 2001; ISBN 087337505X.

The American Bar Association Guide to Wills and Estates: Everything You Need to Know About Wills, Trusts, Estates, and Taxes, Times Books, 1995; ISBN 081292536X.

Software

Personal Recordkeeper (for Windows or Mac) and Quicken Lawyer 2002 Personal Deluxe (for Windows) available at Nolo; call (800) 992-6656 or visit www.nolo.com.

Online

A primer and other very helpful articles are offered by American Express Small Business Exchange at www.americanexpress.com/smallbusiness/.

Booklets

There are many useful tax-related booklets available *free* from the Internal Revenue Service. Just log on to www.irs.gov, then download the PDF files or call (800) 829-3676 to request the print versions. Some titles you may want to ask for are:

Publication 525, "Taxable and Nontaxable Income," which includes information on reporting bartering transactions.

Publication 463, "Travel, Entertainment and Gift Expenses."

Publication 334, "The Small Business Tax Guide."

Publication 552, "Recordkeeping for Individuals," which includes information on what you need to keep for the IRS and how long.

Chapter 16: Healing Trends: Organizing for Health and Fitness

Books

Altars Made Easy: A Complete Guide to Creating Your Own Sacred Space by Peg Streep, Harper San Francisco, 1997; ISBN 0062514903.

Harvard Medical School Family Health Guide edited by Anthony L. Komaroff, M.D., Simon & Schuster, 1999; ISBN 0684847035.

Healthmate Medical Planner: A Practical Guide for Taking Control of Your Health and Having Your Medical Records Always Available Even When Your Doctor Isn't by Kathleen Deremer, Six Ponies Press, 1997; ISBN 0965635058.

Sacred Space: Clearing and Enhancing the Energy of Your Home by Denise Linn, Ballentine Books, 1996; ISBN 034539769X.

Your Child's Medical Journal: Keeping Track of Your Child's Personal Health History from Conception Through Adulthood by Sharon Larsen, Harmony Books, 1999; ISBN 0609802445.

Chapter 18: Calling in the Cavalry: Hiring Others

Books

The Free-Spirited Garden: Gorgeous Gardens That Flourish Naturally by Susan McClure, Chronicle Books, 1999; ISBN 0811821129.

Organizations

National Association of Professional Organizers
P.O. Box 140647
Austin, TX 78714
(512) 206-0151
www.napo.net

Chapter 19: Minimum Maintenance

Books

Alexandra Stoddard's Living Beautiful Together by Alexandra Stoddard, Avon Books, 1991; ISBN 0380709082.

Living a Beautiful Life: 500 Ways to Add Elegance, Order, Beauty, and Joy to Every Day of Your Life by Alexandra Stoddard, Avon Books, 1988; ISBN 0380705117.

Mrs. Sharp's Traditions: Nostalgic Suggestions for Re-Creating the Family Celebrations and Seasonal Pastimes of the Victorian Home by Sarah Ban Breathnach, Scribner, 2001; ISBN 074321076X.

Chapter 20: Organization Styles for Different Lifestyles

Books

After He's Gone: A Guide for Widowed and Divorced Women by Barbara Tom Jowell and Donnette Schwisow, Birch Lane Press, 1997; ISBN 1559724331.

Better Homes and Gardens New Cookbook, Meredith Books, 1996; ISBN 0696201887.

Fannie Farmer Cookbook by Marion Cunningham and Fannie Merritt Farmer, Knopf, 1996; ISBN 0679450815.

Going Solo in the Kitchen by Jane Doerfer, Knopf, 1998; ISBN 0375703934.

Keeping Your Family Close: When Frequent Travel Pulls You Apart by Elizabeth M. Hoekstra, Crossway Books, 1998; ISBN 0891079750.

Serves One: Super Meals for Solo Cooks by Toni Lydecker, Lake Isle Press, 1998; ISBN 1891105019.

The Business Traveler's Survival Guide: How to Get Work Done While on the Road by June Langhoff, Aegis Publishing Group, 1997; ISBN 1890154032.

The Family Puzzle; Putting the Pieces Together: A Guide to Parenting the Blended Family by Nancy Palmer, William D. Palmer, and Kay Marshall, Strom Pinon Press, 1996; ISBN 0891099492.

The New Joy of Cooking by Irma S. Rombauer, Marion Rombauer Becker, and Ethan Becker, Scribner, 1997; ISBN 0684818701.

The Unofficial Business Traveler's Pocket Guide: 165 Tips Even the Best Business Travelers May Not Know by Christopher J. McGinnis, McGraw-Hill, 1998; ISBN 0070453802.

Where's Mom Now That I Need Her? Surviving Away from Home by Betty Rae Frandsen, Kathryn J. Frandsen, and Kent P. Frandsen, Aspen West Publishing and Distribution, 1991; ISBN 0961539011.

Organizations

The National Organization of Single Mothers
P.O. Box 68
Midland, NC 28107
(704) 888-KIDS
www.singlemother.org

This organization helps new members form or join local support groups and publishes "SingleMOTHER," a bimonthly newsletter offering information and advice, plus tips that can save single mothers time and money.

Newsletters

For the two million dads staying home and raising kids, there's "At-Home Dad," an online newsletter edited by Peter Baylies. For a free subscription, go to www.athomedad.com/. There's even information on forming At-Home Dad Playgroups and an At-Home Dad Convention.

Chapter 21: Road Show: Making the Most of Your Vacation

Books

Are We There Yet? Travel Games for Kids by Richard Salter, Random House, 1991; ISBN 0517583046.

Great Games for Kids on the Go: Over 240 Travel Games to Play on Trains, Planes, and Automobiles by Penny Warner, Prima Publishing, 1998; ISBN 0761506268.

Lonely Planet Travel with Children (Lonely Planet Travel Survival Kit) by Cathy Lanigan, Lonely Planet, 2002; ISBN 0864427298.

Travel Bug: A Travel Journal for Kids 7 to 14 by Linda Schwartz, illustrated by Bev Armstrong, Learning Works, 1993; ISBN 0881602566.

Traveling the Lewis and Clark Trail by Julie Fanselow, Falcon Publishing Co., 1998; ISBN 1560444428.

Trouble-Free Travel … And What to Do When Things Go Wrong, by attorneys Stephen Colwell and Ann Shulman, Nolo Press Self-Help Law, 1999; ISBN 0873374789.

Trouble-Free Travel with Children: Helpful Hints for Parents on the Go by Vicki Lansky, Book Peddlers, 1996; ISBN 0916773159.

Catalogs

Christine Columbus
1-800-280-4775
www.christinecolumbus.com

Bon Voyage! Travel Books and Maps
2069 W. Bullard Avenue
Fresno, CA 93711
1-800-995-9716
www.bon-voyage-travel.com

TravelSmith Outfitting Guide and Catalog
(800) 995-7010
www.travelsmith.com

Chapter 22: Getting It Together in the Great Outdoors

Books

Basic Home Repairs by the editors of Sunset Publishing Corporation, 1995; ISBN 0376015810.

Complete Home Storage from the editors of Sunset Publishing Corporation, 1997; ISBN 0376017651.

Creating Storage: Hidden Storage and Rescued Space in the Garage, Attic or Basement from the editors of Sunset Publishing Corporation, 1995; ISBN 0376017686.

The Home Workshop Planner: A Guide to Planning, Setting Up, Equipping, and Using Your Own Home Workshop from the editors of Wood Publications, 1994; ISBN 0696203359.

Chapter 23: Let The Good Times Roll!: Planning the Perfect Party

Books

Einstein's Science Parties: Easy Parties for Curious Kids by Shar Levine and Allison Grafton, John Wiley & Sons, 1994; ISBN 0471596469.

The Best Birthday Party Game Book by Bruce Lansky, Simon & Schuster Merchandise, 1997; ISBN 0671577018.

The Kids' Pick-a-Party Book: 50 Fun Party Themes for Kids, Ages 2 to 16 by Peggy Warner, Meadowbrook Press, 1998; ISBN 0671579665.

The Simple Art of Napkin Folding: 94 Fancy Folds for Every Tabletop Occasion by Linda Hetzer William Morrow & Co., 1991; ISBN 0688102808.

The Ultimate Sleep-Over Book by Kayte Kuch, Lowell House, 1996; ISBN 156563874.

Chapter 24: Ready for Prime Time: Planning Weddings and Reunions

Books

Easy Wedding Planner, Organizer & Keepsake by Elizabeth Llulch, National Book Network, 2000; ISBN 1887169091.

Family Reunion Handbook: A Complete Guide for Reunion Planners by Thomas Ninkovich and Barbara E. Brown, Reunion Research, 1998; ISBN 0961047062.

High School Reunions: How to Plan Yours by Harry McKinzie, McKinzie Publishing, 1995; ISBN 0866260013.

The Complete Idiot's Guide to the Perfect Wedding by Teddy Lenderman, Alpha Books, 1997; ISBN 0028619633.

Organizations

National Association of Bridal Consultants
200 Chestnutland Road
New Milford, CT 06776-2521
(860) 355-0464
BridalAssn@aol.com

Chapter 26: Divine Recreation: More Time for Pastimes

Products

Clotilde is a catalog aimed at needlecrafters and home sewers, with lots of tools for keeping your supplies organized and taking projects with you. Get your catalog by calling (800) 772-2891 or surf to www.clotilde.com.

Atlantic, Inc. specializes in storage solutions for CDs, videotapes, and cassettes. If you'd like the name of a store near you that sells Atlantic's products, phone (310) 903-9550.

Appendix B

Bibliography

Aslett, Don. *Clutter's Last Stand*. Cincinnati: Writer's Digest Books, 1984.

———. *Is There Life After Housework?* Cincinnati: Writer's Digest Books, 1981.

———. *Make Your House Do the Housework*. Cincinnati: Writer's Digest Books, 1986.

———. *Pet Clean-Up Made Easy*. Cincinnati: Writer's Digest Books, 1988.

Berthold-Bond, Annie. *Better Basics for the Home*. New York: Three Rivers Press, 1999.

Breathnach, Sarah Ban. *Simple Abundance: A Daybook of Comfort and Joy*. New York: Warner Books, 1995.

Covey, Stephen R. *The 7 Habits of Highly Effective People: Powerful Lessons in Personal Change*. New York: Fireside/Simon & Schuster, 1989.

Cox, Connie, and Chris Evatt. *Simply Organized! How to Simplify Your Complicated Life*. New York: Perigee, 1988.

———. *30 Days to a Simpler Life*. New York: Plume, 1998.

Culp, Stephanie. *Conquering the Paper Pile-Up*. Cincinnati: Writer's Digest Books, 1990.

———. *How to Conquer Clutter*. Cincinnati: Writer's Digest Books, 1989.

———. *How to Get Organized When You Don't Have the Time*. Cincinnati: Writer's Digest Books, 1986.

———. *Streamlining Your Life: A 5-Point Plan for Uncomplicated Living*. Cincinnati: Writer's Digest Books, 1991.

Davidson, Jeff. *The Joy of Simple Living*. Rodale, 1999.

Dominguez, Joe, and Vicki Robin. *Your Money or Your Life*. New York: Viking Press, 1992.

Edwards, Paul and Sarah. *Working from Home*. Los Angeles: Jeremy P. Tarcher, Inc., 1985.

Elgin, Duane. *Voluntary Simplicity: Toward a Way of Life That Is Outwardly Simple, Inwardly Rich*. New York: William Morrow, 1993.

Gawain, Shakti. *Creative Visualization*. San Rafael, CA: New World Library, 1978.

Gawain, Shakti, with Laurel King. *Living in the Light: A Guide to Personal and Planetary Transformation*. Mill Valley, CA: Whatever Publishing, 1986.

Hunt, Mary. *Debt-Proof Living*, Nashville: Broadman & Holman Publishers, 1999.

Kiechel, Walter III. "Getting organized … the secret is, gulp, making decisions." *Fortune*. March 3, 1986, v. 113, 123.

Linn, Denise. *Sacred Space: Clearing and Enhancing the Energy of Your Home*. New York: Ballantine, 1995.

Longacre, Doris Janzen. *Living More with Less*. Scottsdale, PA: Herald Press, 1980.

McCullough, Bonnie. *Totally Organized: The Bonnie McCullough Way*. New York: St. Martin's Press, 1986.

Mendelson, Cheryl. *Home Comforts: The Art & Science of Keeping House*. New York: Scribner, 1999.

Miller, Timothy. *How to Want What You Have: Discovering the Magic and Grandeur of Ordinary Existence*. New York: Avon, 1995.

Nearing, Helen and Scott. *The Good Life*. New York: Schocken Books, 1989.

Pratkanis, Anthony, and Elliot Aronson. *Age of Propaganda: The Everyday Use and Abuse of Persuasion*. New York: W.H. Freeman and Company, 1992.

The Princeton Language Institute, ed. *21st Century Dictionary of Quotations*. New York: Laurel, 1993.

Rathje, William L. "Rubbish! An archeologist who excavates landfills believes that our thinking about garbage has been distorted by powerful myths." *The Atlantic*. December, 1989, v264, bi6, p99(10).

Robbins, Anthony. *Unlimited Power*. New York: Fawcett Columbine, 1986.

SantoPietro, Nancy. *Feng Shui: Harmony by Design*. New York: Perigee, 1996.

Sher, Barbara, with Annie Gottlieb. *Wishcraft: How to Get What You Really Want*. New York: Ballantine, 1979.

Toffler, Alvin. *The Third Wave*. New York: Bantam Books, 1981.

Wilson, Mimi, and Mary Beth Lagerborg. *Once-a-Month Cooking: A Time-Saving, Budget-Stretching Plan to Prepare Delicious Meals*. Colorado Springs: Focus on the Family, 1992.

Winston, Stephanie. *Getting Organized*. New York: Warner Books, 1991.

Young, Pam, and Peggy Jones. *Sidetracked Home Executives: From Pigpen to Paradise*. New York: Warner Books, 2001.

Index